Open Fields

Open Fields:
Science in
Cultural Encounter

GILLIAN BEER

OXFORD
UNIVERSITY PRESS

OXFORD

UNIVERSITY PRESS

Great Clarendon Street, Oxford OX2 6DP

Oxford University Press is a department of the University of Oxford.
It furthers the University's objective of excellence in research, scholarship,
and education by publishing worldwide in

Oxford New York

Athens Auckland Bangkok Bogotá Buenos Aires Calcutta
Cape Town Chennai Dar es Salaam Delhi Florence Hong Kong Istanbul
Karachi Kuala Lumpur Madrid Melbourne Mexico City Mumbai
Nairobi Paris São Paulo Singapore Taipei Tokyo Toronto Warsaw
with associated companies in Berlin Ibadan

Oxford is a registered trade mark of Oxford University Press
in the UK and in certain other countries

Published in the United States
by Oxford University Press Inc., New York

British Library Cataloguing in Publication Data
Data available

Library of Congress Cataloging in Publication Data
Beer, Gillian.
Open fields: science in cultural encounter / Gillian Beer.
1. English literature—19th century—History and criticism.
2. Literature and science—Great Britain—History—19th century.
3. Science—Great Britain—History—19th century.
4. Great Britain—Civilization—19th century.
5. Darwin, Charles, 1809–1882—Influence
6. Scienc e in literature. I. Title.
PR468.S34B44 1995 820.9' 356—dc20 95-43234
ISBN 0-19-818369-0
ISBN 0-19-818635-5 (Pbk.)

3 5 7 9 10 8 6 4 2

Printed in Great Britain
on acid-free paper by
Bookcraft Ltd,
Midsomer Norton, Avon

Preface

This collection of essays is the result of several years' concern with the ways scientific ideas are realized: realized both in the minds of those who struggle to precipitate them and in their transforming reception by those living alongside, outside the scientific community. Most of my examples are from the nineteenth and early twentieth century but they can throw light, I hope, on current controversies about the place of science in culture. Analytical distance and imaginative re-inhabiting of dilemmas are both needed for any thorough interpretation of how scientific practice draws on as well as affects the life of contemporaries.

In reflecting on these issues I have been fortunate to have the conversation of friends in many fields, and invitations from colleagues in history and philosophy of science, comparative literature, history, anthropology, women's studies, and psychology—as well as scientific societies. In particular, Mary Jacobus, Ludmilla Jordanova, Evelyn Fox Keller, George Levine, Ruth Padel, Simon Schaffer, and Marilyn Strathern may recognize outcomes of some of our conversations here. The essays that have emerged from these encounters, conferences, and lectures have been subsequently published in widely various places and are now drawn together for the first time. I am grateful to the publishers listed below for permission to collect the essays in this volume:

Chapter 1: From Judith Still and Michael Worton (eds.), *Textuality and Sexuality: Reading Theories and Practices* (Manchester: Manchester University Press, 1993).
Chapter 2: The Hilda Hume Memorial Lecture, 1988 (University of London, 1989).
Chapter 3: From Nick Jardine *et al.* (eds.) *Cultures of Natural History* (Cambridge: Cambridge University Press, 1995).
Chapter 4: From Robert Fraser (ed.), *Sir James Frazer and the Literary Imagination: Essays in Affinity and Influence* (London: Macmillan, 1990).

Chapter 5: From John Christie and Sally Shuttleworth (eds.), *Nature Transfigured: Science and Literature, 1700–1900* (Manchester: Manchester University Press, 1989).

Chapter 6: (Cambridge: Cambridge University Press, 1992).

Chapter 7: From George Levine (ed.), *One Culture: Essays in Science and Literature* (Madison, Wis.: Wisconsin University Press, 1987).

Chapter 8: *Notes and Records of the Royal Society of London*, 44 (1990). This is the text of the first lecture on literature and science, sponsored by the Royal Society of Literature, the British Academy, and the Royal Society, and given at the Royal Society on 20 April 1989.

Chapter 9: *AUMLA* (*Journal of the Australasian Universities Language and Literature Association*), 74 (1990).

Chapter 10: From Barry Bullen (ed.), *The Sun is God* (Oxford: Oxford University Press, 1989).

Chapter 11: *Comparative Criticism*, 13, ed. Elinor Shaffer (Cambridge University Press, 1992).

Chapter 12: *Essays in Criticism*, 40 (1990). The F. W. Bateson Memorial Lecture, given in Oxford, 14 February 1990.

Chapter 13: From George Levine (ed.), *Realism and Representation: Essays on the Problem of Realism in Relation to Science, Literature, and Culture* (Madison, Wis.: University of Wisconsin Press, 1993).

Chapter 14: *Ambix*, 41 (March 1994). A version of this chapter was presented to a meeting of the Society for the History of Alchemy and Chemistry on the theme 'Science and Literature', 5 December 1992, at the Science Museum in London.

Extracts from *Square Rounds* by Tony Harrison are reproduced courtesy of Faber and Faber Ltd. 'Schrödinger's Cat Preaches to the Mice' is reproduced from Gwen Harwood's collection *Bone Scan*, courtesy of HarperCollins Australia.

I am continually indebted to the Cambridge University Library and, for the opportunity to undertake the work here, to the British Academy who generously made it possible for me to have two invaluable years' research leave as a British Academy Research Reader. John Beer has been and is an essential companion, for much longer than this volume has taken to grow.

Contents

List of Illustrations

field A region in which a body experiences a force as the result of the presence of some other body or bodies. A field is thus a method of representing the way in which bodies are able to influence each other.

(*Concise Science Dictionary*, Oxford University Press, 1989)

> How sweet I roam'd from field to field,
>   And tasted all the summer's pride,
> 'Till I the prince of love beheld,
>   Who in the sunny beams did glide!

(William Blake, *Poetical Sketches*, 1783)

'In the distant future I see open fields for far more important researches. Psychology will be based on a new foundation, that of the necessary acquirement of each mental power and capacity by gradation. Light will be thrown on the origin of man and his history.'

(From the Conclusion to *The Origin of Species*, 1859)

Introduction

I

Cultural encounter occurs not only between peoples of different ethnic origins but between trades, genders, professional groups, specializations of all sorts in a society. Train-spotters, mothers of babies, astronomers, horse-riders have each their special knowledges and vocabularies; but none of them lives as train-spotter, mother, astronomer, horse-rider alone. Each inhabits and draws on the experience of the historical moment, the material base, the media, and community in which they all dwell. (Indeed they may all be one person, though a busy one.) These multiple subject positions mean that relations never form a single system: what may be perceived as outcrops or loose ends may prove to be part of the tracery of other connections. So, as Marilyn Strathern observes, 'English kin relations do not make an individual person equal to his or her field of relations, let alone a universe of social relations. There is in fact no universe of relationships, any more than personal names or kin terms form universes.'[1] Terms move across from one zone to another, for ideas cannot survive long lodged within a single domain. They need the traffic of the apparently *in*appropriate audience as well as the tight group of co-workers if they are to thrive and generate further thinking. An engrossing question is what happens when *unforeseen* readers appropriate terms and texts.[2]

So these essays all concern the crossings we make as readers between fields (sometimes, it seems, on open ground or over stiles, sometimes crouching beneath barbed wire or plucked by brambles). Two of my epigraphs, one from the *Oxford Concise Dictionary of Science* and one from William Blake, in their very

---

[1] Marilyn Strathern, *After Nature: English Kinship in the Late Twentieth Century* (Cambridge, 1992), 83.

[2] A question explored at large in my *Darwin's Plots: Evolutionary Narrative in Darwin, George Eliot, and Nineteenth-Century Fiction* (London, 1983).

different ways link the idea of the field with that of encounter—
forceful, dangerous, alluring, essential.

Encounter, whether between peoples, between disciplines, or
answering a ring at the bell, braces attention. It does not guarantee understanding; it may emphasize first (or only) what's incommensurate. But it brings into active play unexamined
assumptions and so may allow interpreters, if not always the
principals, to tap into unexpressed incentives. Exchange, dialogue, misprision, fugitive understanding, are all crucial within
disciplinary encounters as well as between peoples. Understanding askance, with your attention fixed elsewhere, or your
expectations focused on a different outcome, is also a common
enough event in such encounters and can produce effects as
powerful, if stranger, than fixed attention.

Some of the same processes of sustaining knowledge and experience that occur through an entire culture occur, then, also in
congeries *within* a culture and the diversity of knowledge-dialects
may set groups at odds with each other. Territory-rights get
involved here, as Carlyle (in a passage I particularly like) observes:

He [the philosopher Dugald Stewart] does not enter on the field to till it;
he only encompasses it with fences, invites cultivators, and drives away
intruders: often (fallen on evil days) he is reduced to long arguments with
the passers-by, to prove that it *is* a field, that this so highly prized domain
of his is, in truth, soil and substance, not clouds and shadow.[3]

Those who work with ideas are always under the pressure of
passions, their own as well as others'. George Eliot's imagined
chess-game in *Felix Holt* (1866), like that in *Alice Through the
Looking-Glass* not long after (1871), figures the disruptive effects of 'passions and intellects' in the power-games of social
control. Rule-bound play assumes passivity in its agents and
objects, but there is parity between players and pieces—and
which is which of players and pieces shifts with the focus of
attention:

Fancy what a game of chess would be like if all the chessmen had
passions and intellects, more or less small and cunning: if you were not
only uncertain about your adversary's men, but a little uncertain also
about your own; if your knight could shuffle himself on to a new square

---

[3] *Thomas Carlyle's Collected Works*, Library Edition (London, 1869–70), *Critical
and Miscellaneous Essays*, i. 92.

by the sly; if your bishop, in disgust at your castling, could wheedle your pawns out of their places; and if your pawns, hating you because they are pawns, could make away from their appointed posts that you might get checkmated on a sudden. You might be the longest-headed of deductive reasoners, and yet you might be beaten by your own pawns. You would be especially likely to be beaten, if you depended arrogantly on your mathematical imagination, and regarded your passionate pieces with contempt.[4]

The first group of essays in this volume explores questions of the boundaries of natural history and the place of the human within it which beset nineteenth-century commentators, particularly Darwin. The same issues were realized anew in the fiction of Thomas Hardy. What is the authority of those native to the environment studied? How is their testimony to be valued when they are also the objects of appraisal? Where is humankind when language is not, or not recognized? How do groups learn from each other when they cannot interpret their signs? These are questions that have not been left behind. They still ballast much present debate in post-colonial studies.[5] So, though my examples in this collection are drawn principally from the nineteenth century, the processes revealed may, I hope, give some purchase on current issues and assumptions.

II

> In the distant future I see open fields for far more important
> researches. Psychology will be based on a new foundation,
> that of the necessary acquirement of each mental power and
> capacity by gradation. Light will be thrown on the origin of
> man and his history.[6]

[4] George Eliot, *Felix Holt The Radical*, ed. Fred C. Thomson, Clarendon Edition (Oxford, 1980), 237.
[5] Homi Bhabha *The Location of Culture* (London, 1994); Peter Hulme, *Colonial Encounters* (London, 1986) and with Neil Whitehead (eds.), *Wild Majesty: Encounters with Caribs from Columbus to the Present Day* (Oxford, 1992); Anthony Pagden, *European Encounters with the New World* (London, 1993); Mary Louise Pratt, *Imperial Eyes: Travel Writing and Trans-Culturation* (London, 1992); Edward Said, *Culture and Imperialism* (London, 1993); Gayatri Chakravorty Spivak, *The Post-Colonial Critic: Interviews, Strategies, Dialogues* (London, 1990); Robert Young, *White Mythologies: Writing History and the West* (London, 1990).
[6] Charles Darwin, *The Origin of Species*, ed. Gillian Beer (Oxford, 1996), 394.

Darwin's arresting prophecy is his one direct reference in the argument of the *Origin* to the position of humankind. Even here, he distances far forwards into the future and back into the extreme past the implications of his theory. The syntax of his sentence allows the reader momentarily to glimpse open fields before they become part of a more abstract process of disciplinary development where new fields open 'for far more important researches'. Psychology, the science most devoted to primates and above all 'man', will be transformed, he declares.

Strikingly, in that formulation 'the necessary acquirement of each mental power and capacity by gradation', Darwin seems imaginatively to set aside any distinction between individual and culture. Indeed, individuals simply do not have time within the single life-span to acquire all the skills necessary to life. The arc of possibility is already formed by the social group into which the baby is born. The individual is endowed with boots, books, bows and arrows, systems of measurement, epistemologies—all the accumulated skills, choices, and experiences made over time go now into their making.[7] In much discussion there is a tendency to emphasize the *acquisition* of intellectual systems, the *presence* of objects, but both boots and measurement systems are prior products of multiple accumulated choices which already enclose the child at birth within a particular group. The diversity of circumstances and past choices inclines to more and more diversity between groups, and to the possibility of their inhabiting widely different environments. The capacity of human groups to flourish in contrasting physical settings is itself largely the product of the human capacity for accumulating and sustaining knowledge over generations. Objects, attitudes, and ideas become intrinsicated in the growing individual. So, of course, do communal prejudices, ignorances, and lacks.

The individual does not need directly to imitate the discoveries of the past. Indeed, that would destroy their efficacy as accumulated knowledge; she or he lives sustained, perhaps controlled, by their outcomes. Direct imitation of current cultural practices and skills, moreover, is most valuable in a slowly changing environment. In a period of rapid change the vital skill to be learnt may be that of how *not* to imitate, yet how not blindly to expunge.

[7] A paper by Robert Boyd given at the Royal Society, April 1995, affected my thinking on these matters.

A peculiarly human advantage is that memory sustained over generations allows us to diverge from the past, not only to mimic it. That divergence may well use parody, the form of imitation that simultaneously claims knowing distance. It may include the trying on, trying out, of materials and methods from other current groups not our own. The constraints of backward imitation are loosened. Bees endlessly replicate geometric marvels but human beings can learn to produce new forms. In doing so, knowledge from the local past and also across to other human groups and *their* pasts may intertwine, or condense, or jar.

Lateral encounter, between groups and individuals alive in the same time but in different initial conditions, allows fresh perception to thrive. The argument of the *Origin* concentrates in the main on those evolutionary factors that prevail across all kinds. But in the key sentences quoted at the outset of this argument Darwin marks out the particularities of human succession—and does so in a way that hints at the cultural component in human evolutionary change and variety. That component had been an important part of his coming to theory, and to what was most particular in his arguments. Survival, extinction, adaptation were dramatized for him on his five year voyage on and off the *Beagle*.[8] His encounters with indigenous groups and his observation and experience of them directed the currents of his thought quite as much as did his encounters with the Galapagos turtles, whose evolutionary significance he understood only later.

The power of responsive mimicry among indigenous peoples encountered during the voyage of the *Beagle* puzzled Darwin and his companions. It made them aware of their own gestures like an unexpected mirror; it drove them into extremes, aping themselves. It brought into question the then prevalent assumption that the European had accumulated complex intellectual skills beyond the range of other tribes. It seems to have amused, disturbed, and discountenanced them, turning into a power-play that could be won by the westerner only by characterizing it as a 'ludicrous habit'. As so often, Darwin's description vacillates between and among admiration, curiosity, pleasure, and brusque resistance.

---

[8] A position developed in my essay 'Darwin: The Insular Condition', in Tim Lenoir (ed.), *Writing Science* (Stanford, 1996).

They are excellent mimics: as often as we coughed or yawned, or made any odd motion, they immediately imitated us. Some of our party began to squint and look awry; but one of the young Fuegians (whose whole face was painted black, excepting a white band across his eyes) succeeded in making far more hideous grimaces. They could repeat with perfect correctness each word in any sentence we addressed them, and they remembered such words for some time. Yet we Europeans all know how difficult it is to distinguish apart the sounds in a foreign language. Which of us, for instance, could follow an American Indian through a sentence of more than three words? All savages appear to possess, to an uncommon degree, this power of mimicry. I was told, almost in the same words, of the same ludicrous habit among the Caffres: the Australians, likewise, have long been notorious for being able to imitate and describe the gait of any man so that he may be recognised. How can this faculty be explained? is it a consequence of the more practised habits of perception and keener senses, common to all men in a savage state, as compared with those long civilized?[9]

The psychological issues raised in this early passage are sidestepped in the *Origin*, but they had already entered powerfully into the fulcrum of thinking that led Darwin to that work, as three of the essays below will argue.

So unsecured and creative are Darwin's reactions in the 1830s that they reach out towards contradictory sequences of thought. A potentiality of his argument here about human mimicry might have led to a theory of decline rather than development ('more practised habits of perception and keener senses' belong to the savage state). It might equally have led to a reordering of developmental scales: the savage state is seen as fresher, as more alive to adaptive possibility, than are the ageing races of 'those long civilized'. Darwin and his companions are encompassed and self-estranged by the Fuegians' mimicry of them. The Fuegians are free to pick and choose among the Europeans' verbal habits, to skim off the surface of language, apparently without understanding, while themselves communicating in a language impossible for Darwin to replicate or match. He wards it off, falling in with the then current understanding of 'mankind' as Caucasian, but he interjects a wary 'according to our notions'.

[9] *Journal of Researches*, Part I, in Paul Barrett and R. B. Freeman (eds.), *The Works of Charles Darwin* (London, 1986), ii. 179–80.

The language of these people, according to our notions, scarcely deserves to be called articulate. Captain Cook has compared it to a man clearing his throat, but certainly no European ever cleared his throat with so many hoarse, guttural, and clicking sounds.
They are excellent mimics . . .[10]

Parodists? Bricoleurs? Free spirits? Not quite, as the later history of Jemmy Button would suggest; but also not examples of simplicity, or of peoples locked onto the only stage of developmental process for which they were fitted.

In the event, it is only much later, and less boldly, that Darwin returns to these dangerous issues, in *The Descent of Man* (1871), when time had lessened the creative confusion of actual encounter. In that time, too, further destruction of these indigenous groups had been perpetrated.

Ruskin, discussing accumulation in *The Political Economy of Art*, observes the power of nations to destroy, here objects, elsewhere humankind and memory:

You talk of the scythe of Time, and the tooth of Time: I tell you Time is scytheless and toothless; it is we who gnaw like the worm—we who smite like the scythe. It is ourselves who abolish—ourselves who consume: we are the mildew, and the flame, and the soul of man is to its own work as the moth, that frets when it cannot fly, and the hidden flame that blasts where it cannot illumine.[11]

What, then, of scientific writing and practice which, despite the conscious conservatism of its methods, so values the new, values it both in investigation and outcome? How does that play in with the stored and compacted? 'According to relativity theory the complete field of force contains besides the ordinary Newtonian attraction a repulsive (scattering) force varying directly as the distance', writes Arthur Eddington in *The Expanding Universe*.[12]

Working with, and within, language is to work with a medium inevitably imbued with the communal past, drenched with what

---

[10] Ibid. 17. Darwin's encounters with the Fuegians figure in several of the essays here—particularly 'Four Bodies on the *Beagle*' and 'Travelling the Other Way', and are alluded to in 'Can the Native Return?' and 'Forging the Missing Link'.

[11] John Ruskin, *The Political Economy of Art: Being the Substance of Two Lectures Delivered at Manchester, July 10th and 13th, 1857* (New York, 1880), lecture 2, 'Accumulation', 57.

[12] Arthur Eddington, *The Expanding Universe* (Cambridge, 1932, repr. Harmondsworth, 1940) 25.

has been. In language others are always implicit, others who have used the same terms in different conditions. How then to reach new ideas, new practices, open fields? These are questions for all creative thinkers, but in the nineteenth century—in ways different from our own—scientists were trying to work with discourses open to their educated peers and drawing on non-technical, even non-mathematical, formulations. They were therefore particularly close to the shared stories of their time and let them move at will in their work, as well as abruptly question-ing them: the term 'work' itself is an example to which I shall return. Science always raises more questions than it can contain, and writers and readers may pursue these in directions that go past science. Such discussions in their turn provide metaphors and narratives which inform scientific enquiry, as I illustrate in some of the essays below. For this is not a one-way process with science as the origin and others as its intellectual beneficiaries only. Scientists work with the metaphors and the thought-sets historically active in their communities. We can see these move-ments to and fro, and across, between scientific and other meta-phors and models—and not only in the *human* sciences.

Ian Hacking cites the example of James Clerk Maxwell's use of the work of the sociologist Quetelet on crowd behaviour and statistics for Maxwell's own thinking through to deterministic laws of gases from the random behaviour of molecules. The philosopher C. S. Peirce then conjectured, from the example of Maxwell's laws, that it would be necessary to postulate a 'universe of chance' which would include the laws of physics themselves.[13] As I suggest in 'The Reader's Wager', the newly stochastic universe is embroiled, for late nineteenth-century people, with issues of class, chance, and desire; and the rise of literary modernism is, I argue in another essay, imbricated with nineteenth century wave-theory.

What emerges in any reading that ranges across differing zones is the *intimacy* between intellectual issues and emotional desires and fears. Sometimes those desires and fears are individual, as often they are communal and historically specific. I have tracked

---

[13] Ian Hacking, 'Probability and Determinism, 1650–1900', in R. C. Olby, G. N. Cantor, *et al.* (eds.), *Companion to the History of Modern Science* (London, 1990), 699–700.

these motions in some of the essays collected here, particularly 'The Death of the Sun' and 'Forging the Missing Link'.

Two questions haunt this collection of essays: How does human encounter, actual or imagined, play into the making of theory? How do people reach new ideas within language, which is so freighted with communal pasts? Together, these raise further questions: about scientific writing and the depth to which it is imbued with cultural experience; about the capacity of human beings to respond to fresh knowledge as experience. And the whole cluster of questions suggests ways in which knowledge-as-experience and experience-as-knowledge are transformed as they move across, beyond, and back and forth from field to field to field.

I

Darwinian Encounters

I

Four Bodies on the Beagle: Touch, Sight, and Writing in a Darwin Letter

Fanatics have their dreams, wherewith they weave
A paradise for a sect, the savage too
From forth the loftiest fashion of his sleep
Guesses at Heaven; pity these have not
Traced upon vellum or wild Indian leaf
The shadows of melodious utterance . . .
Whether the dream now purposed to rehearse
Be poet's or fanatic's will be known
When this warm scribe my hand is in the grave.
(John Keats, 'The Fall of Hyperion')[1]

While some scientists see their endeavour in predominantly adversarial terms, as contests, battles, exercises in domination, others see it as a primarily erotic activity.
(Evelyn Fox Keller)[2]

The 'warm scribe', in Keats's compelling description of the writer's hand, cancels the distance between cold print and body. A hand reaches out from the text, is occupied in the text; brushing aside the print on the page, it makes the reader conscious of the hand's activity in reading as well as writing. We smooth the page, we turn it, each alone. The past body of the writer is here insurgent, meeting the reader's hand, matching it, touching it. The effect is rare, and daring. It relies upon Keats abandoning the dualistic hierarchies of mind and body, having available to him without favour all his five senses. Writing his experiences on the voyage of the *Beagle* some ten years after Keats composed 'The Fall of Hyperion', Darwin shares the

[1] *The Poems of John Keats*, ed. Miriam Allott (London, 1970), 657–8.
[2] *Reflections on Gender and Science* (New Haven and London, 1985), 125.

problematic of empathy that Keats explored: impressions are a ferment, sharing the body, keeping the mind agog, multiplying positions. Yet to survive they must be set down, impacted as ideas, authenticated by alien readers.

In this passage Keats insists that *only* the written gives any hope of survival. The unrecorded lofty dreams with which the savage 'guesses at Heaven' remain incommunicable to those outside the tribe, those born in another time. The writer dead, the hand may survive as idea—but only if that idea holds (and continues to hold) the imagination of many. The arcane world of fanatical belief gives way to time; the circle of disciples dies out. Darwin, energetically observing and writing before the establishment of genetic theory, had to have the patience of the pioneer—the patience not to know for sure within his lifetime 'Whether the dream now purposed to rehearse | Be poet's or fanatic's', whether it would prove to be authentic or delusive.

Like Keats, Darwin started on a medical career and left it part-way through his studies. For both, the problem of pain was a factor in the decision to quit. Before anaesthesia or the practice of hypnosis, before disinfectants, the sights and sounds connected with surgery were terrible indeed. And for the practising doctor not only sight and sound were involved, but touch. The doctor must implicate himself, must use his hands to cause suffering, however much the outcome of that suffering was planned as recovery. The hand is the most conscious, and at the same time the most intimate, point of contact between the individual and the surrounding world. Bodies may be jostled in a crowd, helplessly, but the hand's activities are always in some measure knowing. To reach out; to strike; to stroke; to incise; to inscribe: such are typical activities. And, for the anatomist, to dissect *and* to describe: the hand as scalpel and as pen. Darwin's hand is active in all these ways. He early loved shooting, with its acute eye–hand co-ordination, but he renounced it. His own 'hand' in communication is extraordinarily resistant to interpretation. He writes in a close exquisite calligraphy that appears instantly decipherable at a distance and proves inscrutable close to.

In *Realism, Writing, Disfiguration: On Thomas Eakins and Stephen Crane*, Michael Fried has insisted on the fraught relations between the surgeon's and the painter's and writer's crafts in the activity of representation. In his example, Eakins the painter and Crane the writer work with effects of perspective, of violence to the body, and of prone and upright positions as implicit commentary on the activity of production. The viewer finds it painful either to look at or '*to look away from*' the operation pictured in Eakins's *The Gross Clinic*: 'so keen is our craving for precisely that confirmation of our own bodily reality'.[3]

That confirmation, Fried suggests, is always conflicted and is put under pressure particularly by the thematization in writing and painting of horizontal and upright: 'an implicit contrast between the "spaces" of reality and of literary representation— of writing (and in a sense . . . of writing/drawing)—required that a human character, ordinarily upright and so to speak forward-looking, be rendered horizontal and upward-facing so as to match the horizontality and upward-facingness of the blank page on which the action of inscription was taking place' (ibid. 99–100). For Darwin on the *Beagle*, I shall argue, *prone* and *upright* held particular intensities of meaning. Fried's emphasis on the power-relations of hand, eye, and subject is valuable particularly for its recognition that the *subject* (in both senses) is not only the figure painted or described. It is also the subjectivity and subjection of the viewer or reader experiencing empathetic desire—and the interpellated subjectivities of the writer too. The activity of writing or drawing is figured in that which is described, even while it figures it. As Lacan remarks:

With a two body psychology, we come upon the famous problem, which is unresolved in physics, of two bodies. In fact, if you restrict yourselves to the level of two bodies, there is no satisfactory symbolisation available.[4]

In this essay I shall place at the centre of my argument a quite short passage from a particular letter from among the many that Darwin wrote while on the five-year voyage of the *Beagle*. By doing so, I hope to raise to the surface profound concerns that Darwin can, textually, only glance towards. These concerns are

[3] *Realism, Writing, Disfiguration: On Thomas Eakins and Stephen Crane* (Chicago, 1987), 65.
[4] *The Seminar of Jacques Lacan*, ed. Jacques-Alain Miller, trans. John Forrester, (Cambridge, 1988): Book I, 'Freud's Papers on Technique', 227.

at once sensual, theoretical, political, and sexual.[5] Darwin's difficulty in delimiting any one of these domains is fundamental to his creativity. His extreme openness to sense-experience produces also in his writing a form of nostalgia so intense that it may be called mourning—a nostalgia that acts perhaps as the screen for more enduring grief.

In the letter, three particularly strong and sequent images of naked bodies emerge. The fourth body of my title is Darwin's own. But the number four is here not so much a limit as a multiplier. The bodies Darwin sees in his mind's eye *stand in for*, and symbolically subvert, a range of categories.

The period of his life-writing that I concentrate on here is that of the early 1830s, and the date of the letter I shall cite is 23 July 1834, when the *Beagle* docked at Valparaiso in Chile after a difficult passage more than two years into the voyage and having already visited (among places that disagreeably fascinated and impressed Darwin) Tierra del Fuego and the Falkland Islands. But in order to frame my argument within this time-focus, it is necessary first to set the letter within Darwin's intellectual and emotional experience at that period, and then to look forward to the accomplished form of evolutionary theory that Darwin finally publishes in *The Origin* twenty-five years later.

When Darwin set out on the voyage of the *Beagle*, he was still 22 and not yet a Victorian. This was the period of the Bridgewater Treatises in which God's providence was demonstrated through the natural world and the eye was still held to be the perfect instrument of discernment. Helmholtz's demonstration of the eye's imperfections was still twenty years in the future and first embraced by Darwin twenty years after that, in the last edition of *The Origin*, as evidence for the uncertain processes of natural selection against the model of absolute design. It's as well to register these controlling absences. But, for the later phase of my argument, it is important also to note at the start the surgeon and art-theorist Charles Bell's Bridgewater essay on *The Hand* which

---

[5] I have written about the racial politics involved in a pamphlet essay *Can the Native Return?* (London, 1989; repr. as Ch. 2, below), and about the uses of the first person in such accounts in 'Speaking for the Others: Relativism and Authority in Victorian Anthropological Literature', in R. Fraser (ed.), *Sir James Frazer and the Literary Imagination* (London, 1990), 38–60; repr. as Ch. 4 below.

first appeared while Darwin was on the *Beagle* and which he read on his return.[6] Darwin already admired Bell's work on the fine arts, on anatomy, and on the expression of emotion (a topic that Darwin would much later make his own).[7]

Bell insisted on touch rather than on sight as the 'common sensibility': 'the most necessary of the senses, it is enjoyed by all animals from the lowest to the highest in the chain of existence' (214).[8] Towards the end of the treatise, indeed, Bell compares the excellences of eye and hand and emphasizes that the eye depends on the balance of the whole body. The eye, he argues, is the symbolizing summary sign of that which is already experienced by the hand; the eye therefore relies upon correspondence with the hand. In a sinewy and complex syntax, he places at the climactic point of an extended sentence, the eye's pulse of delay, a moment behind the hand's immediacy: 'the sign in the eye of what is known to the hand' (349).

In Bell's analysis, the image of the eye as camera is jettisoned. In its stead the eye is experienced *from within the body*, as part of a set of muscular rhythms. The efficacy of these rhythms relies upon the body's balance and the equable distribution of our consciousness of the body held in ambient space. The swivelling eye strokes the outer world with the sway of the whole body. The eye's motions become a meta-form of touch, minutely sensible to the 'place, form, and distance of objects':

When, instead of looking upon the eye as a mere camera, or show-box, with the picture inverted at the bottom, we determine the value of muscular activity; mark the sensations attending the balancing of the body; that fine property which we possess of adjusting the muscular frame to its various inclinations; how it is acquired in the child; how it is lost in the paralytic and drunkard; how motion and sensation are combined in the exercise of the hand; how the hand, by means of this sensibility, guides the finest instruments: when we consider how the eye and hand correspond; how the motions of the eye, combining with the

[6] See Sir Charles Bell, *The Hand, its Mechanisms and Vital Endowments as Evincing Design* (London, 1833) (Bridgewater Treatises, no. 4). This work went through six editions by 1860. It is quite likely that it was among the books sent to Darwin while he was on the *Beagle*—but this is not necessary to my argument.

[7] See Charles Bell, *A System of Dissections, Explaining the Anatomy of the Human Body* (Edinburgh, 1798–9), and *Essays on the Anatomy and Philosophy of Expression*, (London, 1806)—from the third edition onwards, this book was called *The Anatomy and Philosophy of Expression as Connected with the Fine Arts.*

[8] I cite page-references to the fourth edition (London, 1837).

impression on the retina, becomes the place, form, and distance of objects—the sign in the eye of what is known to the hand: finally, when, by attention to the motions of the eye, we are aware of their extreme minuteness, and how we are sensible to them in the finest degree—the conviction irresistibly follows, that without the power of directing the eye, (a motion holding relation to the action of the whole body) our finest organ of sense, which so largely contributes to the development of the powers of the mind, would lie unexercised. (349)

The hand, touching, caressing, dissecting, *writing*, is as necessary to Darwin as is the eye for his theoretical purposes and for his life aboard ship. In the particular letter that I examine, the *mind's eye* of memory plays across a repertoire of allusion between the senses, and in particular those of touch and sight.

A good deal of the meaning of the voyage came to Darwin through a polymorphously intense response to sensuous stimuli, and through seasickness. On the voyage of the *Beagle*, even the smallest island gave promise of relief to the endlessly seasick landsman and he seized every opportunity to undertake land journeys. Visiting the almost entirely male community of Ascension Island towards the end of his circumnavigation he commented that: 'Many of the marines appeared well-contented with their situation; they think it better to serve their one-and-twenty years on shore, let it be what it may, than in a ship; in which choice, if I were a marine, I would most heartily agree.'[9] Confinement in an island is, in his view, infinitely preferable to confinement in a ship: celibacy there at least does not include seasickness.

For long-distance travellers by ship, the shipboard life becomes a travelling homeland from which to survey the changing world. But as Darwin continued queasy throughout his five years, it was a shifty homeland. The foreign at least offered terra firma. The British ship, the *Beagle*, offered no island of stability. The emo-

---

[9] *Journal of Researches into the Geological and Natural History of the Various Countries visited by H.M.S. Beagle, under the command of Captain Fitzroy, R.N. from 1832 to 1836* by Charles Darwin, Esq., M.A., F.R.S., Secretary to the Geological Society (London, 1839), 586. The work had first appeared as vol. 3 of the *Narrative of the Surveying Voyages of His Majesty's Ships Adventure and Beagle*, under the editorship of Fitzroy. I quote from the first edition published independently. Soon afterwards it was reissued and became known by the title *The Voyage of the Beagle*.

tional stresses of life on board, in particular his frequently stormy relations with Captain Fitzroy, made disembarking at a succession of islands and territories the more pleasurable. Though five years may now sound like a leisurely pace around the world, to Darwin the recurrent impression was of haste, prematurity, incomplete encounter. The ship exacted departure, or demanded urgent and anxious land-voyages to catch up at the next port of call.

Darwin was on this five-year journey throughout the period of his young manhood and was, very likely, celibate during that entire time. In Darwin, as in Keats his near contemporary, we meet the kind of mind and body on whom nothing is lost, and to whom everything is simultaneously available: sounds, smells, domestic life, the vegetation of remote landfalls, the heat of the day, companionship and cooking, beetles in ditches, the writing of earlier travellers such as Humboldt, the manifold flora and fauna, the luscious single flower, the variety of humankind, the particular encounter. For both of them, sexual congress is absent. On his long land journeys from the *Beagle* this passion of curiosity and response sometimes made progress difficult. The effect as it is described is at once erotic and infantile: 'In England any person fond of natural history enjoys in his walks a great advantage, by always having something to attract his attention; but in these fertile climates, teeming with life, the attractions are so numerous, that he is scarcely able to walk at all' (29).

Like a young child, impressions crowd in so thick that the idea of 'going for a walk' is lost in the immediacy of sensation. Darwin left at home a widowed father and maternal older sisters. His mother had died when he was 8 years old and he retained—remarkably—only one sharp memory of her. When Fox's child later died, Darwin wrote to him that he had not yet himself suffered the loss of a close relative. The degree of denial, repression, or displacement this suggests is indeed remarkable. An unfocused nostalgia for an experience without boundaries, for exploration, even infiltration, may be a response to loss. (Though it is timely to recall that the maternal functions were probably more widely distributed in the kind of household in which he grew up than would be familiar today. Nurses, sisters, servants and—most strikingly—his father all composed a maternal resting place.)

On the voyage of the *Beagle*, Darwin found it hard to do without his family; he suffered homesickness, exacerbated by (and perhaps helping to explain) his persistent seasickness. His balance never made the adaptation to seaboard life. Babies in the womb are held and rocked at ease in amniotic fluid without suffering problems of balance or seasickness. But in that captain's cabin Darwin felt himself reduced at intervals to infantile dependency without comfort. No wonder that he spent as long as possible on shore, seizing every opportunity to have his senses restored to him. Those senses blazed the stronger on land for their recovery. His position on board ship as part naturalist, part gentleman companion to the captain, did not in itself require of him so indefatigable an exploration of the territories and peoples the ship's course touched upon. He chose it.

But his alternating experiences of prone and upright, sickness and equilibrium, made him very aware that observing is never neutral. Darwin knew that observing depends as much upon the body as on the reason, that ear, eye and balance are closely implicated. Like Keats again, he had spent time as a medical student and knew his anatomy. And both these early-bereaved men responded to touch, taste, hearing, smell, as strongly as to sight. The work of mourning can take the form of celebration. Darwin's polymorphous responsiveness to territory (earth, insects, peoples, plants, trees, and pools) serves him for comfort and excitement. Nature for him is 'She' in a more than formal usage. Yet he does not insist on this she-ness as difference.

Darwin's curiosity was intensely libidinous. The two energies—to merge and to classify (loosing the borders of the body into oneness with its environment or eagerly articulating and naming)—are both present to a high degree in his descriptions. He as often describes himself seated or prone as mounted or walking. He places his body in a variety of relations to the physical world. Lying prone is both the naturalist's professional position for observation and, for Darwin, a pleasurable declension into the sensory world. His strong intellectual desire to make links and to discover kinship brings the counter-impulses of merging and of naming into a controllable relationship. His language in the *Voyage of the Beagle* and in the letters of the time often shows the yearning and the embarrassment of categories that he was struggling with.

Darwin was an active letter-writer throughout his five years' travel, as the first volumes of his Correspondence show. He also kept a journal which was later to form the basis of the *Voyage*. Moreover, he had field notes to maintain and specimens to bottle and dispatch with accompanying notes. When he was not travelling, a quite large part of his day, particularly on board ship, was taken up with writing. His most frequent correspondents were his sisters, but he also maintained a lively exchange with a number of co-workers and friends. Letters went and arrived in clumps, sometimes delayed for weeks on either side by the exigencies of transport. One only of these many letters was addressed to his school and college friend Charles Whitley. It is that letter that I dwell on now.

Whitley, much more conservative in opinion than Darwin, had been a crony at college. They both belonged, for example, to the Gourmet or 'Glutton' Club which specialized in eating strange meat: 'the name arose because the members were given to making experiments on "birds and beasts which were before unknown to human palate" . . . hawk and bittern were tried, and their zeal broke down over an old brown owl "which was indescribable" '.[10] Like Darwin at that time Whitley was destined for the Church. The letter under discussion has a certain immediate interest in being his sole communication to Whitley while away (a couple of letters passed between them shortly before he set out on the *Beagle*). The letter proves also to be the repository of much repressed emotional disturbance. Perhaps Darwin was moved to write by a passage in a letter from Catherine Darwin (27 November 1833) which may—like letters from Henslow— have reached him only on arriving at Valparaiso many months later. The letter reminded him of Whitley's active existence and told him of his quite poignantly avid concern for news of Darwin: 'I can't conceive how Mr. Whitley knows all about your plans, movements, discoveries &c, for I don't think you

[10] *The Life and Letters of Charles Darwin, Including an Autobiographical Chapter*, edited by his son, Francis Darwin, in three volumes (London, 1887), i. 169–70. See also *The Correspondence of Charles Darwin*, ed. Frederick Burkhardt and Sydney Smith, (Cambridge, 1985). In a letter of reminiscences written to Francis Darwin, Watkins (then Archdeacon of York) described the Club as making 'a devouring raid on birds & beasts which were before unknown to human palate . . . I think the Club came to an untimely end by endeavouring to eat an old brown owl' (i. 160, n. 1).

correspond with him. Whitley says that two letters of your's have passed though his hands, to other people (not to himself) and that he perfectly longed to break the seal of them, but of course did not' (*Correspondence*, i. 357).

The long silence between them and its sudden breaking seems linked to a crisis of *Heimweh* for Darwin—a crisis which involves not only nostalgia for past scenes but for past selves. Darwin fears that both his youthful self and the imagined future self of his younger years is now irretrievable. Past and future alike are altered beyond recall by the experiences of his protracted journey. 'Body and mind' are in a state disjunct from his settled and carefree past (or a past now imagined to have been settled and carefree). Landing at Valparaiso, the stylish capital of Chile, after a perilous sea-passage after their stay in Tierra del Fuego puts him back in touch with a society more like that from which he came originally, and during his stay there he 'had the good fortune to find living here Mr. Richard Corfield, an old schoolfellow and friend, to whose hospitality and kindness I was greatly indebted'.[11]

But arriving there also marks for him the distance he has travelled from such societies: he is stranded between two—or more—worlds. When in this letter he imagines sexual love and procreation, he turns humorously to the language of Jane Austen. He has no other tongue in which to communicate to his past peers, but that language will not do to represent all that he now needs, knows, and fears to be debarred from.

As he writes, he veers between humour, yearning, amazement, and a curious sequence of images whose juxtapositions tell almost as much as the vignettes themselves. He begins by reminding Whitley 'that there is a certain hunter of beetles & pounder of rocks, still in existence'. Covering his own forgetfulness of Whitley, he remarks that 'it will serve me right, if you have quite forgotten me.—' (*Correspondence*, i. 396).

I do hope you will write to me. ('H.M.S. Beagle, S. American Station' will find me); I should much like to hear in what state you are, both in

---

[11] *Journal of Researches*, 308–9. Ch. 14 ends thus: 'One sight of such a coast is enough to make a landsman dream for a week about shipwreck, peril, and death; and with this in sight, we bade farewell for ever to Tierra del Fuego' (p. 307). Ch. 15 opens: 'July 23.—The Beagle anchored late at night in the bay of Valparaiso, the chief seaport of Chile. When morning came everything seemed delightful' (p. 308).

body and mind.—¿Quien sabe? as the people here say (& God knows they well may, for they do know little enough) if you are not a married man, & may be nursing, as Miss Austen says, little olive branches, little pledges of mutual affection.—Eheu Eheu, this puts me in mind, of former visions, of glimpses into futurity, where I fancied I saw, retirement, green cottages & white petticoats.—What will become of me hereafter, I know not; but I feel, like a ruined man, who does not see or care how to extricate himself.—That this voyage must come to a conclusion, my reason tells me, but otherwise I see no end to it.—It is impossible not bitterly to regret the friends & other sources of pleasure, one leaves behind in England . . . We have seen much fine scenery, that of the Tropics in its glory & luxuriance, exceeds even the language of Humboldt to describe. A Persian writer could alone do justice to it, & if he succeeded he would in England, be called the 'grandfather of all liars'.—

But, I have seen nothing, which more completely astonished me, than the first sight of a Savage; It was a naked Fuegian his long hair blowing about, his face besmeared with paint. There is in their countenances, an expression, which I believe to those who have not seen it, must be inconcevably wild. Standing on a rock he uttered tones & made gesticulations than which, the crys of domestic animals are far more intelligible.

When I return to England you must take me in hand with respect to the fine arts. I yet recollect there was a man called Raffaelle Sanctus. How delightful it will be once again to see in the FitzWilliam, Titian's Venus; how much more than delightful to go to some good concert or fine opera. These recollections will not do. I shall not be able tomorrow to pick out the entrails of some small animal, with half my usual gusto.[12]

And then he turns to request news of friends in common, ending: 'Often & often do I think over those past hours so many of which have been passed in your company. Such can never return; but their recollection shall never die away.—'. The intensity of valediction here, the sense of being like 'a ruined man', affirms that Whitley can act only as a mirror self for a past that Darwin no longer shares, a future that sets off in a different direction. Darwin needs a different pen, now, which will outgo the culture he has left and which that culture could not credit: 'he would in England be called the "grandfather of all liars" '. So his state of unknowing about his old friend, though wryly humorous, also

[12] *Correspondence*, i. 396–7. The oddities of spelling are Darwin's own.

bids farewell to his own past identity. Instead he turns to a different double: the Fuegian seen standing on a rock.

In my discussion I shall concentrate on the three bodies conjured in this passage: the Fuegian, Titian's Venus, and 'some small animal'. They are all, as he writes, absent: fantasies of Darwin's own inscribing eye, hand, and brain. So the fourth body (Darwin's) is/was the only present body. This shifts the question of 'the gaze' into a different dimension. Darwin 'sees' the projected figures as he writes; perhaps his correspondent will see them too—as may that trail of illicit after-readers among whom we must, in this instance, number ourselves, reading a letter addressed to quite another person one hundred and fifty-odd years ago, yet startled into constructing and construing a symbolic sequence of images again in the mind's eye.

Lacan summarizes Sartre's discussion of the gaze in terms of its humanistic premisses:

> The author's entire demonstration turns around the fundamental phenomenon which he calls the gaze. The human object is originally distinguished, *ab initio*, in the field of my experience, and cannot be assimilated to any other perceptible object by virtue of being an object which is looking at me. From the moment this gaze exists, I am already something other, in that I feel my self becoming an object for the gaze of others. (*Seminar*, i. 215)

Among these three mental images only the Fuegian looks back at Darwin; Titian's Venus gazes out of the frame of the picture into a sideways distance that the viewer cannot share; the small animal is already dead, about to be pickled. The three figures are across a spectrum in more than one way: they move from active to passive, from upright to prone, from an interactive gaze to dead upturned eyes, from male to female to unsexed. The Fuegian is animated; the Venus half-reclining; the animal upturned. The Venus is in each of these sequences the hinge category, ambiguously sited: private and communal; womanly and cultural; self-possessed art object; a body never to be touched, paint become flesh in recollection.

In writing the recollected image of his first sight of a savage, Darwin suggests indirectly that the man was far away from him, perhaps seen from ship to shore. The straining of the eye to grip and interpret this figure becomes also a representation that confirms his assumption of extreme cultural distance between them. It also figures the man's resistance to authoritative interpretation. (For nineteenth-century readers the scope of a term like 'savage' was larger than it can now be for us: it includes distance and superiority but need not imply repudiation.) The 'savage' man on his mountainside is represented as 'wild' somewhat in the manner of Thomas Gray's late eighteenth-century poem 'The Bard' about the last prophetic Celts: a member of an earlier and vanishing race whose visions are incommunicable now. This figure cannot be held within even the possibility of Western translation.

The trope of race theory at the time was of other races as children beside the adult Caucasian. But this is a man, aloof, and Darwin is the baffled pupil unable to tap his lore, as well as being the inhibited adult rendered uneasy by the man's 'smeared' surface. Darwin is 'astonished', a word which always includes a strong physical input, a clonk or freezing of the perceiver's bodily frame. Such heartfelt difficulties in tracking kinship, it seems to me, must go to fuel Darwin's much later work *The Expression of the Emotions in Man and Animals*,[13] where he restoratively includes images of animals and of sane and mad people, of young and of old, to affirm the continuities of emotional gesture across species.

In this letter and elsewhere (for this is a scene he returns to), Darwin communicates a sense of fascinated helplessness at finding himself unable to interpret the profound difference of the other man. Gesture is a kinship experienced in the body. Yet it is also a kind of writing, an interchange of meaning stabilized between actor and viewer. Here no *relation*, in the sense of message or narrative, can be established. The other is 'inconceivably wild'. But that which is inconceivable is also here a mirror-image. On his hillside the naked man looks and cries out to the young Darwin. As Darwin recollects it here, they seem to be alone together. Revealingly, closer to the event, he writes of a *group* of men on the mountain.[14] In this dream-like and deso-

---

[13] See Charles Darwin, *The Expression of the Emotions in Man and Animals* (London, 1872).

[14] In *Journal of Researches*, this becomes: 'A group of Fuegians partly concealed by the entangled forest, were perched on a wild point overlooking the sea; and as we passed by, they sprang up, and waving their tattered cloaks, sent forth a loud and sonorous shout' (p. 227). The following page gives a detailed description of their first close encounter with the group.

lated scanning for meaning, an intimate, alienated pair of men emerges: Darwin and the naked Fuegian. And Darwin writes his account with naked hand—had seen his opposite and double with the naked eye.

The topographical and cultural distance Darwin supposes between himself and the Fuegians (though disagreeable to us now) is valuable to him in reaching towards a new theoretical position. It allows Darwin to extend the spectrum of humankind to such an extent that it begins to overlap the distance between humankind and other animals: instead of the severe disjunction between the human and other species enjoined by creationist theory the whole measure can be encompassed, 'we are all netted together'.

Yet the dismay of seeing his own male body figured in so dissimilar a guise, given back to him through observation, estranged, immediately produces in the letter a counter-image of the naked body. This time it is one from Western culture. And it is that of a woman. Again the constraint of the visual distance, the embargo on touching, dominates.

Now he recalls the large and sensuous picture of *Venus and Cupid with a Lute-Player* by Titian (Fig. 1.1), then, as now, centrally placed in a gallery of the Fitzwilliam Museum in Cambridge. The naked Venus faces the viewer but her gaze is dreamily off out of the picture to our right and she has just ceased to play the recorder whose music lies in front of her beside a half-seen viol. Her naked feet rest against the velvet cloak of the lute player, his back to us, his gaze on her. The suggestion is of a body at ease in an ambient atmosphere that sustains and gently warms. Behind the couch a landscape of increasing wildness is in view: near to, a park with Petrarchan deer beneath the trees, a little further off the rough groves of a rising land, and behind them blue and rugged mountains, a savage landscape held in retreat behind the sumptuous presence of the woman's body. Textures and sounds are invoked as part of visual experience.

In the museum—as in watching the man on the rock—distance is insisted upon. But the tactile is aroused. Touching is embargoed and experienced at once. From the distanced voluptuousness of the picture Darwin catches up its references to music (lute, viol, flute) and imagines the more complete satisfactions of the ear engrossed by voice and instruments. *Hearing* will produce a resolution of bodily experience and culture 'much more

FIG. 1.1. Titian, *Venus and Cupid with a Lute-Player* (Fitzwilliam Museum, Cambridge).

than delightful'.[15] The 'uttered tones' of the Fuegian, less intelligible than those of domestic animals, are here assuaged in the hoped for music of his own society—a music that affected him with profound physicality. The first two bodies of the letter also bring to the surface a trouble about the cross-over of fundamental categories: the human and the animal, the sentient and the art object. And the categories of self, kin, and stranger.

In the letter Darwin turns restlessly from the first two bodies to a third. Both these images have proved inscrutable, or at least impenetrable. The figures of the man—here—as Nature, the woman as Culture, produce both yearning and impasse. They remain untouchable. But in his practice as a zoologist Darwin does touch. He also unveils, invades, lays bare the interiority of small creatures: he is all at once dismayed by a sense of intimate contiguity with that body also. Preserving specimens involves disembowelling.

All the bodies he has conjured in this meditation, including his own, seem suddenly present in the 'small animal'. Disturbingly, the Venus in the Titian portrait presents her belly to the viewer in a posture not unlike that of the upturned small animal displayed to the knife. Darwin flinches away from these connections, seeking to put a space between the body of the woman and of the 'small animal'. Thus he half-consciously protects the innocence of his own touching eye, which in memory glances between male and female, between wild body and encultured body, both of them become teasing objects of desire and consternation.

As Evelyn Fox Keller observes in the passage quoted at the outset of this essay, 'some scientists see their endeavour in predominantly adversarial terms . . . others see it as a primarily erotic activity'. Darwin inclined to eroticism yet found himself sometimes engaged in 'exercises in domination'. So it is that the other images—of autochthonous inhabitant, of woman displayed for the pleasure of the gaze—lie behind that of the small

---

[15] Francis Darwin, (n. 10 above), records a friend's memory of the young Darwin's physical response to music: ' "What gave him the greatest delight was some grand symphony or overture of Mozart's of Beethoven's, with their full harmonies." On one occasion Herbert remembers "accompanying him to the afternoon service at King's, when we heard a very beautiful anthem. At the end of one of the parts, which was exceedingly impressive, he turned to me and said, with a deep sigh: "How's your backbone?".". He often spoke of a feeling of coldness or shivering in his back on hearing beautiful music' (p. 170).

animal: just as the word 'guts' is concealed behind the word 'gusto', and the more dignified 'entrails' is substituted: 'I shall not be able tomorrow to pick out the entrails of some small animal, with half my usual gusto.'

The analyst W. R. Bion, in his post-Kleinian essay 'Attacks on Linking', describes the personality that eschews connection.[16] Darwin's bent seems to have been at the opposite end of the spectrum, seeking kinship in the unlike, making links, making *more* than links since that suggests both connection and distance—immersing himself in sensation. And then seeking to taxonomize and describe. In this passage he experiences the terrors of estrangement, of sexual and aesthetic yearning, and also of empathy.

Sex and sexual congress is central to Darwinian evolutionary theory. The pairing of *unlike* in the couple produces diversity of offspring—and that diversity increases exponentially. Other forms of reproduction—hermaphroditism, parthenogenesis, division, for example—produce offspring that replicate the previous generation.[17] Sexual reproduction inclines *away* from any such standard identity. So unlikeness and empathy were as important to him theoretically as emotionally.

When Darwin did eventually precipitate his theory of evolutionary descent, however, he paradoxically did away with the sexual pair as an initiating origin. For Darwin, the originary parental dyad is figured as the one, sexually undifferentiated—and irretrievable: 'the single progenitor.' This move allowed Darwin to distinguish his theory from that, for example, of Edward Forbes who proposed aboriginal pairs reproducing and populating specific biogeographical zones.[18] But it had a further emotional advantage for Darwin. It did away with fixed difference. It also avoided debating the prior claims of male or female parent (perhaps a consolation in his own case).

---

[16] See W. R. Bion, *Second Thoughts: Selected Papers on Psychoanalysis* (London, 1967), 93–109. See also my *Forging the Missing Link: Interdisciplinary Stories* (Cambridge, 1992).

[17] On the voyage, Darwin observed in detail other such forms of reproduction, writing with particular fascination about 'compound animals'; see pp. 15–16, 31, and, esp. 258–62.

[18] See Janet Browne, *The Secular Ark: Studies in the History of Biogeography* (New Haven and London, 1983) for discussion of Edward Forbes's theories.

In his imagination, at the start, there was an 'It': 'the ancient progenitor, the archetype as it may be called, of all mammals, had its limbs constructed on the existing general pattern.'[19] Male and female, masculine and feminine, human and animal, are not yet disparted. 'The first creature' (458), 'the single progenitor', 'one primordial form' (455), 'the common parent' (413): the 'one parent' (457) is never sexed male or female in his writing. It is *hors-sexe*, and almost *hors-texte*.

The progenitor is undescried, irretrievable, but not sexually distanced: both self and mother, self and father identically. Epistemophilia, driving back towards an unaskable question which may include the search for the lost mother, fuels the pleasures and anxieties of Darwin's work. The intensity of his nostalgia for a lost England, a foregone self, shades in the letter to Whitley into an imaging of primary nakednesses: man, woman, animal. The fascination with taxonomy as well as the desire to be at one with the physical world is gratified for Darwin in his *Beagle* voyage, not only by the sensory riches of the journey but by writing.

In writing, the physical hand makes contact with a repertoire of scenes, figures, and emotions already, even amidst the tumult of current impressions, *not* before his eyes. Among these is his old friend Whitley, less figurable to him now than the Fuegian he has encountered: 'I neither know, where you are living or what you are doing.' Whitley represents a familiar world grown exotic: a picturesque and primitive place of green cottages and white petticoats where young men, anticipating priesthood, ate owls together.[20] Darwin's writing hand conjures Whitley as an absence, a point of identification that will now be for ever fictional: *disembodied.*

[19] Charles Darwin, *On the Origin of the Species by Means of Natural Selection or The Preservation of Favoured Races in the Struggle for Life* (1859), p. 416. Page references are to the Penguin Classics edition, ed. John Burrow (Harmondsworth, 1968).

[20] Francis Darwin (n. 10 above) records that the other members of the Glutton or Gourmet Club, besides Darwin and his friend Herbert, were 'Whitley of St. John's, now Honorary Canon of Durham; Heaviside of Sidney now Canon of Norwich; Lovett Cameron of Trinity, now vicar of Shoreham; Blane of Trinity, who held a high post during the Crimean war; H. Lowe (now Sherbrooke) of Trinity Hall; and Watkins of Emmanuel, now Archdeacon of York' (i. 169). Darwin had a lucky escape.

2

Can the Native Return?

My title is a question: 'Can the Native Return?' It may put you in mind of Hardy, and *The Return of the Native* will indeed be a crucial instance in the later part of my argument, forming the centre of a triptych of examples: 'triptych' here not in the devotional sense, but in the original meaning of a set of three writing-tablets hinged together. But I want briefly to set Hardy's theme in a longer literary perspective and then to demonstrate how for the Victorians the idea of the native's return held particularly disturbing cultural possibilities. For one thing, this was a community that set store by emigration as a solution to social problems: the economically enforced journeying of the poor and the disadvantaged did not expect them back. Self-betterment required, in the fullest sense of the word, *displacement*. Novelists understood the dilemma. Elizabeth Gaskell's *Mary Barton* rescues some of the characters at the end of the book for a new life in Canada, thus producing a happy ending which need not pretend that the situation in England has changed for the better. Dickens' *Great Expectations*, in the histories equally of Magwitch and of Pip, probes the nightmares of return.

There were other issues at stake as well. I shall refer to two important and symptomatic non-fictional controversies that raise these further questions. Both illustrate the particular problems of communal self-valuing active for the Victorians in the idea of the return of the native. The cases, to which I shall come a little later in my argument, are those of Jemmy Button and of Sir John Franklin.

December is a good month to talk about natives' return. The uneasy if pleasurable approach of Christmas with its necessary choice of where to be, how long to stay, or whom to ask, brings into sharp focus *place* as the nexus of kinship and the past. Return is not a matter of memory only, it is *going* somewhere.

Indeed the return of the native has as often been an occasion of confusion, bloodshed and dismay as of rejoicing—in literature at least, let us say. From Ulysses and Agamemnon to Pinter's *Homecoming* and Dürrenmatt's *The Visit*, return has unsettled rather than stabilized. The idea of the native's return seems to offer comfort and completion, but it also harbours a confounding paradox. That the native can return seems plain enough, but can he or she return *as a native?*

The act of return includes recognition and estrangement. Hardy in *The Return of the Native* suggests that 'any native home for the holidays' is a kind of toy person, going to church to see and be seen: 'Thus the congregation on Christmas morning is mostly a Tussaud collection of celebrities who have been born in the neighbourhood' (138). Instead of a now-active person, they present a waxwork display, a mere simulacrum of identity. The safest way. Christmas visits, after all, also imply a promise to go away again. Mrs Yeobright is delighted to have her son home for Christmas. Her alarm begins when he shows no sign of leaving afterwards.

Let me start the argument, though, nearer the literary beginnings of our culture. When Ovid pictured the golden age at the beginning of *Metamorphoses* it was of a time when no one travelled, when people were not conscious of boundaries as bounds to be crossed, when all were at one with the place where they were born and satisfied by the beneficent harvests it provided. Ovid's image of change is the shift from vertical to horizontal. The trees, upright in the woods, are cut and lowered, shaped into boats. Fruitful stasis becomes driven movement. That shift of axes begins the history of the world. In its wake comes trade, conflict, invasion, mingling, and travel.

Happiness may take the form of believing that return is possible while freely delaying the journey. Though return to his homeland is Ulysses' overriding desire, the pleasures of the *Odyssey* depend, for the hero as much as the reader, upon the hindrances and delays of that return. But Ulysses does at last get back to his native land, reclaim his wife, and rule again. Penelope's constant unpicking of her weaving during his absence expresses a magical staying of the processes of onward time. Each day simply begins again the business of the previous one, until the completion of her husband's return is achieved. Decay is held off. By repetition and unravelling, strength and youth are sustained and time is impacted.

The insatiable zeal for travel becomes the expression of life itself. Tennyson in the mid-nineteenth century emended Homer's happy close to show instead Ulysses impatient and alienated in a native land where he is no longer *known*, since the meaning of his life has been in his adventures elsewhere:

> It little profits that an idle king,
> By this still hearth, among these barren crags,
> Matched with an aged wife, I mete and dole
> Unequal laws unto a savage race,
> That hoard, and sleep, and feed, and know not me.
>
> I cannot rest from travel . . . (562)

'Unequal laws unto a savage race': it seems as though he feels himself to have returned into an earlier cultural phase.

Doubts about the satisfactoriness of return did not begin with Tennyson's *Ulysses*. It was a persistent topic in eighteenth-century literature: Defoe's *Captain Singleton* and *Robinson Crusoe* and Johnson's *Rasselas* work out counter-possibilities. Captain Singleton has never known a mother and has no idea what 'home' might mean until he forms a friendship with the Quaker, William. Friendship for him gives a possible meaning to the word. At the end of *Rasselas* the return to the happy valley is an image of satiety. (Hardy's mother gave him this masterpiece of disappointment to read when he was 8.)

Gulliver's Travels most fully works through the problems embedded in the idea of the native's return. At the end of *Gulliver's Travels* Gulliver returns, and in a passage less often noted than his account of how he felt about his family, he raises general issues of power and predation. He takes a final leave of his courteous readers, having justified his behaviour against charges that as a traveller he did not pursue with sufficient zeal the enlargement of his Majesty's dominions by his discoveries.

To say the truth, I had conceived a few scruples with relation to the distributive justice of princes upon these occasions. For instance, a crew of pirates are driven by a storm they know not whither, at length a boy discovers land from the topmast, they go on shore to rob and plunder, they see a harmless people, are entertained with kindness, they give the country a new name, they take formal possession of it for the king, they set up a rotten plank or a stone for a memorial, they murder two or three dozen of the natives, bring away a couple more by force as a sample, return home, and get their pardon. Here commences a new dominion acquired with a title *by divine right.* (237)

In contrast, Gulliver will 'return to enjoy my own speculations in my little garden at Redriff'. That sounds very much like the conclusion of *Candide*, cultivating his garden some thirty years later. But Gulliver is not so much cultivating his garden as his speculations. And these are burdened with his alienation from his native land and its inhabitants. Among the rational horses, the Houyhnhnms, he was seen as a member of the race of filthy Yahoos, albeit a Yahoo of unusually docile and teachable propensities: Gulliver steels himself, like an anti-narcissus, to survey his body in the looking glass: 'to behold my figure often in a glass, and thus if possible habituate myself by time to tolerate the sight of a human creature' (238). By such forced recognition he intends to begin the process of reconcilement that may, one day, make of him again a native in his own land.

To him, human beings now are animals, according with the stereotypes by which human beings describe the 'brutes': merely stinking and irrational. But worse, puffed up with human pride. He has earlier within one sentence described the invaders, or explorers, as an 'execrable crew of butchers employed in so pious an expedition', and as 'a modern colony sent to convert and civilize an idolatrous and barbarous people'. In a dizzying series of ironies, the 'barbarous people' become his own family and even himself, stubbornly and self-woundingly gazing into his looking glass. His 'old habits' now are not those of the clan but those learnt on his journeys: 'And although it be hard for a man late in life to remove old habits, I am not altogether out of hopes in some time to suffer a neighbour Yahoo in my company without the apprehensions I am yet under of his teeth or his claws' (238).

In this collapsing pyramid of superiorities Gulliver is left with nobody with whom to identify. He enacts dualism, split between the body of a Yahoo, the mind of a Houyhnhnm—or so he hopes. He is as proud as the rest of the human race he spurns, even while he claims his alienation from it as a sign of virtue.

Swift here savagely decomposes the trope of the return of the native. At one, and at home at last, Gulliver is more profoundly divided than ever, retching with the stench of other human beings, autocratic, imposing, incapable of any healing dialogue with the natives among whom it is now his lot to live.

He just permits his wife 'to sit at dinner with me, at the farthest end of a long table, and to answer (but with the utmost brevity) the few questions I ask her' (238). The subjugated and silenced wife, held far off, is not put in direct parallel with the harmless people plundered by the representatives of a so-called higher civilization that I have quoted from the previous page. But the potential for such a comparison lies only just beneath the surface of the language. Gulliver thinks of himself as the man elevated by travel and by his discourse with the superior Houyhnhnms. He thinks of himself as an educator. But he is, demeaningly, also the token savage, the sample, educated as far as may be into the image of Houyhnhnm civilization but never accepted by them as one of their own. I shall offer another example of that token figure later in this argument in the person of the Fuegian, Jemmy Button. Gulliver has been undermined for life in his native land by the education he has received among the horses. The last irony (though in Swift we can never be sure that we have quite reached the ultimate irony) is that Houyhnhnm civilization con-figures many of the claimed or acclaimed values of Western civilization.

Swift's scarifying version of the native's return puts into jeo-pardy two comforting words: return and native. Their ambi-guities increasingly haunt nineteenth-century fiction, politics, and philosophy. (And I shall not even begin to talk about Nietz-sche nor, directly, Freud, whose concept of *The Return of the Repressed* Perry Meisel well elaborates in his study of Hardy.)

Patriotism—the ideology of the native land—begins when al-ternatives to the native land can be imagined; it brings with it all the rending ills of war and imperialism as well as the apparent blessings of pastoralism and return. The native land is the land of nativity, simply 'the place where I was born'. Knowing it again is a source of intense pleasure. The congruity between being born and a parcel of land makes of the native land a magic place in which identity, body, culture and location are condensed: 'I am native here, And to the manner born'.

Being born needs a mother. The identification between the native land and the figure of the mother (the motherland, the mother-tongue) produces another set of profound associations, played out in a variety of ways by writers of all ideological casts, and, in Hardy's novel, with extraordinary passion.

Re-cognition: knowing again; knowing anew. That is the perfected dream of return: the simple exoticism of the familiar. One of the most famous of Romantic fables of return is the parable contained within the body of Novalis's *Die Lehrlinge zu Sais*. The parable describes a perfect circle, though the circle is also a spiral of understanding. The hero sets out, leaving his familiar loved one at home. He travels to the ends of the earth. The Goddess unveils herself in his sight. Her face is the face of the loved one left behind. He comes back to his native place, seeing it and its inhabitants for the first time, bathed in the light of recognition. Or, the tale of the Swaffham pedlar, alluded to in Hardy's novel. In that folk tale the Norfolk pedlar goes to London Bridge on the impulse of a dream telling him to seek his fortune in London. There he meets another dreamer who has dreamt about a hidden treasure buried in a Swaffham garden. The pedlar completes the circle, goes home, and finds the treasure in his own yard: the treasure includes knowing the place where you began.

That backward return is possible only if the place itself is seen as unchanging. It merges, therefore, into a dream of nostalgia. The native place becomes the past; its recovery gainsays the ineluctable onward movement of time.

Hardy's novel *The Return of the Native* opens not with people but a place, and that place as unchanging as it is possible to conceive: 'The untameable, Ishmaelitish thing that Egdon now was it always had been. Civilization was its enemy; and ever since the beginning of vegetation its soil had worn the same antique brown dress, the natural and invariable garment of the particular formation' (35). This landscape is savage (in the sense of uncultivated), undeveloped, and unchanged since 'the beginning of vegetation'. In natural-historical, and in anthropomorphic terms ('antique brown dress'), it represents the unaltered conditions of the world.

Hardy moves the return of the native from the end of his story to relatively near its beginning, commented on and foreseen from the point of view of the inhabitants. That return becomes the generative act of his fiction. Instead of long-delayed homecoming providing the uneasy calm of closure, as in the eighteenth-century examples I have mentioned, it here sets off the range of interlocking consequences that make the fiction.

Hardy achieves some of his most disturbing effects by extending the emphasis on the dubieties of *return* into the cultural duplicities lodged in the word *native*. These duplicities may seem to us to have been particularly sanguine and unsurveyed in the Victorian period, but, as one reads further into the period, one discovers that they also provided the matter of much contemporary debate. Edward Said's *Orientalism* has tellingly argued that, so far as the construction of knowledge goes, the difficulty for the traveller is that he or she never really leaves home however long the journey. The assumptions of the home culture and language (in Said's argument European culture and language) imbue what can be seen, and precondition what can be valued. But these assumptions are also always contested, I would argue, within the current language of the tribe: for the Victorians here, within the English language, its relations to other tongues then much under debate, and its wide range of discursive dissonances and consonances particularly active—and quite peculiarly active in the language of Hardy's fiction.

But let me first examine a less considered example than anything Hardy could write. To be a native-born Englishman is a state of privilege; to be a native elsewhere is to be a savage. We can hear the play across these two radically opposed senses of the word in R. M. Ballantyne's *The Coral Island* (1858). Newly shipwrecked on their island, the boys settle in comfortably, but 'we did not quite like the idea of settling down here for the rest of our lives, far away from our friends and our native land . . . Then there was a little uncertainty still as to there being natives on the island. But as day after day passed, and neither savages nor ships appeared . . . we set diligently to work at our homestead' (47). Natives *on* the island, not natives *of* the island, one notes. The phrase 'native intruders' is often bandied about at that period (and indeed long after) with no recognition of its contradictoriness. The natives, rather than the boys, are figured as intruders, and the term native is replaced with its pseudo-synonym savages in the next sentence. Peterkin, in a rehearsal of

Gulliver's satiric terms, here nonchalantly used, though not quite without narrative irony, fantasizes their future: 'We'll take possession in the name of the king; we'll go and enter the service of its black inhabitants. Of course we'll rise, *naturally*, to the top of affairs. White men always do in savage countries' (21) (emphasis added). The boys will discover that things are not quite so simple, one should note in fairness to Ballantyne. But the word 'naturally' neatly loads the whole weight of a culture behind an assumption.

It is not necessary to suppose that Hardy is commenting directly on colonialism in his title to perceive that Clym's status as native draws both on the idea of the civilized Englishman and (as the book goes on) on the idea of cultural regression to the savage state. Clym is shown to be in a more advanced stage of development than his neighbours who stayed at home. He is the man educated beyond his original condition, educated for an as yet non-existent future: 'in Clym Yeobright's face could be dimly seen the typical countenance of the future' (156).

Country-dwellers and exotic islanders alike were seen in much mid- and later nineteenth-century anthropological writing (witness Lubbock, Tylor, Spencer) as existing in an earlier phase of cultural development than that reached by cosmopolitan European man. And here I want to draw into my discussion the first of my three examples, a symptomatic mid-nineteenth-century controversy about natives and return. Hardy may have known it. Whether he did or not does not particularly matter for my argument. The case sheds light on the uneasiness in earlier Victorian writing about 'unspoilt' communities and individual development, an uneasiness that certainly *did* tell in Hardy's work. It sheds light too on the problems of telling a story in a language that does not fit its protagonist.

Captain Fitzroy, later to be the captain of the *Beagle* when Darwin was on board as ship's naturalist, first touched land at Tierra del Fuego in 1830. Fitzroy was an earnest Christian. On the first voyage he kidnapped some Fuegians, or as he might prefer to put it, gave them the opportunity of a Western education. When Fitzroy's crew left, they took away with them a small group—in Swift's term, 'a sample'—of people from the tribe, to whom they subsequently gave grotesque jokey names (not content with renaming the land as Gulliver describes, they renamed individuals): Fuegia Basket, York Minster, Boat Memory (who died of smallpox). Among this small band was Jemmy Button, so-called because he had been exchanged for a mother-of-pearl button (Fitzroy, i.444). Jemmy Button had a considerable social success in England and became obsessive about cleanliness and clothing. Together with Fuegia Basket (who had originally been taken hostage by Fitzroy when some of her tribe, in Fitzroy's words, 'approached with the dextrous cunning peculiar to savages', ii.5) he made an apparently smooth transition to English life. Button and Fuegia Basket were even introduced to Queen Adelaide, who gave Fuegia one of her own bonnets, and were taught English and given some education (ii. 12). Fitzroy felt responsible for the Fuegians (as well he might) and for returning them home: Button, in particular, was to return as a missionary to his tribe. So when Darwin set off on the voyage of the *Beagle*, on board were Button, York Minster, and Fuegia Basket dressed in Western habits.

In 1833 the *Beagle* crew landed the Fuegians near where they had taken them and said farewell. A year later they returned to see how things were going. Darwin and Fitzroy both gave accounts of the reunion. Darwin wrote: 'It was quite painful to behold him [Button]; thin, pale, and without a remnant of clothes, excepting a bit of blanket round his waist, his hair hanging over his shoulders; and so ashamed of himself he turned his back to the ship as the canoe approached.' (Embarrassment at the jarring of two cultures and perhaps resentment might seem to us now quite as probable reasons for his action as shame: 'shame' being itself a term symptomatic of Victorian preoccupations.) Darwin continues: 'When he left us he was very fat, and so particular about his clothes, that he was always afraid of even dirtying his shoes, scarcely ever without his gloves and his hair neatly cut.' (Again, the stresses of someone afraid even to dirty shoes meant functionally for walking might lend itself to counter-analysis.) But things improve and 'lastly we found out in the evening (by her arrival) that he had got a young and very nice looking squaw. This he would not at first own to; and we were rather surprised to find he had not the least wish to return to England.' Darwin accounts for Button's reluctance romantically; English honour is thus satisfied.

After that Button was lost sight of. He was said in the English accounts to have 'disappeared', though to himself and his group he had, rather, re-appeared. He had 'gone native' (though whether someone not a native-born Englishman could 'go native' I'm not sure), or he had re-assimilated. Sent back as an educator, his triumph proved to be his capacity to merge again with his home community and to shed alien habits, though Fitzroy and Darwin feared (and in a curious way, perhaps half-hoped) that he had lost his own language. Unlike Gulliver returning from among the Houyhnhnms, Jemmy Button had not been unfitted for life at home by contact with what the European narrators saw as a higher culture.

There is a further stage to Victorian interpretation of this story. Some fifteen years later Jemmy was sighted again. In 1861 W. Parker Snow published an essay in the *Transactions of the Ethnological Society* (vol. i), in which he recounts his re-discovery of Jemmy Button. Snow apologizes persistently for his own tendency to empathize with the Fuegian community, de-murs politely at the more rancorous accounts by earlier travellers of the inhabitants' morals, and gives a touching vignette of Jemmy Button's mixed reactions to their arrival.

Snow is dutifully shocked to see how little of Button's English education remains: 'Yet that same poor creature had been the petted idol of friends here at home, had been presented to royalty, and finally sent back to Fuego as a passably finished man!' (265). ('A passably finished man' is a powerfully ambiguous phrase.) Jemmy has retained some English and taught it to his group: 'It was marvellously strange that he not only retained some knowledge of the English language, but had actually taught a portion of it to his own relations. Unfortunately what they best understood was some of our worst words, though they certainly attached no wrong meaning to what was said.' Jemmy Button's appearance has returned or (as the Victorians might say) *reverted* to that of his tribe. Haunting the controversy is a debate about nature and nurture, about education and adaptation, that still has not died away.

Snow is caught across two responses: he feels that he should be shocked by this sloughing off of 'civilization'; he is delighted by Button's renewed harmony with his tribe. He is inclined to see this as a tribute to human adaptability rather than as demonstrating that other peoples cannot be educated. Like the other commentators, he does not remark their assumption that Western education is to be taken as the only model for development, though A. R. Wallace did so in *Island Life* some years later. Fitzroy, fifteen years before Snow, claimed that Jemmy's 'family were becoming considerably more humanized than any savages we had seen in Tierra del Fuego' (ii. 326). Snow notices, in a glancing and unanalysed aside, that Button's tribe alone was 'treacherous' towards their English visitors. He does not parallel this phenomenon with the treachery they have experienced in the taking away of their people. But he does record the fears of Button's youngest wife, and he does make clear his profound disapproval of removing people from their own culture, whether by force or cajolery. He only half-conceals his deep disquiet about 'what was done and is still being done regarding his people'.

Snow believes his own culture to lay too much sole stress on the development of *mind*: 'The actual difference between a savage and a civilized man is simply in the degree of cultivation given to the mind. In all other respects the savage at home is identical with the savage abroad' (265). The ravages of *mind*, we may recollect, mar Clym Yeobright's beauty: 'The face was well shaped. But the mind within was beginning to use it as a mere waste tablet whereon to trace its idiosyncracies as they developed themselves. The beauty here visible would in no long time be ruthlessly overrun by its parasite, thought . . .' (156).

Throughout Snow's essay the tone is one of mortified puzzlement. Fitzroy, Darwin, and Snow each write and rewrite extensive interpretations of the episode. They were worried and baffled by it. Snow was the most imaginative interpreter, but it is still the failure of interpretation that is the most revealing aspect of the affair. Snow cannot feel what he is supposed to feel; he does not see what he is expected to find; he presents himself therefore as a partial failure—but that self-presentation allows him mordantly to represent the treacheries and blindnesses of his own community. Snow's writing works as James Clifford in *Writing Culture* argues that good ethnography must do: 'Ethnographic truths are thus inherently *partial*—committed and incomplete . . . But once accepted and built into ethnographic art, a rigorous sense of partiality can be a source of representational tact' (7).

So the tale of Jemmy Button is also a tale of Victorian interpretation and counter-interpretation. It seems to be the tale of a native's successful return to his people, coming back as a potential educator, settling in as an ordinary member of the tribe. But we cannot be sure; the mediation of the experience is so inadequate that we never can retrieve Button's experience. Not being able to retrieve it becomes *our* experience, an experience that includes bafflement and remorse. Nor do we inhabit the right language for retrieval: even my necessary mis-calling of him Jemmy Button makes that clear. Who is the native speaker here? And in what language can the tale be told? The poor fit between the language of interpretation and of experience tells its own story.

The Victorian justification for such acts as the taking away of Jemmy Button and his companions was partly religious but partly to be found in the belief in 'survivals'. Remote tribes and, sometimes, country people, were believed to represent intact much earlier phases in the cultural development of humankind. By studying such people the remote past could be revisited. As Edward Clodd, anthropologist and folklorist, put it to Hardy: 'your Dorset peasants represent the persistence of the same barbaric idea which confuses persons and things.' History was still active in the present time, not in the mutated form of continuity and gradual irreversible change, but *unchanged* in its early lineaments. The pockets of inhabitants in isolated places preserved intact earlier forms and traditions. Some of the connections to Hardy's thinking and to his creative building of story now begin to become clearer.

Critics have from time to time objected to the role of the country people in *The Return*, seeing them either as Shakespearean loons or as a somewhat mannered rustic Greek chorus. They are, rather (or also), in Hardy's writing, the surviving and continuing representatives of earlier human life.

Hardy describes the songs, the customs, the superstitions, the speech-styles of these country-dwellers, sometimes in set-pieces as in the mumming episode. He devotes entire scenes to the lighting of the bonfires on November 5th and to the malignant custom of pinsticking employed against Eustacia, who is believed to be a witch in some groups of the country community. The melting of Eustacia's image—so shortly followed by her death from drowning—unsteadies the knowing outsider's assumption that magic is malicious but ineffective. Here, as so often, Hardy establishes contiguous routes to the overdetermined event: through coincidence and witchcraft, or, at the same time, through psychological motive and independent event. Neither form of explanation drives out the other. They appear as parallel languages rather than as opposed interpretations. Present and past belief systems coexist. They do not follow an ordered succession.

In this arrangement, Hardy was pursuing a path rather different from that set out by most of the anthropologists and sociologists of the period: for example, Comte and Spencer (whom Hardy named among his chief intellectual influences) insist on fixed successive phases of culture. Tylor had suggested that the vestiges of earlier belief undermined modern civilizations, and he instanced law, with its rule of primogeniture, and poetry as examples of 'survivals' within current belief-systems. Hardy himself riposted to Clodd's remark that 'the barbaric idea which confuses persons and things', in Clodd's phrase, is 'common to the highest imaginative genius, that of the poet'.

Strikingly, Hardy introduces early in the book the figure of Christian Cantle, an intersex or hermaphroditic figure. The scene in which his predicament is discussed is often read as an embarrassing Victorian comic set-piece. But it can be read along a different grain, taking us with extraordinary rapidity into the value-systems of the local community. The anthropologist Clifford Geertz has recently argued in *Local Knowledge* that attitudes to intersex people offer a means of analysing the central characteristics of diverse cultures. Geertz argues that because intersex or hermaphroditic people challenge sexual divisions in their physical make-up, and thereby gender attributions, their treatment rapidly uncovers the specifying values of particular groups. As Geertz remarks in 'Common Sense as a Cultural System': 'Common sense is not what the mind cleared of cant spontaneously apprehends; it is what the mind filled with presuppositions . . . concludes' (84). Christian reacts with quaking dismay to the talk about the man whom no woman at all would marry and reveals himself as such another one, as he calls himself, a 'maphrotight' (52). ' "Why did ye reveal yer misfortune, Christian?" "'Twas to be if 'twas, I suppose" ' (52).

The reactions to Christian within the immediate group are low-key and humane, though edged with joking condescension. Fairway is forthright: 'Wethers must live their time as well as other sheep, poor soul' (53). In this early scene Hardy pinpoints the matter-of-fact tolerance in the heath community which sees ghosts and hermaphrodites equally as unusual phenomena but native to the place, and therefore to be accepted.

The recording of customs, the allusive speech-patterns, the philological self-awareness of Hardy's composition owe much, as Hardy acknowledged, to the inspiration of his friend William Barnes, poet, folklorist, and philologist. Barnes is often referred to as a local dialect poet, one wholly centred in Dorset; but this is to misunderstand how the relations between local and total were working in Victorian culture. Victorian philology and etymology were preoccupied with the relations between English and other languages within the Indo-Germanic group. The question of common roots between remote tongues was much under discussion. The discursive array within English was being linked to issues of class, of national autonomy, of cultural progression. Barnes tracked between the local and the total. We can see this movement even in a list of some of his books' titles: *A Philological Grammar, grounded upon English, and Formed From a Comparison of More than Sixty Languages* (London, 1854); *Notes on Ancient Britain and the Britons* (1858); *Tiw; or, a View of the Roots and Stems of the English as a Teutonic Language* (1862); *Poems of Rural Life, in the Dorset Dialect* first, second, and third collections, in the 1850s and 1860s; *Early England and the Saxon English* (1869); *A glossary of the Dorset Dialect with a grammar of its word shapening and wording* (1886). Barnes delves into remote history; he considers the relationships of English to other languages, present and past; he investigates the customs of present day country people; he elaborates that which is particular to Dorset in a way that makes it an element in an expansive and systematic enquiry.

The expansion depends upon particularity, but Barnes and Hardy share a swerve or vacillation between experience-near and experience-far language (to use Geertz's terms again). Indeed Hardy has sometimes been criticized for what commentators see as his intrusive allusions to other cultural spheres. His vocabulary ricochets across registers, between language close as touch and removed as latinate legal documents. As readers, we are shifted unendingly between microscopic and telescopic, between very old dialect words and very up-to-date references, particularly in relation to Eustacia. So within the individual observer or reader the phases of past cultural development are enacted synchronically through the language of the novel.

At the end of the description of the 'mummied heathbells of last summer' the paragraph opens: ' "The spirit moved them." ' A meaning of the phrase forced itself upon the attention; and an emotional listener's fetichistic mood might have ended in one of more advanced quality' (78). The allusion is to Tylor's work on the sequence of psychological phases in the past of humankind, but Hardy here invokes the belief also in recapitulation within the individual of the past of human development. He shows the repeated enactment of cultural phases within the present of the reader. Though not, let it be noted, within the native inhabitants of the heathland, other than Clym. Such enactment of earlier phases, after all, assumes (within the Victorian pattern of development) that the reader has come to the highest and last phase of the sequence.

And here I come to the third of my instances, the third writing-tablet of the triptych. One of the strangest and most original of the vacillations between near and far within the book is the recurrent invocation of Arctic scenery and of the idea of the migrating bird, creature of multiple homelands, returning as a native to our land, received as native at the other end of the world as well. This invocation of movement and of temperature-extremes forms unfamiliar sensory experience in the reader and also taps into another troubled Victorian expedition. At the book's opening, Hardy proposes a future for tourism. The extreme and barren Northern lands, Greenland, Thule, and the unmitigated flatness of Flemish landscape, rather than the South, will be the magnet for future human travel he suggests. Egdon is as unchanging as the Arctic, a basic and ultimate natural world which ignores and outscales humankind. It is also a place much frequented and visited by other species. At the beginning of chapter 10 Hardy details the rare birds of the heath: bustards, marsh-harriers, even a cream-coloured courser, an 'African truant' a bird so rare that 'not more than a dozen have ever been seen in England' (and of course shot down as soon as sighted).

Egdon Heath puts a possible traveller (the reader) 'in direct communication with regions unknown to man'. The passage ends with an ordinary mallard who becomes a fabled bird:

A traveller who should walk and observe any of these visitants . . . could feel himself to be in direct communication with regions unknown to man. Here in front of him was a wild mallard—just arrived from the home of the north wind. The creature brought with him an amplitude of Northern knowledge. Glacial catastrophes, snow-storm episodes, glittering auroral effects, Polaris in the zenith, Franklin underfoot,—the category of his commonplaces was wonderful. (108).

The allusion to 'Franklin underfoot' gives access to an unsettling episode of Victorian life, an episode that brought into lurid focus the question of the phases of cultural development. Hardy would have been a boy of about 13 at the height of the controversy in around 1854–5. The senior explorer Sir John Franklin's last Arctic expedition, seeking a Northwest Passage, disappeared in July 1846 and was never found again. A number of following expeditions were sent to rescue them but without success. A reward was offered. And in 1854 Dr John Rae, Chief Factor of the Hudson's Bay company, reported that he had discovered the fate of the explorers. According to his Eskimo informants, they were all dead, and had been driven to cannibalism before they died.

Dickens, among others, was outraged. *Household Words* carried the debate between Dickens and Rae: Dickens accused Rae of trusting the words of savages and Rae replied that these people were native to the region, understood the exigencies of starvation, and were credible witnesses. Rae attacked Dickens's view of the Eskimos 'who seem to be looked upon by those who know them not, as little better than brutes'. He scornfully quotes Dickens's words opposing the summoning of Eskimo witness: 'It may be, (Rae comments) I have only the words of "babbling and false savages who are, without exception, in heart, covetous, treacherous, and cruel" in support of what I say.' Rae then offers a number of anecdotes to illustrate the courage and high-mindedness of his informants. Dickens made the expedition the basis for his play with Wilkie Collins, *The Frozen Deep*, leaving out any reference at all to cannibalism.

Hardy's fugitive allusion to 'Franklin underfoot' here would disturbingly remind the Victorian reader of the return of repressed forms of behaviour under the durance of extreme conditions. Modern man, the well-trained English gentleman, goes to his death responding to the primal drives of hunger and thirst in 'an amplitude of Northern knowledge'. Like Jemmy Button's, though for different reasons, Franklin's account of his experience is missing.

Franklin did not return home; he and his companions, Rae asserted, had instead returned to the bedrock of human survival behaviour. The issue is still debated 150 years on.[1] Rae's argument was subtle: even cannibalism may be ordered into moral scrupulousness, and indeed is so by the Eskimos who are driven to practise it; therefore we should believe their witness *because* they occasionally practise cannibalism themselves and understand the conditions that enforce such behaviour. As we might expect, this argument about Eskimo testimony cut little ice in England. Correspondents in *The Times* were simply aghast. For most of his contemporaries, the English gentleman Franklin had come unbearably close to Frankenstein's monster, who vanishes into the Arctic wastes at the end of Mary Shelley's book—close in more than name. Denial was the only possible response.

But Hardy stirred that memory to different purposes. The dangerous realm in which the English explorers lived and died with so much suffering is the familiar domain of the mallard. The mallard is the wild duck whom we take for granted as a familiar native of the English countryside. The blurring between rural England and the Arctic in the book's allusive system disequilibriates any easy developmental assumptions the reader may bring to the work—and implicitly disturbs Clym's initial enterprise of educating the natives. *Migration* in this work represents the only resilient form of escape and survival: moving seasonally to keep in temper with a supportive environment. In Victorian anthropology the two great categories were the 'settled' and the 'nomadic' tribes. Out of the 'settled' came civilization. But here Hardy suggests a third possibility: the native inhabitants are constantly

---

[1] The question of the fate of the Franklin expedition continues to exercise present-day writers: one suggestion is that they died of lead poisoning from their tinned food. Owen Beattie and John Geiger, *Frozen in Time* (London, 1987) present fresh evidence for the cannibalism theory. For an account of the Rae–Dickens controversy see Ian R. Stone ' "The Contents of the Kettles": Charles Dickens, John Rae and Cannibalism on the 1845 Franklin Expedition', *The Dickensian*, 83 (Spring, 1987), 7–15.

on the move within the confines, or within the range, of the heath. And where in that case (to turn to my last question) is the reader stationed in the life of the writing? How are we made native to the place as well as swerving back upon it? What migratory track are *we* to follow?

Throughout the book Hardy makes us aware of the native inhabitants' power of making sensory discriminations lost to the town-dweller, what he calls 'acoustic pictures' (107): 'they could hear where the tracts of heather began and ended; where the furze was growing stalky and tall; where it had recently been cut; in what direction the fir-clump lay, and how near was the pit in which the hollies grew; for these differing features had their voices no less than their shapes and colours' (107). He makes the ear attentive to the particular character of the heath, and builds a landscape derived not from eye alone but from all the senses, and above all from sound and touch: 'What was heard *there* could be heard nowhere else' (78).

The most intimate expression of physical familiarity between the heath and its denizens is the natives' power of crossing and recrossing it in darkness.

The whole secret of following these incipient paths, where there was not light enough in the atmosphere to show a turnpike-road, lay in the development of the sense of touch in the feet, which comes with years of night-rambling in little-trodden spots. To a walker practised in such places a difference between impact on maiden herbage, and on the crippled stalks of a slight footway, is perceptible through the thickest boot or shoe. (80)

The ear makes acoustic pictures; the foot distinguishes intensities of impact. Scene after scene in this book takes place at night when sound and touch are essential to navigation: Eustacia measures Wildeve's attachment to her by the distance travelled: 'three miles in the dark for me. Have I not shown my power?' (87).

By such means as repeated sensory description, and particularly by awakening the senses usually muffled in reading process, such as touch and to some degree hearing, the novel suggests a kinship of fugitive recall between narrative and characters. That is, the work enters a claim to be at home on the heath on behalf of writer, and reader. Yet at the same time we are to be detached from the heath, observing, surveying. We are to become natives and yet we are still to sustain our outsider's gaze. A degree of empathy and detachment together is produced that goes beyond the chosen methods of anthropology and is perhaps attainable only in the thickness of language of a fiction.

Making the reader a native is brought about by invoking sound, touch, smell, temperature, body-weight, occasionally taste. And by rendering morally equivocal the primary public sense of observation: sight. In this book the virtuous reddleman is a voyeur and Clym is at his most fulfilled when he loses his sight and merges with the heath. The writing intermittently invokes the presence of that feasible but absent observer with whose eye Hardy so often sets the scene. This perspectival eye creates a riddling and erratic distance, calling into question the relationship between sight, truth, and interpretation.

The reader's own act of reading is a sighted act, an act, moreover, that establishes interpretative distance and cultural privilege; our position as observer is reinforced by the repeated interposition of possible watchers, viewers, observers, even quasi-anthropologists, in Hardy's scene-setting. Eustacia, native to Budmouth and child of a foreign, seagoing father, is the most frequent intercessionary figure for the reader, standing in for us, becoming, scribally, identified with the shifting positions of the writing more than any other character. Intermittently we enter the sensory state of being a native. The paradox remains that we do so by means of the process of reading, itself an outcome of an education most of these native inhabitants do not share. The book emphasizes this difference through its allusions across a wealth of reference to be gained solely by means of reading. Obliteration comes to Clym willy-nilly when his eyes fail. He works as a furze-cutter in a congruity of response to the heath that has the quality of bliss as well as of privation. So Clym, the educator and educated, loses for a time the power of reading and writing. But the reader continues to read.

Can other states of consciousness be revived by the act of reading? What, from reading-experience, can we learn about this way of life? And what, within the fiction, can Clym teach to this community? What indeed does Clym believe that he can accomplish by his return? What does he plan to teach? The properties of modern civilization? Discontent? Mathematics? Other languages? Or simply the process of inscription itself—reading and writing—by whose means in his own modern world experience principally survives? The content of his syllabus is never made clear. Yeobright figures himself initially as donor and teacher of new forms of knowledge. He is not an antiquarian, interested in legends and customs in order to preserve them. To that degree he remains a native, taking for granted what would be precious to one from further off.

The mummers, we are told, are part of an unrevived tradition, not of modern folklorism: 'This unweeting manner of performance is the true ring by which, in this refurbishing age, a fossilized survival may be known from a spurious reproduction' (141). Hardy sets the geological authenticity of 'fossilised survival' over against the hotelier's 'refurbishing'. Its value (the 'true ring' of silver as opposed to base metal) is in its unchanged 'survival' from distant oral culture. The word 'unweeting', for unknowing or unconscious, itself summons up a backward trajectory that reaches across lost centuries: archaic words are still current in dialect. 'Unweeting' is used already as archaism in Edmund Spenser's *Faerie Queene* at the end of the sixteenth century. That is, the word is itself a 'survival', vouching for the authenticity of unchanged language, undislodged communities.

In such tradition the originating symbolic systems have vanished within a surplus of decoration. All the energy goes into the decoration not the meaning now. The girls so ornately decorate their chosen men that, what with added scallops and ribbons, it is impossible to tell the Moslem from the Christian characters. The unsymbolic state of the performance is important here. It has become part of quite another ritual—of courtship—not of allusion to the crusades. Hardy is affirming an observation of the mythographer and comparative philologist Max Müller: originating meaning becomes lost and the metaphor employed to describe it takes over a substantive role.

Hardy seems to suggest here, rather, that the originating meaning is not so much lost as sunk beneath observation, imbuing the local culture, as the reddleman is imbued with a red that makes him seem, variously and at once, devil, outcast, and workaday familiar. The reddleman's ambiguities of appearance scare the children and the timid, and he does not quite fit into any of the social categories of the group. He is more symbolic, carrying a freight of diverse significations, than is the mumming play now. He is also, with the hindsight of narrative, shown to be the end of an economic phase, a dodo (as he is called), though not yet an extinct species.

Moreover, the reddleman is a wanderer who roams the heath 'like an unhived bee' (102) or like an Arab (100). Hardy suggests that no clear distinction is to be made between the settled and the nomadic in a community which is so scattered. The settled–nomadic distinction fundamental to the work of many nineteenth-century anthropologists and ethnologists, such as James Prichard, is here replaced by the ideas of 'traversing' and 'migration'. A different psychic and social pattern is suggested. The wild ponies, or heath-croppers, express the endlessly *traversing* spirit of the group. But people in the book walk for a purpose, to destinations, however wayward may seem their route: and all those destinations are within the circumference of the heath. To be forced beyond its range is, for most of these people, a disaster of the kind that Hardy described in 'The Dorsetshire Labourer' and explored in *Tess of the D'Urbervilles*. The birds' free migratory movement becomes heavy-laden when translated into human social and economic terms: the enforced travel of the poor is oppression.

At the end of the book we come back to an image of stasis that we have known at the beginning when Eustacia appeared at the top of the hill like a spike on a helmet. At the end Clym replaces Eustacia as 'the motionless figure standing on the top of the tumulus'. He is preaching, on this last page of the novel, on a text obsessively concerned with the loss of the mother and the desire to re-instate her: 'This afternoon the words were as follows:— "And the king rose up to meet her, and bowed himself unto her, and sat down on his throne, and caused a seat to be set for the king's mother; and she sat on his right hand. Then she said, I desire one small petition of thee; I pray thee say me not nay. And the king said unto her, ask on, my mother: for I will not say thee nay" '(405).

In a book composed of passional triangles, by far the most intense (alternately drenching and arid in emotion) is that between Mrs Yeobright, Clym Yeobright, and Eustacia—mother, son, and wife. I argued earlier that the return of the native figures a return to nativity—to the place of birth, and, further, to the mother who gave birth in that place. Re-entering the mother's womb is impossible; entering the mother sexually is insufficient as well as destructive. Clym is debarred. The impossibility of return, back through childhood, into the womb, is dramatized in the form of the Oedipus story. And that myth is referred to at the moment that Clym discovers that his mother has visited them and was not received by Eustacia. A parallel springs up in the language between Clym's blindness and the self-blinding of Oedipus. And again the imagery of ice enters; here the relentless unchangingness of the landscape dwarfs human emotion:

The pupils of his eyes, fixed steadfastly on blankness, were vaguely lit with an icy shine; his mouth had passed into the phase more or less imaginatively rendered in studies of Oedipus. The strangest deeds were possible to his mood. But they were not possible to his situation. Instead of there being before him the pale face of Eustacia and a masculine shape unknown, there was only the imperturbable countenance of the heath, which, having defied the cataclysmic onsets of centuries, reduced to insignificance by its seamed and antique features the wildest turmoil of a single man. (328)

In this setting the primary Oedipal obsession is linked with the absolute unchangingness of the surroundings, surroundings as unaltered and as absolute as the Arctic, and as mindless of human kind. Clym's zeal as educator is worsted: if there is movement, recursiveness, not progress, is the tide that prevails.

The conflicts between Clym's urge towards the future and his foiled desire to return across time, between the endless re-enact-ment of remorse and the prim commentary on his calling, makes for a grating humour in this last scene. Clym's listeners 'abstrac-tedly pulled heather, stripped ferns, or tossed pebbles down the slope'. 'Yeobright had, in fact, found his vocation in the career of an itinerant open-air preacher and lecturer on morally unim-peachable subjects . . . speaking not only in simple language on Rainbarrow and in the hamlets round, but in a more cultivated strain elsewhere.' Clym, the returning native, resolves into an itinerant. Yet he is still in command of language, now turning it towards the bedrock of human experience, turning away from 'mind': 'He left alone creeds and systems of philosophy, finding enough and more than enough to occupy his tongue in the opinions and actions common to all good men.' The last irony, shifting between benign and rancorous even while you look, is that this unhoused preacher is 'everywhere kindly received, for the story of his life had become generally known'. He is received, as the wanderer and the outcast, instead of as the educator.

In our century, where a characterizing ghastly movement has been that forced on people driven out of their homes as refugees by oppression, war, and famine, and the answering movement has been that of people driven by the longing to re-possess the homeland they have lost, the idea of the return of the native has become laden with kinds of tragedy pitched beyond Hardy's compass in this book. The return Hardy envisages at the end of the novel is, for Clym, one of depletion and loss; but it is also represented as a return from the casuistries of the intellect to a common tongue, a bedrock of concern with the ordinary and profound dilemmas in which people find themselves. A paradox remains within Hardy's writing: such a return can only be enacted by means of the casuistries of the intellect. The formidable range of discourses that Hardy fugitively seizes upon, the haunting immediacy with which he gives the reader bodily access to the heath-dwellers' world relies on written language, in Hardy's work extraordinarily diversified. Communality depends on records, inscribing the traces of an oral culture. Clym wanders within the span of the heath while the reddleman settles down to be a dairy-farmer again. They change places: one ceasing to be a nomad, the other becoming it. Yet this exchange will not satisfy. The final image rankles. Clym, a barren man, is welcomed for his life-story. Like Christian Cantle, he is accepted now as an oddity, outside the line of descent; a tribute (in both senses: palliative offering as well as praise) to the community he had meant to educate.

So, can the native return? For the Victorians, it seems, only at the price of returning to an earlier cultural stage in their development pattern. In Hardy's imagination, as in that of other Victorian writers, return is not possible for the native without the idea of retrogression. The reader, however, enacts all the diverse phases of cultural experience within the span of Hardy's language, not in sequence only but alongside and in contestation with each other. In this way, the novel itself suggests quite another kind of 'survival', and even a different ethnographic pattern.

REFERENCES

Page references within the text are to these editions.

Ballantyne, R.M., *The Coral Island: a Tale of the Pacific Ocean* (London, 1858).

Barnes, William, *A philological grammar, grounded upon English, and formed from a comparison of more than sixty languages* (London, 1854); *Poems of Rural Life, in the Dorset Dialect* (London, 1866); *An Outline of English Speech-craft* (London, 1878).

Brannan, Robert Louis (ed.), *Under the Management of Mr. Charles Dickens His Production of 'The Frozen Deep'*, (Ithaca, New York, 1968).

Clifford, James, and Marcus, George E., *Writing Culture: The Poetics and Politics of Ethnography* (Berkeley, 1986).

Dickens, Charles, 'The Lost Arctic Voyagers', *Household Words*, 2, 9 December 1854; *Great Expectations* (London, 1861).

Fitzroy, Robert, and Darwin, Charles, *Narrative of the Surveying Voyages of His Majesty's Ships Adventure and Beagle, Between the years 1826 and 1836, describing their Examination of the southern Shores of South America, and the Beagle's Circumnavigation of the Globe*, 3 vols. (vols. 1 and 2 by Fitzroy, vol. 3 by Darwin) (London, 1839).

Gaskell, Elizabeth, *Mary Barton* (London, 1848).

Geertz, Clifford, *Local Knowledge: Further Essays in Interpretive Anthropology* (New York, 1983).

Hardy, Thomas, *The Return of the Native*, New Wessex Edition (London, 1975) (First published 1878).

Meisel, Perry, *Thomas Hardy: The Return of the Repressed* (New Haven and London, 1972).

Müller, F. Max, *Lectures in the Science of Language*, 1st and 2nd series (London, 1863–4).

Rae, John, 'The Lost Arctic Voyagers' and 'Dr. Rae's Report', *Household Words*, 23, 30 December 1854.

Said, Edward, *Orientalism* (London, 1978).

Snow, W. Parker, 'A Few Remarks on the Wild Tribes of Tierra del Fuego from Personal Observation', *Transactions of the Ethnological Society of London*, NS vol. 1 (London, 1861).

Swift, Jonathan, *Gulliver's Travels, and Other Writings*, ed. Louis Landa (Oxford, 1976) (First published 1726).

Tennyson, Alfred Lord, *The Poems*, ed. Christopher Ricks (London, 1969).

Tylor, Edward, *Primitive Culture*, 2 vols. (London, 1871).

3
Travelling the Other Way: Travel Narratives and Truth Claims

All narratives take the reader or listener on a journey, and many of them tell the story of a journey too. Narratives are organized to move through time, to transport the reader, and to bring us home again, augmented by the experience and by the knowledge we have acquired. This narrative motion is enacted as much in non-fictional accounts, like the many records of nineteenth-century surveying voyages, as it is in the *Odyssey* or *Gulliver's Travels*. The differences begin when we examine the freight the reader gains by the expedition.

Almost all accounts of travels offer wonders, as well as a record of hardship endured by the narrator and his (usually his) companions. When Othello woos Desdemona he does so with his 'traveller's history' which is also a 'travaillous history': the ear does not discriminate between hardship and travel; their identity is part of the pleasure of the story told and part of its verification. The travel narrative, published or recounted, is a record of survival: the narrator is *here* to tell it in retrospect even as the reader sets out on the journey. That double motion offers reassurance: the experiences undergone, the knowledge gained, the treasure or the specimens preserved, are all trophies for the returning traveller and are proffered also to the reader. Material specimens and treasures are to be had only by proxy, but knowledge is more portable and may become part of the reader's own experience by reading the book. The publication of the 'history' affirms the traveller's re-entry into his initial culture, one presented as shared with the reader. After a spell as alien, the narrator is again homely, caught into current society's processes of exchange and affirmation.

These are some of the implicit assurances offered by travel narrative. But the question of its claim to truth is always ambiguous: travellers' tales are notorious for their self-serving exaggeration. The reader cannot check the authenticity of the monsters described, the adventures lived through. Confusions between actual and imagined voyages are frequent. Some writers, like Daniel Defoe, ransacked the accounts of others and adopted the plain style of authentic record, the careful downplaying of crisis, to such effect that his account of *A New Voyage Round the World By a Course Never Sailed Before* (London, 1725) was accepted as a true record for years after his death, to say nothing of the convincing (but fictional) record of his Colonel Jack's travels in Africa or Robinson Crusoe's make-do and mend on his fortunately fertile island.

The tradition of imaginary voyages is ancient and continuous, and natural-historians on their travels therefore found themselves writing within rhetorical modes that were both enabling and dangerous to their project: enabling because detailed sensory description was valued in the genre, dangerous because such description was easily melded into fantasy and received as playful exaggeration, not controlled observation. Diaries, field notes, samples, and specimens, all the local and immediate evidence of encounter and categorization, therefore became particularly important in vouching for the objectivity of record. Yet at the same time the phenomenological, the personal moment, the record of what is smelt, touched, tasted, seen, and heard by the subject, provides other convincing written evidence of the authenticity of what is told. It also translates as pleasure, one of the most compelling persuasive registers that writing can reach.

The question of the personal becomes a key issue: Who sees? What is seen? What are the conditions of observation? The personal both vouches for and limits the scope of observation and its authority. So the persona adopted by the narrator, or the taken-for-granted social contract between narrator and readers, must be exploited to give the widest possible scope and the greatest possible appearance of objectivity and disinterested access. Freiherr Alexander von Humboldt's (1769–1859) *Personal Narrative of Travels to the Equinoctial Regions of the New Continent, during the Years 1799–1804*[1] provided a formidable

---

[1] trans. H. Williams, 7 vols., (London, 1814–29).

example for nineteenth-century naturalists. His eminent eye, his range of sensuous description, his human contacts, impelled the reader into an identification that was physical and intellectual, specific and generalizing. For Charles Darwin the *Personal Narrative* fuelled his enthusiasm for travel and observation alike and provides a constant point of reference in his description of the Beagle voyage:[2] D'Orbigny is 'second only to Humboldt' (iii. 110) and the phrase 'Humboldt has observed' recurs frequently (e.g. iii. 447). Humboldt's presence in citation also indicated the international gentlemanly community of enquirers.

The title-pages of many a travel narrative reveal the strategies of endorsement adopted. Henry Walter Bates, Alfred Russel Wallace's friend and collaborator, in his title suggests an all-inclusive cornucopia without too much self-consciousness about categories of knowledge; the whole is sustained, and contained, by his self-description as 'the Naturalist': *The Naturalist on the River Amazons: A Record of Adventures, Habits of Animals, Sketches of Brazilian and Indian Life, and Aspects of Nature under the Equator during eleven years of travel.*[3] Bates emphasizes the length of his sojourn ('eleven years') and the range of his interests. He includes events, ('adventures'); systemizing ('habits'); and amateur and contingent observations of other peoples, not claimed as ethnographic studies ('sketches'). He acknowledges different levels and styles of knowledge-acquisition within one person's experience. Though social class is often important in the traveller's self-presentation, it is not so in the Bates example: here, in the late 1860s, his profession ('naturalist') is emphasized.

Earlier, the gentlemanly traveller, such as Louis Antoine, Comte de Bougainville, is assumed in his *Voyage autour du monde* (Paris, 1771) to have a synthesizing gaze that can

---

[2] The first form in which the book we now know as *The Voyage of the Beagle* appeared was as Volume 3 of *Narrative of the Surveying Voyages of his Majesty's Ships Adventure and Beagle, between the years 1826 and 1836, describing their Examination of the Southern Shores of South America, and the Beagle's Circumnavigation of the Globe* (London, 1839). Volume 1 was by Captain P. Parker King and covers the earlier expeditions; volume 2 is by Captain Robert Fitzroy, captain of the *Beagle*, and his account overlaps temporally with that of volume 3 by Charles Darwin. The publisher Henry Colburn produced Darwin's volume as a separate book in the following year as *Journal of Researches into the Natural History and Geology of the Countries visited during the voyage of H.M.S. 'Beagle' Round the World*, and in 1845 a second revised and expanded edition appeared.

[3] 2 vols. (London, 1869).

encompass the discrete findings of field workers and accommodate them to his own large vision. The trust of the authorities that send the traveller out is also imprimatur; the King, the Admiralty, the Royal Society, and, in the period that most concerns me here, the support of the British Association for the Advancement of Science (so we find, for example, in 1831 an account of 'His Majesty's sloop Chanticleer's voyage under Commodore Henry Foster, F.R.S.').

Underpinning these social and intellectual claims to authority, and seemingly largely unobserved by initial writer and reader, is a formation we can afford at present to be sharp-eyed about: that of the imperial and colonizing enterprise. That process may have a religious function: missionaries going forth to convert individuals and cultures. It may be part of land acquisition and conquest. It may also be part of a concern to map the seas, the sounds, the minerals, the rocks, the rivers, the interiors, the peoples of the place. When that exploration is condensed within a pattern of expectation that assumes a range of development in human societies moving from primitive to civilized a particularly ample authority can be claimed, since the civilized is assumed to be the place from which the writer starts and to which he returns. The writing is itself civilization at work on the unruly.

Yet current readers would be self-aggrandizing if they believed themselves to be the first to offer a sceptical critique of the motivation, outcome, and justification of voyages of exploration. Near the end of *Travels into Several Remote Nations of the World, in Four Parts. By Lemuel Gulliver, first a Surgeon, and then a Captain of Several Ships* (London, 1726) Jonathan Swift has Gulliver muse on the 'distributive justice of princes':

> For instance, a crew of pirates are driven by a storm they know not whither, at length a boy discovers land from the topmast, they go on shore to rob and plunder, they see a harmless people, are entertained with kindness, they give the country a new name, they take formal possession of it for the king, they set up a rotten plank or a stone for a memorial, they murder two or three dozen of the natives, bring away a couple more by force as a sample, return home, and get their pardon. Here commences a new dominion acquired with a title *by divine right*.

And Denis Diderot inverts Bougainville's *Voyage autour du monde par la frégate du roi la Boudeuse, et la flûte l'Étoile en*

1766, 1767, 1768, et 1769 (Paris, 1771) in *Supplément au voyage de Bougainville* (Paris, 1773) with an imagined Tahitian's telling account of *his* journey to Europe: a voyage in the reverse direction that was by no means fictional only, as Gulliver's reference to 'samples' suggests, and as the account of the two voyages of the *Beagle* later in this essay will make clear.

The voyages with which this essay is chiefly concerned were those whose prize was represented as knowledge rather than treasure. The categories are, however, not altogether separate. Although the nineteenth-century journeys that set out from Britain to survey the seas and coasts around the world were not piratical, not part of that unconcerned predation that earlier centuries justified as exploration or discovery, they were nevertheless an expression of the will to control, categorize, occupy, and bring home the prize of samples and of strategic information. Natural history and national future were closely interlocked. And natural history was usually a sub-genre in the programme of the enterprise, subordinate to the search for sea-passages or the mapping of feasible routes and harbours.

The prosaic quality of such voyages' enterprise could also become part of the claim to truth-telling. Here, there is to be no surplus adventuring, no high-flown description, but an accurate record of observation and encounter. This level aim assumes that the ship's company has one coherent project and plan in view. But the disturbances manifest in the narrative language describing such voyages undermines that assumption. Fascination with the unfamiliar, fear and loathing, the longing for stable systems of communication, sickness, religious fervour, and the physical pleasures of exploration all pressed across and became part of enquiry and leave their traces in the writing. And so, particularly, do the peoples encountered.

NATURAL HISTORY AND INDIGENOUS PEOPLES

He expressed his regret that so little attention was given to Ethnography, or the natural history of the human race, while the opportunities for observation are every day passing away; and concluded by an appeal in favour of the Aborigines Protection Society.

Among the records of the ninth meeting of the British Association for the Advancement of Science, held at Birmingham in
August 1839,[4] occurs this summary of a paper by the ethnographer James Prichard. It suggests one of the most pressing
issues raised by travels and their narratives in the nineteenth
century and pursued particularly by Prichard. What are the
boundaries of natural history? Are human beings within its
scope? Are they one species or several? Are they separate from all
other species because created as souls by God? And do all, all
savages, have souls? Or are they—here danger lies—a kind of
animal? (If they, then we?)

Elsewhere in this same volume, in the 'Synopsis of Grants of
Money at Birmingham' and under the heading 'Zoology and
Botany' we discover the response to Prichard's appeal:

For Printing and Circulating a Series of Questions and Suggestions for the
use of travellers and others, with a view to procure Information respecting
the different races of Men, and more especially of those which are in an
uncivilized state: the questions to be drawn up by Dr. Pritchard [*sic*], Dr.
Hodgkin, Mr. J. Yates, Mr. Gray, Mr. Darwin [etc.] . . . £5.00. (27)

The grant is among the smallest given, but it is there. The
Aborigines' Protection Society seems to be less a humanitarian
than a natural historical enterprise, though one of an unusual
kind since the subjects observed are also to be the questionnaire's
informants (not something that other botanic or zoological subjects such as kelp or Ascidiae, sloths, ant-eaters, or armadillos
can be expected to perform). That double role of being the
scrutinized subject and the independent respondent is peculiar to
human beings. Over and over again the narratives of voyages
demonstrate how the borders of natural history were blurred by
human encounter and how evolutionary theory profited from
that growing uncertainty about the status of the human in
knowledge and in nature. The zoological and the linguistic appear side by side as parallel kinds of evidence: so, the surgeon
Wilson on the *Beagle*, writes: 'The Fuegian, like a Cetaceous
animal which circulates red blood in a cold medium, has in his
covering an admirable non-conductor of heat'. Alongside is a
vocabulary of Fuegian languages.[5]

4 London, 1840; 'Transactions of the Section', 89.
5 ii. App. 16, p. 143 and App. 15, pp. 135–42.

A review in the *Gentleman's Magazine* of March 1831, (the year that Darwin joined the *Beagle*'s expedition) shows a typical squirm of argument about these matters. The book reviewed is a compendious *Narrative of Discovery and Adventure in Africa, from the earliest ages to the present time: with illustrations of the Geology, Mineralogy, and Zoology*, 'by Professor Jameson, James Wilson, Esq. F.R.S.E. and Hugh Murray, Esq. F.R.S.E.' It is not the geology, zoology, or mineralogy that fascinates and irritates the reviewer but the peoples encountered. The reviewer is writing within the journal's pro-slavery stance:

All savages present to us, in certain respects, tricks, habits, and oddities like monkeys; and it is certain that in artificial acquirements they do not reach the elevation of dancing dogs . . . We are no advocates for the abduction of Africans, because it is robbery, and sometimes consequentially murder . . . but [like impressment or conscription it is] . . . assuredly a means of rendering idle and worthless people useful members of the community. That the African cannot become such useful members at home, is evident from the following tokens of their degrading characteristics as human beings. (237)

Whose 'community' is that to be served? The question does not bear answering. The argument presents 'savages' simultaneously as at the very least *like* animals and yet as degraded human beings. The indigenous inhabitant is here, squeamishly though it is put, to be 'improved' only by removal from home and subjection to 'civilized masters' (237).

Travellers who would have believed themselves heartily against slavery nevertheless commandeered individuals to function as pilots or translators. For example, Robert Fitzroy records a 'boy, whose name, among the sealers, was Bob'. 'Mr. Low had a Fuegian boy on board the Adeona, who learned to speak English very tolerably, during eighteen months that he staid on board as a pilot and interpreter.'[6] Taking local people aboard ship for a time was not altogether unusual: motives varied. One of the most benign was that of Frederick Beechey, as he recounts it in his *Narrative of a Voyage to the Pacific and Beering's Strait, to Co-operate with The Polar Expeditions: performed in His Majesty's Ship Blossom, under the command of Captain F. W. Beechey, RN, FRS, etc in the years 1825, 26, 27, 28.*[7] Beechey

---

[6] ii. 188.   [7] 2 vols. (London, 1831).

came upon a shipwrecked group of Otaheitean islanders who had drifted 600 miles by canoe from their home. He took on board a family, Tuwarri and his wife and children, and the chief of the group and delivered them back to Chain Island. Tuwarri behaves according to the expectations of natural virtue: he is grateful, regrets parting, and is sorry not to be able to 'send some little token of his gratitude'.

These feelings, so highly creditable to Tuwarri, were not participated by his wife, who, on the contrary, showed no concern at her departure, expressed neither thanks nor regrets, nor turned to any person to bid him farewell; and while Tuwarri was suppressing his tears, she was laughing at the exposure which she thought she would make going into the boat without an accommodation-ladder. (236)

Beechey is mortified by the wife's insouciance and eagerness to be gone. Gratitude had, conveniently, long been assumed to be a natural virtue. He also criticizes Tuwarri's lack of curiosity while on board, though he praises his 'strong sense of right and wrong', and he is mildy shocked when Tuwarri 'was not received by his countrymen with the surprise and pleasure which might have been expected; but this may, perhaps, be explained by there being no one on the beach to whom he was particularly attached' (237).

The absence of wonder or surprise was one of the phenomena that most disconcerted Western travellers in their encounters with indigenous people and which they described as most animal-like. Curiosity was so strong a driving force in Western expeditions, and so valued as a disinterested or 'scientific' incentive as opposed to the search for material gain, that the absence of an answering curiosity was felt as rebuff or even insult. Moreover, the reader of the narrative is likely, functionally, to agree with this view unless alerted, since the reading of natural-historical travel narratives is an intensified form of that zealous curiosity that drives all reading.

Captain P. Parker King, the writer of the first volume of the three-volume set that includes Fitzroy and Darwin's accounts of the *Beagle* voyages, is in the main an astute and sympathetic observer. He describes his first encounter with the Fuegians in January 1827, after visiting the Patagonian Indians, linking the terms 'brutes' and 'want of curiosity':

They appeared to be a most miserable, squalid race, very inferior, in every respect, to the Patagonians. They did not evince the least uneasiness at Mr. Sholl's presence, or at our ships being close to them; neither did they interfere with him, but remained squatting round their fire while he staid near. This seeming indifference, and total want of curiosity, gave us no favourable opinion of their character as intellectual beings; indeed, they appeared to be very little removed from brutes; but our subsequent knowledge of them has convinced us that they are not usually deficient in intellect. This party was perhaps stupified by the unusual size of our ships, for the vessels which frequent this Strait are seldom one hundred tons in burden. (24)

King does not quite settle between cowed passivity or, more romantically, dignified remoteness: indeed, he makes the point that interpreting the behaviour of other groups is always risky and unreliable. He repeatedly records the degree to which his own group had to correct their initial impressions and emphasizes that analogies with either animal or Western behaviour-patterns is liable to mislead. As Antony Pagden puts it in *European Encounters with the New World*, one discovery made by travellers is that 'it is incommensurability itself which is, ultimately, the only certainty'.[8]

The need for native interpreters of local languages was therefore pressing. Marshall Sahlins in *Islands of History*[9] has opened up the ways in which entire cultural systems of reference got disastrously caught across each other in Cook's final encounter with the Hawaiians. Western travellers, whether natural historians or not, soon discovered that the apparently universal repertoire of the body and its gestural systems is dangerously unreliable as a measure of meaning and intent. Language, though limited, is less volatile. With our current emphasis on the indeterminacies of language it is striking to realize the degree to which in travel narrative gesture is treacherous, language (even a few words) a blessedly stable resource and coin.

Beechey, for example, gives an account that is amusing if you are not on the spot, of what happened when he tried to persuade the Gambier islanders to dance, having admired their musical instruments. Beechey, hoping to get the islanders to offer their dances in exchange, gets the marines to

[8] (London, 1993), 41.   [9] Chicago, 1985.

go through some of their manoeuvres . . . this, however, had a very different effect from what was intended; for the motions of the marines were misinterpreted, and so alarmed some of the bystanders, that several made off, while others put themselves into an attitude of defence, so that I speedily dismissed the party. (176)

Darwin's much later *The Expression of the Emotions in Man and Animals* (London, 1872) may owe much to his puzzling experiences on the *Beagle* and be in part a final attempt to regulate the irregularities he had there encountered.

DARWIN AND THE FUEGIANS

On board the *Beagle* when Darwin joined the ship's surveying expedition in 1831 as companion to Captain Fitzroy and additional natural historian were seventy-four persons, seventy-three of them men. A girl of 12 or 13 was the only female aboard. Her own name was *yok'cushlu*, but to discover that one must go to a fragment of a vocabulary on page 135 of the Appendix to Volume 2 of the three-volume *Narrative of the Surveying Voyages of his Majesty's Ships Adventure and Beagle*. Elsewhere in the text, both by Fitzroy (volume 2) and Darwin (volume 3), she is always called 'Fuegia Basket' as she had been named on the 1830 passage of the *Beagle* to England. She was one of three Fuegians whose return to their homeland was part of the second expedition's purpose and, so far as Captain Fitzroy was concerned, a compelling incentive. The other two were men, *el'leparu* or York Minster, and *o'rundel'lico* or Jemmy Button. A fourth Fuegian, whose own name is lost but who was hauntingly called 'Boat Memory', had died of smallpox shortly after his arrival in England. It is worth dwelling on the story of the Fuegians' journey to England and return to Fuegia del Tierra, and the subsequent return upon return of Darwin and Fitzroy to the same locality to check their whereabouts, welfare, and behaviour. Later travellers, such as W. Parker Snow, came on Jemmy Button again twenty years later. The story, pieced together, raises a number of important issues that recur in travel narratives, including issues that go into the formation of Darwin's thought. What was the impact of his meeting and acquaintance with these three young people long before he had encountered what he thought of as 'a savage'? And what did Jemmy Button's subsequent history suggest concerning adaptability, survival, and cultural diversity and inheritance?

Captain Fitzroy later glosses his reasons for taking the Fuegians to England in different ways. In his letter to the Admiralty on 23 May 1831, seeking support for his expedition to return the Fuegians to their own country he emphasizes that 'I hoped to have seen these people become useful as interpreters, and be the means of establishing a friendly disposition towards Englishmen on the part of their countrymen, if not a regular intercourse with them'.[10] That secular and diplomatic explanation is overlaid by a religious one as support comes in from a missionary society who send a young man Matthews to accompany the Fuegians, learn language from them, and then use them as a group from which to promote the conversion of their countrymen. (That goes almost disastrously wrong and Matthews has to be rescued by the returning *Beagle*.) Fitzroy back-projects a lofty humanitarian motive, which he universalizes defensively as a 'natural emotion', not capricious behaviour on his part.

Initially, however, it is clear that the various young people were annexed as hostages. Boat Memory and York Minster certainly were so. Fuegia Basket was left behind on board with two other children when women who had been detained escaped by swimming. The other children were returned but Fuegia, showing, Fitzroy asserts, no particular desire to go, was retained. Jemmy Button was conceived as something between hostage and 'interpreter and guide' (ii. 5). While seeking a boat stolen from the *Beagle*, 'accidentally meeting two canoes . . . I prevailed on their occupants to put one of the party, a stout boy, into my boat, and in return I gave them beads, buttons, and other trifles' (ii. 6). Hence the name 'Jemmy Button'.

This shockingly cavalier appropriation of human beings rings ironically alongside Fitzroy's constant complaints about the Fuegians' pilfering. Yet, that fundamental error acknowledged, Fitzroy cared for the young people. He did not display them. He introduced them to his family and friends. He had them educated and looked after and taught certain mechanical skills. He

[10] App. to vol. ii, p. 91.

disliked them being called 'savages'. Fitzroy claimed, oddly, that even their features improved with education. Describing Tekeenica and Alikhoolip people (both Fuegian groups, Jemmy being Tekeenica, the others Alikhoolip), he writes:

The nose is always narrow between the eyes, and, except in a few curious instances, is hollow, in profile outline, or almost flat. The mouth is coarsely formed (I speak of them in their savage state, and not of those who were in England, whose features were much improved by altered habits, and by education). (ii. 175)

Fitzroy's account is riven with contradictions provoked by the gap between his general assertions and his individual reactions: for example, he considers the Tekeenica particularly degraded, yet praises Jemmy Button most highly of his charges. During their stay in England Jemmy Button and Fuegia Basket appeared to adapt to their new conditions, though York Minster remained recalcitrant. Jemmy Button relished shoes and gloves; Queen Adelaide gave Fuegia one of her own bonnets. A phrenological examination performed in London unsurprisingly confirmed 'objectively' the judgements already made on their personalities.[11] These are the assurances the reader is offered, apparently bolstered by the 'factual', sample-like, materials of the various appendices freed from narrative process.

Darwin was not present on the first voyage nor implicated in the decision to take the Fuegians away. He joined the ship on which they were to be returned to their native land. He therefore met the Fuegians in their Western demeanour and outfits. Perhaps the degree of shock that Darwin felt when confronted with 'the inhabitants of this savage land', Tierra del Fuegia, was because he was habituated to the Westernized young people on board ship; certainly his remarks suggest so: 'I could not have believed how wide was the difference between savage and civilized man. It is greater than between a wild and domesticated animal, in as much as in man there is a greater power of improvement' (iii. 228). 'Jemmy understood very little of their language, and was, moreover, thoroughly ashamed of his countrymen' (iii. 230).

Darwin observes that the appalling physical conditions in which the Fuegians live—the cold, the lack of food and heating,

[11] App. 17, pp. 148-9.

the smoke half-blinding them in their wigwams—means that all their energies are engrossed in animal survival:

It is a common subject of conjecture what pleasure in life some of the less gifted animals can enjoy: how much more reasonably the same question may be asked with respect to these barbarians. At night, five or six human beings, naked and scarcely protected from the wind and rain of this tempestuous climate, sleep on the wet ground coiled up like animals. (iii. 236)

The terms in the surrounding passage swerve, registering a disturbance that will not settle: he calls them 'poor wretches', 'barbarians', 'human beings'; 'Viewing such men, one can hardly make oneself believe they are fellow-creatures, and inhabitants of the same world' (iii. 235). But in a footnote Darwin argues that their lack of attainment does not imply inferior capabilities: 'Indeed, from what we saw of the Fuegians, who were taken to England, I should think the case was the reverse' (ibid.).

Darwin's encounters with Fuegians in their native place gave him a way of closing the gap between the human and other primates, a move necessary to the theories he was in the process of reaching. But it came after his experience of Fuegians abroad, since shipboard was a stylized form of England. The individuals, Jemmy, York, and Fuegia, seemed to provide evidence of the human capacity for physical adaptation within the individual life-cycle. What was left moot was the question of descent. What would happen to the next generation? Would Jemmy's children be 'improved' by their father's experience? The answer was unexpected and disconcerting, and is much developed in the second (1845) edition of the *Journal of Researches*.[12]

When Darwin and Fitzroy returned in the February of the succeeding year (1834) they were appalled. A canoe appeared 'with one of the men in it washing the paint off his face'.

This man was poor Jemmy,—now a thin, haggard savage, with long disordered hair, and naked, except a bit of blanket round his waist. We did not recognise him till he was close to us; for he was ashamed of himself, and turned his back to the ship. We had left him plump, fat, clean, and well dressed;—I never saw so complete and grievous a change. (2nd edn., 227)

[12] London, 1845.

The native has gone native.

Instead of admiring Jemmy's survival skills Darwin, like Fitzroy, reads this as degradation. Jemmy tells them 'that he did not wish to go back to England'. Darwin is more satisfied when 'we found out the cause of this great change in Jemmy's feelings, in the arrival of his young and nice-looking wife' (p. 227). York Minster and Fuegia Basket have disappeared, York Minster having robbed Jemmy Button. Only distant and indirect tidings are ever heard of Fuegia Basket: a sealer in 1842 'was astonished by a native woman coming on board, who could talk some English. Without doubt this was Fuegia Basket. She lived (I fear the term probably bears a double interpretation) some days on board.'[13]

So the hope of finding interpreters and guides, of sending back missionaries to convert their own people, came to very little. Instead, the Fuegians acquired some macaronic skills and learnt to trade with language. Jemmy introduced English terms into the vocabulary of his group. Darwin's sentimental (but wary) hope concerning Jemmy's descendants is mocked by actual events:

> Every one must sincerely hope that Captain FitzRoy's noble hope may be fulfilled, of being rewarded for the many generous sacrifices which he made for these Fuegians, by some ship-wrecked sailor being protected by the descendants of Jemmy Button and his tribe! (227–8)

It is easy now to see the absurdity of this high-flown hope, for the Fuegians had no reason to see Fitzroy as a benefactor for stealing them from their homeland.

In a retrospective self-justification Fitzroy cites the reaction of his shipmate Hammond to meeting Fuegians in their own country:

> 'What a pity such fine fellows should be left in such a barbarous state!' it told me that a desire to benefit these ignorant, though by no means contemptible human beings, was a natural emotion, and not the effect of individual caprice or erroneous enthusiasm; and that his feelings were exactly in unison with those I had experienced on former occasions, which had led to my undertaking the heavy charge of those Fuegians whom I brought to England. (91)[14]

[13] 227 n.
[14] A letter from Robert Fitzroy to the Hon. George Elliott, Secretary to the Admiralty, May 23, 1831. Fitzroy, Robert, *Narrative of the Surveying Voyages of His Majesty's Ships Adventure and Beagle, between the years 1826 and 1836, describing their Examination of the Southern Shores of South America, and the Beagle's Circumnavigation of the Globe*, 3 vols., Appendix to Volume II (London, 1839), p. 91.

One further travel narrative gives a wry later vignette of transculturation: W. Parker Snow's *A Two Years' Cruise off Tierra del Fuego, the Falkland Islands, Patagonia and the River Plate: a Narrative of Life in the Southern Seas*.[15] Snow met Jemmy Button 'quite naked, having his hair long and matted at the sides, cropped in front, and his eyes affected by smoke'. He still spoke English and on board the ship wanted to put on clothes and requested a 'knife to cut meat'. Jemmy proved himself adept at immediately re-framing himself in either context. Snow later comments that Jemmy's tribe was the least to be relied on in any dealings, having learnt a double language and behaviour. 'I had never before fallen in with one who had been transplanted to the highest fields of intellectual knowledge, and then restored to his original and barren state.'

Snow shows Jemmy his picture in Fitzroy's *Narrative*:

The portraits of himself and the other Fuegians made him laugh and look sad alternately, as the two characters he was represented in, savage and civilized, came before his eye. Perhaps he was calling to mind his combed hair, washed face, and dandy dress, with the polished boots it is said he so much delighted in: perhaps he was asking himself which, after all, was the best? the prim and starchy, or the rough and shaggy? Which he thought, he did not choose to say; but which I inferred he thought was gathered from his refusal to go anywhere with us again.

The Fuegian encounter continued to raise questions for Western travel narrative about cultural choice and helped to undermine assumptions about improvement and authority.

While the rest of the *Beagle*'s company left familiar England, sailed around the world, explored its people, geology, flora and fauna, and returned home, the Fuegians were performing a counter-motion from Tierra del Fuegia to England and back. They had not chosen to explore the world or discover its properties. They were taken away from familiar Tierra del Fuego to exotic England by guile or force and then, after many adventures, returned more than two years later to a place not quite that from which they had set out. The two journeys, that of Darwin and that of the Fuegians, share one long lap: for him setting forth, for them returning. The Fuegians could compare England and Fuegia: Darwin could not yet do so. They could be not only objects

[15] London, 1857.

of encounter but his informants and authority; and Jemmy Button, at least, we know was so.

It is difficult—impossible—to enter the Fuegians' experience of
this story, though certainly as sentimental to imagine that they
enjoyed nothing as that they relished everything and were grateful for their kidnap. Telling and knowing are ungrounded by this
attempted exchange: what are the natural-historical categories
for these subjects? The reader can know *el'leparu, o'rundel'lico,*
and *yok'cushlu,* if at all, only under the sign of their Western
soubriquets as York Minster, Jemmy Button, and Fuegia Basket.
That process of familiarization and estrangement is repeated in
relation to the language of the *Beagle* voyagers themselves.
Trying to understand the sensibility expressed by the British
sailors in that act of re-naming the Fuegians, re-naming them,
moreover, with those particular nicknames, is likely to make us
register our baffled distance from the shipboard community of
the 1830s more intensely than does anything in the rest of
Fitzroy's urbane or Darwin's ardent prose.

4

Speaking for the Others: Relativism and Authority in Victorian Anthropological Literature

When the Frazer lectureship was founded in 1921 A. E. Housman composed an address to Sir James Frazer in which he compared *The Golden Bough* to a banyan—instead of a single magical branch of parasitic mistletoe it is an exotic tree whose branches drop down new roots.[1] Housman deliberately blends the branch and the book in his eulogy:

The Golden Bough, compared by Virgil to the mistletoe but now revealing some affinity to the banyan, has not only waxed a great tree but has spread to a spacious hospitable forest, whose king receives homage in many tongues from a multitude resorting thither for its fruits or timber or refreshing shade.[2]

This is a jest about the branching growth of the book itself through its successive editions as well as a graceful compliment to the spread of Frazer's reputation.

Yet Frazer's book, though 'wide-waving, many-toned', was no self-generating 'life-tree Igdrasil'.[3] The unpruned forest of the work had spread out its roots and branches not from a seed but a slip—in the horticultural sense of a twig or shoot for grafting. There were trees in the Victorian intellectual forest before Frazer; some of them expanded prodigiously like his: James Prichard's *Researches into the Physical History of Mankind* grew from one volume in 1813, to two in 1836, and became five by 1847.[4] And

---

[1] At Oxford, Cambridge, Glasgow, and Liverpool.

[2] R. Angus Downie, *Frazer and 'The Golden Bough'* (London, 1970), 29.

[3] Thomas Carlyle, *Past and Present* (1843), Everyman edn. (London, 1912), 37.

[4] James Prichard, *The Physical History of Mankind*, 3rd edn., 5 vols. (London, 1836–47).

there were woods too: totalizing systems such as Comte's *Positive Philosophy*, Spencer's *Synthetic Philosophy*, Indo-Germanic and Aryan language theories, Darwin's natural selection, Tylor's fetishism, and, most influentially among Frazer's immediate forerunners, solar mythology, which, in Max Müller's work, referred all interpretations of myth to phenomena of weather and the rising and setting sun.[5] Frazer responded to many of these ideas and systems; but he sought a fresh general explanation that would justify the cross-reading of myths from groups widely separated in time and space and that would stabilize an underlying common significance.

In the first paragraph of the Preface to the First Edition of *The Golden Bough* Frazer combines the matter-of-fact and the arcane, moves between the local and the general, the seasonal and the continuous, to explain—and then to mystify—the work's beginning:

For some time I have been preparing a general work on primitive superstition and religion. Among the problems which had attracted my attention was the hitherto unexplained rule of the Arician priesthood; and last spring it happened that in the course of my reading I came across some facts, which, combined with others I had noted before, suggested an explanation of the rule in question. As the explanation, if correct, promised to throw light on some obscure features of primitive religion, I resolved to develop it fully, and, detaching it from my general work, to issue it as a separate study. This book is the result.[6]

The paragraph is marked by caution and expansiveness, a *pars pro toto* enigma. In Frazer's account a ritualistic magic of proce-

[5] Charles Darwin: *On the Origin of Species by Means of Natural Selection, or the Preservation of Favoured Races in the Struggle for Life* (London, 1859); *The Descent of Man and Selection in Relation to Sex* (London, 1871). T. H. Huxley, *Collected Essays*, 9 vols. (London, 1892–5). F. Max Müller: *Lectures on the Science of Language*, 1st and 2nd ser. (London, 1861, 1864); *Chips from a German Workshop*, 4 vols. (London, 1867–76); *Introduction to the Science of Religion* (London, 1873), Herbert Spencer: *Social Statics; or, The Conditions Essential to Human Happiness Specified and the First of Them Developed* (London, 1851); *Descriptive Sociology; or, Groups of Sociological Facts, Classified and Arranged* (London, 1873–81); Edward Tylor: *Researches into the Early History of Mankind and the Development of Civilization* (London, 1865); *Primitive Culture: Researches into the Development of Mythology, Philosophy, Religion, Language, Art, and Custom* (London, 1871).

[6] J. G. Frazer, *The Golden Bough: A Study in Comparative Religion*, 1st edn., 2 vols. (London, 1890), vol. i, p. vii. For the 'facts' that had come to Frazer's attention, see Robert Fraser, *The Making of 'The Golden Bough': The Origin and Growth of an Argument* (London, 1990), 50–2.

dure (the spring, the course, the happening, the associative motion) combines with the rational (throwing light on the obscure, detaching the specific problem from the general). Together, these imaginative modes produce not a monograph but a work that reaches out endlessly in an effort to exceed its own confines and meet the range of its material.

At the same time, this is a work committed to totalizing explanation, to the discovery of a single system of reference and meaning, such as had already been developed by Darwin in evolutionary terms and in terms of solar myth by Max Müller, and that was being developed, in terms of the unconscious and parent–child dynamics, by Freud, alongside Frazer. Though trained as a classicist, Frazer wrote in *The Gorgon's Head* (1927) that he went to William Thomson's (Lord Kelvin's) lectures at Edinburgh and carried away from Thomson's accounts of thermodynamics 'a conception of the physical universe as regulated by exact and absolutely unvarying laws of Nature'.[7]

The search for parallel mental laws typifies much major Victorian intellectual activity. So Thomas Bendysshe in his 1864 'History of Anthropology' defined the field of anthropology as 'The Science of Man . . . that science which deals with all phenomena exhibited by collective man, and by him alone, which are capable of being reduced to law.'[8] Not for nothing did George Eliot in *Middlemarch* emphasize, and seek to resist, the obsessional seeking after single explanatory systems, conceived as origins, beneath diversity and abundance. That search controls the work of both Casaubon and Lydgate, the one a mythographer, the other a natural scientist. The book's organization counterproposes

[7] J. G. Frazer, *Creation and Evolution in Primitive Cosmogomies and Other Pieces* (London, 1935); quoted in Robert Ackerman, J. G. Frazer: *His Life and Work* (Cambridge, 1987), 14.

[8] T. Bendysshe, 'A History of Anthropology', *Memoirs Read before the Anthropological Society of London*, 1 (1863–4), 335–420. This is a good tight discussion which includes material on early uses of the term 'anthropology' back to 1501. Bendysshe characterizes anthropology as 'The Science of Man . . . that science which deals with all the phenomena exhibited by collective man, and by him alone, which are capable of being reduced to law.' In 1865 T. H. Huxley defined anthropology thus: 'the great science which unravels the complexities of human structure; traces out the relations of man to other animals; studies all that is especially human in the mode in which man's complex functions are performed; and searches after the conditions which have determined his presence in the world'; collected in *Man's Place in Nature and Other Anthropological Essays* (London, 1894), 210.

diversity and abundance, as well as functional similarities, within the community of Middlemarch.[9]

Andrew Lang in *Magic and Religion* (1901) speaks of Frazer's as the 'Covent Garden School of mythologists': 'The new school of mythology does work the vegetable element in mythology hard; nearly as hard as the solar element used to be worked ... The vegetable school, the Covent Garden school of mythologists, mixes up real human beings with vegetation.'[10] In Lang's objection there may also be heard a side-reference to the literary, non-field-work nature of Frazer's undertaking. Frazer remains in armchair control of all the diversity of natural forms he surveys upon the page; not being confronted with them materially, he can 'mix up' real human beings with vegetation.

Frazer is entirely literary in his endeavour, though so much of the material he analyses comes from oral cultures. His imagination is imbued with classical and with English literature, though much of his material has been transmitted through the reports of observers writing in other European tongues. The largess of his work, with its sweeping geographical juxtapositions, its temporal freedom, its invocation of evidence from widely separated cultures, relies upon his own magic stasis. He *needs* not to know the humdrum of field-work and its privileging of one place; he remains a reader of traveller's tales, albeit one who weighs them nicely. He respects the complexity and the strangeness of other societies even while he seeks the elements repeated in them all.

The figure of Prospero haunts the language of *The Golden Bough*, providing Frazer with a never-articulated role, as the magician whose methods are those of reason, and whose goal is to create order out of the unruly elements without denying caprice, chance and accident. Prospero is both dreamer and controller of dreams, curtailing his twin emanations, Ariel and Caliban, and at the last acknowledging death that outgoes knowledge. In the final paragraphs of *The Golden Bough* Frazer contemplates the cooling of the universe, a concept central to the theories of Thomson, whose lectures he had attended:

---

[9] Gillian Beer, 'The Death of the Sun', in Barry Bullen (ed.), *The Sun is God: Painting, Literature and Mythology in the Nineteenth Century* (Oxford, 1989), 159–80 repr. as Ch. 10 below; *Darwin's Plots: Evolutionary Narrative in Darwin, George Eliot and Nineteenth-Century Fiction* (London, 1983).

[10] Quoted in Downie, *Frazer and 'The Golden Bough'*, 54.

In the ages to come man may be able to predict, perhaps even to control, the wayward courses of the winds and clouds, but hardly will his puny hands have strength to speed afresh our slackening planet in its orbit or rekindle the dying fire of the sun. Yet . . . these gloomy apprehensions, like the earth and the sun themselves, are only part of that unsubstantial world which thought has conjured up out of the void . . . They too, like so much that to common eyes seems solid, may melt into air, into thin air.[11]

Revealingly, neither Shakespeare nor the Bible appears in the Index to the First Edition (though one should note that Frazer did not make his own index). They are simply too close to home to be categorized as topics. They permeate the work's discourse and so knit together its assumptions.

Frazer is well aware of the Faustian false promises of scientific explanation and of magic alike. With what may also be an allusion to the image of the seeker after knowledge in seventeenth-century emblem books, stumbling wearily with his stick and his dark lantern after the free and spring-like female figure of Nature, he writes that science and magic both

lure the weary inquirer, the footsore seeker, on through the wilderness of disappointment in the present by their endless promises of the future; they take him up to the top of an exceeding high mountain and show him, beyond the dark clouds and rolling mists at his feet, a vision of the celestial city, far off, it may be, but radiant with unearthly splendour, bathed in the light of dreams.[12]

The multiple allusions, to Moses, to the temptation of Christ, to *Pilgrim's Progress*, to seventeenth-century emblem books such as Michael Maierus's *Atalanta Fugiens*, to a romantic expansion of the reader's own ordinary experience of climbing a hill, all combine to gratify.

Frazer's style is often effusive, always imbued with a shared cultural repertoire which places reader and writer together in the midst of a thronging maze of myth and at the same time at a commanding cultural height above it. His language is constantly caught up into the terms of the assumptions he seeks to analyse; so, in one of his more pithy sentences, he personifies science and magic in kinship and gender terms that reveal a habit of mind he is elsewhere describing as primitive: 'The principles of

[11] *GB A*, 713.   [12] *GB 2*, I, 61–2.

association are excellent in themselves, and indeed absolutely essential to the working of the human mind. Legitimately applied they yield science; illegitimately applied they yield magic, the bastard sister of science.'[13] Magic is both female and illegitimate, disturbing causality.

Frazer's comparative methods in his anthropology draw attention to similarities between the belief systems of remote peoples and rural groups in present-day Europe. His own writing everywhere manifests, though it never draws attention to, the prevalence of magical epistemologies in the culture of his intellectual England, and specifically in the culture of his kind of literary anthropology. This combination of the covert and the all-encompassing, of control and helplessness, characterizes the allure of *The Golden Bough*. On the face of it, after all, it is a little surprising that we are all assembled to discuss Frazer rather than Prichard or Spencer or Lubbock or Tylor, or, particularly, Max Müller. And perhaps their turn will come. These were the figures who shaped the new field of study in the second half of the nineteenth century. The arguments among them and their contemporaries writing in the new specialist journals, as well as in magazines such as *The Nineteenth Century* and the *Contemporary Review*, formed the conditions of study and the problems of method for Frazer's work.

In *The Literary Impact of 'The Golden Bough'* John Vickery gives almost no account of the imaginative enterprise of anthropology before Frazer and so obliterates the lines of affiliation that drew Frazer into, and beyond, the debates of his time. Within the mid-Victorian period there was already an active interplay between anthropological writing and literature, even while anthropology was attempting to determine its own independence and its own limits.

Anthropology was thought of as a new science in the 1860s and not an altogether socially respectable one. George Stocking recounts the anecdote that, when Lubbock was considering becoming president of the newly formed Anthropological Society in 1867, Huxley warned him that 'the title "President of the Anthropological Society" might hinder his attempt to gain a seat

[13] *GB*2, 1, 62.

in Parliament'.[14] Like all novel fields of study, anthropology in the 1860s immediately undertook a double and contradictory task: to shake itself loose from cognate disciplines and to establish antique authority for its enquiry. Choosing your parents and grandparents is a task of self-definition that subject-areas, unlike people, can undertake. They pay for the privilege. The choices of ancestry made may, in the backward gaze of posterity, seem symptomatic rather than 'natural'; ignored lines of kinship may seem disturbingly obvious to later enquirers.

So it is that Victorian anthropology is now seen as evidently implicated in colonialist assumptions; the confidence displayed in evolutionary patterns looks like a strategy for privileging European society. Developmental patterns are arranged with the white, middle-class European male as the crowned personage towards whom the past of the world has been striving. Progress is reconceived as a competitive struggle in which all other cultural groups are inevitably worsted, and civilization is taken to be synonymous with current European forms of society. That at least is the sour image of Victorian anthropology in the 1860s and 1870s that one readily derives from reading a run of journals such as the *Transactions of the Ethnological Society of London*, the *Memoirs Read before the Anthropological Society of London*, the *Anthropological Review* and the *Proceedings of the British Association for the Advancement of Science* (particularly the proceedings of meetings such as that in Nottingham in 1866).

There is no doubt that a concentrated course of reading in anthropological and ethnological journals of the period, such as I have undertaken for this discussion, is both disheartening and exasperating because of the apparently impervious racism which underpins so many of the arguments. It is fruitless, however, simply to bunch together all Victorian anthropological writers as racists. That move flatters ourselves. Moreover, such blanket rejection makes it impossible for us to hear a range of available meanings.

An effort is necessary in order to register the broader range and the subtler nuances available then within terms that now sound simply offensive. Embarrassment in the face of words such as

[14] George W. Stocking, Jr, *Victorian Anthropology* (New York, 1987), 257.

'savages' or 'natives' makes it difficult to discriminate the different registers across which such terms could function for Victorian writers and readers. When, for example, A. R. Wallace in *The Malay Archipelago*, or Robert Louis Stevenson in *In the South Seas* use such words, the pressures within them are very different from those asserted when Wake is working with them.[15] To dismiss all Victorian writers as racist because they use vocabulary that offends us now, or because they all work within a developmental view of human history, has a further powerful disadvantage. It has the effect of absolving present-day readers and allowing us to feel enlightened. The rejection costs us no self-enquiry.

More is to be gained by asking anew some of the questions that Victorians were asking themselves, or were proposing and then shying away from in their writing. Are all races ranged in a developmental order that mimics the development of the individual? Must all change come from without and be brought by Caucasian races? Is Western literature a sufficient resource for describing the life of other peoples? Who are our ancestors? Is humankind absolutely separated from the animals by its possession of language? Do the conditions of the working classes in England lead to racial degradation? Is there continuity between the needs of diverse cultures?

Intelligent unease about anthropology's ethnocentric assumptions began to surface in literature and in ethnography in the period before either Frazer or Freud were writing. Some writers grasped the ways in which ethnography casts light on the home culture. This led to ironic redescriptions of English assumptions and a shrewd recall of the parallels between observers and those remote groups they observed. In much professional anthropological literature the developmental metaphor distanced and empowered the Western observer, and allowed the assumption to prevail that tribal groups lived further back in cultural time. The same premises were active in descriptions of working-class and rural people.

---

[15] See Nancy Stepan, *The Idea of Race in Science: Great Britain 1800–1960* (London, 1982); George W. Stocking, Jr, *Race, Culture, and Evolution: Essays in the History of Anthropology* (New York, 1968); J. S. Haller, *Outcasts from Evolution: Scientific Attitudes to Racial Inferiority 1859–1900* (Urbana, Ill., 1971).

Interested observers, such as natural scientists, missionaries, and colonists, offered first-person accounts that were too often granted the special status of objectivity when quoted in anthropological articles. Natural scientists visited remote areas primarily to seek other than cultural data, stayed only a short time, and rarely knew the language of the locality; missionaries stayed longer, learnt the language, but sought to change radically the habits and belief-systems of the people among whom they dwelt; explorers, like the intermittently discredited du Chaillu, were passing through and seeking a story, a narrative bead in a longer chain; sailors and merchants traded, and tended to keep within the limited repertoire of commercial interchange; colonists inclined to see the native inhabitants as intruders on their own newly acquired territory.

These are not, of course, problems of report peculiar to Victorian anthropology. The evolutionary model may now long have been discarded from anthropological theory (though not from the afterlife of that theory in the assumptions of Western people). The problem of the observer remains recalcitrant. European observers were granted privileged status in the writing of nineteenth-century anthropologists, and not only by those who stayed at home. Field-work is now seen as necessary to professional insight and analysis. But there remains the difficulty of the writer's authorizing presence in the writing. That presence is still often granted authority by expunging any *reference* to the observer, in accord with the ethnographic fiction of the invisible anthropologist. Such issues are at present matter of hot debate, as the writing of James Clifford and the contributors to *Writing Culture* makes clear.[16]

What does now seem strange is the privileging of first-person narratives by travellers, recorded at length, and frequently quite uncritically, in a gentlemanly network of allusion. So, Prichard, for example, cites within a couple of pages Dr Ruppell, Monsieur Costaz, Monsieur Burchell, Mr Daniells. Over and over again the account of the European traveller is accorded the authority of the first-person within the papers in anthropological journals. First-person thus *stands in for* (and so usurps) the utterance of

---

[16] James Clifford and George Marcus (eds.), *Writing Culture* (Berkeley, 1986); and James Clifford, *The Predicament of Culture* (Berkeley, 1988).

the people described. It presents itself—and is presented within the over-narrative—as if it *were* that experience, rather than a partial, possibly mistaken, certainly incomplete, interpretation of it.[17]

This screening means that in reading the journals we are usually presented with a conversation among gentlemanly peers, a conversation that frequently fails in irony, does not sufficiently observe itself, and makes possible that strange and characterizing locution of the time: 'mankind' as meaning white, implicitly middle- and upper-class, Europeans, distinguished from all other ethnic groups.

Prichard's most popular work, *The Natural History of Man*, opens thus: 'The organised world presents no contrasts and resemblances more remarkable than those which we discover on comparing mankind with the inferior tribes.'[18] He insists that all human beings belong to a common species, and he is thus a monogenist; but he still freely uses the discriminator 'mankind'. One may compare C. S. Wake, who opens his paper 'The Psychological Unity of Mankind' in the *Memoirs Read before the Anthropological Society of London* (1867–9) with the passage below. The passage displays the ideological basis of the description of Europeans as mankind: Europeans are the full-grown adult human form; all other races are at an earlier stage on the developmental scale, to be formed and controlled like children.

It is a familiar idea, and one which appears to be now accepted as a truth, that 'mankind' (a term which, in this relation, has probably been used as synonymous with the Caucasian, or Indo-European, race) resembles in its totality an individual man, having, like him, an infancy, a childhood, youth, and manhood. In the early ages of the world man was in his infancy: and from that stage he has progressed, by gradual steps, until now he may be said to have attained—at least in peoples of the European stock—to a vigorous manhood ... The fact, which appears to have hitherto escaped attention, is the present existence of

[17] Robert Louis Stevenson, in *In the South Seas* (London, 1892), 181, recognized that all communication between peoples of different cultures must be radically incomplete: 'Of one thing, besides, I may be sure ... I shall not hear the whole; for he is already on his guard with me; the amount of the lore is boundless.'

[18] James Prichard, *The Natural History of Man: Comprising Inquiries into the Modifying Influence of Physical and Moral Agencies on the Different Tribes of the Human Family*, 2nd edn. (London, 1845), 4.

various families of mankind, exhibiting every stage of the supposed development.[19]

The counter-attempts made by writers in the second half of the nineteenth century to listen to other voices, beneath and beyond those of the dominant interpreters, concern me in this essay. The interrupting of that equable, overbearing conversation among peers can be heard in the work of Mayhew in *London Labour and the London Poor*, Browning's 'Caliban upon Setebos', and—rather differently—in the novels of Grant Allen, particularly *The Great Taboo* and *The British Barbarians*. Other voices can be heard, too, in the work of some anthropologists, such as W. Parker Snow and William Bailey Baker.

Victorian anthropologists were principally concerned with three interlocking topics: the question of kinship between diverse peoples; the question of a developmental hierarchy among races; and the question of language, both as a means of assessing the movements of peoples across the globe, and as a tool for the interpretation of cultural development.[20] Underlying all these topics was an anxiety about the status of humankind and its relationship to other species.[21]

The fascination with the 'missing link' was one mode of controlling the space between man and the animals and preventing any merging. Language was conceived as 'the rubicon', in Müller's phrase, between 'man and the brutes'. A further anxiety also had an evolutionary basis: whether the ordering of human culture was a progressive movement upwards, or whether there is evidence of widespread cultural degeneration, perhaps displayed in the life-styles of nomadic peoples, among others.

[19] C. S. Wake, 'The Psychological Unity of Mankind', *Memoirs Read before the Anthropological Society of London*, III (1867–9), 134.

[20] For a recent discussion of these issues in the nineteenth century see Colin Renfrew, *Archaeology and Language: The Puzzle of Indo-European Origins* (London, 1987); and Martin Bernal, *Black Athena: The Afroasiatic Roots of Classical Civilization* (London, 1987).

[21] Huxley, *Man's Place in Nature*, 89: 'Is he [Man] something apart? Does he originate in a totally different way from Dog, Bird, Frog, and Fish, thus justifying those who assert him to have no place in nature and no real affinity with the lower world of animal life? Or does he originate in a similar germ, pass through the same slow and gradually progressive modifications, depend on the same contrivances for protection and nutrition, and finally enter the world by the help of the same mechanism? The reply is not doubtful for a moment, and has not been doubtful any time these thirty years.'

Another, more pressing, question seems to be locked beneath these anxieties, one that only rarely finds utterance: what is the status of the writer himself? Is he (almost always he) exempt from cultural determinants, perched at the apex of the developmental pyramid? The progression model was often used thus, to suggest that the Caucasian race, latest come, was also the loftiest, and therefore had the surest backward gaze across the history of development. The observer and the writer are doubly authoritative: first-person asserts authenticity, and the writer is an adult representative looking back down into the childhood and adolescence of humankind.

Opposition to this supremacist habit of mind came from what to us may seem unexpected directions. For example, because of its ghastly aftermath, we tend to take it for granted that the Aryan controversy was always about the invention of an élite origin for a favoured group. In the 1860s, however, it seemed threatening in a quite contrary style: it brought to light kinship (and, implicitly, equality) between races whom many commentators would have preferred to keep separate, or to range in a hierarchical sequence with Britain safely at the head. It is a useful corrective to our late-twentieth-century understanding of Aryanism to read the angry and discomfited objections by John Crawfurd, former President of the Ethnological Society, in the 1861 *Transactions of the Ethnological Society of London*. The article concludes thus:

the theory which makes all the languages of Europe and Asia, from Bengal to the British Islands, however different in appearance, to have sprung from the same stock, and hence, all the people speaking them, black, swarthy, and fair, to be of one and the same race of man, is utterly groundless, and the mere dream of very learned men, and perhaps even more imaginative than learned. I can by no means, then, agree with a very learned professor of Oxford [Max Müller], that the same blood ran in the veins of the soldiers of Alexander and of Clive as in those of the Hindus whom, at the interval of two-and-twenty ages, they both scattered with the same facility. I am not prepared, like him, to believe that an English jury, unless it were a packed one of learned Orientalists, with the ingenious professor himself for its foreman, would, 'after examining the hoary documents of language', admit 'the claim of a common descent between Hindu, Greek and Teuton', for that would amount to allowing that there was no difference in the faculties of the people that produced Homer and

Shakespear, and those that have produced nothing better than the authors of the Mahabarat and Ramayana; no difference between the home-keeping Hindus, who never made a foreign conquest of any kind, and the nations who discovered, conquered, and peopled a new world.[22]

Literature is Crawfurd's final court of appeal to his 'English jury'. Empire and the will to conquer become the self-proving mark of racial superiority.

The ability to read Western literature was taken by some observers as the guarantee of a capacity to progress. The debate concerning development was carried on at the British Association for the Advancement of Science in 1866 in papers such as that by John Collinson 'On the Indians of the Mosquito Territory' of Continental America: the king is

a good specimen of what an enlightened Indian can become. His education, received at Jamaica, was quite equal to that of an ordinary English gentleman. With it he had acquired a refined taste hardly to be expected; he was never without one or two volumes of our best English poets in his pocket, and availed himself of every unoccupied moment to peruse them. But I do not want it to be supposed that civilization had made him effeminate in the slightest degree; on the contrary, he was the best shot and canoe's man in the whole country . . . The Woolnas . . . are . . . the most interesting of all the tribes. They are still in their pristine state of barbarity; some of their number who were working for me . . . had actually never before seen a white man.[23]

The assumption here is that improvement means movement towards white culture and barbarity means ignorance of the white man. Yet, despite these ideologically determining assumptions, and locutions, Collinson's argument is also an attempt to break out of the fixing sequence of the developmental metaphor. Whereas others represented such groups as set fast in the 'childhood' of man, he is arguing for the human potential for change,

[22] John Crawfurd, 'On the Aryan or Indo-Germanic Theory', *Transactions of the Ethnological Society of London*, NS 1 (1861), 286–7. Crawfurd's later paper 'The European and Asiatic Races' prompted an interesting reply. See Dadabhai Naoroji, *The European and Asiatic Races: Observations on the Paper Read by John Crawfurd, Esq., F. R. S. before the Ethnological Society on Feb. 14 1866*, read before the Ethnological Society March 27 1866 (London, 1866).

[23] John Collinson, 'On the Indians of the Mosquito Territory', *Proceedings of the British Association for the Advancement of Science*, Anthropological Section (1866), 73–4.

and for the force of environment rather than of cranial measurement.

It would be easy to gather a large number of more extreme instances, including farragos of evidential *non sequiturs* such as Owen Pike's essay 'On the Psychical Characteristics of the English People': Pike argues that the British are descended from the ancient Greeks, not from Germanic races (Hellenes not Huns), and he sets about doing so from material such as the British sense of humour, their love of sports, and even novel-writing by women. This essay was published in the *Memoirs Read before the Anthropological Society of London*. The Pike article typifies the search for illustrious ancestors for the race as a counter to the insistence on 'simian' and 'uncivilized' kin implied in evolutionary theory.

Prichard had already made it clear that those who did not understand the language of the community they entered were likely to make false and fanciful assessments. Tylor later observed in disgust that the hunting and killing of indigenous peoples in Tasmania was made possible because the Europeans heard their language only as grunts and squeals and failed to understand that culture is always present in any human group.

But understanding the language is not quite the same as listening to the utterance. Some did—and were conscious of the difficulties of translation in either direction. In the same issue of *Transactions of the Ethnological Society of London* as contains Crawfurd's attack on Aryanism William Bailey Baker writes on 'Maori Popular Poetry'. He discusses Maori feats of memory, the retention of archaic forms of speech in the poetry, the unfamiliar but complex metric patterns, and the problems for Western listeners structural and otherwise. He accepts the need 'to adopt foreign feelings, views, and prejudices' if Maori opera is to be appreciated; he defends the originals from his translations: 'in criticising a translation we are testing the original in a foreign dress.' He ends his article with a translation of a humorous Maori song which, in its turn, attempts through comedy to translate the exotic. It tells a story

pretty generally believed to be true. A Maori sailor, on his return from England, informed his friends that an English sailor named Haki—Jacky—was possessed of such enormous wealth that the Queen of England fell desperately in love with him . . . finding him inexorable . . . she climbed to the top of the mast of one of her largest frigates, sung

the following words, and cast herself headlong into the sea, uttering the
last exclamation as the waters closed around her—. . .

> Now I climb the topmost height
> Of the tall and slender mast,
> Whence to cast myself down headlong,
> That I may be '*dinner's ready!*'
> For the fishes of the ocean.—
>   Hallo![24]

Baker admires much in the society he describes. In order to come
to terms with the evident complexity, wit, and power of Maori
imaginative life he resorts to a degradationist argument: these are
the last remnants of a former great race, 'and their ideas were
consequently more refined and intelligible to the European
mind'.

It would, then, be false to suggest that Victorian anthropology
offered only the affirmations of cultural imperialism: perceptions
and their ideological contradictions were often held in equi-
poise—as in most periods of history. Edward Tylor, despite his
insistence on a developmental pattern to the emergence of
human culture, always emphasized the congruities between
primitive and advanced culture: indeed, the title *Primitive Culture* (1871) emphasizes, as it were against the odds, that no
human society, past or present, lacks a complex culture of its
own. This is demonstrated, in Tylor's view, in language itself,
that specifically human achievement. Tylor remarks: 'The development of language between its savage and cultured stages has
been made in its details, scarcely in its principle.' Poetry, he
claims, sustains within the present time the systems of savage
thought: 'poetry . . . whose characteristic is that wild and ramb-
ling metaphor which represents the habitual expression of savage
thought, the mental condition of the lower races is the key to
poetry.' Not only poetry but systems of law also, he argues, rely
on 'processes that did not first come into action within the range
of written codes of comparatively cultured nations'.[25]

Legal systems fossilize primitive traditions; Tylor cites the
theory of primogeniture and the only recently abolished

---

[24] W. H. Baker, 'Maori Popular Poetry', *Transactions of the Ethnological Society of London*, I (1861), 58–9.

[25] Tylor, *Primitive Culture*, ii. 446, 43.

Jewish disabilities as examples. For Tylor, human progress towards a reasoned civilization is frequently hampered by these
vestiges of savage thought. Himself a Quaker, he both understood sympathetically the experience of being other to the
dominant culture and distrusted the ritualistic survivals of
myth-systems at work in modern societies, including that of
Britain.

Although he held to the progression, or development, theory of
culture, Tylor was well aware that degradation theory could
present what seemed powerful examples of cultural degeneration. Tylor cites the fanciful examples of the Do-as-you-likes
from Kingsley's *Water Babies*, whose hedonism leads to their
reversion into ape-like creatures without the power of speech.[26]
But he cites also the actual grave injustices of his own society,
which force upon poor people the physical conditions which
drive them into degradation. These effects are then theorized by
degenerationists as universal: the fall of the modern world away
from old high culture, and native peoples as the detritus of lost
civilisations.

Tylor insists that there is no inevitability to social degeneration, nor are native peoples to be identified with slum-dwellers.
The effects of environment on the poor are the responsibility of
modern civilization and can be corrected:

What kind of evidence can direct observation and history give as to the
degradation of men from a civilised condition towards that of savagery? In our great cities, the so-called 'dangerous classes' are sunk in
hideous misery and depravity. If we have to strike a balance between
the Papuans of New Caledonia and the communities of European
beggars and thieves, we may sadly acknowledge that we have in our
midst something worse than savagery; it is broken-down civilisation . . .
The savage life is essentially devoted to gaining subsistence from
nature, which is just what the proletarian life is not. Their relations to
civilised life—the one of independence, the other of dependence—are
absolutely opposite. To my mind the popular phrases about 'city
savages' and 'street Arabs' seem like comparing a ruined house to a
builder's yard.[27]

[26] Ibid., i. 376–7. 'To suppose that theories of a relation between man and the
lower mammalia are only a product of advanced science, would be an extreme
mistake.'

[27] Ibid., i. 43–3. Ackerman, in his biography of Frazer, makes it clear that Tylor
was one of the most important formative influences on Frazer's work.

Tylor holds to his progressivist views but acknowledges in his metaphors (the collapsed ruined house as opposed to the potential houses of a builder's yard) that false class dependencies have produced a desolation among the poor of England of a kind quite different from the independence and the future potential of 'savage' peoples.

A. R. Wallace, co-discoverer of the principle of natural selection and a convinced socialist, went further than Tylor's emphasis on continuity between early and more developed forms of civilization. Instead of seeing the present day as weighed down unprofitably with assumptions descended from the mists of barbarian antiquity, he insists that there have always, throughout time, been 'men both savage and civilised'. In his support he cites the views of Albert Mott in his presidential address to the Literary and Philosophical Society of Liverpool in 1873. Mott argues 'that we have often entirely misread the past by supposing that the outward signs of civilisation must always be the same, and must be such as are found among ourselves'.[28]

The connections between the discourse of racial difference and the discourse of class difference fuelled the work of Henry Mayhew. He opened *London Labour and the London Poor* by setting his enquiry in the context of Prichard's taxonomic ethnography. Before turning to the intimate first-person accounts of life given him by individual people, he frames his enterprise in the context of world-wide categories. Mayhew chooses Prichard's division of humankind into 'the wanderers and the settlers' as his model for description and categorization. The opening sentence reads,

Of the thousand millions of human beings that are said to constitute the population of the entire globe, there are—socially, morally, and perhaps even physically considered—but two distinct and broadly marked races, viz., the wanderers and the settlers—the vagabond and the citizen—the nomadic and the civilized tribes.

The moral die is weighted in favour of the settlers: citizens, not vagabonds. The energy of Mayhew's description, however, goes into the wandering tribes:

The nomadic races of England are of many distinct kinds—from the habitual vagrant—half-beggar, half-thief—sleeping in barns, tents, and

---

[28] A. R. Wallace, *Natural Selection and Tropical Nature* (London, 1891), 424–5.

casual wards—to the mechanic on the tramp, obtaining his bed and supper from the trade societies in the different towns, on his way to seek work. Between these two extremes there are several mediate varieties—consisting of pedlars, showmen, harvest-men, and all that large class who live by either selling, showing, or doing something through the country. These are, so to speak, rural nomads.[29]

The reason for Mayhew's great interest in wanderers rapidly becomes clear. This is an ethnological justification of his own field-work among the wandering tribes of London. Street wanderers have, he asserts,

a greater development of the animal than of the intellectual or moral nature of man . . . they are all more or less distinguished for their high cheek-bones and protruding jaws—for their use of a slang language—for their lax ideas of property—for their general improvidence—their repugnance to continuous labour—their disregard of female honour—their love of cruelty—their pugnacity—and their utter want of religion.

Mayhew's fascinated sympathy with the individual is in tension with his delight in baroquely complex categories:

The Street-sellers of Second-hand Articles, of whom there are again four separate classes; as (a) those who sell old metal articles—viz. old knives and forks, keys, tin-ware, tools, and marine stores generally; (b) those who sell old linen articles—as old sheeting for towels; (c) those who sell old glass and crockery—including bottles, old pans and pitchers, old looking glasses, &c.; and (d) those who sell old miscellaneous articles—as old shoes, old clothes, old saucepan lids &c., &c.[30]

The structure of Mayhew's work depends upon that tension, so that we discover the multifariousness of experience within each category, and thereby get outside the usual Victorian fear of 'the crowd' and 'the mass'. Discussions of *race* in Victorian writing frequently provide a cover for discussions of class, and this is so far Mayhew.

The introduction is no mere attempt to render his task respectable, though it does dramatize the authority of Mayhew's presence by setting him at an extreme intellectual distance from his subjects at the outset. The work itself reverses this procedure: the life-experience of each individual is uttered and recorded

---

[29] Thomas Mayhew, *London Labour and the London Poor* (1861-2; Dover repr. London, 1968), 1.
[30] Ibid. 2-3.

almost without intervention, and without demur. It is, he announces in the Preface, 'the first attempt to publish the history of a people from the lips of the people themselves'. Indeed, so transparent does Mayhew render himself that it is easy for the unwary reader to fail to notice that all London rat-catchers, street-cleaners, Punch and Judy men, and fishmongers, inlay workers, prostitutes, and street-patterers seem preoccupied with their own lineage, their education, and their religious beliefs.

Mayhew has edited out the questions that provoked the responses, just as he has edited out obscenity while rendering individual speech-patterns and dialects. There is, of course, another way of looking at it: that people were preoccupied with their lineage, education, and religious beliefs, while the constraints of class relations meant that they uttered no obscenities in the hearing of a middle-class interlocutor. The truth is probably more erratic than either of these single intepretations allows.

Mayhew's gift was that of acceptance: he does not seek to make judgements about where fantasy enters self-description, and, by the very act of sustained questioning and record, he assures people of the value of their experience and taps a well of memory. He respected the authority of those who talked to him: each is an expert on the work practices in which he or she is involved. We all know and can recount our work, our illnesses, our childhood. Some of Mayhew's urgency is formed by the cross-pull between the experiences held in common and the class divisions between his expected readers and the poor who so eloquently spoke to him. The exotic, his work suggests, is near home, in the next street, not far off on a developmental ladder conveniently placed on the other side of the world.

Kinship and difference was one of the most disagreeable issues posed by anthropology to Victorian people.[31] One famous poem of the period in particular disturbingly concentrates on the ingenuity of human *explanation*, the zeal with which human beings contrive satisfying cosmogonies and cosmologies out of the local

---

[31] Margaret Harkness, who wrote under the pseudonym 'John Law', tellingly deconstructed phrases like 'street Arabs' in her novels of East End London life, such as *A City Girl* (London, 1887) and *Captain Lobe* (London, 1889), later called *In Darkest London*. See Gerd Bjørhovde, *Rebellious Structures: Women Writers and the Crisis of the Novel 1880–1900* (Oslo and Oxford, 1987).

conditions within which they survive. That poem is Browning's 'Caliban upon Setebos or Natural Theology in the Island'. It is a poem about interpretation as well as about the making of myth. It disturbs any easy developmental patterning. Even its epigraph is double-faced: 'Thou thoughtest that I was altogether such a one as thyself.' Ethnocentrism, cultural imperialism, anthropomorphism are jangled in that biblical rebuke. In the poem Caliban speaks at first in the third-person, then, as his account of his conditions makes a shape which he can inhabit, in achieved first-person. The poem is, and was taken to be, a satire on the anthropomorphism of theology. Some critics saw it also as an attack on contemporary science.[32]

Caliban imagines a hierarchy to the world based upon fitful and malign oppression, since that has been his experience of others and of his own desires. The oppression he has suffered has been primarily at the hands of Prospero, the absent figure of the poem. Whereas in Shakespeare's play the *presence* of Prospero grants him authority, here he is a conjured element in Caliban's ruminations. The 'rational' is here a weapon of oppression as well as of self-discovery.

Caliban's utterance is initially declared as the voice of the 'other', of the guttural, the primitive, even the ape-like. But the voice proves to be urgent, articulate, sophistical. It seizes sense-experience and intellectual conflict in sluggish yet passionate movements of mind and body. Caliban does more than curse with the language he has entered. He broods on the issues that were preoccupying theologians and anthropologists alike. He achieves an explanation which is also an impasse.

> Thinketh, He made thereat the sun, this isle,
> Trees and the fowls here, beast and creeping thing.
> Yon otter, sleek-wet, black, lithe as a leech;
> Yon auk, one fire-eye in a ball of foam,
> That floats and feeds; a certain badger brown

[32] 'Caliban upon Setebos' was written during the early 1860s. Boyd Litzinger and Donald Smalley, editors of *Browning: The Critical Heritage* (London, 1970), include in their selection reviews by Walter Bagehot ('mind in difficulties—mind set to make sense of the universe under the worst and hardest circumstances'—275), Edward Dowden ('the natural theology of one who is merely an intellectual animal'—428), and many others. The most extensive Victorian criticism of Browning's poem is to be found in the work of the historian, ethnographer, and literary critic Daniel Wilson, *Caliban: The Missing Link* (London, 1873).

He hath watched hunt with that slant white-wedge eye
By moonlight; and the pie with the long tongue
That pricks deep into oakwarts for a worm,
And says a plain word when she finds her prize,
But will not eat the ants; the ants themselves
That build a wall of seeds and settled stalks
About their hole—He made all these and more,
Made all we see, and use, in spite: how else?
He could not, Himself, make a second self
To be His mate; as well have made Himself:
He would not make what he mislikes or slights,
An eyesore to Him, or not worth His pains:
But did, in envy, listlessness or sport,
Make what Himself would fain, in a manner, be—
Weaker in most points, stronger in a few,
Worthy, and yet mere playthings all the while,
Things He admires and mocks too,—that is it.
Because, so brave, so better though they be,
It nothing skills if He begin to plague.

(ll. 44–67)

Caliban in this poem appropriates the iambic pentameters of Shakespeare's play, the hallowed form of English metrics, and uses it to turn the tables on the reader who assumes him to be a dolt, a fish, a monster, a primitive. Caliban's intricate language gives the lie to any hope that the present-day European has grown beyond the flawed impulses of the past. Lower and higher, present and past, observer and other, all discover themselves in Caliban's lambent and yet spiteful utterance.

But Caliban can imagine a possible future in which the conditions have changed, in which Setebos grows into the higher form, the Quiet, 'as grubs grow butterflies'. That future does not come within the time of the poem. Caliban is still locked within fetishism and sympathetic magic, mind-features here produced by his condition of oppression as much as by his stage of cultural development.

Unlike in most of Browning's monologues, there is no dramatized listener within the poem. We are caught into the mind of Caliban and into the brooding reflexivity of his attempt to manage the universe. Caliban voices the synchronicity of all the phases of mental development; his savage sophistication jumbles that securely upward-moving scale favoured by ethnographers as well as theologians. Browning's poem was written in the early 1860s in the midst of the anthropological controversies concerning development and speciation that I have earlier described.[33]

The first literary responses to Frazer thirty years later were less multi-rooted and more playful. Grant Allen was probably the writer who most immediately used Frazer's work and took it into his own. He quickly perceived that the comparative method made room both for adventure and satire, for the exotic and the homely. In two of his novels particularly he played on Frazerian themes.[34] In *The Great Taboo* a vicar's daughter is cast away with an English gentleman on a cannibal island. They fall overboard from an ocean steamer called *The Australasian*. (Journeying on this fictional boat, incidentally, does seem to be hazardous, as the couple, in W. H. Mallock's *The New Paul and Virginia or Positivism on an Island*, published in 1878, start their adventure when the boiler on a ship of the same name blows up, leaving them castaway on an island where they discover the missing link.)

Allen pays tribute to Frazer in the Preface: 'I desire to express my profound indebtedness, for the central mythological idea embodied in this tale, to Mr. J. G. Frazer's admirable and epoch-making work, *The Golden Bough*, whose main contention I have endeavoured incidentally to popularize in my present story.'[35] He then takes the reader through a very thorough if whimsical course in rituals of sacrifice and taboo, including the rash picking of fruit from the golden bough by the English gentleman:

They were passing by some huts at the moment, and over the stockade of one of them a tree was hanging with small yellow fruits . . . He broke off a small branch as he passed, and offered a couple thoughtlessly to Muriel. She took them in her fingers, and tasted them gingerly. 'They're not so bad,' she said, taking another from the bough. 'They're very much like gooseberries.'

---

[33] Wake (n. 19 above) 134: 'From this sketch of man's mental development, it is seen that it has five chief stages, which may be described as the selfish, the wilful, the emotional, the empirical, and the rational; these several phases will be found to have their counterpart in the mental condition of the several great races of mankind.' (European manhood is, of course, identified with the last of these phases.)

[34] Grant Allen, *The Great Taboo* (London, 1890), and *The British Barbarians* (London, 1895).

[35] Allen, *The Great Taboo*, p. i.

The eating of the fruit has broken taboo and a tornado immediately ensues. The story is something of a farrago of inconsistencies. In the copy I read a late-nineteenth-century hand has pointed out in the margin how often Allen forgets the taboo against touching. But Grant Allen reserves his fundamental joke to the end. Having survived horrors and vicissitudes too numerous to recapitulate, the English pair are rescued from the island and marry on the way back to England. The last scene takes place in a London drawing-room where Muriel's aunt receives them. Her one worry about their experiences is different from theirs: ' "how dreadful . . . that you and Felix should have been all these months alone on the island together without being married." . . . Mrs Ellis sat still in her chair and smiled uncomfortably. It affected her spirits. Taboos, after all, are much the same in England as in Boupan.'[36]

This insistence on the primitive nature of social inhibition was Grant Allen's strongest belief, and in *The British Barbarians* he takes the joke out beyond jest: the book opens with the comic encounter between the hero and a young man, a stranger, who asks him for directions to a lodging-house and enquires whether there are any rituals or taboos to be observed when entering such a house. Of course not, says our hero astonished. Next day he meets the young man again, who tells him sadly that he had forgotten to mention the essential ritual: no entry without baggage.

The stranger, called the Alien, proves to be an anthropologist from the twenty-sixth century who has come back through time to observe primitive British society of the late nineteenth century. Allen has seized the cultural relativism implicit in Frazer's associative methods and in the richness with which Frazer represents complex beliefs from widely divergent times and places.

Frazer's emphasis on the fruitfulness of association offset the rigidly developmental movement of many contemporary ethnologists and anthropologists. It allowed him to develop a copious comparativism. The power of association that he praised in the human mind was also his primary mode of organizing argument. He could move freely as a mind-traveller across time and space within the scan of a single thought.

[36] Ibid. 96, 280.

This apparently unsystematic procedure had methodological and ideological advantages: it liberated his work from the ruthless developmentalism that led earlier writers such as Crawfurd to think a comparison between Indian and Greek classic texts absurd. His comparative method set loose powers at odds with the severely developmental and law-bound world-set within which he yet believed himself to work.

Frazer's enterprise was entirely book-bound, dependent on description derived from the work of others rather than on field-work or direct observation.[37] His language was replete with allusions to English literary sources. Thus he bound up the remote tribal customs he described into a half-familiar imaginative world indebted to Shakespeare and to a strong idea of England, as well as to classical sources. In his case, ethnocentrism was opened out by associationism. He could inhabit and link the imaginative processes of many human groups—so far as he could understand them. In the process, his native land and its customs were made strange. Like Grant Allen's twenty-sixth-century anthropologist, Frazer encouraged English readers to look askance at their own landscapes, values and experiences. What in Allen was realized as comedy, in Frazer became part of an arcane and tragic world. That world was inhabited by peoples from all ages and places, variously imaginative, synchronously imagined.

---

[37] In 'Out of Context: The Persuasive Fictions of Anthropology', the 1986 Frazer Lecture at the University of Liverpool, Marilyn Strathern offers an account of Frazer's literariness and its relation to his audience as part of an important larger discussion of modernist assumptions in anthropology.

5

Darwin and the Growth of Language Theory

My title embeds an assumption that my argument will pry out again: 'the *growth* of language theory'. Is knowledge, then, an organic process, its accretions and transformations more than metaphorically like that of the organism? Such taken for granted locutions as 'growth' illustrate how readily the discourse of one field is appropriated by another. The case I want to examine is one of more conscious appropriation and re-appropriation: that between Darwinian evolutionary theory and language theory. During the last 150 years these two major fields of human enquiry have drawn upon each other's evidences, and, even more, upon each other's metaphors, as I shall demonstrate. Equally striking—though harder to demonstrate empirically since this phase of theory-making relies upon the *absence* of material—is the desire for autonomy which has, from time to time, involved repudiating and suppressing links between the fields. There are often sound intellectual reasons for such disengagement. However, it also seems that for theory to conceive itself as authentic and to establish itself as free-standing, it needs to obliterate traces of dependence and to repudiate analogies with other fields of learning. Such suppressed dependencies may re-emerge later, generating fresh topics of enquiry. This pattern of interchange and autonomy will also be seen to have significance for appraising claims to self-sufficiency in scientific language.

The general assumption in twentieth-century histories of language theory is that such theory in the mid-nineteenth century was dependent on Darwinian evolutionary theory. Einar Haugen in *The Ecology of Language*, writing in the light of Chomskyean linguistics, notes the evolutionist and ontogenic models which informed philological discussion in the later nineteenth century:

'it was common to speak of the "life of languages", *because the biological model came easily to a generation that had newly discovered evolution*' (my italics).

They had their life-spans, they grew and changed like men and animals, they had their little ills which could be cured by appropriate remedies prescribed by good grammarians. New species evolved in the course of their 'progress', often as a result of competition which ensured the survival of the fittest . . . Today the biological model is not popular among linguists . . . Other metaphors have replaced the biological one, generally in response to the strong constructive aspect of our industrial civilisation.[1]

Haugen here characterizes a system of description which we might associate with Max Müller, in his *Lectures on the Science of Language* (1861), or with George Whitney's *The Life and Growth of Language* (1875). Whitney's title emphasizes an organic metaphor, though Ferdinand de Saussure admired him particularly for his emphasis on the arbitrariness of the sign. 'The essential difference, which separates man's means of communication in kind as well as degree from that of other animals, is that, while the latter is instinctive, the former is, in all its parts, arbitrary and conventional.'[2] Controversy raged between the mythographer and Sanskrit scholar, Müller, the language theorist, Whitney, the physical scientist, George Darwin, and the anthropologist, Tylor, in the *Contemporary Review* in the years 1872–5 over the 'organic evolution' as opposed to the 'institution' model of language. Whitney favoured the 'institution' model and insisted that Darwinism and the science of language were separate enquiries. He attacked Schleicher's *The Darwinian Theory and the Science of Language* (Weimar 1863) which sought to identify the two and said that 'the relation between the two classes of phenomena is one of analogy only, not of essential agreement'.[3] In his seminal *Course in General Linguistics* (1915) Saussure placed Whitney at the start of a methodological sequence which led to modern linguistics: he was followed by the German neogrammarians, thanks to whom 'language is no longer looked upon as an organism that develops

---

[1]　Einar Haugen, *The Ecology of Language* (Stanford, 1972), 326.
[2]　William Whitney, *The Life and Growth of Language* (London, 1875), 282.
[3]　William Whitney, *Language and the Study of Language* (London, 1867), 47.

independently but as a product of the collective mind of linguistic groups'.[4]

The controversy concerning the usefulness of paralleling evolutionary and language theory has continued. In *Language and Mind* Noam Chomsky insists

> There is nothing useful to be said about behaviour or thought at the level of abstraction at which animal and human communication fall together ... This ... is often overlooked by those who approach human language as a natural, biological phenomenon; in particular, it seems rather pointless ... to speculate about the evolution of human language from simpler systems—perhaps as absurd as it would be to speculate about the 'evolution' of atoms from clouds of elementary particles.[5]

Chomsky emphasizes discontinuity between other species and the specifically human power of language. In this passage, he polemically shifts the term evolution from a neutral concept into a fanciful wrong-headed metaphor, ascribing a merely fairy-tale explanatory power to it by his second example with its destabilizing quotation marks, ' "evolution" of atoms'.

Twentieth-century workers in linguistics and historians of language-study have emphasized the dependence of mid-nineteenth-century linguistics on the evolutionary and organic metaphors. Implicated in that general view may be an unacknowledged assumption of primacy for the more 'scientific' field—the study of language depends upon the study of biology. However, more is revealed if we reverse the emphasis: much important nineteenth-century scientific work, particularly that of Lyell in geology and Darwin in evolutionary theory, drew upon the new models of language development. Within Darwin's own thought we can observe him using language theory as metaphor, as model, and as illustration, and as an example of evolutionary process. We can see also the problems of argument this created for him late in his career.

In an earlier essay I suggested that 'cross-category movement of concepts' is 'most active in areas of unresolved conflict or problem. It signals the significant anxieties of a period ... the

---

[4] Ferdinand Saussure, *Course in General Linguistics*, introd. J. Culler (London, 1974), 5.
[5] Noam Chomsky, *Language and Mind*, enlarged edn. (New York, 1972), 70.

function of transposition may be as much to disguise as to lay bare.'[6] My present argument moves on to consider further implications arising from that position. One always central debate in the past 150 years has been 'man's place in nature', and language theory and evolutionary theory have been the two fields most preoccupied with this question. Two controversies in particular created connections between language theory and the biological sciences. One question was whether humankind uniquely possessed language and was thereby manifestly of a different order from all other living creatures. The second was whether a genealogical organization was the correct mode of categorizing the relationships of different languages.

Descartes had earlier argued that language was what distinguished *homo sapiens* from beasts, since even the stupid and insane could put words together so as to convey their thoughts, whereas the most perfect and thriving animals could not do the same. This, he held, proved that animals had no reason, since so little reason was needed to enable men to talk (*Discourses on Method and Meditations*, 1637). Locke had seen that any enquiry into the origin of language would be an enquiry into 'the very origin of the human race', and the point was taken up and quoted by Lord Monboddo in *Of the Origin and Progress of Language*, (1773–92.)[7] In that work, Monboddo shifts the barriers between man and beast, claiming the orang-utan, though silent, as a member of the family of man.

Monboddo's insistence that the orang-utan 'belongs to our species' is based on an ordering of development which places the orang-utan at the point just before the acquisition of speech, the point of 'the invention of certain arts', particularly those of defence.[8] After language, asserts Monboddo, comes government and laws. Monboddo adopted a developmental view of species which he linked specifically to language acquisition. In his novel *Melincourt*, Thomas Love Peacock, writing in 1816, creates a marvellous parody of Moboddo's theory, both sympathetic and

---

[6] Gillian Beer, 'Anxiety and Interchange: *Daniel Deronda* and the Implications of Darwin's Writing', *Journal of the History of Behavioural Sciences*, 19 (1983), 31.

[7] Lord Monboddo, *Of the Origin and Process of Language*, 6 vols. (Edinburgh, 1773–92), i. 154.

[8] Ibid., i. 272.

acute. He does so in the figure of Sir Oran Haut-Ton—the impeccably silent, chivalrous orang-utan hero who is a thorough gentleman, skilled in the arts of defence and rescue, though not yet having acquired the skills of speech since he was brought to England from his native Borneo.

In August 1838 we find Darwin, who had been reading Monboddo and Horne Tooke, signalling to himself in his notebooks with cryptic boast the strength of that theory which he was in the throes of realizing: 'Origins of man now proved.—Metaphysics must flourish.—He who understand baboon would do more toward metaphysics than Locke.'[9] Darwin compared man's separation of himself from other species to the vile alienation involved in slavery. Max Müller, in *The Science of Language* (1861), responds to the implications of Darwin's theory as to an attack on the special status of humankind: 'There is *one* barrier which no-one has yet ventured to touch—the barrier of language ... no process of natural selection will ever distill significant words out of the notes of birds or the cries of beasts.'[10] Darwin, who had ventured to touch that barrier privately in the 1830s, ('Were signs originally musical!!!??')[11] discussed it publicly ten years after Müller's book in *The Descent of Man* (1871) where he argues that both sexual selection and natural selection have developed the human power of speech. Though the question of whether signs were originally musical may seem a familiar one, following Rousseau, the excitement with which Darwin proposes the question suggests that he reached it by his own observational and theoretical pathways. Alluding to Müller's claim that 'the use of language implies the power of forming general concepts; and that as no animals are supposed to possess this power, an impassable barrier is formed between them and man', Darwin claims, that, on the contrary, animals 'have this power, at least in a rude and incipient degree'. He argues that human language is most probably a result of 'the continued use of the mental and vocal organs leading to inherited changes in their structure and functions'—changes which have widened the gap between song, the calls of birds, the imitation of natural

---

[9] 'The Notebooks on Man, Mind and Materialism', in Howard Gruber and Paul Barrett, *Darwin on Man* (London, 1974), 281.
[10] F. Max Müller, *Lectures on the Science of Language* (London, 1861), i. 357.
[11] Gruber and Barrett, 382–3.

sounds, warning cries, and reasoned speech.[12] In the Notebooks thirty years before, he had argued for 'some necessary connexion between things and voice', and in emphasizing the musical beginnings of human speech, delightfully epitomized the relation between sexual selection and a fine voice.[13] The first arts of music and the developed arts of language were in his view continuous: 'A Melody on flute & epic poem, opposite ends of series of harmonious prose.'[14] Music is antecedent to language; intonation and pitch precede semantics. His is not simply a theory of onomatopoeia; the run of the voice, he argues, is itself a primary means of communication, and the beauties of such communication give an evolutionary (sexually selective) advantage to the most skilled musicians, whether animal or human.

The transformation of languages through time became a disciplined topic by the beginning of the nineteenth century. The second debate which informed language theory from the beginning of the nineteenth century was of equally great importance to Darwin, since it bore on methods of classification, and on genealogical patterns of knowledge and descent. Languages were now conceived as having descended from previous lost forms. Monboddo observed,

I think it probable, that all the languages spoken in Europe, all Asia, if you will, and some part of Africa, are dialects of one parent-language which probably was invented in Egypt . . . Some, I know, are very fond of the system of an universal language; but when they come to prove it by facts, by the languages themselves, I think they fail very much . . . Whatever therefore we may believe of there having been once but one language upon the face of the earth, we must, I think, allow, that it is now either totally lost in a great part of the earth, or so depraved and corrupted as no longer to be known.[15]

Hans Aarsleff, one of the most productive of recent historians of linguistics, asserts: 'It is universally agreed that the decisive turn in language study occurred when the philosophical, a priori method of the eighteenth century was abandoned in favor of the historical, a posteriori method of the nineteenth.'[16]

[12] Charles Darwin, *The Descent of Man* (1871; repr. London, 1901), 135.
[13] Gruber and Barrett, 334.
[14] Ibid. 334.   [15] Monboddo, 476.
[16] Hans Aarsleff, *The Study of Language in England, 1780–1860* (Princeton, NJ, 1967), 127.

From the middle of the eighteenth century onwards there was a movement in the study of the history of language away from the view of language as a fixed structure towards the concept of language as a growing and developing medium. We can see this at the level of single words in the great interest of etymology. (Whewell was at the centre of an active Etymological Society at Cambridge in the early 1830s while Darwin, his great admirer, was an undergraduate there and later Darwin's cousin and friend, Hensleigh Wedgwood, produced an etymological dictionary in the 1850s and 1860s). Another, and most important level of debate, was that of comparative grammar, which in England took its impetus from the work of William Jones and was established in the major studies of Franz Bopp. Both Bopp and Jones were Sanskrit scholars. Their work emphasized kinship and filiation between the languages in the Indo-European system, and emphasized too the idea of what Darwin was later, in another context, to call the 'single progenitor'—a lost mother tongue previous to Sanskrit. Alexander Hamilton in his review of Bopp's *Conjugations System* in the *Edinburgh Review*, May 1820 (a journal which Darwin regularly read), remarked that 'Schlegel first indicated to his countrymen the sources of unexplored truths concealed in that distant region [India] and the important discoveries to which they might probably lead, in tracing the affiliation of nations, the progress of science, and the transactions of that mysterious period which precedes all history, [as] but that of one remarkable family.'[17] (This seems to have been Darwin's earliest acquaintance with German language theory.)

In *The Origin* Darwin turns to comparative grammar, and to the different rates at which languages change, to make clear what is novel in his ideas: evolutionary genealogy would explain the relations of diverse languages. And, as important, not all forms (linguistic or organic) need change greatly in an evolutionary system.

It may be worth while to illustrate this view of classification, by taking the case of languages. If we possessed a perfect pedigree of mankind, a genealogical arrangement of the races of man would afford the best classification of the various languages now spoken throughout the

[17] Alexander Hamilton, 'Review of Bopp, *Conjugationssystem*', *Edinburgh Review*, 33 (1820), 431.

world; and if all extinct languages, and all intermediate and slowly changing dialects, had to be included, such an arrangement would, I think, be the only possible one. Yet it might be that some very ancient language had altered little, and had given rise to few new languages, whilst others (owing to the spreading and subsequent isolation and states of civilisation of the several races, descended from a common race) had altered much, and had given rise to many new languages and dialects. The various degrees of difference in the languages from the same stock, would have to be expressed by groups subordinate to groups; but the proper or even only possible arrangement would still be genealogical; and this would be strictly natural, as it would connect together all languages, extinct and modern, by the closest affinities, and would give the filiation and origin of each tongue. In confirmation of this view, let us glance at the classification of varieties, which are believed or known to have descended from one species.[18]

Genetic terms (stock, varieties, filiation) move freely to and fro across the description of language and descent.

Darwin uses linguistic theory here not only as a metaphor but also as an *example*, an 'illustration' of evolutionary processes. In the 1830s he had already been reading language theory, as we know from his notebooks and his reading lists. The names of Locke, of Dugald Stewart, Monboddo, Horne Tooke, Brougham, Hensleigh Wedgwood, all appear.

Hensleigh Wedgwood, Darwin's cousin and friend, published an extensive technical exposition of Grimm's achievement in the *Quarterly Review* in 1833.[19] The same issue of the journal opened with a review of four of the Bridgewater Treatises, those of Whewell, Kidd, Bell, and Chalmers. Darwin was away on the voyage of the *Beagle* at that time but later in the 1830s, when he settled in London, he was in almost daily contact with Wedgwood, who was by then at work on his etymological dictionary. It is likely that Darwin read his cousin's only published article, given his current interest in the subject and the close ties between

[18] Charles Darwin, *On the Origin of Species by Means of Natural Selection* (London, 1859), ed. John Burrow from 1st edn. (Harmondsworth, 1968), 406.

[19] Hensleigh Wedgwood, 'Grimm on the Indo-European Languages', *Quarterly Review*, 50 (Oct. 1833), 169–89. This is the only periodical publication by Wedgwood noted by the Wellesley Index. He worked on his etymological dictionary from 1833 onwards and it was published in three volumes, 1859–67. Edward Manier in *The Young Darwin and his Cultural Circle* (Dordrecht, 1978) comments on Darwin's relation to some of the dictionary's definitions, such as the several meanings of the term 'struggle'.

them. He could not, in any case, have failed to become aware of the importance of Grimm's work for Wedgwood's enterprise. In the review article Wedgwood makes clear the fundamental importance of Grimm's achievement for other workers in language theory, and he does so using unselfconsciously the genetic discourse ('descendant', 'stock') which Darwin raises to the level of argument in the passage quoted from *The Origin* above.

Wedgwood opens his discussion by praising Grimm's thoroughness:

the illustrious scholar Grimm, has here given us, under the modest title of *a German grammar*, a thorough history not only of his own language, but of that of every descendant of the Gothic stock throughout Europe, tracing, at the same time, every inflection in every dialect through every intermediate stage up to the earliest period of which any literary monuments remain![20]

Grimm's achievement is the more remarkable, Wedgwood observes, because its thoroughness does not draw on an even spread of material *evidence*. It relies instead upon the discovery of fundamental *laws*. Herein lies the crucial attraction and challenge of language theory as a thought model for Darwin during the period in which he was organizing his theory. The gaps in the fossil record were a notorious problem in assaying evidence and in arguing for a consecutive history of law bound change.

Wedgwood makes the comparison with the fossil record, (which he represents as relatively complete) and suggests that the linguistic record is harder to recuperate and to interpret:

like the organic remains of the external world, these particles were formed of the most striking portions of the sentences which they represent, whilst the more perishable portions have mouldered away. In some respects the fossil remains have met with a more fortunate destiny than these relics of the immaterial world, for, whilst the former have for the most part been preserved by the protecting soil in which they were embedded, so that a skilful anatomist has little difficulty in deciding to what portion of the skeleton of living animals they correspond, the latter, from their everyday and universal use, have been worn, until, like pebbles on the beach, they have lost every corner and distinctive mark, and hardly a vestige remains to indicate their original form. Yet even here we are not left entirely without traces which may enable us to form some conjecture of the origin of one or two of these pronouns.[21]

[20] Wedgwood, 169.   [21] Ibid. 175.

Wedgwood emphasizes the morphological similarity between past and present life-forms which, he argues, allows 'a skilful anatomist' to interpret the fossil record. Darwin, in the course of his next twenty years' work, became ever more conscious of the gaps in the record and of the problem of discriminating between 'true affinity' and mere similarity. He needed to construct a historical register, and to formulate laws governing change, as it seemed Bopp and Grimm had already done in their own field.

Wedgwood's article also touches on a topic which came to have a particular theoretical interest for Darwin: that of animal communication. This topic suggested strong connections between evolutionary and language theory, particularly in the matter of continuity between humankind and other species. Henry, Lord Brougham's *Dissertations on Subjects of Science Connected with Natural Theology* (1839) in particular excited Darwin because of Brougham's emphasis on the continuity between the powers of abstraction in animals and human kind: 'says animals have abstraction because they understand signs.—very profound.—concludes that difference of intellect between animals and men only in kind. Probably very important work.'[22]

What Darwin did *not* understand in Brougham's work was his emphasis on the arbitrariness of the sign. We now connect this idea with the work of Saussure (who, as I have earlier indicated, drew on Whitney). But in Brougham we see how certain elements of language theory, which were to become of the first importance for twentieth-century work, were already available for discussion before 1840, in the long wake of Locke, though Darwin could not use all of them.

I think we may go a step further; have not animals some kind of language? At all events they understood ours. A horse knows the encouraging or chiding voice and whip, and moves or stops accordingly. Whoever uses the sound, in whatever key of loudness, the horse acts alike. But they seem also to have some knowledge of conversational signs. If I am to teach a dog or a pig to do certain things on a given signal, the process I take to be this. I connect his obedience with reward, his disobedience with punishment. But this only gives him the motive to obey, the fear of disobeying. It in no way can give him the means of connecting the act with the sign.

[22] Gruber and Barrett, 342. Entry c.Jan. 21, 1839.

Now connecting the two together (action and sign), whatever be the manner in which the sign is made, is Abstraction; but it is more, it is the very kind of Abstraction in which all language has its origin—the connecting the sign with the thing signified; for the sign is purely arbitrary in this case as much as in human language.[23]

In Darwin's copy in the Cambridge University Library he has drawn a line beside this passage and has written 'Don't understand'. What did Darwin not understand or resist understanding? He needed and could use Brougham's emphasis on common origins and on animal intelligence. Animals understand signs; so do human beings: this demonstrates a common power of abstraction. Darwin's problems concern the move from the idea of *abstraction* to that of *language* (and this indeed has continued to be a problem of theory and practice for workers with primates and language).

His theory was at the time preoccupying him with continuity and connection: evidence of discontinuity and arbitrary relations might therefore, one might argue, not be within the current comprehension of his creativity. But something further is going on here. The recognition and suppression taking place concerns Brougham's insistence on semiotic arbitrariness as the prototype of abstraction. The relation between signifier and signified is, Brougham suggests, arbitrary in animal communication as in human language. This suggests a continuity of possible development and capacities between them. However, the arbitrariness of relationship between signifier and signified seems to be the point that Darwin baulks at. He believed in the musical basis of language, which could imply either a mimetic or an abstract relation of 'things and voice' (see note 13 above). Darwin *needed* not yet to make up his mind concerning the question of the basis of language, and for this reason he believes himself not to have understood Brougham's argument. What are the major ideological pressures and indecisions focused here? It may be that he felt reluctant to 'cross the Rubicon' (as Müller held language to be between men and animals) but this is unlikely as some of his most insistent private writing in the 1830s exuberantly emphasizes the connection. When he came to publish, he dealt with the

[23] Henry Brougham, *Dissertations on Subjects of Science Connected with Natural Theology*, 2 vols. (London 1839), i. 195–6. Darwin notes this discussion in the index he made in his copy.

'diplomatic' problem of man's place in nature by leaving out the example of man in the argument, though not the language, of *The Origin*. This social difficulty is not by itself a sufficient explanation. The reason for his delay in understanding, I believe, has more to do with the problem of stabilizing his views on the origin of language itself. Until he had worked further through the evidence for multiple evolutionary change, he could not afford to settle a particular question of origins, lest it curtail his thought across a broader field.

Major theories, it seems, must always *leave out* certain relevant questions. Creativity not only connects but excludes (in the interests of coherence and of uncertainty) resources apparently relevant to the current project. Those left-over resources may well later move back to the centre of a long-term debate.

Let us look now at two particular examples of the way in which Darwin's reading of language theory gave him terms to work with and problems to brood upon. Edward Manier has written concisely but revealingly about Darwin's views on language in *The Young Darwin and his Cultural Circle*; through my brief analysis here I hope to suggest the intimacy with which language theory and evolutionary theory were inter-implicated, metaphors and models moving freely back and forth, providing projects and hopes as well as difficulties.

The problem of essentialist versus developmentalist views of language is succinctly set out in Dugald Stewart's essay 'On the Beautiful'. He cites Diderot on the word *beau* in the *Encyclopédie*, who, 'after some severe strictures on the solutions proposed by his predecessors, is led, at last, to the following conclusions of his own, which he announces with all the pomp of discovery;—"That beauty consists in the perceptions of relations" '. This, Stewart says, originated in an enduring prejudice 'that when a word admits of a variety of significations, these significations must all be *species* of the same *genus*, and must consequently include some essential idea common to every individual to which the generic term can be applied'. He counterproposes that this is 'a supposition founded . . . on a total misconception of the nature of the circumstances, which, in the history of language, attach different meanings to the same words; and which often, by slow and insensible gradations, remove them to such a distance from their primitive or radical sense, that no ingenuity can trace the successive steps of their progress'.[24]

One notes in this passage the suggestion of *unconscious* processes of change ('slow and insensible gradations'), just as, later, Darwin, in *The Origin* contrasts the consciousness of artificial selection against the improvement and modification which 'surely but slowly follow from this unconscious process' of *natural* selection.[25] We note too the transformation from the 'primitive or radical sense'; the refusal of any static taxonomy, 'some essential idea common to every individual to which the generic term can be applied': a refusal also of an essentialist view of *species*, what Darwin later called 'the vain search for the undiscovered and undiscoverable essence of the term, *Species*'.[26]

Darwin's new taxonomy took the view that not all characteristics need be identical to establish species. That refusal of essentialism present in Stewart's language theory is a necessary precondition of an evolutionist biology, but, strikingly, Dugald Stewart glosses over as being beyond discovery the phases by which words change: 'no ingenuity can trace the successive steps of their progress.' The genetic enquiry was *left over* to be undertaken later in other fields.

Bopp and Grimm set out not only the *resemblances* but the *kinships* between languages. They showed that resemblance may in fact indicate separation. Their argument was based on the 'presenting as natural transformations (through inheritance) of a single mother tongue, Indo-European'.[27] The original 'mother tongue' (like the 'single progenitor' of Darwin's theory) can be known only by reconstruction: most scholars did not believe that Sanskrit was itself the mother tongue; Darwin emphasized the irrecoverable forms of 'the one parent'.

In the third Anniversary Discourse, of 1786, William Jones had suggested that many languages, and, in particular, Sanskrit, Greek, and Latin, would have to be considered as having 'sprung from some common source, which, perhaps no longer exists'.[28]

[24] Dugald Stewart, 'On the Beautiful', *Collected Works of Dugald Stewart*, ed. William Hamilton (Edinburgh, 1854), v. 192, 193–5; 'Of language', iv. 6, 115.
[25] Darwin, *Origin*, 148.   [26] Ibid. 456.
[27] Oswald Ducrot and Tzvetan Todorov, *Encyclopaedic Dictionary of the Sciences of Language* (Oxford, 1981), 9.
[28] William Jones, *The Works of Sir William Jones* (London, 1799), i. 26.

Bopp provided a programme of linguistic research which would analyse the grammatical structures of several languages, comparing their morphology and illustrating the common laws of change.

Many resemblances are evident at first sight, others are discovered by more careful investigation, and the more closely we analyse the recondite structure of the kindred tongues, the more we are surprised to find them constantly developed by the same principle . . . It will be well to avail ourselves [he writes later] of the first grammarians, and beginning with the simplest elements, contemplate the roots developing themselves under our own sight, as we may say, into various ramifications.[29]

Again, we can see at work here an organization of knowledge which will prove to be of immense worth for the development of later evolutionary and developmental theory, 'roots developing themselves . . . into ramifications': the branching diagram of Darwinian theory shares its pattern with that of the comparative grammarians of the earlier nineteenth century. As Martin Rudwick has shown, Lyell found the metaphor from contemporary language theory of great worth in helping to organize his geological information and also in helping him to escape from the blinkered empiricism of the geological society of his period.[30] The emphasis both upon unreclaimable origins and upon the establishment of the regularity of laws of change through phonetic laws were crucial as thought models for later workers in different fields. As Ducrot and Todorov make clear, the new emphasis in language theory on *inheritance* meant that the filial relationship between languages was expressed through differences, not only through *resemblances*: 'The belief in natural change will lead . . . to a search for proofs of kinship within the differences themselves.'[31]

[29] Franz Bopp, *Über das Conjugationssystem der Sanskritsprache in Vergleichung mit jenem der griechischen, lateinischen, persischen, und germanischen Sprachen, nebst Episoden des Ramajan und Mahabharat in genauen, metrischen Übersetzungen aus den Originaltexten und einigen Abschnitten aus den Vega's*, ed. K. J. Windischmann (Frankfurt/Main, 1816). Edition introduced by E. F. K. Koerner (Amsterdam, 1974), pp. x, 14, 19. This work was first translated into English in 1845.

[30] Martin Rudwick, 'Transposed Concepts from the Human Sciences in the Early Work of Charles Lyell', in *Images of the Earth*, ed, L. J. Jordanova and Roy Porter (Chalfont St Giles, 1979), 67–83.

[31] Ducrot and Todorov, 7.

Etymology was the oldest form in which such linguistic change had been recorded, but it was possible to produce more than one convincing etymology for a single word, and difficult ever to establish an authoritative sequence of change. Although etymology was the first focus of work on language development, and remained a crucial concern, it was the demonstration of phonetic laws that made possible the newest enquiries into filiation. Genetics, as Darwin was well aware, was not yet sufficiently advanced to be able to demonstrate the laws of transformation. It had not yet, that is to say, reached the degree of specificity that Bopp and Grimm had already achieved in linguistic morphology. Language study therefore provided not only metaphors and illustrations but also a hopeful model for future research. It seemed to promise the transformation of 'chance' into 'as yet unknown laws' (always Darwin's goal).

Darwin, surveying the paucity of the geological record, saw the scientist's activity as a 'decipherment' of 'characters'. The history of the world is also a linguistic history, a palimpsest, riddled with gaps and lacunae—a record incomplete and fitful, 'written in a changing dialect'.

For my part, following out Lyell's metaphor, I look at the natural geological record, as a history of the world imperfectly kept, and written in a changing dialect; of this history we possess the last volume alone, relating only to two or three countries. Of this volume, only here and there a short chapter has been preserved; and of each page, only here and there a few lines. Each word of the slowly-changing language, in which the history is supposed to be written, being more or less different in the interrupted succession of chapters, may represent the apparently abruptly changed forms of life, entombed in our consecutive, but widely separated formations.[32]

Darwin transposes the old idea of 'the book of nature' into a new historical register, emphasizing the book as 'a history of the world', a history whose script and language itself changes over time, and, furthermore, he describes it as a document which is itself a physically damaged product of historical change, now tattered and incomplete, with pages and whole chapters missing.

The major methodological problems produced by the degree of interpenetration of language theory and evolutionary theory

[32] Darwin, *Origin*, 136.

became manifest, however, in the *Descent of Man*, where Darwin uses as independent sources of evidence what are in fact common terms, genetic and linguistic, which have been shifting to and fro between the two fields of study. The shared discourse makes for self-proving argument. Discussing the formation and origins of language, Darwin cites first Lyell, then Müller, then by allusion his own earlier writing as it has been appropriated by Müller:

A language, like a species, when once extinct, never, as Sir C. Lyell remarks, reappears. The same language never has two birth-places. Distinct languages may be crossed or blended together. We see variability in every tongue, and new words are constantly cropping up . . . The survival or preservation of certain favoured words in the struggle for existence is natural selection.[33]

Analogy has lost its analogical function here. It was high time for the two fields to declare their independence of each other, to assert the autonomy of their studies and to obliterate for a while the lines of filiation. Their imagistic interconnections were beginning to flaw argumentative procedures, producing only a self-verifying interchange. The ricochet of terms to and fro between language theory and evolutionary theory was making the apparent proof of congruity too easy.

Evolutionary theory henceforth turned towards genetics, and linguistics to synchronic laws. Saussure remarks that the German neo-grammarians 'fought the terminology of the comparative school, and especially the illogical metaphors that it used. One no longer dared to say, "Language does this or that", or "life of language" since language is not an entity and exists only between speakers.' But he wisely goes on to remark that to refuse metaphor entirely and '*to require that only words that correspond to the facts of speech be used, is to pretend that these facts no longer perplex us*' (my italics).[34] Any suggestion that a field of study is authoritatively 'factual' and autonomous, Saussure suggests, will be more misleading than accepting the provisionality of metaphor. This important insight recognized that 'left-over' metaphors may initiate further creative thinking.

Some of the metaphors which haunted the nineteenth-century debates have very recently become productive again, and the

[33] Darwin, *Descent*, 318–19.   [34] Saussure, 65.

relations between linguistics and 'man's place in nature' have entered creativity anew. In *Speaking of Apes, a Critical Anthology of Two-Way Communication with Man*, edited by T. and J. U. Sebeok, Jane H. Hill opens an essay on 'Apes and Language': 'How shall anthropological linguistics assess the significance of the recent experiments with apes and language? The question is a momentous one. The answers may imply a paradigm shift, with Plato finally giving way to Darwin.'[35] Or, as Darwin had already exuberantly and secretly written in the 1830s, 'Plato ... says in Phaedo that our "imaginary ideas" arise from the preexistence of the soul, are not derivable from experience.—read monkeys for preexistence.'[36]

Hill continues: 'Ten years ago, the answer from most established scholars to the question, "Do other animals have language?" would have been an unequivocal "No". Chomskyean rationalism dominated American linguistics and insisted on ... "*discontinuity theory*"—the argument that humankind is not continuous in its abilities with other species.'[37] Chomsky argued for the innate and unique specialization of the human brain to include the capacity for working with grammatical structures common to all languages.

The 'discontinuity' element in Chomsky's theory, which he shares with much earlier workers like Müller, to whom language was a Rubicon between man and 'the brute', has come under increasing scrutiny and criticism in the past ten years. Charles Osgood in 'What is a language?' argues that the chimpanzee Washoe in fact met five of his six criteria for language (non-random recurrency of forms, reciprocality, pragmatics, semantics, and combinational productivity), and that the sixth, syntax, might be not so much absent as unrecognizable and novel, 'based on social relationships'.[38]

Charles Snowdon, in 'Linguistic and psycholinguistic approaches to primate communication', argues against a dichotomy 'between simple, stereotyped, fixed communication systems in

---

[35] Jane H. Hill, 'Apes and Language', in *Speaking of Apes, a Critical Anthology of Two-Way Communication with Man*, ed. T. and J. U. Sebeok (New York and London, 1980), 331.

[36] Gruber and Barrett, 324.   [37] Hill, 331.

[38] Charles E. Osgood, 'What is a Language?', in *The Signifying Animal: The Grammar of Language and Experience*, ed. Irmengard Rauch and Gerald F. Carr (Bloomington, 1980), 18.

human beings'. He concludes, nevertheless, 'there is no identity between the natural communication system of any primate and the natural communication system (including language) of human being'. He then adds a crucial sentence: 'Nor is there any biological reason to assume an identity of communication systems between species.'[39] The levelling organization of his argument, which implies that we can hope only to describe points of congruity or of overlap between communication systems which differ across many species, all of them unique, is a valuable check. It guards against our interpreting all other species as aspiring towards the human condition.

The interpretative habits which irritated Darwin in human thought prove again to be both spur and stumbling-block for the new study of animal communication. The field is recognized both as a branch of evolutionary theory and of language theory. One dramatic concentration has been on the attempt to teach *human* language to other primates. The ideological elements which may hamper such an enterprise have been pinpointed by a number of commentators. Such elements are present in the approach both of those who criticize and those who work within the programme. These habits are the placing of humankind at the unique centre of significance (as well as of signifying), the tendency to anthropomorphism, and hierarchical assumptions.

For example, in the collection *Language in Primates: Perspectives and Implications* contributors bring out the anthropocentrism which constantly endangers fresh enquiry in evolutionary and linguistic theory.[40] In the Introduction the editors assert that: 'Any definite answer to the question of whether the apes are communicating in ape language experiments is likely to tell us more about our anthropomorphic understanding of communication than about the ape's behaviour.' William C. Stokoe, in 'Apes Who Sign and Critics Who Don't' argues for what may prove an infinite delay in undertaking such studies: 'Only a science of man

---

[39] Charles T. Snowdon, 'Linguistic and Psycholinguistic Approaches to Primate Communication', in *Primate Communication*, ed. Charles T. Snowdon, Charles H. Brown, and Michael R. Petersen (Cambridge, 1982), 212, 235.

[40] Judith de Luce and Hugh T. Wilder (eds.), *Language in Primates: Perspectives and Implications* (New York, 1983). See Introduction, p. 12, William C. Stokoe, 'Apes who Sign and Critics who Don't', 147.

and woman will be able to test the premise that is often taken as axiomatic in other behavioural sciences—ultimately a theological premise—that human creation was unique and that human behaviour, especially language, is cut off from any evolutionary continuum.' In another important collection, *The Meaning of Primate Signals*, Roy Harris satirizes the anthropocentric conditions of such experimental programmes: 'Arguably, human infants would fare no better at the language game if subjected to comparably bizarre experiments (involving removal from natural habitat, control by members of another species, force-feeding with a relentless diet of gobbledegook, insistence on an unnatural medium of expression etc.).'[41] Harris's argument, it should be noted, is itself based on anthropomorphism.

Some of the assumptions within which, and against which, Darwin was working remain to be debated anew. But what, in the period of his enquiries, was often argued to be only a metaphorical link between evolutionary theory and language theory, proves now to be substantive. Animal communication and human language has turned out to be a controversial growing point in evolutionary and linguistic theory. The particular development of the chimpanzee's vocal tract makes utterance difficult and the absence of right or left hemisphere dominance tells against the development in primates of powers of communication along lines identical with those of human speech or language. Richard Passingham, for example, attempts to answer the question of how it comes about that chimpanzees can acquire linguistic skills, though conditions in the wild do not require them to do so and therefore such skills would not be favoured in evolutionary terms. He suggests that it is their general high intelligence which 'enables them to learn any tasks intelligently'. This leads him to conclude that Chomsky may have overestimated 'the extent to which the capacity for learning language depends on areas specialized for this purpose'.[42]

In such work, and in that of writers in the 1970s such as Colin Beer in the collection *Origin and Evolution of Language and*

[41] Roy Harris and Vernon Reynolds (eds.), *The Meaning of Primate Signals* (Cambridge, 1983), Roy Harris, 'Comment', 204.

[42] Richard Passingham, 'Specialization and the Language Areas', in *Neurobiology of Social Communication in Primates: An Evolutionary Perspective*, ed. Horst D. Steklis and Michael J. Raleigh (New York, 1979), 222.

Speech or Donald Griffin, *The Question of Animal Awareness.*
Evolutionary Continuity of Mental Experiences,[43] the organic
and evolutionary questions raised for Darwin by nineteenth-
century linguistics have moved again into a substantive status
after a period as an obliterated metaphor. Erased filiations can
be renewed, and can give fresh impetus to further fields of
enquiry.

[43] S. R. Harnad, H. D. Steklis, and J. Lancaster (eds.), *The Origin and Evolution
of Language and Speech* (New York, 1976); Donald Griffin, *The Question of Animal
Awareness: Evolutionary Continuity of Mental Experiences* (New York, 1976).

6

Forging the Missing Link:
Interdisciplinary Stories

Interdisciplinary work crosses over between fields: it trans-
gresses. It thus brings into question the methods and materials of
differing intellectual practices and may uncover problems *disguised* by the scope of established disciplines.

Forms of knowledge do not readily merge; they may lie
askance or cross-grained. But that does not imply failure. Dis-
analogy can prove to be a powerful heuristic tool. Indeed, it is
important not too readily to pair particular disciplines since that
ignores indirection, the shared and dispersed other forms of
experience and knowledge active in the time.

Interdisciplinary studies do not produce closure. Their stories
emphasize not simply the circulation of intact ideas across a
larger community but transformation: the transformations
undergone when ideas enter other genres or different reading
groups, the destabilizing of knowledge once it escapes from the
initial group of co-workers, its tendency to mean more and other
than could have been foreseen.

Problems remain. How thoroughly interdisciplinary is it
possible to be? Are we lightly transferring a set of terms from one
practice to another, as metaphor, *façon de parler*? Are we appro-
priating *materials* hitherto neglected for analysis of the kind we
have always used? Or are we trying to learn new *methods* and
skills fast, which others have spent years acquiring? The key
questions in another discipline may at first glance seem banal,
since the incomer is ignorant of the resistances that have produced and shaped them. That superior glossing of other people's
controversies is one hazard in interdisciplinary work; the opposite temptation is to succumb to the glamour of the horizon.
Those most sceptical about their own disciplinary practices are
sometimes inclined to embrace the practices of an adjacent discipline too reverentially.

Yet it is this willingness—even eagerness—to yield to, pay tribute to, the methods of other intellectual undertakings that first opens up most interdisciplinary work. Learning how to work with fresh methods and materials vivifies intellectual enquiry. After all, we ordinarily, in our daily lives, experience interdisciplinarity, and function across multiple, conflicting, epistemologies: these are not untried skills. The move to textualization in a variety of areas is offset by the recognition that written culture can never be autonomous, or complete. Writing *occurs* as reading, and reading takes place as enactment amidst other stimuli—what you are looking at, what you hear, what you consume and cook, what the news is at present, what the season, and what the political system within which your life is constructed.

No community can be sufficiently described in its own terms. Its characterizing difficulties escape the terms available for description within that particular community; and that applies also to disciplinary communities. If we work solely within the terms and categories established by our initial training—or even our own current theory—we may find ourselves caught in a monstrous self-referentiality. As the post-Kleinian psychoanalyst Winnicott put it in a letter to his fellow-analyst Hanna Segal: 'I am concerned that you shall not spoil it all by getting into some sort of ugly state in which you are sitting perched up on top of a Mount Everest of an internalised good breast.'[1] The outsider's eye offers fresh insight, the visitor construes questions different ly. But such construction can function only through a thorough attempt to understand the terms inhering in the culture (or the discipline) approached.

Our initiating professional skills are diverse. We should be ware, it seems to me, in the pleasure of learning new practices, of renouncing or undervaluing our long learnt skills—which for those trained in literary studies is our skill as questioning *reader* Making things happen, precipitating change, has recently bee the business of the ivory tower, not directly, but by an insisten questioning of categories and of assumptions embedded in language.

Some stories declare themselves late, in narratives caught together out of the concerns of another (present) moment in

[1] Donald Winnicott, *The Spontaneous Gesture: Selected Letters of D. W. Winn cott*, ed. F. Robert Redman (Cambridge, Mass., 1987), 26.

time. Such stories may appear only if we put together in our own signifying moment materials from several past disciplinary or discursive zones. These significant constellations tend to be composed of ideas that at the time were *moved on* compulsively within the community, rather than being steadied for contemplation. Such ideas are characterized by what I would call *under-interpretation*, in which anxieties and preoccupations never find full realization within a single text.

Over-interpretation is a familiar (and cherished) outcome both of anxiety and of hermeneutics: the itch to notice everything, to control by constant re-playing, to reach out towards further and further signifying possibilities. These are symptoms alike of lovers, semiologists, and attentive readers. Such over-interpretation is necessary to those brooding on cultural change. But within the historical period in which such change is occurring, avoidance, deflection, and denial may be quite as marked as attentiveness. That is what I mean by my term under-interpretation. So a phrase, like 'the missing link', may crop up all over the place without ever quite being argued through or narrativized. This insistent *moving on* of an idea from field to field is a mark of profound shared disquiet within a community. Out of such recurrent but discrete formations wraith-like narratives emerge, blocked or tabooed at the time, realizable now.

The fascination with the 'other', and with the process of othering, has gone alongside the rise of interdisciplinary studies. The two may be connected. The concept of the 'other' still grants centrality to the subject-position of the speaker and may even continue the process of occupation and colonization that it decries. Perhaps we need another term now, something closer to what Salman Rushdie praises as mongrelization or others as creolization. The story I am about to tell bears on the process of othering and its anxieties. It has a turn, but not an ending. It raises questions about authentication and styles of belief. To tell it I shall draw on material from Victorian scientific writing, poetry, cartoons, feminist novels, and religious tracts.

In my title *forging* bears both its meanings: connecting and counterfeiting. The 'missing link', a hypothetical type between two life forms, particularly between mankind and other primates, was an immensely popular idea in the mid- and later nineteenth century—and into our own. Both Darwin and Huxley emphatically denied that any link was missing in the evolutionary process. But in journalism, fiction, poetry, cartoons, and popular entertainment the idea took hold and the being was often figured as a monster or a racial 'other'. From the start it was a popular, journalistic, even jokey notion, one more often encountered in cartoons than in scientific papers. Those were more likely to have titles such as this, from the *Journal of the Ethnological Society of London* in 1856: 'Ethnological Remarks upon Some of the More Remarkable Varieties of Human Species Represented by Individuals Now in London'.[2] Though their subject-matter may be—as in this instance—people exhibited in freak shows.

It is no accident that the fascination with the missing link and the rise of the detective novel occur in the same historical period. The phrase 'the missing link' suggests a heuristic search, for a lost link in a chain of reasoning, as much as the search for the evidence of physical remains. It came also rapidly to signify outlandish, even monstrous creatures, as yet undiscovered and, quite probably, *fraudulent*. The search for the missing link therefore frequently shifts from the interpretation of physical vestiges to the detection of human agents.

Indeed, in Conan Doyle's *The Hound of the Baskervilles* at the end of the century the solution to the mystery is condensed by Sherlock Holmes into finding what he calls the missing link: this turns out to be at once an essential part of a chain of evidence *and* the discovery that the missing evidential link is an atavistic man who has reverted to an older, more violent, type. Philosophers have made much of the congruence between Peirce's concept of 'abduction' (backward hypothesizing: what Huxley called, alluding to Voltaire, 'the method of Zadig') and the proceedings of Sherlock Holmes. Peirce himself emphasized the function of abduction in evolutionary theory.[3] The detective novel, with all its playful miscluing of the reader's attention, still

---

[2] R. G. Latham, *Journal of the Ethnological Society of London*, 4 (1856), 148, quoted in Robert Bogdan, *Freak Show: Presenting Human Oddities for Amusement and Profit* (Chicago and London, 1988), 188.

[3] Umberto Eco and Thomas A. Sebeok (eds.), *The Sign of Three: Dupin, Holmes, Peirce* (Bloomington, Ind., 1983). Thomas Henry Huxley, 'On the Method of Zadig: Retrospective Prophecy as a Function of Science', in *Science and Culture* (London, 1881), 128–48.

promises that by the time we have read to the end we shall also have reached back to secure origins. A sufficient explanation of how things came to be will be provided by means of this revisionary backward reading. The insistence on stable recovery of initiating acts was at odds with (perhaps was an attempt to find comfort against) the lostness of origins figured in nineteenth-century geology and evolutionary theory.[4]

In this essay I shall suggest some of the ways in which the idea of 'the missing link' functioned among British Victorians, not only in the manifest context of palaeontology and evolutionary theory but in the implications it bore for race and class, and sometimes gender. What anxieties did the 'missing link' conceal or propagate? What were its politics? Why did it need to stay missing? The idea of the missing link condensed past with future, looking forward with excitement to the solution of a mystery from the infinitely remote past. That at least was its overt narrative trigger. Lévi-Strauss has argued that whereas the myths of older cultures tend to be spatial, those of more recent cultures are temporal.[5] In structural terms the idea of the missing link is clearly temporal (the link went missing long ago), but it also bore for the Victorians a freight of conflicted political meanings that called on spatial terms: particularly those of distance and closeness between kinds, classes, and peoples. It raised questions of boundaries: what's in, what's out; the object and the abject.

Categories always have in them an element of chosen kinning and exclusion. Both Darwin and Huxley pointed out that no observer outside humankind would have invented a special category for man as opposed to other primates. So the link might be missing for one of two contrasted reasons: (1) that everything is connected and therefore no gaps are to be found. The gaps are simply in our present knowledge; (2) that humankind is quite separate from all other species and therefore nothing can be found to close up the gap. In either case the search for one intermediate form would be fruitless. Yet, of course, the search remains a compelling one, still producing controversy and still straining questions of class and category. Is *Homo habilis* (handy man) to be distinguished from *Australopithecus* on any but

---

[4] See my 'Origins and Oblivion in Victorian Narrative', in *Arguing with the Past* (London, 1989), 12–33.

[5] In an interview with Paolo Caruso, *Atlas*, 11 (Apr. 1966), 246.

behavioural (and therefore genetically suspect) grounds? And is Leakey's team guilty of categorial sleight of hand, revising the minimum size of brain necessary to qualify as a specimen of the genus *Homo*?[6]

Among Victorian people two contradictory intellectual ideals prevailed: synthesis and development. Synthesis is enacted in the present; development is enacted over time. Both may seem to be socially neutral concepts but as the notion of the missing link can demonstrate they were in fact freighted with emotions, denials, and class, race, and gender assumptions—as strong ideas always are.

In narrativizing the past the cusp of the story was a 'not there', a 'missing link'. Could things hang together without it? Or, to turn the question round, was its absence *necessary* to the story being mounted? How else to begin? How else to keep the story of humankind autonomous? The idea of the link implies clasp and closure not reach and bridging. The climax of anticipated discovery—finding the link—was one that could produce dread and delay rather than fulfilment. Victorian satirists made much of the absurd features of a search for the missing link between human and other forms—and conservative writers like W. H. Mallock pooh-poohed the insistence on the material descent of humanity. In *The New Paul and Virginia: or Positivism on an Island*, Mallock shipwrecks the high-minded secular preacher Paul on an island with the hedonistic and married Virginia:

Virginia was preparing, with a rueful face, to resume her enjoyment of the higher pleasures, when a horrible smell, like that of an open drain, was suddenly blown in through the window.

Virginia stopped her nose with her handkerchief. The Professor's conduct was very different.

'Oh, rapture!' he cried, jumping up from his seat, 'I smell the missing link.' And in another instant he was gone.

Paul returned in about a couple of hours, again unsuccessful in his search.

'Ah!' cried Virginia, 'I am so glad that you have not caught the creature!'

'Glad!' echoed the Professor, 'glad! Do you know that till I have caught the missing link the cause of glorious truth will suffer griev-

---

[6] See discussion in Roger Lewin, *Bones of Contention: Controversies in the Search for Human Origins* (Harmondsworth, 1991).

ously? The missing link is the token of the solemn fact of our origin from inorganic matter. I did but catch one blessed glimpse of him. He had certainly a silver band about his neck. He was about three feet high. He was rolling in a lump of carrion. It is through him that we are related to the stars—the holy, the glorious stars, about which we know so little.'

'Bother the stars!' said Virginia.[7]

Mallock has here in his sights John Tyndall who in 'The Use of the Imagination in Science' had recently insisted on the uninterrupted sequence of matter from the sun to the human. To Mallock the preoccupation with the missing link is pernicious reflexivity: a symptom of godless self-absorption.

In one sense, then, what I am discussing falls within the domain of nineteenth-century natural history, in another, within that of romance. It is the shiftiness of the categories that is one source of interest; also, the ways in which the contiguity between categories of natural history and romance makes it possible for people to elide the question of *how* you believe in history. The search for the missing link has the character of quest-romance, but of a modern sort: the quest for the missing link has as its covert goal the finding that the link is *not there*. Certainly the heritage industry, now, fills some of the same space, a warding-off that has all the appearance of a coming-near. Part of the pleasure of theme-parks is that they don't demand full belief. They tantalizingly offer to bring the past *to* us. And they are yet manifest forgeries or pastiches, even declaring themselves as such. They shroud the past, precisely by offering it a coat of fresh (acrylic) paint.

The instance I'm about to analyse shows how, sometimes, doubtful authenticity—even inauthenticity—may be a desired characteristic of some sought-for explanation or origin. Fraudulence and disconfirmation become pleasures. Anxiety is comforted by deflection. Indeed, one could even argue that the search for the missing link (absence and creature at once) is an epitome of 'différance', in Derrida's term: difference and deferral at once.

The fascination with 'the missing link' has certainly produced some spectacular forgeries, of which the Piltdown Man is perhaps the most famous. The connection between the detective search for human agents and for early life-forms re-emerges here. A skull and pieces of bone were found in 1912 in a Sussex gravel pit, and, nicely, Teilhard de Chardin was one of those who found remains: in his case, a canine tooth at Piltdown in 1913. The hoax was finally exposed in 1953, as a result of new physical and chemical dating techniques. The mystery of its perpetrator continues: a recent book has argued that he was, in fact, the then head of the British archaeological establishment, Sir Arthur Keith: a feat of supposed detection whose pleasure is analogous to the purported discovery that Jack the Ripper was the Prince of Wales.[8]

Though the example I'm using was in its heyday of half-belief in the later nineteenth century, I hope that the discussion may uncover some communal narratives still pertinent to our current concerns. The question 'what is a monster?' and the apparently related question 'where is the boundary between mankind and the animal?' haunt literature and theory from the writing of Lord Monboddo in the late eighteenth century to H. G. Wells's *The Island of Dr Moreau* in the late nineteenth (a work that comes out of the Victorian anti-vivisection debate as much as the debate on eugenics). In Wells's novel the forced hybrids between animals and humans, bred in pain, living in slavery, raise the question of what is human not only by their appearance but by the light they cast on the 'inhumanity' of the experimenters, the shifting identifications of the narrator.

The phrase 'the missing link' figured nineteenth-century anxieties, not only about our relationships to other life-forms, but about a variety of social relations within and beyond European culture. It is an idea that has not ceased to haunt writers.[9] Doris Lessing's novel *The Fifth Child* (1988) describes a being who is both monster and ordinary child, emerging from some ancestral buried strain to disrupt a modern nuclear family. There seems to be in the Lessing fable a troublingly nineteenth-century

[8] Frank Spencer, *The Piltdown Papers 1908–1955: The Correspondence and Other Documents Relating to the Piltdown Forgery* (London, 1990).

[9] Donna Haraway, *Primate Visions: Gender, Race, and Nature in the World of Modern Science* (London, 1989), analyses the twentieth-century history of primate study in terms of issues of gender and species and includes discussion of fiction, e.g. the chapter 'Reprise: Science Fiction, Fictions of Science, and Primatology'. Harriet Ritvo, *The Animal Estate: The English and Other Creatures in the Victorian Age* (Cambridge, Mass. 1987).

genetic construction of development and progress passing through phases from the primitive to the civilized, a condensing of ontogeny and phylogeny, with the primitive phase viciously seeking vengeance on the achieved harmony of the modern family: though that institution also is satirized. Kathryn Dunne's much-praised novel, *Geek Love* (1989), on the contrary, described a family of freaks lovingly designed by their parents with a cocktail of drugs, to boost the failing fortunes of the family circus.

There may be a particular value in analysing some of the significations of the missing link in the nineteenth century at the present moment. We need to think through the politics of reproduction and technology, and such undertakings as the human genome project, with all the evidence we can command. That evidence will include fictions: novels like Jeannette Winterson's *Sexing the Cherry* (1989), which works inventively on grafting, fostering, maternity, and monsterdom by means of fantastic transformations and historical transplants between seventeenth-century and present-day England.

Monsters and missing links are, of course, by no means necessarily the same thing (especially since one of the characteristics of what are clinically described as monsters is the lack of the power to reproduce). The distinction between them was not, however, readily apparent in nineteenth-century England before genetics. Thus two diverse ideas—connection and encroachment—are both sheltered within the phrase 'the missing link'. In the wake of palaeontological and evolutionary theory the matching of ontogeny (the life-cycle development of the single organism) and phylogeny (species development) has been one of the most powerful new metaphors of the past 150 years. The ontogenic metaphor is of immense antiquity, but the matching is new. It is only recently that the politics also of ontogeny (of assuming that the 'developmental' shape for the single life-span is a matter controlled by biology not culture) has been coming under scrutiny.[10]

The pairing of individual and species development was what excited mid-nineteenth-century people. Take, for example, a

[10] John R. Morss. *The Biologising of Childhood: Developmental Psychology and the Darwinian Myth*, foreword by Rom Harre (Hove, 1990).

British Association for the Advancement of Science paper of 1862, where Robert Dunn argued that all other races were arrested at various phases of the embryonic Caucasian: 'the Negro exhibiting the imperfect brow, projecting lower jaw, and slender bent limbs of the Caucasian child some considerable time before its birth, the Aboriginal Americans representing the same child nearer birth, and the Mongolian the same new born.'[11] If such ingenuity could go into incorporating and literalizing the power relations between different human groups, ensuring dominance for the European, we should not be surprised perhaps by the inventiveness with which the barriers between humankind and other species were policed in language.

The barrier between 'man' and 'brute' (to use the nineteenth-century terms, neither of them now ideologically satisfying) became a contested borderland. The phrase 'the missing link' precedes Darwin, but evolutionary theory destabilizes static taxonomy. Evolution takes place through change and individuation and Darwin insisted that there is no essence to species. It's hard, therefore, to discriminate securely between productive variation and endstopped monstrosity. It's a good deal harder if, as was the case for mid-nineteenth-century people, laws of genetic inheritance have not yet been established.[12] In *The Origin* Darwin remarked that 'monstrosities cannot be separated by any clear line of distinction from mere variations'.[13] A monster may be a form out of accord with the environment in which it must live. Change the environment, the monster (it seemed) may become

---

[11] Robert Dunn, 'Some Observations on the Psychological Differences Which Exist Among the Typical Races of Man', *Report of the Thirty-Second Meeting of the British Association for the Advancement of Science: held at Cambridge in October 1862* (London, 1863), 'Transactions of the sections', 146. See also C. S. Wake, 'The Psychological Unity of Mankind', *Memoirs Read Before the Anthropological Society of London*, vol. 3 (1867–9), 134, and discussion in my 'Speaking for the Others: Relativism and Authority in Victorian Anthropological Literature', in Robert Fraseru (ed.), *Sir James Frazer and the Literary Imagination: Essays in Affinity and Influence* (London, 1990), 38–60; repr. as Ch. 4 above. Cf. Robert Young, *White Mythologies: Writing History and the West* (London, 1990).

[12] For discussion of fictional monsters see Chris Baldick, *In Frankenstein's Shadow: Myth, Monstrosity, and Nineteenth-Century Writing* (Oxford, 1987). See also Adrian Desmond, *The Ape's Reflection* (London, 1979) and his *Archetypes and Ancestors: Palaeontology in Victorian London 1850–75* (London, 1982).

[13] Charles Darwin, *On the Origin of Species by means of Natural Selection, or the Preservation of Favoured Races in the Struggle for Life* (London, 1859). Edn. cited ed. John Burrow (Harmondsworth, 1968), 72.

apt, even normative. That is one reason for the sense of encroachment in the phrase 'the missing link'. But in much writing the separation between the human and other creatures is taken for granted, with the human always at the top of the hierarchy. Consider the following passage from Alfred Russel Wallace's journal while working in the Brazilian forests in the 1850s a little before he, like Darwin, conceived the idea of natural selection. Wallace and his companion came upon a troop of monkeys:

Presently we caught a glimpse of them skipping about among the trees, leaping from branch to branch, passing from one tree to another with the greatest ease. At last one approached too near for its safety. Mr Leavens fired, and it fell, the rest making off with all possible speed. The poor little animal was not quite dead, and its cries, its innocent-looking countenance, and delicate little hands were quite child-like. Having often heard how good monkey was, I took it home, and had it cut up and fried for breakfast.[14]

Here the sentences run almost seamlessly on, the sensibility swivelling on the word 'good': the childlike creature becomes not 'a good monkey' but 'good for food': consuming replaces sympathy. The eye boggles momentarily as the words fall into a new structure: the structure of feeling that places humankind apart from and above all other life-forms, able to use them at will.

When Darwin published *Of the Origin of Species by Means of Natural Selection* in 1859 he excluded humankind, as he put it, 'diplomatically', from his argument, though not from his language. His earlier writing in *The Voyage of the Beagle* had, however, emphasized the distance between now-extant 'savage' and 'civilized' peoples as a strategy, perhaps, for closing up the distance between species—a move which would become necessary as he formulated his evolutionary theory. Describing the Fuegians of Wollaston Island he observed:

These were the most abject and miserable creatures I anywhere beheld . . . these Fuegians in the canoe were quite naked, and even one full-grown woman was absolutely so. It was raining heavily, and the fresh water, together with the spray, trickled down her body. In another harbour, not far distant, a woman, who was suckling a recently born

---

[14] Alfred Russel Wallace, *A Narrative of Travels on the Amazon and Rio Negro, with an Account of the Native Tribes, and Observations on their Climate, Geology, and Natural History of the Amazon Valley* (London, 1853), 42.

child, came one day alongside the vessel, and remained there out of mere curiosity, whilst the sleet fell and thawed on her naked bosom, and on the skin of her naked baby! These poor wretches were stunted in their growth, their hideous faces bedaubed with white paint, their skins filthy and greasy, their hair entangled, their voices discordant, and their gestures violent. Viewing such men, one can hardly make oneself believe that they are fellow-creatures, and inhabitants of the same world. It is a common subject of conjecture what pleasure in life some of the lower animals can enjoy; how much more reasonably the same question may be asked with respect to these barbarians! At night, five or six human beings, naked and scarcely protected from the wind and rain of this tempestuous climate, sleep on the wet ground coiled up like animals.[15]

Darwin insists here, in disagreeable terms, on the closeness of human and animal. In an unfavourable environment, he argues, it is hard to distinguish one form of life from the other. His terms vacillate uneasily: 'abject and miserable creatures', 'poor wretches', 'men', 'fellow creatures', 'barbarians', 'human beings'. He recoils and leans towards the people he describes. He is puzzled, even dismayed, by the obduracy of curiosity, here in the naked mother. She surveys him as he does her; but her gaze is characterized as 'mere curiosity' while he 'beholds' and 'views'. Being the 'other' comes hard to Western man.

In *The Origin* he made no such direct references to human conditions or human kind. The effect was to reserve the question of where human beings stood in relation to other forms of nature. It was, just, possible for the physical similarities between man and other animals to continue to be ignored by those bent on doing so, particularly because—as was often pointed out by Darwin's opponents—the fossil record was faulty in the extreme, with great gaps in the evidence.

Darwin himself was well aware of this problem, likening the geological findings to a museum with paltry and unsystematic

[15] In the first version of this passage no reason is adduced for the woman's behaviour and animals are described as 'less gifted' instead of 'lower': *Narrative of the Surveying Voyages of His Majesty's Ships Adventure and Beagle* (London, 1839), vol. III. That version persists in the 1839, 1840 editions. It is only in the second (1845) edition 'corrected, with additions' that the changes are made: *Journal of Researches into the Natural History and Geology of the Countries Visited During the Voyage of HMS Beagle Round the World under the Command of Capt Fitzroy, R.N., By Charles Darwin, 2nd edition, corrected, with additions* (London, 1845), 213. Why does Darwin after ten years comment on the woman's 'mere curiosity'?

records, and the earth to a tattered book with pages missing. This allowed him, at the same time, to hold the view that no link *was* missing between the human and other primates, or between the multitude of life forms past and present (as he wrote in an 1838 notebook 'We are all netted together'). What is missing is surviving physical evidence of those links—and that lack opens 'a wide door for the entry of doubt and conjecture'.

In very many cases, however, one form is ranked as a variety of another, not because the intermediate links have been found, but because analogy leads the observer to suppose either that they do now somewhere exist, or may formerly have existed; and here a wide door for the entry of doubt and conjecture is opened.[16]

The missing link is an absence, a wide door, a gulf, as well as a cross-over, a chiasmus or creature.

In 1863, with the publication of Huxley's anthropological essays *Man's Place in Nature*, the challenge of likeness and continuity could no longer be evaded. But the missing link is always *about* to be found—and at the place and in the culture held to be furthest from the writer's own.

The phrase 'the missing link' is noted first in the *Oxford English Dictionary* in the context of geology rather than zoology (though with the advent of palaeontology the two studies were closely connected). The citation is from Lyell's *Elements of Geology* in 1831, though there must be many earlier. The metaphor's physical referents are here more starkly expressed: 'A break in the chain implying no doubt many missing links in the series of geological monuments which we may some day be able to supply.'[17]

The visual image that lies at the back of the expression is that of a chain, not a tree: a single succession rather than the Darwinian branching diagram. It goes back, that is, to the idea of the *scala naturae*, and it can be expressed either vertically (with God, the King, Man, at the top), or horizontally, with a sequence of living forms from obsidian to humankind—or it can incline diagonally upward to express the mounting satisfaction of proceeding towards the human, as in Chambers's *Vestiges of Creation*. That notion of purposive sequence is reinforced by the common image for causality: 'a chain of events', bringing out

---

[16] *Origin of Species*, 103–4.   [17] *Oxford English Dictionary*, 1818.

again the connections between heurism and creature in the idea of the missing link. Indeed, the probability theorist John Venn suggested in *The Logic of Chance* (1867) that it would be better to substitute 'the rope of events' for 'the chain of events', since that more effectively figured the multiple intertwining of cirucmstances.[18] In all these positionings of the chain, humankind—particularly *man*kind—is seen as the last link and becomes the endpoint towards which the chain has been making.

That is not the only capacity of the metaphor, of course. Chains can be added to; they are not endstopped. Further links may be coupled to what goes before. But the vast amount of attention directed to the *missing link* has the effect of deflecting the gaze from that possibility. It turned the eye back through time. It fixed attention on the gap between man and what the Victorians usually, in such settings, called 'the brutes'. It fixed man as the endpoint, and it puzzled over the miracle of how he proceeded there.

What distinguishes humankind from other life-forms?—is it physical shape, reason, language? Descartes had earlier (1637) argued that language was what distinguished *homo sapiens* from beasts, since even the stupid and insane could put words together so as to convey their thoughts, whereas the most perfect and thriving of animals could not do the same. This, he held, proved that animals had no reason, since so little reason was needed to enable men to talk. Lord Monboddo in *Of the Origin and Progress of Language* (1772–92) took up Locke's point that any enquiry into the origins of language would be an enquiry into 'the very origin of the human race'. Monboddo shifted the boundaries, claiming that the orang-utan, though silent, was a member of the family of man.[19]

This disturbing of the boundaries (or what Max Müller later called the 'Rubicon' of language between human and animal) attracted much anxious ridicule and made of the orang-utan a disputed brother, a bar sinister in human self-figuring. Thomas

---

[18] John Venn, *The Logic of Chance* (London, 1866), 228.
[19] See my 'Darwin and the Growth of Language-Theory', in John Christie and Sally Shuttleworth (eds.), *Nature Transfigured: Science and Literature, 1700–1900* (Manchester, 1989), 152–70; repr. as Ch. 5 above. This essay demonstrates the ways in which Darwin drew on language theory as he precipitated his ideas in the 1830s.

Love Peacock in *Melincourt* (1816) offered a benign and acute parody which inverts the later class assumptions about the missing link as a filthy aberration. Sir Oran Haut-Ton (the high-toned or distinguished) is the impeccably chivalrous and silent hero who rescues the lady in distress, though he has not yet acquired the skills of speech since arriving in England from his native Borneo. He is, of course, an orang-utan. Intriguingly, the work often taken to be the founding text of detective fiction, Edgar Allan Poe's 'The Murders in the Rue Morgue' (first published in *Graham's Magazine* in 1841) creates its mystery by transgressions of classification and expectation. The murderer escapes by impossible routes and is heard speaking in a foreign tongue, which each listener recognizes as a language, but always a different one, that he or she does not know. The murderer, here, is again an orang-utan—the illicit brother admitted dangerously to familiarity with humankind.

The emphasis on the *missing* link both suggested that such a link might in the future be found and yet emphasized the break between mankind and the 'lower orders' of nature. Chains are two chains, not one, without a link. The fascination with the idea of the link was also often a dread of finding it. Once found, mankind would indissolubly be part of the material order. So long as the gap remained, mystery prevailed and the supremacy of the human could remain intact. Perhaps for that reason, the 'missing link' was most often imagined as monstrous, a discovery to be dreaded not welcomed.

This confusion between the idea of the monster and of the missing link is further illuminated if we turn to post-Kleinian psychoanalytic theory. The psychoanalyst W. R. Bion in his essay on 'The Rejection of Links' opens by commenting on 'the psychotic part of the personality . . . the destructive attacks which the patient makes on anything which is felt to have the function of linking one object with another.'[20]

In order to understand the functions of the idea in Victorian thought we need to ask suppressed questions of the metaphor. Why was the missing link not figured as Messiah, as the doubled human and divine of Christ? That idea moves through the disturbing last line of Yeats's poem as the Messiah, animal-like,

---

[20] Paper read before the British Psycho-Analytical Society, 20 Oct. 1957.

'slouches towards Bethlehem to be born'. And why was it usually represented as male? This gender attribution reinforced the connection with a sport or monster, whereas a female creature would suggest the possibility of reproduction, and raise the suspicion that the missing link might already have been assimilated into an inheritance that humankind inescapably shared, the damage have been done. Maleness was necessary to ward off that imagination.

The human 'missing links' displayed at fairs, aquariums, and so-called museums were disabled people, sometimes deaf and dumb, larger or smaller than the norm, more hairy, with more toes and fingers, an extra limb or a particoloured skin. Above all, they were people animalized by imprisonment, by the spectators' gaze, by being cast as the 'other'. Robert Bogdan offers compelling examples in *Freak Show*: William Henry Johnson, an African American born in the eastern United States, was exhibited for many years as 'What is it? Or The Man-Monkey'. Bogdan quotes from an 1860 publication for the American Museum describing him as 'a most singular animal, which though it has many of the features and characteristics of both the human and the brute, is not, apparently, either, but, in appearance, a mixture of both—the connecting link between humanity and brute creation'.[21] Here, in a freakish setting, the link can be claimed as *connecting*.

The human psyche may need always the monstrous to reject, that other which lurks inside the self to be split off as enemy. The desire to expel, reify, and control was certainly not peculiar to the Victorians, but in their case it took a particular physical and argumentative form which went, in covert ways, into the enterprise of imperialism. Then-new and powerful scientific theory had a counter-emphasis; indeed, it asserted, in evolutionary argument, both the closeness of the human to other animal species and the value of diversity. Out of variety come new evolutionary possibilities. The monster may be the favoured form when environmental conditions change. That chain of reasoning is felt as threatening; thus, paradoxically, the new epistemology gives birth to a monstrous creature.

---

[21] Bogdan, *Freak Show*, 136. Bogdan also here quotes the more specific and distancing claim of his keeper that he was 'a connecting link between the wild native African and the brute creation'.

The missing link bears a freight of curiosity, reluctance, and disgust, what Ruskin called 'the filthy heraldries which record the relation of humanity to the ascidian and the crocodile'.[22] Implicit in the metaphor of heraldry is the idea of bodily generation, of lineage and descent, though, as Gerard Manley Hopkins for one, saw, there was no need to assume a direct line from monkey to mankind. Writing to his mother (an interesting recipient for the letter), Hopkins remarked in 1874: 'I do not think, do you know, that Darwinism implies necessarily that man is descended from any ape or ascidian or maggot or what not but only from the common ancestor of ascidians, the common ancestor of maggots, and so on: these common ancestors, if lower animals, need not have been repulsive animals. What Darwin himself said about this I do not know.'[23]

Hopkins's reassurance to his mother makes it clear that a physical, aesthetic, even sexual distaste, is present for many Victorians in the idea of kinship with other animal species. In *Structural Anthropology* (London, 1977), Lévi-Strauss argues that the Oedipus myth

has to do with the inability, for a culture which holds the belief that mankind is autochthonous . . . to find a satisfactory transition between this theory and the knowledge that human beings are actually born from the union of man and woman . . . the Oedipus myth provides a kind of logical tool which relates the original problem—born from one or born from two?—to the derivative problem: born from different or born from same? (212)

What Lévi-Strauss there presents as a 'derivative problem: *born from different or born from same?*', is the primary problem for the Victorians. The missing link is figured always as a *negative creature*, formed phantasmally out of resistance to connection between classes and kinds. That distaste becomes a haven for social class and race prejudice also, enacting the snobbish phrase 'keeping one's distance'.

A class- and race-ridden fastidiousness is lodged in many of the cartoons that cluster upon the idea, most of which appear in the 1870s after the publication of Darwin's *The Descent of Man*

[22] John Ruskin, *Love's Meinie* (Keston, Kent, 1873), 59.
[23] *Further Letters of Gerard Manley Hopkins*, 2nd edn. ed. Claude Colleer Abbott (London, 1956), 128.

(1871). One of the most politically complicated of these did not appear until two years after *The Descent*.[24] Entitled *The Descent of Man* (Fig. 6.1), it pictures two men in the smoke-laden atmosphere of, perhaps, a gentleman's club. The location is emphatically a masculine domain. The exchange reads:

FIGURATIVE PARTY: 'So long as *I* am a man, sorr, what does it matther to me whether me *Great-Grandfather* was an anthropoid ape or not, sorr!'

LITERAL PARTY: 'Haw! Wather Disagweeable for your *Gwate Gwand-Mother*, wasn't it?'

The man sitting on the table, to whom the viewer's eye is drawn, is a condensation of an ape, a typical Victorian representation of an African, and Darwin himself, with receding forehead and overhanging eye-brows. That figure is the 'figurative party'. The typography claims that he is also Irish. So there he is, oppressed and lowly, but perched high—and full of ontological assurance ('What does it matther to me?'). The top-hatted smoker, sitting below him, speaks with the effete 'r'-less accents of the aristocracy. He is the 'literal party' as perhaps befits a class obsessed with the anxieties of pedigree and land-inheritance. He is also provocatively insistent that descent implies sexual congress: 'wather disagweeable for your gwate gwandmother.' The threat of matrilineal descent, which may already have absorbed the missing link and closed up the gap between human and other species, English and other races, aristocracy and other classes, is again at issue here.

Among my selection of illustrations the first to appear was 'A Logical Refutation of Mr Darwin's Theory' (Fig. 6.2).[25] The tranquil domestic scene figures difference, division, and paternal anxiety. The father, hairy with pointed ears, sits on a low cushion at the feet of his wife who grasps a girl-child to herself in a madonna-and-child pose. He 'has been reading passages from the *Descent of Man* to the wife he adores, but loves to tease'. His command of knowledge is assumed.

JACK: 'So you see, Mary, baby is descended from a hairy quadruped with pointed ears and a tail. We *all* are!'

---

[24] *Punch, or the London Charivari* (24 May 1873), 217.
[25] *Punch* (1 Apr. 1871), 130.

MARY: 'Speak for *yourself*, Jack! *I'm* not descended from anything of the kind, I beg to say; and baby takes after me. So, there!'

The straining italics urge and repudiate connection. Is he the father? Need there *be* a father? Cuckoldry and parthenogenesis thrive. Women are seen as dangerously sexed or dangerously a-sexual.

And so are those female evolutionary dead-ends, mermaids, much loved of Victorian story-tellers and mockers of science. In August of the same year *Punch* carried a piece 'The Mermaid no Myth' which was quizzical about the quality of the evidence presented at British Association meetings and about evolutionary links:

Mermaids have been seen on the coasts of Scotland by respectable persons, who told a gentleman, who at the late meeting of the British Association told a scientific audience what they said. Nobody present questioned a statement about which there can, of course, be no question among zoologists.

The Mermaid (Siren canora) is one of the connecting links of which too many are missing, between Man and the Marine Ascidiae. She is a pneumono-branchiate animal, and as there are no males, constitutes an instance of true parthenogenesis.[26]

Small wonder that the showman Barnum 'made up' mermaids (of which there are still examples in the London Science Museum and the Cabinet of Curiosities at the Brighton Museum: see Fig. 6.3). Buckland's mermaid is a late arrival in his book of curiosities, appearing for the first time in 1873. Like the 'nondescript', which breaches categories (Fig. 6.4), the pleasure given is half-belief and disconfirmation.[27] Forgeries titillate and fictionalize, offering the dangerous moment of belief, the relief of retraction.

Nor has that pleasure died away, as a more recent mermaid-story suggests.[28] The *Montreal Sun* in September 1990 carried a picture and account of a mermaid recovered by a Russian trawler. The photograph shows a smiling baby, covered with heavily drawn-on scales, and with mouth and eyes lengthened towards a distinctly fishy appearance. This baby from Atlantis of course

[26] *Punch* (26 Aug. 1871), 79.
[27] A 'nondescript' here is a creature not yet given a scientific description. Buckland is probably joking across the non-technical meaning: an unnoticeable person or object.
[28] *The Montreal Sun* (4 Sept. 1990), 23.

THE DESCENT OF MAN.

Figurative Party. "SO LONG AS *I* AM A MAN, SORR, WHAT DOES IT MATTHER TO ME WHETHER ME *GREAT-GRANDFATHER* WAS AN ANTHROPOID APE OR NOT, SORR!"

Literal Party. "HAW! WATHER DISAGWEEABLE FOR YOUR *GWATE GWAND-MOTHER*, WASN'T IT?"

FIG. 6.1. Cartoon from *Punch*, 1873 (courtesy of the Mistress and Fellows of Girton College, Cambridge).

Fig. 6.2. Cartoon from *Punch*, 1871 (courtesy of the Mistress and Fellows of Girton College, Cambridge).

FIG. 6.3. Barnum's Mermaid (illustration in the author's possession).

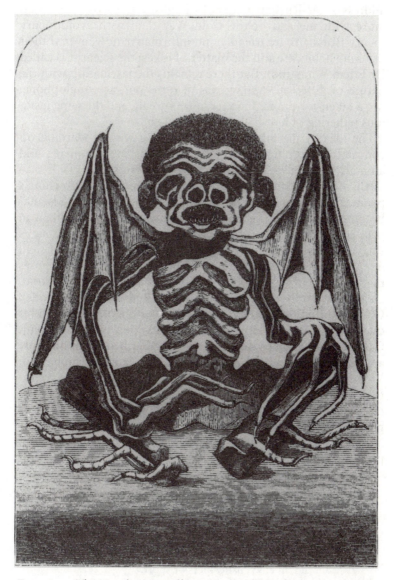

FIG. 6.4. 'The Nondescript' (illustration in the author's possession).

addresses her Russian finders in English. The story has to do more with the end of the Cold War than with evolutionary theory (Russians are friendly and informative now, even if their drinking habits are still the matter of jokes: the scientist is called Dr Ethan Winograd). But there remains the fascination with the nature of difference (Atlanteans, it turns out, are Anglophone: not a taken-for-granted matter in Montreal), and the same insidious tethering of half-belief to political ends.

The idea of the missing link becomes a way of warding off connection, keeping hypothetical the kinship of humans and animals, or of races, or even of social classes.

It is in this setting that the fuller implications of Browning's poem 'Caliban upon Setebos or Natural Theology in the Island' become apparent.[29] (In the recent re-positioning of Caliban in post-colonial theory this poem has not yet had its full due, but as I have written about it elsewhere (see Chapter 5, above) I shall not dwell on it here.) Caliban, in Browning's poem, supposes that God is a more primitive monster, unable to breed his kind, creating a world 'in spite' (maliciously and against the odds). Caliban formulates a cosmology and a cosmogony based on his own experience of oppression, colonization, and resentment. Caliban is a 'nondescript', a never-yet-described form: not only a 'primitive' but an 'advanced' thinker. The familiar emphasis in Victorian ethnology on the 'older races' surpassed by the youthful Caucasian (who represents a perfected form of reason) is mocked here. The matrilineal Caliban's utterance shows complex philosophical thinking working in a 'primitive' mind uttering pithy, cramped, and sibylline insights in Shakespearian pentameters:

> He made all these and more,
> Made all we see, and us, in spite: how else?
> He could not, Himself, make a second self
> To be his mate; as well have made Himself:
> He would not make what he mislikes or slights,
> An eyesore to Him, or not worth his pains:
> But did, in envy, listlessness or sport,
> Make what Himself would fain, in a manner, be—

[29] See my 'Darwin and the Fictions of Development', in David Kohn (ed.), *The Darwinian Heritage* (Princeton, NJ, 1986), 543–88 and my 'Speaking for the Others'.

Browning's poem became the inspiration for the only thorough nineteenth-century consideration of the linguistic politics lodged in 'the missing link'. The Scots-Canadian writer Daniel Wilson produced a long study entitled *Caliban: the Missing Link* (1873) which sets Shakespeare, Browning, and evolutionary ideas side by side.[30] It is the only counter-example I know to the general tendency to figure the missing link fleetingly, obliquely, and askance.

But there were other ways of reading. How did women writers and Socialists relate to the idea of the missing link? In the same year, 1859, that Darwin published *The Origin of Species* the first report of the discovery of Neanderthal Man was published in an out-of-the-way journal by a German schoolteacher, Johann Carl Fuhlrott. Fuhlrott's discovery was by some dismissed as a pathological specimen—a human being distorted by rickets, the disease of the malnourished poor. In that same year there appeared also a small book by L.N.R. (Ellen Rangard) called *The Missing Link: or, Bible-Women in the Homes of the London Poor*.[31] Here we encounter a use of the 'missing link' that seems independent of Darwinian theory, though drawing on evolutionist concepts. This work gives an account of the degraded conditions of the poor, as she calls them 'the sunken sixth', and of the ignorance of these conditions among the middle and upper classes who, when they become aware at all of the poor, see them as bundles of rags in their path. Of St Giles in London she writes: 'Know, then, that St Giles's is nothing but the sample of a vast world unvisited, and supposed unvisitable, by the better classes, which lies behind the screen of their respectable dwellings' (8). The 'screen' of the 'respectable dwelling' blots out the squalor of the streets to the rear of them. The 'sunken sixth' are, she points out, not beggars so much as functionaries in the bourgeois world. She quotes an article from *The Times*, 9 April 1857: 'Many of them are the people who do the hard work of this metropolis . . . They are not the beggars, but the porters, at our doors. To their dirt we owe our cleanliness; and they are the scapegoats of a thousand pollutions' (6). Her programme is for a '*Native Female Agency*, drawn from the classes we want to serve and instruct'

[30] Daniel Wilson, *Caliban: the Missing Link* (London, 1873).
[31] [Ellen Rangard], *The Missing Link: or, Bible-Women in the Homes of the London Poor by L.N.R.* (London, 1859).

which 'has hitherto been a MISSING LINK, and that such supplementary work might now perfect the heavenly chain which shall lift the lost and reckless from the depths of their despair' (272).

The discourse quite openly draws on that of the missionary to so-called primitive peoples. As so often in Victorian writing, race and class terms seem interchangeable, and the writing position of the text is that always of the Caucasian at the top of the *scala naturae* or the high bourgeois looking down into the pit. Indeed, in the third of a set of pamphlets called *The Missing Link Tracts* (1871), by L.N.R. again, we read: 'Well might Dr. Livingstone say, on his last departure from his native shores, "If I were not a Missionary to Africa, I would be a Missionary to the poor of London".'[32]

But Ellen Rangard is questioning that stratification and observing it. The force of the *native* female here is somewhat different from any crude primitivist use of the term. Here the 'missing link' emphasizes closeness and the lateral, an attempt to move away from hierarchy: 'it has been a mission of *Women to Women*, and of *Women of their Own Class*, which was very much wanted, as was evident by its ready acceptance: it was a Missing Link' (285). The most important enterprise, she argues, is to help the people to help themselves, and the missing link is the working-class woman who can act to stir and question. Elsewhere in the *Tracts* she points out that even essays such as 'Immortal Sewerage' (1853) assume that the *men* of the gutter are to be spoken to whereas her search is 'after the woman'. 'Why was this *Missing Link* not thought of long ago?' (272).

She ends her work by commenting on the stratification of society, calling on the terms of taxonomy and geology to make her point: 'In this England of ours we live so much in classes and in strata of society, as observing Americans tell us, that we have hitherto been content not to enlarge our experiences, or to look beyond our own horizon' (286). Underlying the language ('not the beggar but the porter at our doors') is the parable of Dives and Lazarus, the rich man and the beggar.[33] Even with their positions inverted Dives still expects Lazarus to make himself

[32] No. 3, *How Wears the Missing Link?* (London, 1871), 9–10. No. 4 is called *Link after Link: Bible-Women Nurses.*
[33] *Luke* 16: 19–26.

useful. The 'great gulf' fixed in the parable is often referred to in Victorian writing as a necessary gulf, between man and 'the brutes'. Darwin sardonically observes that just as the whites seek to justify slavery by making the black man another species, so humans justify their exploitation of animals by affirming distance of descent from them. To Rangard the missing link is high as well as low: 'In our view it is the Bible itself that is the grand Missing Link between heaven and earth'.[34] Her 'link' is present, active, not set back in the past.

Ellen Rangard's writing may already have brought to mind Dickens's *Bleak House*, written a few years previously. Dickens, like these religious writers, uses the image of links and gulfs. The ignored presence of connections in the world, particularly between different social classes, is a recurring theme in Dickens's writing—and is fundamental to the plotting of his novels. Refusing to recognize that people are connected is in his novels a form of wickedness as well as danger. Haunting the many versions of this repudiation in *Bleak House* is the story of Dives and Lazarus. So Jo, the little crossing sweeper, unable to read or write, is the point of connection and crossing, the chiasmus, between the fatalities of widely different groups in the story. He is less advanced, Dickens suggests, than is the drover's dog: 'He and Jo listen to the music, probably with much the same amount of animal satisfaction. But otherwise how far above the human listener is the brute!'[35]

What connexion can there be, between the place in Lincolnshire, the house in town, the Mercury in powder, and the whereabouts of Jo the outlaw with the broom, who had that distant ray of light upon him when he swept the church-yard step? What connexion can there have been between the many people in the innumerable history of this world, who, from opposite sides of great gulfs, have, nevertheless, been very curiously brought together!

Jo sweeps his crossing all day long, unconscious of the link, if any link there be. (185)

Jo is the missing link in the plot of intrigue, the unknown and unknowing witness. The lack of recognition of the missing link

---

[34] *How Wears the Missing Link?*, 3.
[35] Charles Dickens, *Bleak House* (London, 1853). Edn. cited, ed. Norman Page, introd. J. Hillis Miller (Harmondsworth, 1971), 275.

easily folds into an idea of unconsciousness. Jo is also the pa-
thetic pathway for disease which, through him, touches the
middle classes, the innocent and sympathetic Esther among
them. So the missing link is in Dickens's figuration the crossing
sweeper, the point of exchange—a figuration that precedes the
appearance of *The Origin of Species*.

Another woman writer, Margaret Harkness who published as
John Law, later took up some of the issues explored by Dickens
and by L.N.R. Strikingly, in her naturalist novel *Captain Lobe*
(1889) the voice of the missing link is itself heard, perhaps for the
first time in fiction. It is the voice of the present-day poor and the
handicapped, those ignored by a factitious 'civilisation'. In her
novel an alliance is formed between feminists and forgotten
people. A midget feels himself to be a monstrosity and is comforted by the feminist Jane Hardy's vision of a future in which
room will be made for the handicapped: ' "I ain't a man" said the
midget sorrowfully. "I ain't nobody. Sometimes I says to myself
as I'm the missing link, as I'll come back again as a dog or
something." '

The idea of the missing link, I have argued, was as much a way
of reinforcing distance as it was of seeking out connection. The
fictional nightmares it generated are all concerned with *forced
connections*, internalized kinships. Perhaps the most striking
figuration of the fear that boundaries are unstable and that, in
the developmental metaphor of evolution, the primitive past may
not be safely past, is Robert Louis Stevenson's 'Dr Jekyll and Mr
Hyde'. Hyde, the ugly, muscle-bound, and stunted alternation of
Jekyll, can at first be conjured and laid at will. Jekyll's nature is
mixed, good and evil, intellect and animal. Hyde's is unmixed
evil. His uninhibited presence overmatches the tentative, so-
cialized Jekyll. The sickening turn from Jekyll's mastery comes
when one day he wakes to find hands on his sheet, hairy and
powerful, unlike his own sleek townsman's fingers. How to keep
Hyde hidden becomes the anguish of the story. He will burst out,
to trample categories as well as children.

No longer is the monsterized missing link safely distanced as a
past, a myth, a phantasm. In this fiction he is much of man, now,
urging his way through the skin and mind of sedate city-dwellers:
the return of the repressed, not of the erased or the extinct.
'Jekyll and Hyde' is an extraordinarily masculinist story: women

exist here only on its peripheries, as gloomy housekeepers, lost kin. Self-birthing becomes nightmare.[36]

The attempt to keep the missing link in the distant past, already extinct, became less and less viable as the century drew to its close. Samuel Butler's *Unconscious Memory* includes a translation of Ewald Hering's work on memory first delivered as a lecture in 1870. In this essay, Hering—with whom Butler concurs—argues that the 'chain of living beings' is the result of an accretion of *memory* as instinct, coming down in a direct line of descent from an initiating organic matter: 'every organised being now in existence represents the last link of an inconceivably long series of organisms . . . at the beginning of this chain there existed an organism of the very simplest kind, something, in fact, like those which we call organised germs.' Where Hering and Butler part company with Darwin is in their belief in inherited acquired characteristics, a form of unconscious memory: 'the development of one of the more highly organised animals represents a continuous series of organised recollections concerning the past development of the great chain of living forms, the last link of which stands before us.'[37] Memory thus becomes not a means of distancing the missing creature but the motive-power for an identification with it. In such a re-definition, time is not fixed and irreversible: memory can traverse heuristically the distances between the earliest moments and now, because the information is conceived as continuous, embedded in the body and unconscious.

The idea of mythic simultaneity underlies much modernist writing, from *The Waste Land* to *Between the Acts*: the suggestion is that it is possible to re-awaken memory traces and experience identification, not with the present moment only, but with primal 'archetypal' forms of experience. Such an understanding of memory makes the idea of the missing link an impossibility, since all previous experiences and recollections have been internalized without loss.

---

[36] 'The Strange Case of Dr Jekyll and Mr Hyde' (1886). Elaine Showalter offers a fascinating analysis of the story in her *Sexual Anarchy: Gender and Culture at the 'Fin de Siècle'* (London, 1991). For the history of anxieties about degeneration in Europe see Daniel Pick, *Faces of Degeneration: A European Disorder, c.1848–c.1918* (Cambridge, 1989).

[37] Samuel Butler, in *Unconscious Memory*, first published 1920 but written much earlier.

This position is crucial both for Jung and for Freud. Freud argued as late as the 1930s that, through neuroses, we can tap back into the conditions of primitive man. In *Civilisation and its Discontents* he writes:

As a rule the intermediate links have died out and are known to us only through reconstruction. In the realm of the mind, on the other hand, what is primitive is so commonly preserved alongside of the transformed version which has arisen from it that it is unnecessary to give instances as evidence.[38]

Stephen Jay Gould argues in *Ontogeny and Phylogeny* that recapitulation theory was not so much disproved as rendered without effect in twentieth-century biology. Yet it always depends upon the group as to whether a belief is inoperative. Among biologists a belief in the homology between the development of a single organism and a species may now be inconsequential. But in a number of displaced forms it still haunts us. Instead of, in Tennyson's line, 'let the ape and tiger die', in the twentieth century we have the modernist comedy of Bernard's long soliloquy at the end of Woolf's *The Waves*.

There is the old brute too, the savage, the hairy man who dabbles his fingers in ropes of entrails; and gobbles and belches; whose speech is guttural, visceral—well, he is here. He squats in me. Tonight he has been feasted on quails, salads, and sweetbread. He now holds a glass of fine old brandy in his hand. He brindles, purrs and shoots warm thrills down my spine as I sip. It is true he washes his hands before dinner, but they are still hairy. He buttons on trousers and waistcoats, but they contain the same organs . . . That man, the hairy, the ape-like, has contributed his part to my life.[39]

In modernism, the missing link was no longer previous, obliterated; it informed the present and troubled it. Putting away the missing link in time had been a means of keeping control. Holding the gap open in space also maintained the distance between social classes and human races. Temporal distance lessened the power of otherness. In Victorian conjurations the missing link was *extinct* if it ever had existed. It could be denied, or

---

[38] Sigmund Freud, *Civilization and its Discontents* (London, 1930; rev. edn. 1963), 5.
[39] Virginia Woolf, *The Waves* (London, 1931). Edn. cited, ed. Gillian Beer (Oxford, 1992), 241–2.

expunged, or fantasized. Even if its successors were alive they were at the other end of the developmental metaphor of nineteenth-century race theory: across the world in space and—by implication—time.

The politics of heritage (that comforting form of history) demanded always the miniaturizing of the missing link. In *Studies on Hysteria* Freud reported his patient Frau Emmy von N. as suffering from 'zoopsia, macropsia, and zoophobia' (i.e. she saw animals not really there; they grew bigger; she feared them).[40] The 'missing link' rationalized such monsters of the subconscious and held them at bay, as different. The fear disguised was not, in the end, of otherness but of *sameness*: the 'other' of social class, or racial theory, or primate life, might prove to be indistinguishable from those who set out to describe it. *Inauthenticating*, keeping belief wavering, making monsters, or fictions, proved in this case to be a more intense need than authentication or discovery.

[40] Sigmund Freud, *The Standard Edition of the Complete Psychological Works*, ed. J. Strachey (London, 1955), vol. 2 (1893–5) 'Studies on Hysteria', Case 2 'Frau Emmy von N.', 48–105, esp. 62–5.

7
Problems of Description in the Language of Discovery

Discovery is a matter not only of reaching new conclusions but of redescribing what is known and taken for granted. Scientific enquiry constantly revives questions which are answered both in science and literature at changing levels of description. Description must find ways out of the circle of current presumptions if it is to create knowledge or fresh insight. Yet all description draws, often unknowingly, upon shared cultural assumptions which underwrite its neutral and authoritative status and conceal the embedded designs upon which describing depends. How can the language of scientists and of poets (in the broadest sense) resist such designs and disturb teleological patterns which may otherwise lock their project into the circle of the foreknown? How much do the discursive strategies of scientists and poets have in common? Are we able to pinpoint stable distinctions between scientific communication and poetic communication in relation to the problem of describing? These are questions I shall consider by means of example in this essay.

Much recent work on 'science and literature' has emphasized those features which the two enterprises have in common, particularly in their relation to language. We can note and reaffirm that the discourses begin together, and continue to draw on common cultural sources. But without at all dissenting from that insistence on setting close together categories of knowledge that have been misleadingly polarized, I want in this essay to analyse differences as much as similarities between the discourse of scientists and poets. The status of description in the two discourses allows us to focus the question of difference: I shall suggest that professional scientific writing has to rely on tacit agreements with a projected readership to a degree that literature evades, and that the shifting of linguistic levels has notably different functions in literary and in scientific communication.

Though kinds of evidence and levels of description may change, some questions have a way of remaining intact to be answered creatively again:

the ideas of time and space—or how we came by those ideas—or of what stuff they were made—or whether they were born with us—or we picked them up afterwards as we went along—or—whether we did it in frocks—or not till we had got into breeches—with a thousand other enquiries and disputes about INFINITY, PRESCIENCE, LIBERTY, NECESSITY, and so forth, upon whose desperate and unconquerable theories so many fine heads have been turned and cracked.[1]

The great physicist James Clerk Maxwell put it another way in his paper 'Molecules' given to the British Association for the Advancement of Science in 1873. His problem is how to describe the new concept, 'molecule', since 'no one has ever seen or handled a single molecule' and molecular science is 'one of those branches of study which deals with things imperceptible by our senses, and which cannot be subjected to direct experiement'. He does it by framing his study of this 'smallest possible portion of a particular substance' at first with the largest unanswered questions:

The mind of man has perplexed itself with many hard questions. Is space infinite, and if so in what sense? Is the material world infinite in extent, and are all places within that extent equally full of matter? Do atoms exist, or is matter infinitely divisible?

The discussion of questions of this kind has been going on ever since men began to reason, and to each of us, as soon as we obtain the use of our faculties, the same old questions arise as fresh as ever. They form as essential a part of the science of the nineteenth century of our era, as of that of the fifth century before it.[2]

He ends his analysis by discovering a complete rhetorical congruity between the characteristics of molecules and the desired characteristics of the moral and physical universe in which he has

---

[1] Laurence Sterne, *The Life and Opinions of Tristram Shandy, Gent.*, ed. G. Saintsbury (London, 1912), 136.

[2] James Clerk Maxwell, 'Molecules', *Nature* 8 (1873), 441. Collected in Noel G. Coley and Vance M. D. Hall (eds.), *Darwin to Einstein: Primary Sources on Science and Belief* (London, 1980), 86.

faith. Molecules, he declares, are unchanging, 'the foundation stones of the material universe remain unbroken and unworn':

They continue this day as they were created, perfect in number and measure and weight, and from the ineffaceable characters impressed on them we may learn that those aspirations after accuracy in measurement, truth in statement, and justice in action, which we reckon among our noblest attributes as men, are ours because they are essential constituents of the image of Him Who in the beginning created, not only the heaven and the earth, but the materials of which heaven and earth consist. (p. 86)

The questions Maxwell raised at the outset are allayed rather than answered. The description of a novel concept has here been permitted by its familiarization; but the activity of that description, as Maxwell himself acknowledges, is not so much 'scientific' in the Baconian sense ('subjected to direct experiment') as it is speculative and persuasive. It persuades by calling upon the argument from design. Molecules, it proves, are God's characters (as so often in Victorian science, the senses of 'characteristics' and 'inscribed codes' combine). They are understandable as having complete congruity with a foreknown order: they vouch for, and are vouched for by, that order. The circle of description is complete. The discovery of such fortunate congruity gives pleasure, and still persuasively does so even to those of us who do not share the beliefs relied upon by Maxwell. The pleasure here depends upon individual moral assurance and communal reassurance, but that is by no means always the case in the activities of poets or of scientists.

Wordsworth's insistence in the 1802 Preface to the *Lyrical Ballads* on the inseparable association of knowledge and pleasure takes us straight to a profound conjunction in the work of scientist and creative writer. 'We have no knowledge, that is, no general principles drawn from the contemplation of particular facts, but what has been built up by pleasure, and exists in us by pleasure alone ... The knowledge both of the Poet and the Man of Science is pleasure.' The passage points also to a central paradox in their achievements. 'However painful may be the objects with which the Anatomist's knowledge is connected, he feels that his knowledge is pleasure', just as the poet studying the 'infinite complexity of pain and pleasure' experiences 'an overbalance of enjoyment.'[3] The 'happy ending' of successful theorizing, satisfactory experiment, achieved work of art, creates pleasure. And so—at least since the Middle Ages—does the process, or story, of discovery. Such pleasure has no inherent accord, as Wordsworth points out, with the processes observed or the outcome of the narrative.

Enigma and its resolution have an allure which has coloured the popular image of the scientist in literature itself, where he frequently figures (as Augustine Brannigan also has noted) as the transgressor.

Science directed its attention to a quasi-physical 'nature' or underlying order of things which had a characteristic intrigue associated with it. And because of the mystery associated with nature, the procedure of its becoming known came to exhibit a dramatic social significance. Consequently we find a curious feature in accounts of scientific discoveries; they are recurrently characterised as being bizarre achievements made by eccentric personalities under curious circumstances, often having horrible consequences.[4]

The scientist in narrative, moreover, can figure the narrative's own intense desire to break the bounds of encoded story and discover meaning not hitherto admitted to consciousness. Faust and Dr Frankenstein flout the stories permitted in their cultures. The scientist is perceived as system breaker as much as system maker. His role as demystifier is less celebrated than his role as magic individual—and indeed the power of the creative thinker to outgo the evidence and to generalize convincingly from not-yet-adequate data is a powerful fact of scientific history. So Einstein writes of Niels Bohr's achievement with an emphasis upon 'miracle' and 'unique instinct', and in his final metaphor from music reminds us of the powers of Thomas Mann's Doctor Faustus:

That this insecure and contradictory foundation was sufficient to enable a man of Bohr's unique instinct and tact to discover the major laws of the spectral lines and of the electron-shells of the atoms together with their significance for chemistry appeared to me like a miracle—and

---

[3] William Wordsworth, *Lyrical Ballads* (1798–1805), ed. George Sampson (London, 1940), 24–5.

[4] Augustine Brannigan, *The Social Basis of Scientific Discoveries* (Cambridge, 1981), 2–3.

appears to me as a miracle even today. This is the highest form of musicality in the sphere of thought.[5]

Wordsworth's distinction between scientist and poet insists on 'uniqueness' and on the resulting solitariness in the scientist—quite in contrast with the teamwork we now habitually associate with scientific activity. It is worth reminding ourselves that Wordsworth's term 'the Man of Science' itself marks a new isolating of 'scientific' from other intellectual and creative activity. What we now call 'science' was still called philosophy earlier in the eighteenth century, while in the Middle Ages the seven sciences or arts were the Trivium (Grammar, Logic, Rhetoric) and the Quadrivium (Arithmetic, Music, Geometry, and Astronomy). It is not until 1840 that Whewell remarks: 'We need very much a name to describe a cultivator of science in general. I should incline to call him a Scientist.'[6] That 'name to describe a cultivator of science' begins to privilege as well as demarcate a particular method of coming to know and allows summary description of an enclosed professional group. Wordsworth's emphasis on the separation of the scientific thinker from the rest of humankind has continued to be a source of unease—an unease which finds its focus in the nature of scientific language.

Claude Bernard, in his great methodological work *Introduction à l'étude de la médecine expérimentale* (1865), distinguishes between art and science in contrary terms: 'l'art, c'est moi; la science, c'est nous.' He insists on the communality of the scientist's enterprise as well as of his material. He expresses this sense of a shared culture by means of images of the household, and at the same time suggests the 'irregularity' of the scientist's pathways to knowledge which disturb the sociogeography of the house. 'La science de la vie . . . c'est un salon superbe tout resplendissant de lumière, dans lequel on ne peut parvenir qu'en passant par une longue et affreuse cuisine.'[7] The only route to the brilliantly lit drawing room of truth, in this surreal household

[5] Albert Einstein, 'Autobiographical Notes', in P. A. Schilpp (ed.), *Albert Einstein: Philosopher-Scientist*, vol. 1, (London, 1970), 45–7.
[6] William Whewell, *The Philosophy of the Inductive Sciences* (London, 1840), i. 113.
[7] Claude Bernard, *Introduction à l'étude de la médecine expérimentale* (1865), ed. F. Dagognet (Paris, 1966), 39–40.

(which is our household), is through a long and bloody kitchen: the kitchen of animal experiments.

Scientists, including Einstein, have continued to claim the authority of 'we', but that first-person plural contains a shifting population. Does it represent the physical conditions of life experienced by all animate beings? Does it represent humanity in general? Does it refer to the sub-community of scientific workers, or, more exactly, to the specific discourses agreed among them to convey technical information? Each of these questions may be answered in the affirmative, but rarely all at the same time.

OWNING AND OBSERVING

In 'The Daemon of the World' Shelley projects a possible future, in which man gives up his separation from other forms of life and thereby discovers the fullest powers of mind:

> All things are void of terror: man has lost
> His desolating privilege, and stands
> An equal amidst equals: happiness
> And science dawn though late upon the earth.[8]

What Shelley calls man's 'desolating privilege'—the desire to set ourselves apart from all other phenomena of the material world, to claim special status, and to exercise control through knowledge—has been a matter of wry commentary in many forms of writing, as in these lines from Donne's 'An Anatomy of the World':

> For of Meridians, and Parallels
> Man hath weav'd out a net, and this net throwne
> Upon the Heavens, and now they are his owne.[9]

That claim to 'own', to possession, is more openly mocked by Darwin in the notebooks of the 1830s: 'Mayo (Philosophy of Living) quotes Whewell as profound because he says length of days adapted to duration of sleep in man!! whole universe so

---

[8] Percy Bysshe Shelley, *The Complete Poetical Works*, ed. T. Hutchinson (Oxford, 1934), 10.
[9] John Donne, *The Poems of John Donne*, ed. Herbert Grierson (Oxford, 1912), i. 239.

adapted!!! and not man to Planets—instance of arrogance!!!'
The human desire to know about the universe and so subjectively
to make it 'his own' readily merges into the claim of human
centrality to the universe. Darwin caustically analyses the further
implications of such claims to dominance; writing of man's
insistence on special status and denial of kinship with other
animals, he observes: 'Has not the white man, who has debased
his nature and violated every such instinctive feeling by making
slave of his fellow Black, often wished to consider him as another
animal.—it is the way of mankind.'[10] The separation of the
observer too readily becomes the separation of the oppressor.

The paradox for both scientific and literary writer is that
writing is itself the inscription of human distinctiveness. No
other animals write, and the events of the physical world are
language-free. Human language is necessary for our apprehension and description of events beyond the human. Yet at the
same time language is anthropocentric, persistently drawing the
human back to the centre of meaning. It thus both exaggerates
the power of the human and blurs the limits of our perception of
what lies beyond. But it has also, through scientific knowledge,
greatly extended our control over the non-human.

Language is therefore both a limiting condition on knowledge
and a liberating discipline which makes possible the formulation
of knowledge. Thus, we are told that John Tyndall had an
extraordinarily developed mental awareness of relations in
space, which helped to advance his work on radiation. That
talent was trained by the language of Milton's epic of cosmic and
syntactic spaces, *Paradise Lost*.

English grammar was the most important discipline of my boyhood.
The piercing through the involved and inverted sentences of *Paradise
Lost*, the linking of the verb to its often distant nominative, of the
relative to its transitive verb, of the preposition to the noun or pronoun
which it governed, the study of variations in mood or tense, the
transpositions often necessary to bring out the true grammatical structure of a sentence, all this was to my young mind a discipline of the
highest value, and a source of unflagging delight.[11]

---

[10] Howard E. Gruber and Paul H. Barrett, *Darwin on Man: A Psychological Study
of Scientific Creativity Together With Darwin's Early Unpublished Notebooks*
(London, 1971), 455, 450.

[11] John Tyndall, *Fragments of Science for Unscientific People* (London, 1868), ii. 92.

What Tyndall valued was the intensification of linguistic organization in a great writer, the pace of whose work plays off the syntax of the reading eye moving from line to line, against the energetic demands of metre, and against the act of rationalization implicit in the completed syntactical ordering of each sentence and verse paragraph. This complex multiple ordering in Milton's writing often includes a delay and accumulation so extreme that it rouses the reader's *attention* both to his own activity of syntactic speculation and to the writer's spatial organization of sense.

Certain conditions of language bear particularly hard on the scientific writer whose domain of enquiry, unlike that of literature, is not primarily or necessarily the human. Language is anthropocentric; it is also historically and culturally determined; it is never neutral; and it is multivocal. It potentiates diversity of meaning. At the same time, not all potential significations are active. One of the most remarkable powers of the human mind—less often commented on than its power to proliferate senses—is its power to exclude, or suppress, feasible meanings. The terms of agreement between writer and implied reader can for the time being select and exclude significations. Thus 'races' and 'wild aboriginal stock' may be taken to refer solely to cabbages in a sentence like this, from *The Origin of Species*: 'It seems to me not improbable, that if we could succeed in naturalising, or were to cultivate, during many generations, the several races, for instance, of the cabbage, in very poor soil (in which case, however, some effect would have to be attributed to the direct action of the poor soil), that they would to a large extent, or even wholly, revert to the wild aboriginal stock.'[12] However, as I have argued in *Darwin's Plots*, such an agreement is neither permanent nor inclusive: signification may be controlled and focused within a like-minded group (particularly any professional group), but the excluded or left-over meanings of words remain potential.[13] They can be brought to the surface and put to use by those outside the accord or professional 'contract', as well as by those future readers for whom new historical sequences have intervened.

[12] Charles Darwin, *The Origin of Species*, ed. John Burrow (Harmondsworth, 1968), 77.
[13] Gillian Beer, *Darwin's Plots: Evolutionary Narrative in Darwin, George Eliot, and Nineteenth-Century Fiction* (London, 1983).

y or spiteful or homosexual, as these are attributes o[
[r]e complex than genes: human organisms.[15]

[suc]cessful' one-level language that Rose, et a[l
[mi]ght be encountered in any number of Nature: [
[te]chnical address to like-minded and similarl[y
[...]rs, emphasizing specification of meaning an[d
[m]eans of entry to non-specialists. The enclosin[g
[u]nity is a necessary condition for assuring stabl[
[T]he unreliable 'amateur' reader is kept ou[
[i]s hoped, the range of other potential significa[
[...] he or she may endow the scientist's parsimo[n
But, as Rose indicates, as soon as scientifi[
[a]cross levels of language and reference, the a[
[m]ny and neutrality of description are shake[n
[...] that the shared assumptions of the group beg[
[d]eed, the language he characterizes is very unli[k
[...] meet in Harvey or Lyell or Darwin or Cle[r

[...]zes that 'the language to be used at any time
[th]e purposes of the description; the muscle physi[c
[...]ed in a different aspect of the question of t[
[...]tch from the ecologist or evolutionary biolog[i
[...] their difference of purpose should define t[
[...]cription used' (p. 282). Yet he also insists [
[co]mplementary description just as Wadding[to
[ha]ve done. Stephen Gould has gone farther a[
[...]ly on the need for multi-level description, b[
[...]ion as endemic to any understanding of inter[a
[...]vels of organization.[16] He sees this interacti[
[...] essential to the evolutionary process. Goul[
[...] the question of how to describe such inter[a
[...]king the 'individual' the normative unit of [
[...] would misleadingly reproduce in the the[
[...]bedded in the language available for descr[
[...]s with his emphasis on free interaction with[
[...] Rose is here, properly, emphasizing the n[

[...]n Kamin, and R. C. Lewontin, Not in Our Genes (Harmo[n
[Gou]ld, 'Darwinism and the Expansion of Evolutionary The[
[...]80–7.

Senses shift to and fro from periphery to centre, both in history and in the action of the particular reader. They are not fixed at particular points on the spectrum. Furthermore, any radical new theory will itself have the effect of disturbing the 'taken for granted' elements in the language it employs.

The attempt to control and curtail the power of language within scientific activity can be seen in this century in two contrary modes. One is that of linguistic positivism; the other is the recent fashion for highly impressionistic terms, such as 'charm' and 'quark'. If we turn to the work of early positivists such as Ernst Mach and then Leonard Bloomfield, we find an insistence on the univocal and the unireferential, as in Mach's *The Analysis of Sensations and the Relation of the Physical to the Psychical* (1914) and Bloomfield's *Linguistic Aspects of Science* (1939). Mach, in fact, reached the position that because mathematics is a linguistic system which cannot be directly referred to observable entities or events, it must be cleansed from scientific theory. For example, he held that concepts such as 'plus,' 'sum,' or 'differential' were meaningless because without empirical referent. Paradoxically, his views would have returned scientists to the situation of nineteenth-century workers such as Darwin who had very little mathematical training or mastery. Darwin compensated for this lack by a combination of stupendously accretive observation cross-hatched with a powerful multivalent discourse. But Darwin also saw that all observation is theory-laden and therefore subject to interpretative sentences: 'No facts without theory', he wrote. The naïve positivistic equivalence between object and event, or utterance, presupposes a single necessary theoretical outcome. This problem has led to the contrary mode of impressionistic or whimsical naming which is fashionable in high theory today: words such as 'charm', 'quark', or 'black hole' deliberately evade severe equivalence in order to allow space for correction and enhancement without the need constantly to replace and to move on from terms. One Nobel Prize winner informed me that his research group had deliberately favoured terms such as 'beads' and 'bumps' while working on their project because any prematurely analytical terms might have hampered the speculative multiplicity of their work, or else resulted in their having to abandon and replace their terminology at embarrassingly frequent intervals. Language is a heuristic tool but it may best function at the frontiers of scientific knowledge by adopting a mode which sounds strangely belletristic. Severe one-to-one equivalence may prove to be paradoxically less exact as a working tool than the larger term during the period of theory formation.

We can, moreover, see how difficult it is for even workers like Bloomfield, with his praise of parsimony of signification, to avoid the mythic or affective in their discourse. Because he repudiates metaphor and multivalency, he cannot bring it under control as a necessary element in discourse. He remarks:

> The use of language in science is specialized and peculiar. In a brief speech the scientist manages to say things which in ordinary language would require a vast amount of talk. His hearers respond with great accuracy and uniformity. The range and exactitude of scientific prediction exceed any cleverness of everyday life: the scientist's use of language is strangely effective and powerful. Along with systematic observation, it is this peculiar use of language which distinguishes science from non-scientific behaviour.[14]

The curtness and severity at first described (and implicitly praised) is then (without any signalled shift) extended into something romantically potent by using the intensive 'strangely' with 'effective' and adding 'powerful' as a larger parallel term for 'effective'. As a result of these shifts, when the word 'peculiar' recurs in the next sentence its sense has expanded from that of 'specific' to include that of 'mysterious'. The discourse is already beginning to undermine the positivism of the proferred argument. Bloomfield's attack on connotative language has recourse to unremarked, emotive metaphor which takes its power from the kind of language he represents himself as repudiating: 'It is our task to discover which of our terms are undefined or partially defined or draggled with fringes of connotation, and to catch our hypotheses and exhibit them by clear statements, instead of letting them haunt us in the dark.' The rapid succession and confluence of metaphors there—draggled fringes, hunter/collector, catching and exhibiting, the haunting night thoughts, hardly dispel the shamanistic linguistic world he seeks to escape. It is no wonder that he feels the need for 'a redefinition

[14] Leonard Bloomfield, *Linguistic Aspects of Science, International Encyclopedia of Unified Science*, no. 4 (Chicago, 1939), 1, 4.

of speech-forms'
"seven" and "thir
connotation' (p. 47

To Bloomfield, t
part of the commu
practice reveals ho
cess must depend
tempt to exclude
simply in an unsta
discourse. Just as
metaphor to be 'a
into a mythic adve
kers seeking to mi
party to such adve
work makes clear
ment and descripti
a close profession
exclusion. Not wh
on its reception, w
tion will be tempo
powerful.

LE

Steven Rose, Leo
account of an im
technical 'descript
without implying
can be applied wit

Conventional scien
confined to descript
ly easy to describe t
molecules in the la
biology. What is n
moving from one la
a level the properti
units of which it is
them . . . these orga
relevant at one leve

be selfish or ang
wholes much mo

The 'quite su
here specify m
concentrated t
prepared reade
offering few m
within a comm
signification.
and thereby, it
tions with whic
ious discourse.
writers move a
parent autono
One might add
to be visible. In
that which we
Maxwell.

Rose emphas
contingent on t
ogist is interest
frog-muscle tw
or biochemist;
language of de
the need for c
and Toulmin h
insisted, not or
on such descrip
tions between
across levels as
argument raise
tion without m
scription, whic
assumptions en
tion and at od
privileged level

[15] Steven Rose, Le
worth, 1984), 278.
[16] Stephen Jay G
Science, 216 (1982),

for scientists to clarify their purposes and to regulate their language in such a way that they make no hubristic or deterministic claims drawn from unanalysed anthropomorphism. His account relies upon accord between writer and reader, what Toulmin in 'The Construal of Reality' calls the 'polis' of the scientific community.[17]

Description depends upon such accord since what is considered necessary to be described is culturally determined, as well as to some extent genre-determined. The stories of the culture, or 'themata', as Gerald Holton calls them,[18] go largely *undescribed*: symmetry, simplicity, development, hierarchy, chance, provide models, ideals, and implied narratives in science as much as literature. If symmetry is the ideal of scientific elegance, it is likely to be extensively observed and studied; if simplicity is anticipated it will be found. But from time to time, such sequestered stories move out from beneath description into debate, as has recently been the case with work such as that of T. F. H. Allen and Thomas B. Starr on hierarchy.[19]

The apparent neutrality of description is the source of much of its authority; it is openly informative, but it is also more covertly predictive. Description stands *in place of* assertion and prediction and, as Thomas Kuhn remarks in *The Structure of Scientific Revolutions*, 'there are important contexts in which the narrative and the descriptive are inextricably mixed'.[20] Even more important, description works at an agreed *upper* level of specification, and ignores (and is often ignorant of) shared and unmarked assumptions. When we describe the taken-for-granted we change its status: 'an old yellow car *on wheels*'; the last phrase is either redundant or crucial. This observation does not, of course, apply only to scientific discourse; it is powerful throughout literary language. Beckett gains many of his most disturbing effects by detailed recounting of reflex actions of the body usually left undescribed.

[17] Stephen Toulmin, 'The Construal of Reality', in W. J. T. Mitchell (ed.), *The Politics of Interpretation* (Chicago, 1982), 99–117.
[18] Gerald Holton, *The Thematic Origins of Scientific Thought* (Cambridge, Mass., 1973).
[19] T. F. H. Allen and Thomas B. Starr, *Hierarchy: Perspectives for Ecological Complexity* (Chicago, 1982).
[20] Thomas Kuhn, *The Structure of Scientific Revolutions*, 2nd edn. (Chicago, 1970).

Empson's poem 'Doctrinal Point' observes precisely the false triumph of teleology in description. Describing becomes a form of designing and is used to infer design as inherent to the universe. Using metaphors from natural growth and development, the project of both scientist and poet becomes self-fulfilling. How can we distinguish design from description? How prevent 'the Assumption of the description', since description creates its own transcendental level? Through the multiplying senses of *assumption* he shows this transformation at work.

> The god approached dissolves into the air.
>
> Magnolias, for instance, when in bud,
> Are right in doing anything they can think of;
> Free by predestination in the blood,
> Saved by their own sap, shed for themselves,
> Their texture can impose their architecture;
> Their sapient matter is always already informed.
>
> Whether they burgeon, massed wax flames, or flare
> Plump spaced-out saints, in their gross prime, at prayer,
> Or leave the sooted branches bare
> To sag at tip from a sole blossom there
> They know no act that will not make them fair.
>
> Professor Eddington with the same insolence
> Called all physics one tautology;
> If you describe things with the right tensors
> All law becomes the fact that they can be described with them;
> This is the Assumption of the description.
> The duality of choice becomes the singularity of existence;
> The effort of virtue the unconsciousness of foreknowledge.[21]

'The Assumption' of the description raises into essence what began as account—and it presumingly, or 'assumingly,' uses its own 'assumptions' as a means to authority without bringing them into question: so Empson suggests, in the caustic second verse of a poem which opens in sumptuous enjoyment of the aptness of the magnolia to its own performance, the perfect

[21] William Empson, *Collected Poems* (London, 1955), 39–40. Empson's poem is collected in a useful anthology, *Poems of Science*, ed. John Heath-Stubbs and Phillips Salman, which in its chronological arrangement shows the changing common themes of science and literature, from Copernican cosmology to relativity theory.

accord of possibility and purpose, form and information, sap and sapience.

Eddington had commented on the tendency of the mind to recover its own anticipated patterns from the universe, what Empson calls 'tautology': 'The mind has by its selective power filled the processes of Nature into a frame of law of a pattern largely of its own choosing; and in the discovery of this system of law the mind may be regarded as regaining from Nature that which the mind has put into nature.'[22] Or, as Einstein suggests: 'All concepts, even those which are closest to experience, are from the point of view of logic freely chosen conventions, just as is the case with the concept of causality.'[23] Toulmin has recently emphasized that the loss of the detached spectator 'out there' has been a characteristic movement in recent scientific thinking.[24]

This loss, while it may remove some of the dangers of 'owning,' further complicates and destabilizes the concept of description. If the observer is always necessarily a part of what he or she observes, no authoritative distance can be sustained. ('How describe the world seen without a self?' asks Virginia Woolf.) Etymologically, as Toulmin also observes, the word 'theory' recalls the idea of the observer or symbolic representative since the *theoros* was the delegate sent by the city sage to consult the oracle. The loss of spectator status makes also for a loss of theoretical 'space'; it leads to 'implication' or folding in.

Darwin's sturdy sense of a thronging physical world only partly within the domain of human reason is further tempered in Einstein's essay on Clerk Maxwell in the collection perhaps riddlingly entitled *The World as I See It*: 'The belief in an external world independent of the perceiving subject is the basis of natural science. Since, however, sense perception only gives information of this external world or of "physical reality" indirectly, we can only grasp the latter by speculative means. It follows from this that our notions of physical reality can never be final.'[25]

[22] Arthur Eddington, *The Nature of the Physical World* (Cambridge, 1928), 224.
[23] Einstein, in Schilpp (ed.), *Albert Einstein*, 13.
[24] Stephen Toulmin, *The Return to Cosmology: Postmodern Science and the Theology of Nature* (Berkeley, 1982).
[25] Albert Einstein, *The World as I See It* (London, 1935), 60.

Umberto Eco, among others, has entered an important *caveat* on the question of 'ingenuous transposition' from one field to another:

Epistemological thinkers connected with quantum methodology have rightly warned against an ingenuous transposition of physical categories into the fields of ethics and psychology (for example, the identification of indeterminacy with moral freedom) . . . Hence it would not be justified to understand my formulation as analogy between the structures of the work of art and the supposed structures of the world. Indeterminacy, complementarity, noncausality are not *modes of being* in the physical world, but *systems for describing it* in a convenient way.[26]

Scientists seek to delimit the application of their terms and respect the exigencies of their topic. But at the same time it is essential to recognize that any such containment of meaning will be local and temporary. It may allow a satisfactory completion of a phase of discussion and demonstration, but it cannot be held enclosed once it is read by other readers or in a different context of discussion. And this is not a matter of careless or ignorant reading by those outside the technical argument (though it may sometimes also be that); it is that the insurgency of signification, the perception of fresh relations, is inherent to all language—though most particularly to that intensified form of discourse which we call 'literary language.'

Literary language moves, often openly, and with great flexibility from level to level, achieving much of its intensity by means of allusion and connotation across levels. Such language opens out connections which technical discourses exclude from notice and, Rose suggests, at their most honest must abjure considering. The free and multiple movement across levels in literary language is its characteristic resource for discovery. As Waddington emphasized in *The Nature of Life*, for any adequate appraisal of complexity many kinds of description are needed.[27] An example of such unfolding, reconnecting, and enwebbing is to be found in the opening of Adrienne Rich's poem 'Waking in the Dark':

> The thing that arrests me is
> how we are composed of molecules

[26] Umberto Eco, *The Role of the Reader* (Bloomington, Ind., 1979), 66.
[27] C. H. Waddington, *The Nature of Life* (London, 1961).

(he showed me the figure in the paving stones)

arranged without our knowledge and consent

 like the wirephoto composed
 of millions of dots

 in which the man from Bangladesh
 walks starving
   on the front page
   knowing nothing about it

which is his presence for the world[28]

The human body as 'molecules,' and the 'millions of dots' which compose the newspaper photograph of the starving man, are both seen as part of an order which denies 'our knowledge and consent'. The shift from molecules to information suggests a congruity between them which does not need to be voiced. What *is* voiced is the sense of exposure and helplessness that the poet feels both in her arranged body and in her unwilled act of voyeurism, looking at the man starving 'on the front page, knowing nothing about it'. The human body is exposed, not only to a watcher out there, but in its predetermined composition irrelevant to will or individuality. She is 'arrested'—imprisoned as well as startled. In the poem there lurks also a recognition that the starving man knows nothing of either the poem or its language, that print, as much as those other 'millions of dots' of the wirephoto, cannot connect with the man's starvation. Knowledge is not solution; the power to perceive connections may itself be a trap which has no issue.

CONSTRUING AND PREDICTING

The enterprises of scientist and of writer both act out the paradox that narrative implies teleology even when its argument denies it. The acknowledgement of the foreknown in the imprinting of writing; the process of discovery which has now become disclosure; the fact that the book ends (even when the argument of the ending is peremptory and unresolved): all this makes for

---

[28] Adrienne Rich, *Poems, Selected and New, 1950–1974* (New York, 1975), 18.

an organization in which the future is already disposed, and is thus apparently under the control of the writer's description at least, if not of his free choosing. Narrative implies successful prediction. Greimas, indeed, argues that each semantic unit, each word, carries a potential narrative. So the 'fisherman' implies all the possibilities of his employment: 'Le pêcheur porte en lui, évidemment, toutes les possibilités de son faire, tout ce que l'on peut s'attendre de lui en fait de comportement; sa mise en isotopie discursive en fait un rôle thématique utilisable par le récit.'[29] But he mitigates the apparent determinism of a single fixed narrative programme by emphasizing that it is not until the last page of the narrative that 'le personnage de roman . . . déploie sa figure complète . . . grâce à la mémorisation opérée par le lecteur' (the character of the novel . . . is fully revealed . . . by the act of memorization undertaken by the reader).

The attempt to break out of a prediction-dominated narrative was one of the most important features of the French New Novel (Pinget's *Passacaille*, for example), and the attempt was strongly connected to a distrust of the anthropomorphism of language, particularly in the work of Robbe-Grillet.

In another work which allures the reader with a promise of a system, enigmatically disappointed, or enigmatically delayed, *The Crying of Lot 49*, Thomas Pynchon examines the problems of the observer, within the system or outside of it, and of the self-referential nature of any cyclic system. The heroine here is named deterministically but multiply. She is Oedipa Maas (Maze, Mass, Ma's). Instead of the traditional male scientist exploring a female 'Nature,' we are shown a woman exploring an information system dominated by male scientists, psychoanalysts, playwrights, and writers. The 'maze' she enters turns out to be a closed system in which not only the topics but the materials of the writing are part of a sinister chain, economic, political, scientific, literary. Cigarette filters, and the ink with which the writer writes, the printer prints, are products of the bones of

---

[29] 'Obviously, the fisherman contains within himself all the possibilities of his occupation, every type of behaviour that one could expect of him through the fact of him as fisherman; by putting him into discursive isotopy, he is given a thematic role that can be put to use by the *récit*.' Algirdas Julien Greimas, 'Les actants, les acteurs et les figures', in Claude Chabrol (ed.), *Sémiotique narrative et textuelle* (Paris, 1973), 174.

drowned and murdered men. Here, information theory, religious language, and entropy are overtly linked. Clerk Maxwell becomes a kind of fairy godfather within the work; his concept of a 'demon' which outplays the entropic system provides a counter-notion of design (though one whose vagrancy is very different from the benign accord in the Maxwell essay quoted earlier).

'Entropy is a figure of speech, then,' sighed Nefastis, 'a metaphor. It connects the world of thermodynamics to the world of information flow. The Machine uses both. The Demon makes the metaphor not only verbally graceful, but also objectively true.'

'But what,' she felt like some kind of heretic, 'if the Demon exists only because the two equations look alike? Because of the metaphor?'

Nefastis smiled; impenetrable, calm, a believer. 'He existed for Clerk Maxwell long before the days of the metaphor.'[30]

Coincidence proves—or seems—to be coded warning: 'What, tonight, was chance?' Free invention, it appears, is no longer possible for scientist or writer:

How can you blame them for being maybe a little bitter? Look what's happening to them. In school they got brainwashed, like all of us, into believing the myth of the American Inventor—Morse and his telegraph, Bell and his telephone, Edison and his light bulb, Tom Swift and his this or that. Only one man per invention. Then when they grew up they found they had to sign all their rights to a monster like Yoyodyne; got stuck on some 'project' or 'task force' or 'team' and started being ground into anonymity. Nobody wanted them to invent—only perform their little role in a design ritual, already set down for them in some procedures handbook. (pp. 63–4)

And yet at the book's conclusion there remains just the possibility of what Eddington calls 'anti-chance', the cheater or demon in the system. Joseph Bertrand, the great mathematician, remarked that 'Chance has neither consciousness nor memory': the specific powers of human intelligence are exactly those of consciousness and memory. The problem, common to scientists, poets, and other people, which Pynchon here disturbs is how to represent chance without knitting it into a language whose conditions inevitably imply teleology. The reader's eagerness to discover system is employed by Pynchon so that we

[30] Thomas Pynchon, *The Crying of Lot 49* (Harmondsworth, 1967), 77–8.

zealously uncover multiple systems which will not accord: this systematic or asystematic dance becomes itself the narrative figuring of narrative's problem. The nature of discovery may be predetermined by the conditions for its description. The refusal to describe, as well as overdescription (as in the jammed plotting of the Jacobean tragedy), draws our attention to the designs implicit in construal and the predictions implicit in recounting.

EXCHANGES BETWEEN POETS AND SCIENTISTS

Scientific ideas and writing are often of most value within literature precisely where the risks of translation are great. We should not look for stable one-to-one correspondences between scientific exposition and literary creation. Works of art press on the uncontrolled implications of science, while new scientific ideas, theories, and products make it possible to articulate what has earlier been taken for granted (and therefore was not available to be recounted, so embedded was it in assumptions beneath the level of description). Sometimes the level of allusion vanishes again as scientific theories change.

New scientific and technical knowledge allows the poet to contemplate with fresh intensity intransigent questions which grip language in all generations. For example, the intervention of a new scientific meaning for a word poignantly marks the shifting of levels in John Donne's 'A Nocturnall upon S. Lucies Day. Being the Shortest Day' (first published in 1633). Subsequent changes in the signification of the word cluster 'nocturnal' and 'nocturne,' as well as the disappearance of the object referred to, have disguised Donne's substantive meaning here. The most common form is and always has been adjectival, 'of or pertaining to the night', as the *Oxford English Dictionary* puts it. So we speak of a 'nocturnal animal'. As a substantive the *OED* lists first, as obsolete and rare, the sense 'a night-piece' and instances *only* the title of Donne's poem for this sense. The next, more substantial, listing, beginning in the seventeenth century (1627), is an 'astronomical instrument adapted for taking observations by which to ascertain the hour of the night'.

The poem is an act of mourning which takes place on the shortest day of the year (13 December, old style), that day when

there would be most need to keep time's bearings in the dark.
Lucy was the saint associated with light. The 'nocturnall' was,
when Donne wrote, a very recently invented instrument.
   The poem opens:

> Tis the yeares midnight, and it is the dayes,
> *Lucies*, who scarce seaven houres herself unmaskes
> The Sunne is spent, and now his flasks
> Send forth light squibs, no constant rayes;
> The Worlds whole sap is sunke.

The poet mourns the death of a woman. The poem itself becomes
the poet's 'nocturnall', an instrument for telling the time, keeping
his bearings as he moves through the darkness of grief.

> I am re-begot
> Of absence, darknesse, death; things which are not.

He is, yet, 'Of the first nothing, the Elixer grown'.

> But I am by her death, (which word wrongs her)
> Of the first nothing, the Elixer grown;
> Were I a man, that I were one,
> I needs must know; I should preferre,
> If I were any beast,
> Some ends, some means; Yea plants, yea stones detest
> And love; All, all some properties invest;
> If I an ordinary nothing were,
> As shadow, a light, and body must be here.

Shadow implies light, but he is beyond all such renewal. Donne
intensifies the expectation of the return of light and the coming
of dawn by combining in his night-piece the new instrument, 'the
nocturnall', and an allusion backward to the old monastic form
of service, matins, which took place at 3:00 a.m., long before
dawn, and consisted of three 'nocturns', each of which brought
the hour nearer to the light. But within this poem day never
returns, 'nor will my Sunne renew'. It ends:

> Since shee enjoyes her long nights festivall,
> Let mee prepare toward her, and let me call
> This houre her Vigill, and her Eve, since this
> Both the yeares, and the dayes deep midnight is.

The 'nocturnall' becomes the poem's only measure. Since Donne's time, works like Chopin's 'Nocturnes' and Whistler's 'Nocturnes' have reinforced for the modern reader the idea of a dreamy impressionistic composition not at all in key with Donne's poem. Donne is never obscure or vague, though sometimes difficult when we do not know enough. Here, as elsewhere, he intensifies emotion by the tension between senses within a word and by bringing current scientific material into close relation with older world pictures.

Distrust of the simultaneity of reading levels distinguishes scientific discourse from the ideals of other forms of creative writing. The shifting of levels, which in scientific discourse may blur exact description, yet brings to our attention the excluded or taken-for-granted elements in the social language of theory. When they are writing outside the tight circle of fellow professionals, the best scientific communicators excel by using the possibilities of current literature. It is a commonplace that Freud used the techniques of Victorian narrative to structure his recounting (and perhaps they structured his understanding) of his case histories, 'The Wolf-Man' being the most discussed example. We can certainly measure the extent of that reliance on current literary reference if we set Freud's narratives against the postmodernist narrative form of D. W. Winnicott's case history, *The Piggle*.[31] But an equally remarkable congruity, at the level this time of style rather than of form, can be found in other fields than those of psychoanalysis, fields less obviously centred upon the human subject.

Take the passage below. Are we reading Virginia Woolf? Here not only the lucid description of hesitation, the combination of hyperbole and matter-of-fact statement, may lead us to believe that we are reading Woolf: there is also the matter of sentence length and of the paced gaps between the sentences. If we know her work well we are likely immediately to think across to the discourse of Rhoda in *The Waves*, standing always on the threshold, seeking the permanent; 'Putting my foot to the ground I step gingerly and press my hand against the hard door of a Spanish inn':[32]

[31] D. W. Winicott, *The Piggle* (London, 1977).
[32] Virginia Woolf, *The Waves* (New York, 1959), 319.

I am standing on the threshold about to enter a room. It is a complicated business. In the first place I must shove against an atmosphere pressing with a force of fourteen pounds on every square inch of my body. I must make sure of landing on a plank travelling at twenty miles a second round the sun—a fraction of a second too early or too late, the plank would be miles away. I must do this whilst hanging from a round planet headed outward into space, and with a wind of aether blowing at no one knows how many miles a second through every interstice of my body. The plank has no solidity of substance. To step on it is like stepping on a swarm of flies. Shall I not slip through? No, if I make the venture one of the flies hits me and gives a boost up again; I fall again and am knocked upwards by another fly and so on. I may hope that the net result will be that I remain about steady; but if unfortunately I should slip through the floor or be boosted too violently up to the ceiling, the occurrence would be, not a violation of the laws of Nature, but a rare coincidence.[33]

Eddington's *The Nature of the Physical World*, from which this passage is taken, was written in 1927, giving him slightly the priority over *The Waves*. Virginia Woolf read Eddington, certainly. Did Eddington read Woolf? Very probably, although I know of no direct evidence. The congruity, however, has more than one significance: it demonstrates that ways of viewing the world are not constructed separately by scientists and poets; they share the moment's discourse. This particular instance, moreover, makes clear that we would be mistaken to read Virginia Woolf as an isolated sensibility, edged with madness, unaware of the movements of thought, the reshaping of the physical world, in her time. Her 'waves' are also those of light, of time, of Einstein and Eddington:

The progress of a wave is not progress of any material mass of water, but of a form which travels over the surface as the water heaves up and down . . . These forms have a certain degree of permanence amid the shifting particles of water. Anything permanent tends to become dignified with the attribute of substantiality . . . Ultimately it is this innate hunger for permanence in our minds which directs the course of development of hydrodynamics, and likewise directs the world-building out of the sixteen measures of structure.[34]

Virginia Woolf's achievement, like that of hydrodynamics, comes from the attempt to describe anew that hunger.

[33] Eddington, *Nature of the Physical World*, 342.   [34] Ibid. 242.

The 'hunger for permanence' Eddington sees as another deluding constituent of the human imagination which leads us to discover in the universe the patterns that our minds have put there. The utmost resourcefulness and probity of language are needed, both by scientists and poets, to outwit the tendency of description to stabilize a foreknown world and to curtail discovery. Notwithstanding the requirement for precise expression of procedures and results, it becomes clear that—in the phase of experiment and again in the phase of communication—scientists need to have recourse to the linguistic dexterity, and sometimes even the instability of reference, with which literary language recognizes multiple simultaneous levels of event and meaning.

8
Translation or Transformation? The Relations of Literature and Science

The theme of this chapter, 'the presentation of science through literature', might suggest a one-way traffic, as though literature acted as a mediator for a topic (science) that precedes it and that remains intact after its re-presentation. That is not how I understand the relations between the two. I shall emphasize interchange rather than origins and transformation rather than translation. Scientific and literary discourses overlap, but unstably. Victorian writers, scientific and literary, held to the ideal of the 'mother-tongue'; in our own time the variety of professional and personal dialects is emphasized instead. Yet the expectation lingers that it should be possible to translate stably from one to another. This expectation may prove unrealistic.

More is to be gained from analysing the transformations that occur when ideas change creative context and encounter fresh readers. The fleeting and discontinuous may be as significant in our reading as the secure locking of equivalent meanings. Questions can change their import when posed within different genres. Recognizing scientific reference within works of literature may not be as straightforward a business as it seems. To put it at its most direct: how do we recognize science once it is in literature? Can such reference to scientific material be drained again of its relations within the literary work and returned to autonomy?

Neither literature nor science is an entity, and what constitutes literature or science is a matter for agreement in a particular historical period or place. The activities of scientists, and their social and institutional bases, have changed enormously over the past 100 years. More, on the face of it, than those of the writer of literature. But the English language now bears a freight of meaning from very diverse national groups across the world. That is an important change. The present internationalism of both science and literature makes for curious crossplays. I shall examine some examples later in this argument. The movement towards mathematicization has enhanced hopes of a stable community of meaning for scientists at work; the spread of English makes for often delusive accords between different communities of meaning.

In the first part of the chapter I concentrate on some sought-for correspondences between scientific and literary language; in the second part I examine some recent examples of the transformation of scientific materials in literary works. Such analysis reminds us forthwith of the apparent ease with which, in language, we inhabit multiple, often contradictory, epistemologies at the same time, all the time.

AUTHORITATIVE LANGUAGES

In the mid- and late nineteenth century the humanities were still in the ascendant in school and university studies, whereas now the appeal to authority is usually in the direction of science. In that way our present situation differs also from that described thirty years ago by C. P. Snow in *The Two Cultures*.[1]

The language available alike to nineteenth-century creative writers and scientists had been forged out of past literature, the Bible, philosophy, natural theology, the demotic of the streets or the clubs. Scientists as various as James Clerk Maxwell and Charles Lyell habitually seamed their sentences with literary allusion and incorporated literature into the argumentative structures of their work (as Lyell does Ovid and Clerk Maxwell, Tennyson.) The first number of the scientific journal *Nature* (4 November 1869) opened with a set of aphorisms culled from Goethe and selected by Huxley. Huxley describes the journal's aim as 'to mirror the progress of that fashioning by Nature of a picture of herself, in the mind of man, which we call the progress

[1] C. P. Snow, *The Two Cultures and the Scientific Revolution* (Cambridge, 1959).

of Science'.[2] 'Progress', 'fashioning', 'picture', 'mirroring', 'Nature herself': the securing of enquiry by means of a stable accord with a sacrilized external world is reinforced by the journal's epigraph from Wordsworth:

To the solid ground
Of nature trusts the Mind that builds for aye.

'Ground' in this scientific context condenses the senses 'earth' and 'argument'. That epigraph, with its accompanying image, continues as the bannerhead of the journal, past Maxwell, past Einstein, for almost 100 years. In 1957 it was shorn of its image but it was retained on each volume title-page until 1963, when its anachronism must at last have seemed greater than its annealing powers.

To the Victorians, whether preoccupied with science or literature or politics—and however conscious they might be of the fickleness of signification—the concept of the mother-tongue was crucial. In the case of English the 'mother-tongue' was idealized as the English of past literature above all. Scientific writers in the Victorian period were immersed in the general language of the tribe, yet needed to formulate their own stable professional dialects with which to communicate with each other. By that means they would be able to change the level of description so as to engage with new theoretical and technical questions. They would also limit the range of possible interpretation, and, it was their hope, misinterpretation. But they were reluctant to allow writing on scientific issues to remain on the linguistic periphery. They thus claimed congruity with poetry, perceived as the authoritative utterance within current language.

Victorian middle- and upper-class language was formed by what we might call a parental diad: not only the mother-tongue but the father-tongue shaped the dominant educational ideology. Classical languages played a central role in the education system, a system reserved almost entirely for boys until the late nineteenth century and taught to them by men. The practice of Victorian scientists of citing classical writing in their work serves several functions: some social, some illustrative, some argumentative. Such allusion effortlessly claimed gender and class

[2] T. H. Huxley, *Nature*, (1869).

community with a selected band of readers; it implied a benign continuity for scientific enquiries with the imaginative past of human society; it could figure the tension between objectivity and affect.

In our own time writers on discourse have emphasized the heterogeneity of dialects within the apparently common tongue, the way in which we never can quite securely translate from one professional or social group to another the intensity, or vacuity, of terms. Terms may be precise and full in one domain, meagre in another, transformed in yet another: 'matter' would be a simple example, or 'select'. Words are also subject to ontological decay: what starts precise and bounded may become neutralized, or soggy. When George Eliot's novel *Daniel Deronda* first appeared, both R. H. Hutton and George Saintsbury objected in their reviews to the description of the heroine's 'dynamic glance' as being pedantic and over-scientific.[3] Hardly the objection that such a clichéd phrase would raise now.

Words are impressed with the shared assumptions, with the things *not said* of each group, just as much as they are with their shared assertions. But none of us is a member of one social and linguistic group only. We live, therefore, in a variety of conflicted epistemologies. Scientific workers strive to contain their procedures within a single epistemological frame, but cannot exempt them from further and other construals. We experience every day, and we condense that experience in speaking and listening, as co-workers, shoppers, friends, researchers, women or men, perhaps parents, lovers, certainly political activists or quietists, members willy-nilly of local, national, and global communities at a particular moment in historical time. Some terms transfer across all these zones, particularly those terms that have to do with kinship, commerce, measurement, conflict. They shift scale and energy as they go.

Much literature of the late twentieth century is proudly parodic, presenting puns as the profoundest rather than the lowest form of wit. The preference for improbable simultaneities that hold unlike together goes alongside the emphasis in wave–particle theory on unreconciled complementarity. As Edwin Morgan puts it in the briefest of his six particle poems:

[3] Collected in D. Carroll (ed.), *George Eliot: The Critical Heritage* (London, 1971), 369, 374.

The particle that decided
got off its mark, but died.[4]

The word 'decided' by the act of decision withers to its four last letters i d e d and 'died'. How to explain such proximities? Gerald Holton speaks of the 'themata' of a period, a term which is an attempt to move away from the concept *Zeitgeist* with its inherent animism.[5] The banishing of *Zeitgeist* has usefully uncovered a series of difficulties: how to describe the relations between intellectual fields within a historical period? How to relate them to social and economic movements? How to articulate the interactions between apparently remote preoccupations? How to analyse the close written relations between authors who probably never read each other's work? How to explain the concurrent appearance of similar ideas in science and in literature without inevitably forging causal links? And how to avoid stabilizing the argument so that one form of knowledge becomes again the origin of all others?

Major changes have taken place since the time of the controversy over the 'two cultures'. Scientific events are now the daily currency of our newspapers. A great writer, Primo Levi, has, in *The Periodic Table* and other works, demonstrated that being human and being a scientist may be the same heroic task when the worst comes.[6] A number of working scientists, as well as many philosophers, have analysed the potency of language in their own practice. Writers as various as François Jacob and Michel Serres have emphasized the simultaneity of science and myth as systems for containing (and constraining) possibility.[7] Some scientists have expressed scientific controversy and theory in non-mathematical terms accessible to general intelligent readers: one thinks, among others, of Stephen Jay Gould, Stephen Weinberg, Steven Rose, Stephen Hawking, Ilya Prirogine, Richard Dawkins.

[4] E. Morgan, *Poems of Thirty Years* (Manchester, 1982), 388.

[5] G. Holton, *The Thematic Origins of Scientific Thought: Kepler to Einstein* (Cambridge, Mass., 1973).

[6] P. Levi, *The Periodic Table* (London, 1985).

[7] F. Jacob, *The Possible and the Actual* (New York, 1982), 9: 'myths and science fulfil a similar function: they both provide human beings with a representation of the world and of the forces that are supposed to govern it. They both fix the limits of what is considered as possible.' M. Serres, *Hermes: Literature, Science, Philosophy* (Baltimore and London, 1983), esp. 'The Origin of Language: Biology, Information Theory, and Thermodynamics', 71–83.

Such writing joins a powerful tradition of re-imagined science, represented among the Victorians by writers such as John Tyndall, T. H. Huxley, James Clerk Maxwell, Richard Proctor, W. K. Clifford. In our own century no one has surpassed the condensed lucidity of Eddington who, for the time of reading, allows the reader to comprehend scientific problems well beyond his or her intellectual reach, though it has to be acknowledged that the burst of clarity is not secure for ever. Alongside him in the late 1920s and 1930s were figures such as James Jeans and Julian Huxley and H. G. Wells, who elucidated scientific questions in such a way that readers were aware not of the remoteness but of the urgent closeness of those questions to the practical, emotional, political, and economic issues particular to the times. They were made aware, too, of endlessly recurring issues in human society and in life beyond the human.

C. P. Snow's claim that 'the intellectual life of the whole of Western society is increasingly being split into two polar groups' excluded further intellectual and cultural groups from consideration.[8] Intellectual life does not take place only among literary intellectuals and physical scientists, though those milieux happened to be the ones that Snow knew best. His neglect of other intellectual and artistic concerns falsified the map from the outset. Now, since the expansion of higher education in Britain in the 1960s, his complaints (salient perhaps at the time and, indeed, helping towards the expansion) seem to treat remotely of a dwindling class of literatures, *not* our main problem now. (Though it was striking to see Peter Ackroyd's novel *First Light* (1989) taken to task by reviewers for poeticizing the Uncertainty Principle.[9])

Another, more general though shifty, source of understanding has become available. The power of television to represent scientific thinking in the form *simultaneously* of words and images has opened access to issues hard properly to represent in words alone. I am sure that working scientists flinch at some of the simplifications and misprisions that result, since at some point algebra must begin, but the spirited leap of enquiry generated both by the works of high popularization and by translation for the screen means that scientific work at present enters the con-

---

[8] Snow, *Two Cultures*, 3.   [9] P. Ackroyd, *First Light* (London, 1989), 3.

course of interpretation rapidly and powerfully. It becomes part of the imaginative currency of the community. It is set in multiple interpretative relationships and helps to construe the times. All the more, science has itself to become more conscious of how it depends on language and on society.

Indeed, the new alliances between scientists and humanists in a bleak economic and educational environment in this country for higher education should not make us too sanguine; they may themselves be a symptom of the extent of the danger we face, which obliges the sinking of real differences.

In preparing the lecture on which this chapter is based I was ruefully aware of that concourse of dialects—that diversity of assumptions and foreknowledge—active in such a group as that which formed its audience. I am not a scientist: my concern is language, representation, and reception. Our special skills do not fall in line with each other. But we do not need to disguise or discard these incongruities. No 'ingenuous transposition' (in Umberto Eco's words) is possible from one genre to another.[10] But neither should transformations be seen as errors or wastage. Snow wrote scornfully of poets: 'Now and then one used to find poets conscientiously using scientific expressions, and getting them wrong—there was a time when "refraction" kept cropping up in verse in a mystifying fashion.'[11] Perhaps the key word there is 'conscientiously', but it seems unlikely that Snow would have liked such fleeting allusions any better had he acknowledged their hedonism. He was hoping, it seems, for perfect gridding.

The reception of ideas outside the immediate circle of co-workers hardly ever is systematic. Many simultaneous kinds of description are necessary; such descriptions do not all converge; understanding works as often recursively as progressively. In scientific writing as in other creative writing we are reading forms of description; to quote Umberto Eco again: 'Indeterminacy, complementarity, noncausality are not *modes of being* in the physical world, but *systems for describing it* in a convenient way'.[12]

[10] U. Eco, *The Role of the Reader* (Bloomington, Ind., 1979), 66.
[11] Snow, *Two Cultures*, 16.
[12] Eco, *Role of the Reader*. For a discussion of the functions of description see G. Beer 'Problems of Description in the Language of Discovery', in G. Levine (ed.), *One Culture: Essays in Science and Literature* (Madison, Wis., 1987), 35–58.

Faraday made this same point about how the authority of language misleads once terms are received as 'physical truths'. In a letter to Maxwell on the problematical significance of the term *force*, he remarks 'experimentalists on force generally . . . receive that description of gravity as a physical truth, and believe that it expresses all, and no more than all, that concerns the nature and locality of the power. To these it limits the formation of their ideas, and the direction of their exertions' (23 November 1857).

Faraday continues, despite his awareness of the cramping effects of terminology, by asking Clerk Maxwell whether it may not be possible for mathematicians to express their 'conclusions . . . in common language as fully, clearly, and definitely as in mathematical formulae? . . . translating them out of their hieroglyphics, that we also might work upon them by experiment.'[13]

SEEKING A COMMON TONGUE

A recurrent game of courtesy and reassurance played between scientists and other creative thinkers and writers is that of equalizing their concerns, seeing the diversity of their projects as yet part of a common pursuit. So Schrödinger in the 1930s takes up the concept *homo ludens* and speaks of the essential human 'surplus' that is play, seeing it expressed in card games, literature, conversation, the making of scientific theory.[14] So Helmholtz in the 1870s, having warned against the use of empty big words and the easy manufacture of hypotheses, asserted: 'The first discovery of a new law, is the discovery of a similarity which has hitherto been concealed in the course of natural processes. It is a manifestation of that which our forefathers in a serious sense described as "wit", it is of the same quality as the highest performances of artistic perception in the discovery of new types

---

[13] L. Campbell and W. Garnett, *The Life of James Clerk Maxwell* (London, 1882), 289–90.

[14] E. Schrödinger, *Science and the Human Temperament* (London, 1935), 23. See E. M. MacKinnon, *Scientific Explanation and Atomic Physics* (Chicago and London, 1982) for helpful discussion of the views on language of Bohr, Heisenberg, Schrödinger, and Einstein. See also B. R. Wheaton, *The Tiger and the Shark: Empirical Roots of Wave–Particle Dualism* (Cambridge, 1983) for an excellent account of the epistemological debates among physicists in the 1920s and 1930s.

of expression.'[15] The emphasis in Helmholtz's remark is on simultaneity and diversity as together forming fresh concepts, just as wit in poetry condenses absolutely for the moment what has seemed separate, and that in language may separate again. Eighty-odd years later than Helmholtz, Heisenberg, drawing on his discussions with Bohr, turns not to the compression of wit but to the expansiveness of natural language (that is, conversational speech) as his point of comparison with the discursive practices of science: 'one of the most important features of the development and analysis of modern physics is the experience that the concepts of natural language, vaguely defined as they are, seem to be more stable in the expansion of knowledge than the precise terms of scientific language, derived as an idealization from only limited groups of phenomena.'[16] The 'vagueness' in natural language in Heisenberg's terms is a result of multivocality, the way in which a single word may cover a broad range of significations. From among these, the most needed meaning of the moment will be sharply held in focus while the rest remain in shadow. The shadowing, but not evanishing, of countersignifications is a sought effect in much literature, an effect that often dramatizes the re-emergence of repressed senses.

For communication among scientific workers, however, a necessary condition for professional interchange is usually held to be a stable locking of single signification. That is one reason why Peter Medawar in his tonic lecture of 1968 on science and literature flouted the courtesies between the two domains and curtailed the high-minded modesty of expressions such as those I have just quoted: 'The case I shall find evidence for is that when literature arrives, it expels science.'[17] The nub of his argument was his mistaken association of 'rhetoric' only with 'obscurity'.

It is always, let us note, easier to descry rhetoric in retrospect and to analyse the persuasive elements in theories no longer current. But the hope that, within language, words or syntax can be detained within the order of single meaning relies upon a tight

[15] H. Helmholtz, 'On Thought in Medicine', in his *Popular Lectures on Scientific Subjects* (second series) (London, 1884), 227.

[16] W. Heisenberg, *Physics and Philosophy: The Revolution in Modern Science* (New York, 1958), 200.

[17] P. Medawar, 'Science and Literature', in his *Pluto's Kingdom* (Oxford, 1982), 43.

contraction of readership, rather than on the terms employed. Bertrand Russell's tart account in *The Scientific Outlook* of the linguistic problems of physics touches on the helpless largess of language: 'Ordinary language is totally unsuited for expressing what physics really asserts, since the words of everyday life are not sufficiently abstract. Only mathematics and mathematical logic can say as little as the physicist means to say.'[18]

When Bruno Latour and Steve Woolgar studied the life of a lab for a year as anthropologists, their first strong observation was that they were watching a tribe addicted to inscription. They write:

After several further excursions into the bench space, it strikes our observer that its members are compulsive and almost manic writers . . . This appears strange because our observer has only witnessed such diffidence in memory in the work of a few particularly scrupulous novelists . . . Our anthropologist is thus confronted with a strange tribe who spend the greatest part of their day coding, marking, altering, correcting, reading, and writing.[19]

Unsurprisingly, the workers in the lab vehemently resisted this description of their activities. Their writing was *about* something, something out there, they argued, and inscription was simply an agency, not in itself an end.

The implicit contrary was with imaginative writing that draws on no stable ulterior world and makes of the activity of writing a topic as well as a medium. Leaving aside for now the improbable assumption that the composition in science of a world 'out there' eschews rhetoric, we may yet assent to a difference between the linguistic position of creative writer and scientist. For one thing, the scientist is involved with many more semiological and gestural systems in the work-place than is the writer: in particular, apparatus, the time-span of an experiment, co-workers in conversation, observers. Creative writing emphasizes writing process and calls attention to the reader's activities as reader. The scientific paper, with its tightly ritualized succession of sections, its invariant procedures of description, claims an authoritative retrospect towards the knowledge it produces.

---

[18] B. Russell, *The Scientific Outlook* (London, 1931), 85.
[19] B. Latour and S. Woolgar, *Laboratory Life: The Construction of Scientific Facts*, 2nd edn. (Princeton, NJ, 1986), esp. 45–53.

Closure has already been completed, as the expression 'writing up' as opposed to writing, claims. The process of experiment, research, thinking, however, is continuing alongside, and there is a sense in which the scientific paper is simply a shedding from that more fundamental and complex activity. For that reason, the notion bruited in the late 1980s in justification of government cutbacks in research spending, that it is possible to tap into others' research by means of the scientific literature alone is quite misguided.

One of the primary functions of technical language is to keep non-professionals out. There are good reasons for this desire. The closed readership enables precise conceptual exchange and continuance. The sustained achievement of agreed meaning may, however, be at the cost of effective secrecy, even, at worst, of mandarin enclosure. That is one reason (though there are others) why the laboratory has been so often represented in Gothic mode as a secret place where arcane events take place (as in Mary Shelley's *Frankenstein*), where personality is voided (as in Nigel Dennis's *Cards of Identity*), or even where the bounds of the human are undermined in a Sadeian promiscuity of hybridization (as in H. G. Wells's *The Island of Dr Moreau*). In much science fiction the laboratory becomes a dystopic site where experiments release threatening forms of the future. This Faustian, or occult, characterization is associated with the exclusion of outsiders and the difficulty of interpreting the unfamiliar semiological systems of the lab. Latour and Woolgar offer themselves as comic versions of the naïve observer unable to interpret along the grain of the community's assumptions and therefore able to descry activities of which the tribe is unaware, refusing to interpret those activities in terms acceptable to the tribe's internal systems. Very recently, in her collection of poems *Electroplating the Baby*, Jo Shapcott has alluded to and subverted Latour and Woolgar further in her poem 'Love in the Lab'. The lovers undermine classification by removing the last vestiges of language, tearing the labels off all the jars.[20]

Literature cannot, even if it would, take on the task of technical translator when scientists find themselves from time to time in the dilemma that their scrupulousness has sustained agreed

---

[20] J. Shapcott, *Electroplating the Baby* (Newcastle-upon-Tyne, 1988), 42–3.

meaning but rendered their knowledge and purpose inscrutable to others beyond the trained circle.

Fortunately, however, language, even technical language, is potentially transgressive. As soon as terms get outside the interactive eyes of co-workers, unregarded senses loom up. In *Darwin's Plots* I demonstrated the effects of this phenomenon by analysing some of the contradictory significances that Darwin's writing acquired in broader Victorian culture. So, for example, Darwin reserves the word 'race' in a discussion in *The Origin of Species* to the cultivation of cabbages, but cannot corral it long in that garden-plot.[21]

Sometimes scientists have chosen to draw common terms into technical functions and so to assert a continuity with ordinary experience while designating a specific new signification. We see that phenomenon in the current fashion for bellelettristic terms such as 'quark', 'charm', and 'black hole'. Such terms allow ontological leeway while theory is being formed; the novelty of the terms does not prematurely foreclose theoretical possibilities, as a more rigorously positivist terminology would do. Such transposed terms also significantly open up highly technical usages to the creative reception—and sometimes misprision—of non-scientists who may thus pursue implications not bounded by the initiating theorems.

Questions of nomenclature in the later nineteenth century became connected with current movements in language theory and nationalist practice. For example, P. G. Tait, reviewing W. K. Clifford's *Elements of Dynamic Part I: Kinematic* in *Nature* in 1878, is disturbed by the variety of 'new and very strange nomenclature' and records his dismay at 'an apparently endless array of such new-fangled terms as Pedals, Rotors, Cylindroids, Centrodes, Kites, Whirls, and Squirts! . . . Something, it seems, *must* be hard in a text-book—simplify the Mathematic, and the Anglic (i.e. the English) immediately becomes perplexing'.[22]

Clifford was, in fact, much influenced in his linguistic practice by the work of the philologist, poet, and folklorist William Barnes and by Barnes's attempt to winnow the foreign elements

---

[21] G. Beer, *Darwin's Plots: Evolutionary Narrative in Darwin, George Eliot, and Nineteenth-Century Fiction* (London, 1983).

[22] P. G. Tait, review of *Elements of Dynamic Part I: Kinematic* by W. K. Clifford, in *Nature* 2 (1878), 91.

from English and retrieve a folk-tongue, conceived as forthright, egalitarian, poetic, and truth-telling. Here, scientific discourse claims authority from a revivified common tongue. Very recently, Benoit Mandelbrot (1982) announces that for his fractal geometry he has invented a set of domesticated Gothic terms that combine the grotesque and the humdrum in ways that reassure and yet break bounds. He coins words from what he calls 'the rarely borrowed vocabularies of the shop, the home, and the farm. Homely names make the monster easier to tame. For example, I give technical meaning to *dust, curd,* and *whey*.'[23] Elsewhere in the essay he offers 'Cross Lumped Curdling Monsters' and 'Knotted Peano Monsters, Tamed'.

A verbal mimesis of his own theoretical work is implied, in which the random, the inordinate, the non-Euclidian is granted an appropriate language that bulges, miniaturizes, and grows gargantuan, constantly shifting across registers of scale and distance to achieve its imaginative effects. He domesticates and enchants his terms. By these means a non-mathematical reader can glimpse the implications of the theorems that are interspersed between the sentences.

LOCAL AND TOTAL REFERENCE

One of the problems in critical exposition and analysis is the desire to offer an account that will penetrate the entire system of a work and riddle its completeness. A kind of professionalism seems to be implied by such an enterprise, and, of course, sometimes it is. But there is a need, if we are to appraise the presences of scientific ideas and activities in literature, to take account also of the local: the fugitive allusion, the half-understood concept, the evasive reference whose significance takes us only some way. I shall show material of that kind gathering power from its fleetingness in Don DeLillo's *White Noise,* one of the most reviewed of recent novels.[24] But equally, fundamental narrative

---

[23] B. Mandelbrot, *The Fractal Geometry of Nature* (San Francisco, 1982) 5, 125. For an analysis of chaos theory in relation to literature see Katherine Hayles, *Chaos Bound: Orderly Disorder in Contemporary Literature and Science* (London, 1990).

[24] D. DeLillo, *White Noise* (London, 1986).

hopes and fears may be renewed and re-shaped by the implications of current scientific theories: for the nineteenth-century
reader, descent and variation; for ourselves, information-theory
and entropy.

How shall we discern such shifts of signification at work?
These re-interpretations of significant story may be expressed in
the ordering of the narrative rather than declaring themselves in
the language of the text; they may be figured in disarrangements,
for example, of what Propp took to be the necessary and universal syntax of story-telling.[25] Pynchon's *The Crying of Lot 49*
might serve as an example there.[26] Or, the implications of scientific enquiry may be pursued obsessionally so as to stretch the
reader's experience beyond the ordinary registers of sense-experience. Stanislaw Lem's *Fiasco* is a powerful instance of this
capacity.[27]

It turns out not always to be a simple matter to re-distil ideas
absorbed into other formations. The implications of scientific
ideas may manifest themselves in narrative organizations. They
may be borne in the fleeting reference more often than in the
expository statement, condensed as metaphors or skeined out as
story, alive as joke in the discordances between diverse discursive
registers. Lightness and suspicion may tell more than scrutiny
and exposition.

Scientific material does not have clear boundaries once it has
entered literature. Once scientific arguments and ideas are read
outside the genre of the scientific paper and the institution of the
scientific journal, change has already begun. Genres establish
their own conditions which alter the significance of ideas expressed within them. When concepts enter different genres they
do not remain intact. Readerships, moreover, are composed not
only of individuals but of individuals reading within a genre. So,
for example, those whose profession happens to be science do
not read novels or poems simply *as scientists* but as readers
newly formed by the possibilities of the genre within which their
reading is engaged. The readerships implied by the forms and
language of novels and poems are more various than those
implied by scientific papers.

[25] V. Propp, *Morphology of the Folktale*, 2nd edn. (Austin, Texas, 1968).
[26] T. Pynchon, *The Crying of Lot 49* (Harmondsworth, 1967).
[27] S. Lem, *Fiasco* (London, 1987).

Yet, although each genre establishes expectations, these expectations cannot be enforced. No genre can preclude the reader's invocation of other knowledge, other questions, than those manifestly indicated by the text. Such other knowledge, other questions, lie latent in the work's terms and forms, waiting for the apt and inappropriate reader. There is, therefore, always the possibility of a vacillation of meaning, a chording of significance, that will break through generic constraints, whether the genre be that of poem, drama, novel, scientific paper.

Lem, moreover, touches on a paradox always at play in narrative, even at its most unruly: its tendency to align itself with a purposive explanation of the world it describes. Narrative and propositional prose alike have difficulty in paying attention to the non-purposive:

here nothing served a purpose—not ever, not to anyone—and that here no guillotine of evolution was in play, amputating from every genotype whatever did not contribute to survival, nature, constrained neither by the life she bore nor by the death she inflicted, could achieve liberation, displaying a prodigality characteristic of herself, a limitless wastefulness, a brute magnificence that was useless, an eternal power of creation without a goal, without a need, without a meaning.[28]

Not only single lexical items but whole arguments may have residual and unused resources available to those outside the first circle of reception and debate. Left-over questions implicit in scientific theories may pose themselves anew, or for the first time, in terms that draw upon further—sometimes quite other—resources within a historical moment. The left-over or unraised questions that later surface have most often to do with social order, survival, authority, and the quarrel between providence and chance. That is to say, the questions are not themselves framed in terms that will yield once and for all to confirmation or disconfirmation. The questions provoked by scientific writing are recurrent questions that outgo current answers but adopt the terms of current theory.

So, in his highly-praised novel, *White Noise*, Don DeLillo's serious comedy about fear of death finds its terms in 'waves and radiation' (as the first book is entitled), in the release of noxious gases, the change in weather patterns, and in the bricolage of

---

[28] Ibid. 30.

information flowing in through many technological channels. It stills from time to time upon the question of the married pair:

Who will die first?

This question comes up from time to time, like where are the car keys. It ends a sentence, prolongs a glance between us. I wonder if the thought itself is part of the nature of physical love, a reverse Darwinism that awards sadness and fear to the survivor. Or is it some inert element in the air we breathe, a rare thing like neon, with a melting point, an atomic weight?[29]

The novel's characters find comfort in the homely high-tech profusion of the supermarket where peripatetic consumers discover taxonomic order and global plenitude upon the shelves (the supermarket is, I would suggest, the modern Great Exhibition). There, social encounters with acquaintances are brief, benign, spontaneous, and non-committal. The ephemeral sumptuousness of the supermarket staves off closure. Because its description invokes lists, it promises endlessness. All the more does dread of death lurk in its aisles, DeLillo suggests.

What, we may ask, does science contribute to this work? The novel certainly includes no expository account of scientific developments, nor more than allusive gestures towards wave–particle conundrums and information theory. But the writing depicts a society whose determining circumstances are the direct outcome of applied science: the train loaded with toxic chemicals, the excellent swift flight of foodstuffs to the supermarket shelves, their gleaming preservation, the radio, the television and telerecorder, the telephone—all those insistent and contingent carriers of messages, few of which are designed for any one recipient, many indeed eerily self-contained in their endless outflow of information. The 'incessant bombardment of information' needs the occasional catastrophe to break it up. 'We're suffering from brain fade', argues one character: 'The flow is constant . . . Words, pictures, numbers, facts, graphics, statistics, specks, waves, particles, motes. Only a catastrophe gets our attention.'[30]

Surface and depth have become indistinguishable; the old spatial hierarchies inconsequential. The irresoluteness of the novel's narrative voice eschews explanation: the family man who speaks

---

[29] DeLillo, *White Noise*, 15.   [30] Ibid. 66.

the tale is head of Hitler Studies at the College on the Hill and evidences no sense of difficulty about the bland lack of connection between his academic studies and his life. The society imaged is, moreover, one whose deepest disquiets are the outward ripples of fundamental scientific theory, particularly the insistence in entropy on increasing disorganization, and the simultaneous life and death of space-time phenomenology. The novel refuses decisive futures, closures, is punctuated by the barren poetry of overheard utterances from radio and television shorn of context. *Déjà vu* is the first clinical symptom experienced by victims of the chemical catastrophe that takes place in DeLillo's novel. The reference in this novel to *déjà vu* is *both* to the nature of parody and to the temporal-causal problems raised by the work of Bohr, Heisenberg, and Schrödinger.[31]

Schrödinger's cat is a frequent presence in modern literature, giving the title to Robert Anton Wilson's cult trilogy of the early 1980s[32] and working as fable in a piece such as this by the distinguished Australian poet, Gwen Harwood.[33]

Schrödinger's Cat Preaches to the Mice

Silk-whispering of knife on stone,
due sacrifice, and my meat came.
Caressing whispers, then my own
choice among laps by leaping flame.

What shape is space? Space will put on
the shape of any cat. Know this:
my servant Schrödinger is gone
before me to prepare a place.

[31] A. Eddington, *New Pathways in Science* (Cambridge, 1935): 'As a conscious being I am involved in a story. The perceiving part of my mind tells me a story of the world about me . . . As a scientist I have become mistrustful of this story. In many instances it has become clear that things are not what they seem to be. According to the story teller I have now in front of me a substantial desk; but I have learned from physics that the desk is not at all the continuous substance that it is supposed to be in the story' (p. 1). Cf. also B. Russell, *The ABC of Relativity* (London, 1926), 226: 'What we know of the physical world . . . is much more abstract than was formerly supposed . . . Of the bodies themselves . . . we know so little that we cannot even be sure that they are anything: they *may* be merely groups of events in other places, those events which we should naturally regard as their effects.'

[32] R. A. Wilson, *Schrödinger's Cat*, I: *The Universe Next Door* (London, 1980); II: *The Trick Top Hat* (1981); III: *The Homing Pigeons* (1982).

[33] G. Harwood, *Bone Scan* (London, 1988), 26–7.

So worship me, the Chosen One
in the great thought-experiment.
As in a grave I will lie down
and wait for the Divine Event.

The lid will close. I will retire
from sight, curl up and say Amen
to geiger counter, amplifier,
and a cylinder of HCN.

When will the geiger counter feel
decay, its pulse be amplified
to a current that removes the seal
from the cylinder of cyanide?

Dead or alive? The case defies
all questions. Let the lid be locked.
Truth, from your little beady eyes,
is hidden. I will not be mocked.

Quantum mechanics has no place
for what's there without observation.
Classical physics cannot trace
spontaneous disintegration.

If the box holds a living cat
no scientist on earth can tell.
But I'll be waiting, sleek and fat.
Verily, all will not be well

if, to the peril of your souls,
you think me gone. Know that this house
is mine, that kittens by mouse-holes
wait, who have never seen a mouse.

Is the cat alive or dead? Observing falsifies the answer, Schrödinger suggests. Harwood here wittily provides a false solution
from another scientific domain: the cat is never safely dead
because kittens are born with the same genetic information,
watching by mouse-holes before they have encountered a mouse.
And is God ever safely dead? The invocation at once of biblical
language and of Schrödinger's thought-experiment condenses
sardonically the menace of returning authority, of descent and
instinct as recurrent power, of time disturbed.

This double dread, of order and disorder, is a powerful cultural story—perhaps the most powerful in the period of postmodernism since it emphasizes at once the random and the energy of secret plotting. Like another major American novel, Thomas Pynchon's *The Crying of Lot 49*, with its invocation of Maxwell's Demon both as part of the plot and an image for plotting, DeLillo (and in some measure Harwood) turn the reader's attention upon the intrinsication of scientific and literary intelligence, intelligence in both senses, as percipience and spying.

INTERCONNECTION AND INTERNATIONALISM

The alarm in much recent writing is less about the separation of two cultures than about their volatile implication. That may be more typical of American literature than of writing in England. It certainly has something to do with the knowledgeability of a society where many universities routinely run courses generically known as 'Physics for Poets' and scientists must take courses in literature. But although education systems differ, the internationalism of literature in English, like the internationalism of science, is now compelling. This has produced thematics of its own.

The internationalism of both science and literature sets up new tensions between the local and the total. The dreads of particular nations within supranational culture are focused in the figure of the spy; even more, of the double-agent whose loyalties can never be pinned down. Scientists and writers have allegiances within and beyond national boundaries. Moreover, contradictory ideals are composed within the international community of science: both the rapid free movement of information within the professional community and the competitive secrecy of teams seeking to outdo others. In creative writing in English a different but not wholly unrelated phenomenon can be observed. That phenomenon is the now supranational availability of English as a lingua franca, and also as a literary language with very diverse ideological and creative meaning for writers in particular countries: in India, in the United States, in the Philippines, in Nigeria, in the Caribbean, in Scotland, for example. It is no longer possible even to pretend that English belongs exclusively to the English and it is necessary now to speak of literature in English as much as English literature. The spy story, with its accoutrements of high-tech information, its trafficking in secret fundamental scientific research, is a new myth generated by the national against supranational struggle. Frequently its function is to give satisfying vent to a base nationalism that finds itself forbidden expression in polite ideological society.

Tom Stoppard's play *Hapgood* includes that level of meaning, though it has other, more sophisticated tasks.[34] Stoppard uses the vocabulary and ideas of quantum mechanics to organize his drama—or is the drama an allegorized lecture in quantum mechanics? The play is peculiarly tender towards some forms of English society, such as prep schoolboys playing football. The drama zealously works out the image of the spy, of intelligence and observation, of polyglot communities and the secret command of other tongues, the superposing of contradictory possibilities. The title, Hapgood, proffers reversed indications: 'Good Hap', lucky chance; and uses the designed lucky chance that the word *happens* to sound like (but is not quite identical with) the name of the scientist-theologian Habgood, Archbishop of York. The compactedness of the title is an indication of the close-wrought, yet skittish quality of the play. There is no reason to expect a solemn or respectful treatment of scientific ideas in literary works.

Stoppard's theatrical pyrotechnics are as closely controlled, and as vacillating, as any proper realization of Heisenberg's uncertainty principle could aim to be:

KERNER: The particle world is the dream world of the intelligence officer. An electron can be here or there at the same moment. You can choose; it can go from here to there without going in between; it can pass through two doors at the same time, or from one door to another by a path which is there for all to see until someone looks, and then the act of looking has made it take a different path. Its movements cannot be anticipated because it has no reasons. It defeats surveillance because when you know what it's doing you can't be certain where it is, and when you know where it is you can't be certain what it's doing: Heisenberg's uncertainty principle; and this is not because you're not looking carefully enough, it is because there is *no such thing* as an

---

[34] T. Stoppard, *Hapgood* (London, 1988). Stoppard prefaces the play with an epigraph from Richard Feynman's *The Character of Physical Law*.

electron with a definite position and a definite momentum; you fix one, you lose the other, and it's all done without tricks, it's the real world, it is awake.

HAPGOOD: Joseph, please explain to me about the twins.

KERNER: I just did but you missed it.[35]

The dramatic problem Stoppard encounters is that the speed of exposition and enactment leaves the audience, like many of the characters, bemused. And the solution (which has to do with multiple sets of twins) baffles the viewer in a way that rebuffs the apparent contract of the 'detective story' to provide a solution permitting a stable tracking back to explanatory origins.

Of course, that is also the point of the play. It enacts the salient difficulties of the theory to which it refers. A familiar trope of stagecraft and of fiction (the twins, the doubles, familiar to us from Shakespearean comedy on) here produces an ironic strain not only between verbal practices but between the possible styles of enactment within scientific theory and in drama. For if the drive in the discourse of quantum physics has been to obliterate the picture and the model, images are inevitably re-introduced by the physical presence of bodies on a stage. The shift of genre produces a transformation that jars with the attempt verbally to translate the concepts of physics.

How then do we recognize the activities of science in literary works if translation will not suffice and transformation may invert the initiating meaning? Fugitive reference need not imply slight meaning. To discover the effects of scientific activity in literary works we need to look not for explanatory or systematic discussion but rather for ironic doubling of reference or the disturbing of authoritative story.

The anthropologist Clifford Geertz in 'Common Sense as a Cultural System' sets different authoritative stories on a level with each other, and with what he sees as the improvident claims of common sense to universality: 'Like *Lear*, the New Testament, or quantum mechanics, common sense consists in an account of things which claims to strike at their heart.'[36] Lyotard has argued that our age is characterized by the break-up of grand narratives,

[35] Ibid. 48.

[36] C. Geertz, *Local Knowledge: Further Essays in Interpretive Anthropology* (New York, 1983), 84.

the loss of authority for scientific knowledge and language alike. His claim is, naturally, the grandest narrative of all: the *Über-*narrative that reflects on *Götterdämmerung*. He claims the end-position, from which summary and fade alike can be conjured.[37] But authoritative narratives have a way of re-forming. Fundamental assumptions may leave slight traces on the surface of writing. Sometimes assumptions declare themselves instead in the ordering of narrative or in the juxtaposition of diverse sorts of language. New orderings of knowledge will be sprung within the tensions of form as well as of description, abutting, sometimes merging with, but always casting light upon prior constructions of meaning, their decay, their tenacity.

Science is not a single origin, with literature, or sociology, or economics, or philosophy as its interpretative followers. Nor are any of these fields alone the necessary prior or initiating condition of knowledge. We all learn stories from each other—language takes its meaning from interaction. The scientist works with the ideal stories already available (hierarchy or simplicity, for example). Sometimes he or she adds a new one, or, more often, revises the imaginative meaning and explanatory power of an old one. The excitement generated among non-scientists by chaos theory is an instance: chaos theory calls attention to observed but excluded irregularity, asymmetry and flux. That it has developed alongside deconstruction, with its refusal of parameters of interpretation, its obdurate relativism, is as intriguing as is the rediscovery of plate-tectonics at the height of the fashion for Derridean epistemology, with its emphasis on ungrounding.

Are such analogies just a play of words? I do not believe so. But neither do I believe that it is possible to produce a stable causal sequence to account for these temporal relations. Alongside such proximities one can detail technical permitting factors. The need to drill deep for oil, and the development of the technology to do so; the development of computers and their capacity to record fractals; these are crucial explanatory factors in placing the moment of theory-precipitation. But the technical account does not drive out the interactive account. There is no necessary

---

[37] J-F. Lyotard, *The Post Modern Condition: A Report on Knowledge* (Manchester, 1984).

competition between these explanatory forms. Loose accords have their significance too. Scientists and writers dwell in the land of the living where multiple epistemological systems interlock, overlap, contradict, and sustain our day-by-day choices. At present we are again in a moment when scientists are accepting the risks of uncontrolled reception. Writing that had initially sought and required the autonomy of the specialist group is now rapidly and copiously re-interpreted by wider and diversified groups of writers and readers. Literature also, like scientific activity, is now very consciously working across an international system of intertextuality with novels and plays from many countries rapidly translated into English. This further extends the degree to which the English language bears the determining forces of many, and various, communities.

Such free reception is not likely to leave scientific problems intact within the expository terms already established by scientists. Rather, the transformed materials of scientific writing become involved in social and artistic questioning. That questioning is enacted sometimes at the level of semantics, sometimes of form or of broken story. Transformations and imbalances reveal as much as congruities. Such enquiry must not be subordinated to current demands in our society for predetermined relevance, nor can its success be measured by discovering identity between the different domains. The questioning of meaning in (and across) science and literature needs to be sustained without seeking always reconciliation.

9

Parable, Professionalization, and Literary Allusion in Victorian Scientific Writing

Victorian scientific writing frequently invokes literary allusion or knits parable into argument. What were the functions of these invocations? What light can they throw on the social, ethical, intellectual, and even economic conditions of Victorian science? And how do they relate to the processes of professionalization? Language is a large institution. Within it diverse groups define their identities. The major debate among Victorian language-theorists in the 1860s and 1870s concerned whether language was to be understood as organic and evolutionary or interactive and institutional. Nowhere in the course of that debate was the ideal of 'the mother-tongue' disputed. Victorian people took it for granted that they shared, and should share, a common tongue, and that scientists must aim to write in an accessible style for a diversified readership.

What, then, were the in-groups and out-groups formulated implicitly in Victorian scientific writing? Writing accessibly may, after all, be seen equally as a power-sharing or a power-seeking activity. What kinds of authority were scientists like James Clerk Maxwell or Joseph Hooker or Thomas Henry Huxley claiming for their writing? Who were they addressing and who excluding?

These are the questions that concern me in the argument that follows. I shall seek to demonstrate how literary allusion and parable bear out the following conclusions: that scientific discourse had an uneasy (and productive) relationship with the established authoritative narratives of the Bible and literature; that the process of professionalization among Victorian scientists knit in class and gender assumptions; that Victorian scientists were caught between the goals of objectivity and affect, and that they found ways, through literary reference, to poise necessary contradictions in their work. These are not all novel observations, but studying discourse will allow us a more secure understanding of some of the issues at stake within Victorian intellectual culture.

Let me begin by analysing a scientific parable that precisely addresses the in-group/out-group question: the relation of inhabitant and observer, or how knowledge is formed and changed within a society.

At the 1866 Nottingham meeting of the British Association for the Advancement of Science Joseph Hooker, one of the key figures in the Victorian scientific community, concluded his major lecture on the origins of insular flora with a parable.[1] The parable was a narrative form much favoured by Victorian writers, scientific and literary. It had more meanings than homily. It was often used as a satiric weapon for getting under the listener's or reader's guard, insinuating distance, and separating the group from its habitual self-image. Its humour protected the speaker from giving offence: the playfulness of the form (as well as its religious credentials) reinserted the speaker into the community from which telling the story simultaneously detached him (or, much less frequently, her). The parable also offered enigma: the unlocked meaning of the conclusion is never quite commensurate with the suggestiveness of the story.

Hooker's parable can serve us as a vantage-point from which to begin surveying some of the stresses within Victorian experience that I have summarized in the terms observing and inhabiting. The topic and site of Hooker's main address was island bio-geography. The island-form focuses with particular intensity on the relations of observer and inhabitants. Hooker prefaced his parable by emphasizing 'that the scientific study [of] the principles of life, whether in their structural or functional aspects . . . is not yet recognised as a branch of a liberal education'.[2] The assembled company listening to his lecture is privileged—and yet set apart from the educational mainstream of the time which is

---

[1] Joseph Hooker, 'Insular Flora', *Report of the British Association for the Advancement of Science, Nottingham Meeting, 1866* (Nottingham, 1866), 225–7.

[2] Ibid. 227.

still dominated by the humanities, particularly the classics: the scientists form a new professional tribe.[3]

This is his parable:

You have all read of uncivilised races, who regard every month's moon as a new creation of their gods; who they say eat the old moons, not for their sustenance, but for their glory, and to prove to mortals that they can make new ones—and they regard your denials that their gods do monthly make new moons as equivalent to denying that they could do so if they would.

It is not so long since it was held by most scientific men, and is so by some still, that species of plants and animals were (like the savages' moons) created in as many spots, and in as great numbers as they were first found in, at their native places. To deny that species were thus created, was in many persons' opinion, regarded as equivalent to denying that they could be so created.

And I have twice been present at the annual gatherings of tribes in such a state of advancement as the above, but after they had come into contact with the missionaries of the most enlightened nation of mankind. These missionaries attempted to teach them, amongst other matters, the true theory of the moon's motions, and at the first of these gatherings, when the subject was described by them, the presiding Sachem shook his head and his spear. The priests first attacked the new doctrine, and with fury: their temples were ornamented with symbols of the old creed; and their religious chants and rites were worded and arranged in accordance with it. The 'Medicine men', however, being divided amongst themselves (as Medicine men are apt to be in all countries), some of them sided with the missionaries, many from spite to the priests, but a few, I could see, from conviction; and putting my trust in the latter, I, for one, never doubted what the upshot would be.

Upwards of six years elapsed before I again visited that country, and was present at another annual gathering of the same tribes; and I then found the presiding Sachem treating the Missionaries' theory of the moon's motions as an accepted fact, and the people applauding his avowal of the new creed.

Do you ask me what tribes these were, and where their annual gatherings were held, and when? I will tell you. The first was in 1860,

---

[3] At the BAAS meeting at Birmingham in 1865 the General Committee referred to evidence given to the Parliamentary Committee on the Public Schools Bill by scientists such as Huxley, Tyndall, Carpenter, and Hooker which demonstrated 'the zeal and energy with which the cultivators of science continue to remonstrate against the system, which still unhappily prevails in many of our schools, of ignoring the claims of science'. The schools referred to are 'our great public schools'. *Report of the Proceedings at the Birmingham Meeting* (London, 1865), 3.

when Mr. Darwin's derivative theory of species was first brought before the bar of a scientific assembly, and that the British Association at Oxford; and I need not tell those who heard our presiding Sachem's address last Wednesday, that the second was at Nottingham.

Hooker's parable winningly allows his audience to guess their own discomfiture, and so to triumph in some modest measure over it. He represents a convincingly 'uncivilised', or uncooked, cosmogony for his fictitious tribe; their gods eat raw moons. He makes strange—and thereby recognizable—the suppositions of those who opposed evolutionary theory. (He was Darwin's closest scientific co-worker.) He slyly draws out the approximations between the so-called primitive and the advanced intellectual reception of ideas (denial, delay, and then that which has been impossible becomes taken for granted), and he includes a comforting dig at doctors—always useful sacrificial victims in story. The drama of the narrative relies on the observer's absence and return: the process by which minds have changed remains deliberately mysterious. Community is preserved: the whole group within the story now agrees to what it earlier ridiculed.

Hooker *dares* his listeners outside the story, gathered theatrically as they were in Nottingham that afternoon in a mirror image of those described within the tale. He employs the physical parallel between the moot or scientific meeting (or—to put it another way—the discursively self-selected group) to dare his audience to dissent from his narrative moral. The conclusion of his tale affirms the likeness between the behaviour of his listeners and that of the tribe within the story.

Of course, Hooker comes well out of this: tellers of parables usually do. He uses the ethnocentric assumptions of the scientific group against them. The joke consists in applying to the privileged professional assembly, committed to the value of objective truth, a rule-bound analysis derived from another, then new and controversial, subject-field: that of anthropology. Indeed, observers of ritual behaviour might observe that when, at the previous meeting of the BAAS, the anthropologists had sought to establish a separate section devoted to anthropology independent of either geology or geography, they were worsted by the rituals of committee reasoning against change. It was argued that this was the first such request in thirty-four years: to allow it would have others scrambling to follow suit (the floodgates argument); the association at present had seven sections (the magic number argument); they owed a duty to visit smaller cities and towns which could not conveniently house a larger gathering (the pseudo-egalitarian argument)![4]

Hooker represents scientists as a primitive tribe, visited not only by missionaries but by the apparently neutral first-person observer whose position in the story is opaque, or transparent (according to which metaphor for invisibility one prefers and where one stands in the controversy concerning the place of the author in ethnography currently being argued out among writers such as James Clifford and Clifford Geertz).

Hooker's story changes scientists and science into the passive *objects* of observation. It thus denies them their favoured active role, exempt from social analysis, in which they are pursuing, inspecting, and intervening in, a subject nature. The tenor of the story would seem to accord with Feyerabend's proposal in *Against Method* (1975) that 'basic scientific ideas are protected by taboo reactions which are no weaker than are the taboo reactions in so-called primitive societies . . . the similarities between science and myth are indeed astonishing'.[5] Or the observations of the Nobel Prize-winning biologist François Jacob who comments in *The Possible and the Actual* (1982) that, in some respects at least, 'myths and science fulfil a similar function: they both provide human beings with a representation of the world and of the forces that are supposed to govern it. They both fix the limits of what is considered as possible.'[6] Hooker's story suggests that the taboos concerning the possible can finally be broached by revolutions in belief; and in this he seems in agreement, rather, with Thomas Kuhn's paradigm-shift theory.[7]

But Hooker is also a man of his time. That is revealed in the linchpin of the narrative: he takes it for granted that the missionaries are right! The apparent cultural relativism of his tale nevertheless relies upon a shared assumption of abiding incongruity between uncivilized and civilized man. The indigenous inhabitants are wrong and must be educated by particularly advanced

---

[4] Ibid. 5.

[5] Paul Feyerabend, *Against Method* (London, 1975), 298.

[6] François Jacob, *The Possible and the Actual* (New York, 1982), 9.

[7] Thomas Kuhn, *The Structure of Scientific Revolutions*, 2nd edn. (Chicago, 1970).

representatives of advanced races. The structure of his story, in fact, relies on evolutionary assumptions (as did many Victorian anthropologists). Thus it is, covertly, a self-proving construct. Its over-narrative takes for granted that different races are positioned on an ascending developmental scale. Its concealed, anagogic topic is the reception of evolutionary theory. The two levels coincide.

Furthermore, the favoured incomers (the scientists who got it right) have priestly status. That status, for scientists and for creative writers, was one of the burdens that Victorian culture laid on the shoulders of intellectuals. The abrasion between the discourses of theology and of science, and the attempt to reconcile or claim each other's terms, made for a troubled alliance between religious and secular levels of description. Matthew Arnold argued that literature was now obliged to take on the emotional and intellectual tasks of religion. Huxley claimed the transformation of those tasks for science. Tennyson sought to voice communal suffering and communal hope out of painfully private experience and deep introspection; George Eliot saw the artist's task as essentially being to enlarge our sympathies. In scientific writing of the time, particularly that addressed to a broader audience but including many articles and scientific papers in journals such as *Nature* and, a little later, *Mind*, we can track the same straining towards the mission of interpreting for the whole community. For example, in Huxley's only faintly ironic title *Lay Sermons*; in Clerk Maxwell's 1863 essay on molecules, with its conclusion that the 'ineffaceable characters impressed' on molecules (their endurance, integrity, and 'faith') teach the congruity between our noblest human attributes and 'the image of Him Who in the beginning created . . . the materials of which heaven and earth consist'. We see it also in the astronomer Richard Proctor's essay 'The Past and Future of the Earth'; or in the mathematician W. K. Clifford's (to our ears) strangely titled essay, 'Cosmic Emotion'.[8] Clifford, in his essay 'The Aims of Scientific Thought', says that he aims to 'bridge over' the divide between scientists and others in order that 'this so-called outer world may see in the work of science only the

[8] W. K. Clifford, *Lectures and Essays*, ed. Leslie Stephens and Frederick Pollock, 2 vols. (London, 1901), i. 140.

putting in evidence of all that is excellent in its own work,—may feel that the kingdom of science is within it'. The unselfconscious appropriation and re-casting of the biblical saying that the kingdom of God is within us makes it clear that some Victorian scientific writers wished to claim an almost complete congruity between scientific and religious sentiments. And Jim Moore has shown, in more sociological terms, the degree to which Charles Darwin took on the role of squarson, a Victorian condensation of the roles of squire and parson.[9]

When we analyse the extent and kinds of writing undertaken by Victorian scientists we should not, equally with such ideological incentives, disregard the incentive of money. Unless Victorian scientists had independent means, like Darwin, or a university professorship, like Clerk Maxwell, they were extremely underfunded. Workers like Forbes and Tyndall and Proctor, to say nothing of Huxley, earned much of their income, and the funding for their research, from high journalism and the lecture-circuit. They earned money by popularizing, and earned reputation by technical writing—but the two modes were not severely separated. In the configuration of Victorian scientific writing we can see the forces of popular reception at work: John Tyndall, in particular, spent much energy in his later years fighting the issue of religious faith and materialism in the generalist journals, and resting his agnostic argument on the meta-religious nobility of materialism.[10]

Victorian intellectual ideals set up a tension between, on the one hand, intellectual synthesis, demonstrated at its most extensive in Herbert Spencer's many-volumed *Synthetic Philosophy*, and, on the other, classificatory systems. Taxonomy claims to include everything, but does so by articulating separate groups; synthesis equally claims to include everything, but by emphasizing relations and connections. These diverse ideals set up, equally, tensions between the ethical drive towards open communication and the desire for closed communities of adepts. The wonderful inclusiveness of generalist journals at that time, from the *Literary Gazette and Journal of Belles Lettres, Science, and Art*, to the *Contemporary Review* and the *Nineteenth Century*,

---

[9] James Moore, *The Post-Darwinian Controversies* (Cambridge, 1979).
[10] See the essays collected in his *Fragments of Science: A Series of Detached Essays, Addresses, and Reviews*, 2 vols. (Longmans, London, 1899).

meant that philosophers, lawyers, evolutionary theorists, politicians, astronomers, physicists, novelists, theologians, poets, and language theorists all appeared alongside each other, more often with the effect of bricolage than synthesis, true enough. But their lying alongside on the page encouraged the reader to infer connections between their activities by the simple scan of the eye and by the simultaneous availability of diverse ideas.

This availability tended towards (and perhaps relied for comfort on) the expectation that it would yet be possible to uncover general laws. Such laws would stabilize all knowledge. The accessibility of widely diverse kinds of knowledge fostered the belief that language is held in common. The readerly community of the educated mid-nineteenth century in Britain assumed that it could rely on gaining access to whatever knowledge was current even within specialist groups. It was consequently often taken for granted that words retain the same signification across widely divergent fields. Yet some Victorian writers played knowingly on such expectations, particularly in the form of parable, as in John Ruskin's practical title, *Notes on the Construction of Sheepfolds*, of which the *Literary Gazette* plaintively remarks:

If any country gentleman has ordered this work to be sent down from town in his next monthly literary packet, he will find he has made a mistake, which, if the book were larger, would put him not a little out of temper. It is of ecclesiastical, not of agricultural, sheepfolds that Mr. Ruskin treats.[11]

Ethics and technology here play hide and seek in language.

Scientists needed a language with (to quote Huxley) 'a definite and constant signification'.[12] They were actively composing professional groups and moving into professional discursive practices. In the period from 1850 to 1880 new institutional bases were being formed, but the private laboratory and the independent scientific worker were not yet things of the past. The pressure was between the need to delimit terms and the desire to dislimn boundaries between enquiries. That desire to cross disciplinary bounds was itself part of the insistence on kinship in evolutionary thought.

[11] No. 1,783 (Mar. 1851), 219.
[12] Thomas Henry Huxley, *Lay Sermons, Addresses and Reviews* (London, 1903), 119.

Scientific writers were immersed in the liberal language of the tribe (liberal in the sense of being available to anyone educated to a standard sufficient to read the general journals of the time). Yet scientists needed to formulate their own stable professional dialects with which to exchange agreed meanings, and to confine and hold steady those meanings, within the professional group. By that means they would be able to change the level of description so as to engage with new theoretical and technical questions. They would also limit the range of possible interpretation, and, it was their hope, misinterpretation. Technical language, or jargon, excludes the inexpert, with their tendency to multiply and destabilize the significations of specific terms. Such destabilizing may be the source of new insights for a broader cultural group, but it is always disconcerting for the generative group of co-workers.[13]

As Huxley figured it, the alternative to being the interpreter is to be powerless. Like Hooker, he uses the parable story of primitive ignorance; that ignorance is, in Huxley's example, shown to be dwelling within 'many of the best minds of these days'. In his essay 'The Physical Basis of Mind' he wrote:

They watch what they conceive to be the progress of materialism, in such fear and powerless anger as a savage feels, when, during an eclipse, the great shadow creeps over the face of the sun. The advancing tide of matter threatens to drown their souls; the tightening grasp of law impedes their freedom.[14]

The continuity between savage and modern thinker is here also a reinforcement of the argument that Huxley is mounting in the essay for the physical basis of all life, with its insistence on continuity between all forms of life. He describes 'the community of faculty' reaching from lichen to botanist. But at the same time his parable-metaphor of the savage and the eclipse assumes a developmental and progressive organization, in which the modern thinker is to feel shame at discovering an identity with past primitive forms of thought as if a necessary distance from the primitive has been forgone. A telling advantage of development

---

[13] This argument is developed more fully in my 'Translation or Transformation? Relations of Literature and Science', *Notes and Records of the Royal Society* (Jan. 1990); repr. as Ch. 8, above.

[14] *Lay Sermons*, 123.

theory for those who sought authority was that it provided a temporal distance from which to observe. Its rhetoric could cast a powerful glance backwards over the stages by which western man has come into his self-designated high position among the forms of life. This temporal hierarchy countered the emphasis in the same theory on kinship and connection, and it preserved a privileged place for the observer. Occurring late in time, such observation was itself held to be the crowning outcome of development.[15]

Huxley's own position on the continuity between species and between different life-forms did not prevent him from figuring blacks and women as debarred by nature's old Salic law from 'the highest places in civilization'. Indeed, he argued that it was safe to give every opportunity to women and 'other races' since they would never be able to challenge the inherent superiority of European manhood or—save in the rarest of exceptional cases—reach positions of high creativity or authority. Giving them freedom was good for the psychic health of men, and carried very little risk of loss of privilege.[16] And when Lyell appealed to him, by means of yet another parable, to favour the admission of women to the Geological Society in 1860, he opposed the plan on the grounds that:

five-sixths of women will stop in the doll stage of evolution to be the stronghold of parsondom, the drag on civilization, the degradation of every important pursuit with which they mix themselves—'intrigues' in politics, and 'friponnes' in science. If my claws and beak are good for anything they shall be kept from hindering the progress of any science I have to do with.[17]

Huxley is willing—in language at least—to take on the female role, of harpy, in order to keep the women out. He wants to preserve the groups of scientific adepts intact, unobserved and not infiltrated by outsiders. We may note here a paradox which is also observed in *Gentleman of Science*, though in a different

[15] One example among many of this attitude is C. S. Wake, 'The Psychological Unity of Mankind', *Memoirs Read Before the Anthropological Society of London 1867–9*, vol. 3 (London, 1870), 134–47.
[16] Huxley, 'Emancipation—Black and White', *Lay Sermons*, 17–23.
[17] Leonard Huxley, *Life and Letters of Thomas Henry Huxley*, 2 vols. (London, 1900), i. 212.

context.[18] Observing is a strong and objective activity when undertaken by professional men, but it seems that strength and objectivity may be undermined by the presence of other, un-initiated observers, whether they be workers or women. One can see this in the marginal position of the lady associates at the BAAS and the embarrassments of the special meeting laid on at Nottingham for working-men.[19]

In both cases, these outgroups are admitted on sufferance, in particular circumstances, as a local privilege—and to listen, not to comment. The reaching out of the professionals towards these others is thus also a dramatization of their exclusion. Workers and women are cast as peripheral, powerless. Yet their scrutiny of scientific practice or scientific discourse is felt as disturbing. In the passages above, that scrutiny is represented as an uncom-prehending gaze, either feckless or menacing.

The menace of that scrutiny was experienced by scientists partly as a result of the very openness of scientific discourse at the time: their terms were available for misprision or misappro-priation. The overt terms that Victorian scientists shared with other social groups formed a paradox for the professionalizing workers, who were aware of the highly specialist context of construal within which their apparently liberal utterances were functioning.

The language available alike to nineteenth-century creative writers and scientists had been forged out of past literature, the Bible, philosophy, natural theology. In our own time writers on discourse have emphasized the heterogeneity of dialects with-in the apparently common tongue, the way in which we can never quite securely translate from one professional or social group to another the intensity, or vacuity, of terms. Terms may be precise and full in one domain, meagre in another: dynamic would be a simple example. (When *Daniel Deronda* first appeared Gwendolen's 'dynamic glance' was criticized as being an over-scientific and abstruse description.)

---

[18] Jack Morrell and Arnold Thackray, *Gentlemen of Science: Early Years of the British Association for the Advancement of Science* (Oxford, 1981).

[19] 'The British Association and the Working Classes', *Report of the BAAS* (Nottingham, 1866), 299–300. The meeting was delayed, so that 'some were heard who were going away use the word "insult" ' and there were, more generally, 'muttered complaints . . . that the great mass of the people were shut out from the advantages of the visit of the Association'.

Words are impressed with the shared assumptions, with the things not said of each group, just as much as they are with their shared assertions. Just as we inhabit continuously conflicting epistemologies, so none of us is a member of one social and linguistic group only. We experience every day, and we condense that experience in speaking and listening, as co-workers, shoppers, friends, researchers, women or men, perhaps parents, lovers, political activists or quietists, certainly members willy-nilly of local, national and global communities at a particular moment in historical time. Some words transfer across all these zones: terms of kinship, commerce, measurement, conflict. The terms themselves shift scale and energy as they go.

Thomas Carlyle, writing out of the Scottish experience of his upbringing and the German experience of his reading, had challenged his own time by a blast against established categories of knowledge and language in his first masterpiece *Sartor Resartus*. The opening sentence runs: 'Considering our present advanced state of culture, and how the Torch of Science has now been brandished and borne about, with more or less effect of five-thousand years, and upwards'; it ends eight lines further on with surprise that 'nothing of a fundamental character . . . has been written about clothes.' Science is then praised and dismissed:

Man's whole life and environment have been laid open and elucidated; scarcely a fragment or fibre of his Soul, Body, and Possessions, but has been probed, dissected, distilled, desiccated and scientifically decomposed . . . every cellular, vascular, muscular Tissue glories in its Lawrences, Majendies, Bichats.[20]

Key-words then begin to flee across categories: 'tissue', as body, clothing, argument; property, as possession and characteristics; fact, as stable observation and act accomplished. Some odd category errors are unmasked: 'In all speculations they have tacitly figured man as a Clothed Animal; whereas he is by nature a Naked Animal.'

Metaphor, translation, chiasmus, heterogeneity of reference: such are the modes by whose means Carlyle transports the reader from the fixed grid of here and now. He makes metaphors

[20] Thomas Carlyle, *Collected Works*, Library Edition (London, 1869–70), *Sartor Resartus*, 4.

manifest. He insists on the corporeal, on language as producing physical affects: fear, excitement, bodily recognition of past persons. (In his work on fantasy, Todorov has characterized its method as prolonging the moment of hesitation between interpretations and has reminded us that the removal or varying of categorical boundaries itself 'represents an experience of limits'.) Carlyle was greeted by his contemporaries as a philosopher and a historian, but his method is never analytical. His enterprise was a formative force in the Victorian search for synthesis and (apparently contradictorily) for taxonomic refinement.[21]

Carlyle was much cited and read by scientists, as well as by the fiction writers, politicians, and activist workers of his time. We know from reading Darwin's notebooks, for example, that Darwin read Carlyle's works as they came out, with strong enthusiasm and frequent exasperation. Fiona Erskine has recently further demonstrated the extent of the friendship between them during Darwin's years in London.[22] Carlyle's writing brought (and brings) home to the reader the extent to which the displacement of a term from its accustomed context may transform our secure inhabitant's gaze into that of the estranged observer. His bravura with language fascinated and often repelled his contemporaries; but before we start conceiving him as a contemporary of our own, it is necessary to note that he never doubted that there was a hierarchy of value among terms, nor did he dislodge the idea of language as finally unitary, and God-given.

If we turn from his work to that of recent discourse-theorists we begin to understand better, I think, some of the ways in which Victorian linguistic ideals affected the writing of science as much as of literature. In 1981, in 'Rhizome', Deleuze and Guattari articulated the problem of communality of understanding thus: 'there is no language in itself, nor any universality of language, but a concourse of dialects, patois, slangs, special languages. There exists no ideal "competent" speaker-hearer of language any more than there exists a homogenous linguistic com-

[21] Tzvetan Todorov, *The Fantastic: A Structural Approach to a Literary Genre* (Ithaca, NY, 1975), 77, 93. See also Philip Rosenberg, *The Seventh Hero: Thomas Carlyle and the Theory of Radical Activism* (Cambridge, Mass., 1974), and for a development of this section of the argument: 'Carlylean Transports' in my *Arguing with the Past: Essays in Narrative from Woolf to Sidney* (London, 1989).

[22] Fiona Erskine, 'Darwin in London', unpublished Ph.D thesis, Open University, 1988.

munity.'[23] They continue: 'There is no mother-tongue, but a seizure of power by a dominant tongue within a political multiplicity.' (The writing here, it will be noted, harbours the glamorous violence it uncovers. The takeover bid, the military coup, disguises its power as maternal and originary: Deleuze's assertion carries the same threatening force.) The image of the concourse of dialects oversimplifies matters, for dialects do not only assemble but overlap, sometimes amicably, sometimes with cross-set tensions.

The analysis of discourse I have just quoted would, I believe, have been quite unfamiliar, and not very useful, to Victorian writers. That was so even for those like Carlyle who relished the shiftiness of discursive categories and the misfits of implication when translating from one language to another. To the Victorians, whether preoccupied with science or literature or politics, the concept of the mother-tongue was still crucial. In the case of English, that maternal language was represented as the English of past literature above all. English literature was then seen as that which binds up the ideal of English nationhood and history.

For evolutionary studies, philology was treated as an arm of genetics; in cultural studies regional writers, particularly the Dorsetshire poet and language-theorist William Barnes, set out to winnow English from its foreign elements and retrieve a folk-tongue, conceived as forthright, egalitarian, and poetic. We can see the effects of Barnes's work in the writing of the mathematician W. K. Clifford, who translates 'the doctrine of the nature of human knowledge, *Erkenntnis-theorie*', as 'Ken-lore' and writes of co-operation as 'bandwork' (*Cosmic Emotion*, 270, 293). Clifford also illustrates the action of natural selection by quoting Swinburne's 'Songs before Sunrise'—and was not unusual among Victorian scientists in such an appropriation of literary texts.[24]

Victorian middle- and upper-class writing, however, was formed not only by the mother-tongue alone but by a parental diad: the father-tongue shaped the dominant educational ideology. By this I mean that the classical languages played a central role in the education system. This system was reserved almost

[23] Giles Deleuze and F. Guattari, 'Rhizome', *Ideology and Consciousness*, vol. 8 (1981), 49–71.
[24] Clifford, *Lectures and Essays*, ii. 270, 293.

entirely for boys and taught to them entirely by men. Science was peripheral to the educational programme (as were women), but most scientists of the time had first been trained within its confines (as women had not). So the practice of Victorian scientists of citing classical writers in their work, as Lyell does Ovid, for example, serves several functions, some social, some illustrative, some argumentative. First, such reference breathes effortless (and perhaps helpless) class and gender claims: it makes an appeal to the cohesion of those who have shared an education. Further, classical allusion establishes the accretive and benign power of scientific enquiry, emphasizing its continuity with the past. Classical reference and quotation serve to place the current scientific text close to the ancient philosophers and poets, then still at the authoritative centre of written culture. Such cross-reference presents not only a professional but a human spaciousness, and it reinforces the observing role of the writer, who can appraise relations across time. Lyell, indeed, held that the power to re-imagine the remote past was the characterizing property of human reason. Classical reference, as he employs it, forms a bridge back towards the earliest reaches of human civilization.

But the relations of Victorian scientific writers to past literature were not tactical or social only. The direct pleasures of reading, of a well-stored memory, are evident everywhere. Literature, especially English literature, offered also, as I have suggested elsewhere of Darwin's reading, *stories* by whose means to imagine the world, and organizations which potentiated fresh relations.

Poetry offered particular formal resources to think with. Poetry works by cross-setting a considerable number of systems in simultaneity (natural speech word order, metric units, line units, grammatical units, cursive syntax—all play across each other). By means of metre in particular, and sometimes by rhyme, the poet sets up multiple relations between ideas in a style closer to the form of theorems than of prose. And if this sounds remote from the business of science consider the example of John Tyndall, whose work on radiation had, he suggested, been enhanced by an unusually developed mental awareness of relations in space, trained by his early reading of Milton's epic of cosmic and syntactic spaces, *Paradise Lost*:

English grammar was the most important discipline of my boyhood. The piercing through the involved and inverted sentences of Paradise Lost, the linking of the verb to its often distant nominative, of the relative to its transitive verb, of the preposition to the noun or pronoun which it governed, the study of variations in mood or tense, the transpositions often necessary to bring out the true grammatical structure of a sentence, all this was to my young mind a discipline of the highest value, and a source of unflagging delight.[25]

Milton's language clenched mother-tongue and father-tongue together into an extraordinary energy. Within his work words constantly oscillate between their Latin and their English significations, unsettling and expanding the scope of language to make room for descriptions of the universe since its formation out of chaos. It is not surprising that the ambitiousness and mastery of his epic should have drawn those seeking to gain a new centrality for the scientific imagination. It is to Milton's work that Tyndall turns in his essay on the use of the scientific imagination: 'the study of natural sciences goes hand in hand with the culture of the imagination . . . We have been picturing atoms and molecules and vibrations and waves which eye has never seen nor ear heard, and which can only be discerned by the exercise of imagination.'[26]

Milton, Wordsworth, and to a surprisingly lesser extent, Shakespeare: these are the three poets most frequently quoted in Victorian scientific writing. Among contemporaries, scientific writers invoke Walt Whitman, Browning, Swinburne—but above all, and by far the most frequently, Tennyson. Tennyson was, Huxley held, the 'first poet since Lucretius . . . who has taken the trouble to understand the work and tendency of the men of science'. Huxley even asserted that 'the insight into scientific method shown in Tennyson's In Memoriam' was 'quite equal to that of the greatest experts' (if Wilfrid Ward's reminiscences are to be believed).[27]

Huxley wrote an ode on the death of Tennyson which was published in the *Nineteenth Century* alongside contributions from

[25] For further discussion of this passage see my 'Designing and Describing: A Problem in the Language of Description', in *One Culture: Essays in Science and Literature*, ed. George Levine (Madison, Wisc., 1988).

[26] John Tyndall, 'On the Scientific Uses of the Imagination', *Fragments of Science: A Series of Detached Essays, Addresses and Reviews*, 2 vols. (London, 1899), ii. 202.

[27] Quoted in *Life and Letters of Thomas Henry Huxley*, ii. 337.

other intellectuals such as Frederic W. H. Myers, F. T. Palgrave of *The Golden Treasury*, James Knowles, philosopher and editor of the *Nineteenth Century*, and the poet Aubrey de Vere. The first verse, spoken in the voice of Westminster Abbey, runs:

> Bring me my dead!
> To me that have grown,
> Stone laid upon stone,
> As the stormy brood
> Of English blood
> Has waxed and spread
> And filled the world,
> With sails unfurled.
> With men that may not lie;
>   With thoughts that cannot die.

Huxley was pleased that all the words in his poem were understandable by working-men; he did not comment on its imperialism.[28]

Tennyson was a member of the Royal Society, among his other honours, and seems to have been adopted by the scientific community as a confrère, but also as one who voiced underlying troubles. Such troubles could thus be set a little apart and veiled by poetic form while yet being represented within scientific prose. Just as T. S. Eliot's 'This is the way the world ends Not with a bang but a whimper' has come to have a clichéd and yet profound presence in our own broad culture, so

> An infant crying in the night:
> An infant crying for the light:
> And with no language but a cry

appears in scientific, as well as other, settings. It becomes an accepted description of the anxiety in Victorian experience and the inadequacy of language to cope with the new understanding, evolutionary and thermodynamic, of the universe.[29]

---

[28] *The Nineteenth Century*, 32 (1892), 831–44.

[29] *The Poems of Tennyson*, ed. Christopher Ricks (London, 1969), 909. Cf. the Presidential Address to the 1866 BAAS Biology section, p. 69: 'We are probing into the very deepest recesses of nature, and inquiring into her closest secrets. We feel ourselves here almost to be

> Children crying in the darkness,
> Children crying for the light,
> And with no language but a cry.'

Tennyson's plangent lines express an unexpectedly tremulous self-image: no triumphalism here. The expanding of individual death into the idea of the death of whole species in the concept of extinction, as well as the idea of the ebbing of the sun's energy, make for an undertow of sadness in Victorian thought, a current that is constantly and determinedly countered by an insistent coupling of development with progress. Tennyson's great poem of bereavement, *In Memoriam*, condenses personal grief with a profound generalization of that grief as natural order:

> 'So careful of the type?' but no.
> From scarped cliff and quarried stone
> She cries, 'A thousand types are gone:
> I care for nothing, all shall go . . .'[30]

Incorporating poetic elements in scientific writing could give voice in communal form to the underlying affective problems with which Victorian scientists were engaged, yet from which they needed to sustain some distance. But poetry could not undertake all the functions of scientific language, nor could scientific writing encompass the same range of problems as literature. The fragmented and intermittent nature of literary allusion is an apt reminder that the two forms of writing cannot cohere absolutely. Yet the reverberation of the unwritten in such allusion, the reminiscence of other meanings, other contexts, forms a serious bond with the reader who is assumed to respond through full, foreknown reading to the isolated, telling fragment.

Literary allusion does not by any means always function as interruption or interjection in Victorian scientific prose. Sometimes it is seamed apparently effortlessly into the flow of argument. James Clerk Maxwell's Rede Lecture on the telephone, for example, quotes Tennyson's 'The Princess', and comments that 'the line of force is more like one of Milton's spirits, which cannot

> In their liquid texture mortal wound
> Receive, no more than can the fluid air.'

He praises the application of Bell's system to the education of the deaf and dumb by changing the context of Samson's affliction: 'I

[30] *Tennyson*, 911.

cannot conceive a nobler application of the scientific analysis of speech, than that by which it enables those to whom all sound is

> expunged and rased
> And wisdom at one entrance quite shut out

not only to speak themselves, but to read by sight what other people are saying.'[31] Milton matches the sinew of Maxwell's prose. Maxwell is the canniest and most articulate analyst of the linguistic problems of the scientist seeking to address an audience beyond his immediate peers.[32] Maxwell's own enterprise is underpinned by his religious confidence. Unlike many of his contemporaries, he never doubts the benign disposition of final authority. In his belief, God organized a world whose ultimate physical characteristics bear witness to a sustaining order. The business of the scientist is to manifest that order in his work. To do so it is necessary, in Maxwell's view, to formulate a style capable of stable communication.

So, he praises Rankine, who developed

a singular power of bringing the most difficult investigations within the range of elementary methods. In his earlier papers, indeed, he appears as if battling with chaos, as he swims, or sinks, or wades, or creeps, or flies,

> 'And through the palpable obscure finds out
> His uncouth way;'

but he soon begins to pave a broad and beaten way over the dark abyss, and his latest writings shew a power of bridging over the difficulties of science.[33]

That this is the description of Satan's malign journey to tempt Adam and Eve gives Maxwell no ostensible qualms. He excises the context, save for a tremor of teasing inappropriateness that gives zest to the compliment. He concentrates on 'bridging over the difficulties of science'. Perhaps, though, there is preserved in the allusion a sense of the chaotic and the darkened, of all that

---

[31] *Scientific Papers of James Clerk Maxwell*, ed. W. D. Niven, 2 vols. (Cambridge, 1890), ii. 748, 752.

[32] Not only his scientific papers but his correspondence illustrate his alertness to problems of language. See Lewis Campbell and William Garnett, *The Life of James Clerk Maxwell with a Selection from his Correspondence and Occasional Writings and a Sketch of his Contributions to Science* (London, 1882).

[33] *Scientific Papers*, ii. 663.

remains uncontrolled and unknown, on either side the 'broad and beaten way' of contemporary knowledge. The line he first cites appears within the following passage:

> With heads, hands, wings, or feet pursues his way,
> And swims or sinks, or wades, or creeps, or flies:
> At length a universal hubbub wild
> Of stunning sounds and voices all confus'd
> Borne through the hollow dark assaults his ear
> With loudest vehemence.[34]

The obliterated lines give voice to the discursive cacophony in the realm of Chaos and Night, those forces that Milton calls the 'Ancestors of Nature'. These 'sounds and voices' form a menacing undertext in Maxwell's account of the communicative struggles of scientists. They also presage, in another tongue, recent chaos theory to which Maxwell's work on entropy and information would, in the afterlife of knowledge, make its unwilled contribution. Parable and allusion not only worked as tactic and resource in Victorian scientific writing. They could also harbour anxieties and insights that tapped the further implications of current scientific theories, beyond the range for which experiment could vouch.

[34] John Milton, *Paradise Lost*, ii. 949–54.

III

Victorian Physics and Futures

10

'The Death of the Sun': Victorian Solar Physics and Solar Myth

Many Victorians, including Darwin himself, were disturbed by the apparent contradiction between the 'progressive' implications of evolutionary theory and the emphasis in the physics of Helmholtz and Thomson on the ageing of the sun, which would eventually make the world too cold for life.[1] Physics, mythography, and the ordinary fear of death converged in late-nineteenth-century imaginations. Such condensations form most readily at a point of contradiction. In this essay I shall examine some of the attempts made to moralize the conclusions and bring under control the anxieties generated by early solar physics. The contradictions between evolutionary ideas of sustained development and physicists' theories of the dissipation of energy, as well as the more specific debate between them concerning the age of the earth, gave urgent propinquity in Victorian thinking to apparently disassociated ideas. This activity is first particularly notable in the 1870s. John Tyndall, in 'The Scientific Use of the Imagination' (1870), connects 'Natural Evolution' with the sun as the source of all consequent energy:[2]

For what are the core and essence of this hypothesis? Strip it naked and you stand face to face with the notion that not alone the more ignoble

---

[1] Darwin concludes *The Origin of Species* by emphasizing the stability of cosmic conditions equally with the paradoxical production of ever higher and more various forms from adversity: 'Thus, from the war of nature, from famine and death, the most exalted object which we are capable of conceiving, namely, the production of the higher animals, directly follows. There is a grandeur in this view of life, with its several powers, having been originally breathed by the Creator into a few forms or into one; and that, whilst this planet has gone cycling on according to the fixed law of gravity, from so simple a beginning endless forms most beautiful and most wonderful have been, and are being evolved'. The reference to the creator is not in the first or some later editions. I quote from Charles Darwin, *The Origin of Species* (London, 1872), 420.

[2] John Tyndall, 'The Scientific Use of the Imagination', in *Uses and Limits of the Imagination in Science* (London, 1870), 47.

forms of the horse and lion, not alone the exquisite and wonderful mechanism of the human body, but that the human mind itself—emotion, intellect, will, and all their phenomena—were once latent in a fiery cloud . . . But the hypothesis would probably go even further than this. Many who hold it would probably assent to the position that at the present moment all our philosophy, all our poetry, all our science, and all our art—Plato, Shakespeare, Newton, and Raphael—are potential in the fires of the sun. We long to learn something of our origin. If the Evolution hypothesis be correct, even this unsatisfied yearning must have come to us across the ages which separate the unconscious primeval mist from the consciousness of to-day.

In 1876 Darwin wrote in the *Autobiography* he prepared for his family of his dismay at the view now held by most physicists, namely that the sun with all the planets will in time grow too cold for life.[3]

Believing as I do that man in the distant future will be a far more perfect creature than he now is, it is an intolerable thought that he and all other sentient beings are doomed to complete annihilation after such long-continued slow progress. To those who fully admit the immortality of the human soul, the destruction of our world will not appear so dreadful.

But Darwin did not count himself among such religious believers.

In this argument I shall conclude by considering speculatively some of the reasons for the popularity of Darwin's last published work, *The Formation of Vegetable Mould through the Action of Worms, With Observations on their Habits* (1881): 'This is a subject of but small importance; and I know not whether it will interest any readers, but it has interested me,' Darwin wrote shortly before its publication.[4] Yet between November 1881 and February 1884 8,500 copies were sold and it went on outselling all his other works. What were the intellectual and emotional needs which contributed to its enthusiastic reception? The processes of interpretation in a culture are the results of multiple needs and anxieties—and so, we may agree at the outset, is the later process of reinterpretation and pattern-seeing in which I am here engaged as well. I shall return to this problem of methodo-

---

[3] *Autobiographies of Charles Darwin and Thomas Henry Huxley*, ed. G. de Beer (London, 1974), 153-4.

[4] *Charles Darwin: His Life Told in an Autobiographical Chapter and in a Selected Series of his Published Letters*, ed. Francis Darwin (London, 1892), 52.

logy and insight later in my argument: suffice it to say here that we are not exempt from the instability of interpretation, nor from its blindness to its own sources.[5] Let us first look in more detail at the specific controversy between the geologists and the physicists which made physical theory a talking-point in the 1860s and 1870s.

During the 1860s the findings of William Thomson, later Lord Kelvin, and of Charles Darwin came directly into conflict, though this was only the most public phase of disagreements between geologists and physicists over the preceding thirty years. The major argument was about the age of the earth and the age of the sun. Darwin and Lyell's theories demanded an immense prolongation of the age of the earth in order for evolutionary process to have taken place according to the mechanism (natural selection) and in the manner (uniformitarianism) that they argued. If Thomson's ageing of the sun according to his physical calculations of the rate of dissipation of energy from the sun's source were correct, there could not have been sufficient time for Darwinian evolutionary processes to have taken place. Thomson believed the sun to be cooling without renewal of its energy. In his article in *Macmillan's Magazine* on 'The Age of the Sun's Heat', which made his ideas available to a wide public, Thomson particularly attacked Darwin's calculations of the time necessary for the geological 'denudation of the Weald'.[6]

We may therefore consider it is rendered highly probable that the sun's specific heat is more than ten times, and less than 10,000 times, that of liquid water. From this it would follow with certainty that this temperature sinks 100 per cent in some time from 700 years to 700,000 years.

What then are we to think of such geological estimates as 300,000,000 years for 'the denudation of the Weald'? Whether it is more probable that the physical conditions of the sun's matter differ 1,000 times more than dynamics compel us to suppose they differ from those of matter in our laboratories; or that a stormy sea, with possible channel tides of extreme violence, should encroach on a chalk cliff 1,000 times more rapidly than Mr. Darwin's estimate of one inch per century? . . . It seems, therefore, on the whole most probable that the

[5] For discussion of related issues, see Paul de Man, *Blindness and Insight: Essays in the Rhetoric of Contemporary Criticism* (New York, 1971).

[6] William Thomson, 'On the Age of the Sun's Heat', *Macmillan's Magazine*, 5 (Mar. 1862), 388–93, 391–2, 393. For a full discussion of Thomson's career and views, see Joe D. Burchfield, *Lord Kelvin and the Age of the Earth* (London, 1975).

sun has not illuminated the earth for 100,000,000 years and almost certain that he has not done so for 500,000,000 years.

The sun was thought to have a store of heat which it gradually gives out. How long can this store last? How long has it already lasted? Helmholtz suggested that the source of sun's heat was not combustion (of oxygen and hydrogen) but contraction. In 'Observations on the Sun's Store of Force' (1854) Helmholtz wrote:

If the mass of the sun had been once diffused in cosmical space, and had then been condensed—that is, had fallen together under the influence of celestial gravity—if then the resultant motion had been destroyed by friction and impact, with the production of heat, the new world produced by such condensation must have acquired a store of heat not only of considerable, but even of colossal, magnitude . . .

He is here considering the problem of an age for the sun greater than known resources could account for:

. . . We may, therefore, assume with great probability that the sun will still continue in its condensation, even if it only attained the density of the earth—though it will probably become far denser in the interior owing to the enormous pressure—this would develop fresh quantities of heat, which would be sufficient to maintain for an additional 17,000,000 of years the same intensity of sunshine as that which is now the source of all terrestrial life.

He offers reassurance: combustion 'would be sufficient to keep up the radiation of heat from the sun for 3021 years. That, it is true, is a long time, but even profane history teaches us that the sun has lighted and warmed us for 3000 years, and geology puts it beyond doubt that this period must be extended to millions of years.'[7]

Helmholtz calls on evidence from geology as his *starting-point* in the search for an extended source of the sun's heat. Thomson, on the other hand, prefers swingeingly to cut back the allowance of time demanded by geology and to use this cutback incidentally to undermine evolutionary theory. In his article 'On a Universal Tendency in Nature to the Dissipation of Mechanical Energy' (1852), Thomson concludes that there is 'at present in the material world a universal tendency to the dissipation of

7 Collected in Hermann Helmholtz, *Popular Scientific Lectures*, trans. E. Atkinson (London, 1872), ii. 312–25, and extracted in A. J. Meadows (ed.), *Early Solar Physics* (Oxford, 1966), 99–102.

mechanical energy', and that 'most probably the sun was sensibly hotter a million years ago than he is now'.[8] Hence, he argues, geological speculations assuming somewhat greater extremes of heat, more violent storms and floods, more luxuriant vegetation, and hardier and coarse-grained plants and animals in remote antiquity are more probable than those of the extreme quietist or 'uniformitarian' school.

Darwin was disturbed by Thomson's attack on his geologically based time-scale. In the second edition of *The Origin* he responded to the anonymous review in *Saturday Review* which questioned his calculation of denudation of the Weald—that same matter taken up by Thomson in his 1862 *Macmillan's* article.[9] Darwin wrote repeatedly about his trouble with Thomson's views: 'Thomson's views on the recent age of the world have been for some time one of my sorest troubles'.[10]

In *Myths and Marvels of Astronomy* the astronomer Richard Proctor opens his chapter on 'Suns in Flames' thus:[11]

In November 1876 news arrived of a catastrophe, the effects of which must in all probability have been disastrous, not to a district, or a country, or a continent, or even a world, but to a whole system of worlds. The catastrophe happened many years ago—probably at least a hundred—yet the messenger who brought the news had not been idle on his way, but has sped along at a rate which would suffice to circle the earth eight times in the course of a second. That messenger has had, however, to traverse millions of millions of miles, and only reached our earth November 1876. The news he brought was that a sun like ours was in conflagration.

After an account of the present conflagration and of past observations Proctor ends the chapter on an upbeat, assuring his readers that our sun is likely to persist yet awhile: '. . . we may

---

[8] William Thomson, 'On a Universal Tendency in Nature to the Dissipation of Mechanical Energy', *Philosophical Magazine*, 4 (1852), 304–6, 306.

[9] The question was first raised by John Phillips in *Life on Earth: Its Origins and Succession* (London, 1860). James Croll, the author of *On Geological Time* (London, 1868) and *Climate and Time* (London, 1875), supported Darwin.

[10] *Alfred Russel Wallace: Letters and Reminiscences*, ed. J. Marchant (London, 1916), i. 242.

[11] R. A. Proctor, *Myths and Marvels of Astronomy*, new edn. (London, 1896), 160, 190. Proctor, one of the most productive of scientific journalists and a respected astronomer in his own right, published a number of volumes which took up the ethical and imaginative problems raised by scientific knowledge, for example, *Our Place Among Infinities* (London, 1875).

fairly infer a very high degree of probability in favour of the belief that, for many ages still to come, the sun will continue steadily to discharge his duties as fire, light, and life of the solar system.' But the doubt has been raised and was raised repeatedly in this period.

Max Müller was the most influential of Victorian mythographers; his work on language and on myth signification dominated interpretation before Frazer and Freud. In *Lectures on the Origin and Growth of Religion* (1878) Müller cites the work of John Tyndall on radiation as a way of claiming a specific territory for his own researches on solar myth. He emphasizes the centrality to scientific enquiry of recent work on the sun:[12]

> Not even the most recent scientific discoveries described in Tyndall's genuine eloquence, which teach us how we live, and move, and have our being in the sun, how we burn it, how we breathe it, how we feed on it—give us any idea of what this source of light and life, this silent traveller, this majestic ruler, this departing friend or dying hero, in his daily or yearly course, was to the awakening consciousness of mankind. People wonder why so much of the old mythology, the daily talk, of the Aryans, was solar:—what else could it have been?

Müller here is almost certainly referring to Tyndall's *Six Lectures on Light* (1873), which gives an account of contemporary solar physics. Müller's usual shifty eloquence claims more than it states: the sun is quasi-scientifically equated with godhead by that rolling in of the biblical phrase 'we live, and move, and have our being' to describe our relationship to the sun. Müller's well-known inability to imagine other topics of conversation among early peoples apart from solar myth is neatly mocked by Andrew Lang: 'Savages, like civilised people, are much more interested in making love, making war, making fun, and providing dinner, than in the phenomena of nature.'[13] But Müller himself had worried long about the obsessional singleness of his topic: 'Is everything the Dawn? Is everything the Sun? This question I had asked myself many times before it was addressed to me by others . . . but I am bound to say that my own re-

---

[12] Max Müller, *Lectures on the Origin and Growth of Religion* (London, 1878), 207–8.
[13] Andrew Lang, Introduction to *Grimm's Household Tales*, ed. M. Hunt (London, 1884), vol. i. p. xxiv.

searches lead me again and again to the dawn and the sun as the chief burden of the myths of the Aryan race.'[14]

Without, I hope, falling into Müllerian monomania, I want to suggest that conversation among articulate Victorians about solar physics and the prospects for life on earth in a cooling solar system worked, as half-formulated anxieties will, to generate much imaginative thought and production and that the power of Müller's work and its enthusiastic reception draws on displaced anxieties: we can see some of the very varied literary responses in works such as *Middlemarch, Two on a Tower, Tess of the D'Urbervilles, After London,* and *The Time Machine.* In Müller's system all linguistic and mythological signification leads back towards the sun and the phenomena of weather, and to the fear of non-recurrence. He claimed that primitive peoples constantly feared that the sun would not rise again. In her *Darwinism in Morals* (1872), Frances Power Cobbe, speaking of the presence of subconscious thought, recounts a terrifying dream which goes deep into the current imagery of her culture: the loss of faith in *recurrence,* the loss of any assurance of 'eternal return', the recognition that oblivion is not only the matter of the past but of the future:[15]

I dreamed that I was standing on a certain broad grassy space in the park of my old home. It was totally dark, but I was sure that I was in the midst of an immense crowd. We were all gazing upward into the murky sky and a sense of some fearful calamity was over us, so that no one spoke aloud. Suddenly overhead appeared through a rift in the black heavens, a branch of stars which I recognised as the belt and sword of Orion. Then went forth a cry of despair from all our hearts! We knew, though no one said, that these stars proved it was not a cloud or mist which, as we had somehow believed, was causing the darkness. No; the air was clear; it was high noon, and *the sun had not risen!* That was the tremendous reason why we beheld the skies. The sun would never rise again!

Max Müller's solar mythography was so powerful because it gave expression to covert dreads then current: it cast itself as past enquiry but expressed current fears.[16]

[14] Max Müller, *Lectures on the Science of Language,* second ser. (London, 1864), 520.

[15] *Darwinism in Morals and Other Essays* (London, 1872), 343.

[16] Cf. my discussion of this passage in a different context in 'Origins and Oblivion in Victorian Narrative', in *Sex, Politics and Science in the Nineteenth-Century Novel: Selected Papers from the English Institute,* ed. R. B. Yeazell (Baltimore and London, 1986), 78–80. The passage represents the genesis of the present essay.

To take first a later example of powerful counter-interpretation in which both analyst and analysand have recourse to the discourse of solar myth: in Freud's 'Notes on a Case of Paranoia' (1911) Schreber dreads the end of the world as a result of a permanent cooling of the sun, 'a process of glaciation owing to the withdrawal of the sun'. Schreber's 'delusional privilege' will be the power to look directly at the sun, which in Freud's analysis, overriding the feminine gender of *die Sonne*, signifies the father.

The eagle, then, who makes his young look into the sun and requires of them that they shall not be dazzled by its light, is behaving as though he were himself a descendant of the sun and were submitting his children to a test of their ancestry. And when Schreber boasts that he can look into the sun unscathed and undazzled, he has rediscovered the mythological method of expressing his filial relation to the sun, and has confirmed us once again in our view that the sun is a symbol of the father.

Freud reinterprets what he calls this 'solar myth' into parental myth:

Schreber makes it easy for us to interpret this solar myth of his. He identifies the sun directly with God, sometimes with the lower God (Ahriman), and sometimes with the upper . . .
The sun, therefore, is nothing but another sublimated symbol for the father; and in pointing this out I must disclaim all responsibility for the monotomy of the solutions provided by psychoanalysis. In this instance symbolism overrides grammatical gender—at least so far as German goes, for in most other languages the sun is masculine. Its counterpart in this picture of the two parents is 'Mother Earth' as she is generally called.

Schreber's myth-economy is produced out of elements generated from late nineteenth-century anxieties—recast into a personal form.[17]

We might take as rough end-dates for the constellating activity I am here examining the publication in 1847 of Helmholtz's essay *Über die Erhaltung der Kraft* and the conclusion to Frazer's *The Golden Bough* (1915). Frazer's first volume appeared in 1890, the twelfth and last in 1915, well after the discovery of radioactivity but with its imaginative space unaffected by the

---

[17] Sigmund Freud, 'Notes on a Case of Paranoia', in *The Pelican Freud Library* (Harmondsworth, 1979), ix. 190, 207, and 222. Daniel Schreber's memoir of his illness was published as *Denkwürdigkeiten eines Nervenkranken* (Leipzig, 1903).

realization of the implications of this new form of energy. In his final paragraphs Frazer looks forward ecstatically to the future sweep of science, only to halt in the realization of cosmic ending, before coming to rest in that comforting fabulatory dissolution of Prospero's great speech.[18]

The dreams of magic may one day be the waking realities of science. But a dark shadow lies athwart the far end of this fair prospect. For however vast the increase of knowledge and of power which the future may have in store for man, he can scarcely hope to stay the sweep of those great forces which seem to be making silently but relentlessly for the destruction of all this starry universe in which our earth swims as a speck or mote. In the ages to come man may be able to predict, perhaps even to control, the wayward courses of the winds and clouds, but hardly will his puny hands have strength to speed afresh our slackening planet in its orbit or rekindle the dying fire of the sun. Yet the philosopher who trembles at the idea of such distant catastrophes may console himself by reflecting that these gloomy apprehensions, like the earth and the sun themselves, are only part of that unsubstantial world which thought has conjured up out of the void, and that the phantoms which the subtle enchantress has evoked today she may ban tomorrow. They too, like so much that to common eyes seems solid, may melt into air, into thin air.

Everything, it turns out, is mind: and this mentalism is the new escape from death.

Between these points in time lies the work of Thomson, Darwin, and Müller—alongside Frazer lies Freud. It is not my purpose in this essay to argue simply for points of agreement and disagreement among these theorists in several fields. Rather I shall demonstrate how an imaginative idea—the death of the sun or 'Balder Dead' to quote the title of one of Matthew Arnold's poems on the Norse myth—increased in intensity and range of meaning once it was accorded scientific status and was generating scientific controversy.[19]

---

[18] James Frazer, *Balder the Beautiful* (1913), in *The Golden Bough* (London, 1907–15), xi. 306–7.

[19] Carlyle gave a synopsis of the Balder legend in *Heroes and Hero-worship* (London, 1841)—the legend from the *Edda* of the death of the sun-god leading to *Ragnarök*, the twilight of the gods, was very like that explored by William Morris in 'Sigurd the Volsung', and by Richard Wagner in *The Ring*. Arnold's poem was published in 1853, and is a Christianizing of the myth in which Balder is identified with Christ. The poem ends with a vision of a new earth, 'More fresh, more verdant than the last'.

The reception of ideas outside the immediate circle of co-workers is not systematic. This realization may be a nuisance for those of us raised in scholarly habits of mind but its acceptance is a precondition for any worthwhile analysis of the movement of ideas across fields within a historical culture. We must not look for intact ideas being transferred from setting to setting: ideas rarely remain intact when they change context. Instead, we need to study how ideas are re-imagined in response to other needs and to the thickness—in Geertz's term—of enquiry and debate elsewhere. We need also to be aware of the inertia of old thoughts to which new ideas can be accommodated. Deepest habits of mind often leave only slight traces on the surface of writing. We need to look as much at movements across from sentence to sentence as at what is contained within any single sentence, and to watch how substantive theories become metaphors in another field. Nor should we forget how far our acts of interpretation are powered and bound by shared needs in our own culture.[20] To most intelligent Victorian readers physics could become intelligible only in a popular conceptual form. Moreover, the absence of a formal scientific education meant that scientific ideas tended to be received by non-scientific Victorians in the mode of dreads and dreams as well as intellectual conundrums. The result is that ideas of 'force' and 'energy', arguments concerning the age of the earth and the cooling of the sun, passed rapidly into an uncontrolled and mythologized form. In addition, prominent Victorian scientists saw it as part of their function to impart their ideas to untutored readers in an accessible form and so wrote not only for technical but for general cultural journals.

[20] Jacques Derrida in 'White Mythology: Metaphor in the Text of Philosophy', in *Margins of Philosophy* (Brighton, 1982), 213, argues that 'any expression of an abstract idea can only be an analogy. What is metaphysics? A white mythology which assembles and reflects Western culture: the white man takes his own mythology (that is, Indo-European mythology), his *logos*—that is the mythos of his idiom, for the universal form of that which it is still his inescapable desire to call Reason.' A remarkable example of the simultaneity of mythic and scientific thought in metaphysics is Michael Serres's conclusion to his essay 'The Origin of Language: Biology, Information Theory, and Thermodynamics', where he says: 'Nothing distinguishes me ontologically from a crystal, a plant, an animal, or the order of the world; we are drifting together towards the noise and the black depths of the universe, and our diverse systemic complexions are flowing up the entropic stream toward the solar origin, itself adrift' (J. V. Harari and D. F. Bell (eds.), *Hermes: Literature, Science, Philosophy* (Baltimore and London, 1982), 83).

Some Victorian scientists, for example, Tyndall, Proctor, and W. K. Clifford specialized in the teasing out of theorems into imaginatively illuminating ideas for those to whom the succinct elegance of mathematical formulation is a hermetic tongue. The world as argued by geological and evolutionary theory (specifically that of Hutton, Lyell, and Darwin) must have begun very much longer ago than biblical Mosaic accounts had suggested. But the death of the sun, according to Thomsonian physics, was not put farther off; on the contrary, it was rendered historically foreseeable. Instead of the timeless apocalypse of Revelations, physicists were busy computing the number of years left for life on earth—they ranged from twenty-one years more to several million. In his 1862 article in *Macmillan's Magazine* on 'The Age of the Sun's Heat', Thomson puts it thus: 'As for the future, we may say, with equal certainty, that inhabitants of the earth cannot continue to enjoy the light and heat essential to their life, for many million years longer, unless sources now unknown to us are prepared in the great storehouse of creation' (393). The number, 'several million years more', is reassuring, but the curtailing form of the sentence, 'cannot continue to enjoy the light and heat essential to their life', is alarming.

The death of the sun was far off, true enough, but, in the time of the imagination, a million or two of units cannot stave off immediacy. The *event* is more imaginable than its distance. People do not spend all day worrying about the extinction of the universe; they have other matters on hand. That is true even for us, in our more immediate nuclear crisis (which, in its turn, has raised into my consciousness a hitherto not much discussed trouble in Victorian imagination). Such thoughts tweak the memory and disturb the serene continuity of a future beyond the self which, for the Victorians at least, had seemed to be newly vouched for by the continuous descent and proliferation of evolutionary history. Such thoughts may fasten themselves about available myths: cosmic deaths prefigure as well as post-date our own. Proctor, in his article on 'The Past and Future of our Earth', seeks to reassure his readers of the continuity of the future by an appeal to the concepts of absolute time and space.[21]

[21] R. A. Proctor, 'The Past and Future of Our Earth', *Contemporary Review*, 25 (1974), 74–99, 91.

Thereafter, during ages infinite to our conceptions, the great central orb will be (as now, though in another sense) the life of the solar system. We may even look onwards to still more distant changes, seeing that the solar system is itself moving on an orbit, though the centre round which it travels is so distant that as yet it remains unknown. We see in imagination change after change, cycle after cycle, till

> Drawn on paths of never-ending duty,
> The worlds—eternity begun—
> Rest, absorbed in ever glorious beauty.
> On the Heart of the All-Central Sun.

But in reality it is only because our conceptions are finite that we thus look forward to an end even as we seek to trace events back to a beginning. The notion is inconceivable to us that absolutely endless series of changes may take place in the future and have taken place in the past; equally inconceivable is the notion that series on series of material combinations, passing onwards to ever *higher* orders,—from planets to suns, from suns to sun-systems, from sun-systems to galaxies, from galaxies to systems of galaxies, from these to higher and higher orders, absolutely without end,—may surround us on every hand.

In the argument of this passage, it is notable that Proctor moves into poetic allusion in order to blur the question of the collapse of the universe, which may thus be perceived poetically as the tranquillity of God. Note also how by the interposition of the word 'higher' he implies progress as well as progression:

It has been said that progression necessarily implies a beginning and an end; but this is not so where the progression relates to absolute space or time. No one can indeed doubt that progression in space is of its very nature limitless. But this is equally true, though not less inconceivable, of time. Progression implies only relative beginning and relative ending; but that there should be an absolute beginning or an absolute end is not merely inconceivable, like absolute eternity, but is inconsistent with the necessary conditions of the progression of time as presented to us by our conceptions.

In the same issue of the *Contemporary Review* James Hinton, in an article on 'The Religious Emotions', has resort to a mentalist argument to escape the universality of matter and force as characterizing the universe.[22] 'To science the world is no more mech-

---

[22] James Hinton, 'Professor Tyndall and the Religious Emotions', *Contemporary Review*, 25 (1974), 93–9, 91.

anical than it is coloured, or warm: as colour is an idea derived from a mode of our Sensation, so also, fully as much, is force, or mechanical necessity.'

Incongruities were manifest, then, between the new physics (with its insistence on increasing disorder in entropy and on the running down of the sun, already in a period of desuetude), and Darwinian theory (with its emphasis on development and upon increasing complexity as a means to sustained diversity of life). Such incongruities could provide a bolt-hole for determined optimists (it is all just a matter of description), but the awkwardness of fit, and even contradiction between them, also meant that they were readily trapped back into human reference and human problem. Huxley, in 'The Physical Basis of Life' (1868), uses the savages' fear of their sun darkening as an analogy for the modern fear of materialism. And later, in Social Diseases and Worse Remedies (1891), he comes to see that the final threat is not the incongruity of evolutionary theory and physics but their congruity:[23]

. . . it is an error to imagine that evolution signifies a constant tendency to increased perfection. That process undoubtedly involves a constant remodelling of the organism in adaptation to new conditions; but it depends on the nature of those conditions whether the direction of the modifications effected shall be upward or downward. Retrogressive is as practicable as progressive metamorphosis. If what the physical philosophers tell us, that our globe has been in a state of fusion, and like the sun, is gradually cooling down, is true; then the time must come when evolution will mean adaption to an universal winter, and all forms of life will die out, except such low and simple organisms as the Diatom of the arctic and antarctic ice and the Protococcus of the red snow.

Mythography, linguistics, physics, and biology were all public subjects of debate in the 1860s and 1870s rather than being confined only to specialist journals. Thomson, as we have seen, published one of his major essays, 'On the Age of the Sun's Heat', in Macmillan's Magazine in March 1862. Huxley published in a wide variety of magazines. The mythographer Müller, the folklorist Lang, the anthropologist Tylor, and Whitney the language theorist, as well as the physical scientist George Darwin, carried on their quite savage debates about linguistics in relation

[23] T. H. Huxley, 'The Struggle for Existence in Human Society (1888)', in Social Diseases and Worse Remedies (London, 1891), quoted from Collected Essays (London, 1906), ix. 199.

to mythographic and anthropological methodology in *The Nineteenth Century* in the 1870s and weighed the differing claims of linguistic and ethnological methods. Darwin did not make contributions to generalist journals but *The Origin* and *The Descent of Man* were best-sellers. As a result there could be a free and rapid movement of ideas among specialists and in the general public. It is worth noticing, for example, that in the issue of the *Fortnightly Review* in 1873 in which Andrew Lang mounted his first attack on Müller's solar mythology, 'Mythology and Fairy Tales', there was also a review of Helmholtz's *Popular Lectures on Scientific Subjects* with an introduction by John Tyndall. The collection, the reviewer records, includes his essays 'On the Interaction of Natural Forces' and 'Conservation of Force'. These two essays the reviewer concludes: 'treat the subject with special reference to the practical euthanasia of force in mechanical work, and discuss the problem of perpetual motion in its widest bearing, on the future prospects of the mechanism of the universe'.[24]

At their meeting in 1875 Thomas Hardy and Leslie Stephen talked, so Hardy tells us in his *Journal*, of 'theologies decayed and defunct, the origin of things, the constitution of matter, the unreality of time . . . and the staggering fascination of the new theory of vortex rings'.[25] George Eliot, in her journal, copies out passages from Clerk Maxwell's address to the British Association in which he advanced his theory of ring vortices. This theory added a third mode of movement to the current argument about time and catastrophism. First, Darwin's theories suggested development, expansion in variation, even progress. Second, Thomson's theories emphasized an ageing and cooling world which was inevitably proceeding towards the period when it would be too cold for life on earth. The sun expended but did not renew its energies. Clerk Maxwell's work on molecules, on the other hand, emphasized *unchangingness*, neither the outward and upward movement associated with evolutionary ideas, nor the downward motion of *Sonnenuntergang*, the final setting of

[24] Andrew Lang, 'Mythology and Fairy Tales', *Fortnightly Review*, NS 8 (1893), 618–31. Lang argues for a progressive and evolutionary account of myth with fetishism as a stage in all myth-making, rather than Müller's organization, which Lang sees as a theory of dissipation and degeneration. 'If this be so,' he said, 'the myths of the dawn and the sun, can no longer be considered *primary*.' The review of Helmholtz is printed in *Fortnightly Review*, NS 8 (1873), 664–5.

[25] Florence Hardy, *The Early Life of Thomas Hardy* (London, 1928), 139.

the sun. 'If a whirling ring be once generated . . . it will go on forever . . . and could never be divided or destroyed', wrote Maxwell in 1870 in one of the passages George Eliot copied out. And in his essay on 'Molecules'[26] he made it clear that such a process could have nothing to do with evolution: 'No theory of evolution can be formed to account for the similarity of molecules, for evolution necessarily implies continuous change, and the molecule is incapable of growth or decay, of generation or destruction.' He concludes that essay with a reassertion of the argument from design:

Natural causes, as we know, are at work, which tend to modify, if they do not at length destroy, all the arrangements and dimensions of the earth and the whole solar system. But though in the course of ages catastrophes have occurred and may yet occur in the heavens, though ancient systems may be dissolved and new systems evolved out of their ruins, the molecules out of which these systems are built—the foundation stones of the material universe—remain unbroken and unworn.

They continue this day as they were created, perfect in number and measure and weight, and from the ineffaceable characters impressed on them we may learn that those aspirations after accuracy in measurement, truth in statement, and justice in action, which we reckon among our noblest attributes as men, are ours because they are essential constituents of the image of Him who in the beginning created, not only the heaven and the earth, but the materials of which heaven and earth consist.

The indivisibility of molecules has a mythic function. It becomes a way of sustaining the mind drifting towards dissolution with the cooling sun. The indivisible world is steadfast even when life-giving light dies out.

Nor did physicists read only physics. Maxwell offers a tongue-in-cheek solar mythological reading of *Middlemarch*. He reports to his friend Campbell, professor of Greek at St Andrews, a meeting of the Philosophical Society, a revealing name for the principal Cambridge scientific society.[27]

The Cambridge Philosophical Society have been entertained by Mr. Paley on Solar Myths, Odysseus as the Setting Sun, etc. Your Trachiniae

[26] James Clerk Maxwell, *Scientific Papers*, ed. W. D. Niven (Cambridge, 1890), ii. 377.
[27] Lewis Campbell and William Garnett, *The Life of James Clerk Maxwell, with a selection from his writings* (London, 1884), 295–6.

is rather in that style, but I think Middlemarch is not a mere unconscious myth, as the Odyssey was to its author, but an elaborately conscious one, in which all the characters are intended to be astronomical or meteorological.

Rosamond is evidently the Dawn. By her fascinations she draws up into her embrace the rising sun, represented as the Healer from one point of view, and the Opener of Mysteries from another; his name, Lyd Gate, being compounded of two nouns, both of which signify something which opens, as the eye-lids of the morn, and the gates of day. But as the sun-god ascends, the same clouds which emblazon his rising, absorb all his beams, and put a stop to the early promise of enlightenment, so that he, the ascending sun, disappears from the heavens.

Dorothea, on the other hand, the goddess of gifts, represents the other half of the revolution. She is at first attracted by and united to the fading glories of the days that are no more, but after passing, as the title of the last book expressly tells us, 'from sunset to sunrise', we find her in union with the pioneer of the coming age, the editor . . .

There is no need to refer to Nicholas Bulstrode, who evidently represents the Mithraic mystery, or to the kindly family of Garth, representing the work of nature under the rays of the sun, or to the various clergymen and doctors, who are all planets. The whole thing is, and is intended to be, a solar myth from beginning to end.

Note how well Maxwell picks up the Müllerian etymological insistence (lyd-gate) and the mixture of explanation and unexplanation 'they are all planets'. The analysis is not entirely facetious—there are evident allusions in *Middlemarch* to solar myth: Casaubon (rather too early) worrying about other men's solar deities, Will's sunny Apollonian locks:[28]

Poor Mr. Casaubon himself was lost among small closets and winding stairs, and in an agitated dimness about the Cabeiri [fertility gods] or in an exposure of other mythologists' ill-considered parallels, easily lost sight of any purpose which had prompted him to these labours. With his taper stuck before him he forgot the absence of windows, and in bitter manuscript remarks on other men's notions about the solar deities, he had become indifferent to the sunlight.

The final book is called 'Sunset and Sunrise'. The sun does rise again. At sunrise Dorothea sees determinedly demythologized, though generalized, human beings—the emphasis is on the manifold, the complex, the extending, rather than the drawing all

---

[28] *Middlemarch*, cabinet edition (Edinburgh and London, 1878–80), i. 303.

back upon a single source. Although *Middlemarch* respects the work of the solar mythologists, it preserves always a sense of the relative. No one explanation can encompass all the phenomena of the world. Just as Lydgate poses a question in physiology not quite in the form required by the waiting answer, so does Casaubon. His seemingly old-fashioned and anachronistic obsessions in myth theory were not 'scientific', but *Middlemarch* brings into doubt also the 'scientistic' claims of solar mythologists with their single explanatory system. Clerk Maxwell, with his usual brilliant immediacy, has picked up the hints concerning solar mythological controversy implicit in the book, and his jest concurs with *Middlemarch*'s own refusal of the overweening explanatory power that Müller and his followers claimed. This example also makes it clear that scientists and writers imbibed each other's materials: solar physics and solar myth were separate enquiries certainly, but beneath the surface they stirred some of the same troubles.

It was not until the turn of the century that new sources of energy for the sun were experimentally established, thereby resolving the quarrel between geologists and physicists about the age of the earth. Curé and Laborde (*Sur la chaleur dégagée*) discovered that radium salts constantly release heat, thereby unveiling the unknown source of heat which Thomson had somewhat dismissively prophesied. By 1904 Rutherford was convinced that radioactivity overthrew Thomson's results. The imagery of darkness and the dying sun comically, and perhaps unawares, permeates Rutherford's account of the reception of his ideas at the Royal Institution:[29]

I came into the room, which was half dark, and presently spotted Lord Kelvin in the audience and realized that I was in for trouble at the last part of the speech dealing with the age of the earth, where my views conflicted with his. To my relief, Kelvin fell fast asleep, but as I came to the important point, I saw the old bird sit up, open an eye and cock a baleful glance at me! Then a sudden inspiration came, and I said Lord Kelvin had limited the age of the earth, *provided no new source of heat was discovered*. That prophetic utterance refers to what we are now considering tonight, radium! Behold! The old boy beamed upon me.

[29] Quoted from Arthur Eve, *Rutherford* (Cambridge, 1939), 107. Rutherford's paper was entitled 'The Radiation and Emanation of Radium'.

Rutherford's speech ends:

The discovery of the radio-active elements, which in their disintegration liberate enormous amounts of energy, thus increases the possible limit of the duration of life on this planet, and allows the time claimed by the geologist and biologist for the process of evolution.

That is to take the story towards its end and to show another *Ragnarök* or *Götterdämmerung*, as the old Thomson, by now Lord Kelvin, beams on the theory which spells the end of his own—however much his prophetic role is flatteringly exaggerated by Rutherford. The discovery of radioactivity relieved anxieties about the imminent death of the sun—but the happy end of that story was to prove the start of another and more terrifying one with which we are all-too familiar. Thermodynamics both distances Huxley's 'universal winter' by replenishing the sun's heat, and brings it near through nuclear fission.

But while the question of the sun's age still hung in the balance and foreshortened time, we can see varying attempts to reassure, as well as various unconscious appropriations of the assumptions of solar physics into solar myth. Perhaps the most pleasing example of a leap in interpretation which covers an unrecognized assumption or concern is that of Müller's follower Sir George Cox in *Aryan Mythology*, where he offers a solar analysis of the Wolf and the Seven Little Kids (the analysis is criticized by Lang in the same Introduction to *Grimm's Household Tales* cited earlier). Lang emphasizes the modernity of the clock-case and criticizes Cox for placing so much emphasis upon it:[30]

If, then, we interpret the tale by regarding the clock-case as its essential feature, surely we mistake a late and civilised accident for the essence of an ancient and barbarous legend. Sir G. W. Cox lays much stress on the affair of the clock-case. 'The wolf', he says, 'is here the Night, or the Darkness, which tries to swallow up the seven days of the week, and actually swallows six. The seventh, the youngest, escapes by hiding herself in the clock-case; in other words, the week is not quite run out, and before it comes to an end, the mother of the goats unrips the wolf's stomach, and places stones in it in place of the little goats who come trooping out, as the days of the week begin again to run their course.'

---

[30] Andrew Lang, Introduction to *Grimm's Household Tales*, vol. i. p. xvii; *The Mythology of the Aryan Nations* (London, 1870), i. 358.

THE DEATH OF THE SUN

Lang quips: 'Surely a clock-case might seem . . . a good hiding-place, even to a mind not occupied at all with the sun.' Tylor rather surprisingly allows:[31] 'We can hardly doubt there is a quaint touch of sun-myth in a tale which took its present shape since the invention of clocks.'

What is the unanalysed connection in both Cox and Tylor's minds which makes the link between the feature of the clock and solar myth? There is no manifest association. The answer surely is that, according to then contemporary physics, the sun, like the seven-day clock, is running down. The happy ending of the seventh day recovered is not available in the physical world. The sun, as the new theory of the dissipation of energy had made very clear, cannot be rewound like a clock. The hidden grounds of interpretation here conceal a contemporary anxiety which is displaced and healed by the solar analysis of the Grimm *Märchen*. Lang's sceptical puzzlement as to why the clock should be seen as an essential feature of the story leads on to an explanation that even he could not observe because it was too specific to the culture he shared with Tylor and Cox. Interpretation tells as much about the needs of the interpreter and the current culture as about its material—and the concerns of a present-day interpreter brings to the surface hitherto unobserved mythic patterns which have as much to do with our own predicaments as those of the past, but which are not thereby devalued.

In the light of that argument let us look at the Earthworm essay anew. Darwin's last book marked a return in his own mind to his earliest professional self. He thought of himself initially as a geologist and was secretary to the Geological Society of London in the late 1830s. It was in geology also that he made his only major theoretical blunder, in his 1839 paper on the 'parallel roads' of Glen Roy. He tended, perhaps, as the controversy over the denudation of the Weald also shows, to rely in geology overmuch on Lyell's views. He had first thought academically about worms in a geological context. In 1837 he read a paper 'On the Formation of Mould' to the Geological Society of London.[32] The report ends: 'The author concluded by remarking that it is probable that every particle of earth in old pasture land has

<hr>

[31] Edward Tylor, *Primitive Culture* (London, 1871), i. 341.

[32] Charles Darwin, 'On the Formation of Mould', *Proceedings of the Geological Society of London*, 2 (1837–8), 574–6.

passed through the intestines of worms, and hence, that in some senses, the term "animal mould" would be more appropriate than vegetable mould.' When, more than forty years later he returned to the theme, Darwin entitled his volume, judiciously: 'The Formation of Vegetable Mould, Through the Action of Worms, with Observations on their Habits. The worm is, in Darwin's argument, not only the lowliest but the most enduring life-form, living out of sight of the sun, endlessly turning the soil of the world and fructifying it. Like Maxwell's account of the molecule, Darwin's account of the worm emphasizes unchangingness. Maxwell writes of the molecules' steadfastness.[33]

But though in the course of ages catastrophes have occurred and may yet occur in the heavens, though ancient systems may be dissolved and new systems evolved out of their ruins, the molecules out of which these systems are built—the foundation stones of the material universe—remain unbroken and unworn.

So writes Darwin in the course of his concluding paragraph.[34]

It is a marvellous reflection that the whole of the superficial mould over any such expanse has passed, and will again pass, every few years through the bodies of worms. The plough is one of the most ancient and most valuable of man's inventions; but long before he existed the land was in fact regularly ploughed, and still continues to be thus ploughed by earthworms.

The lowest common denominators of matter then known (the molecule) and of life (the earthworm) become matter of consolation. Continuity persists through change. Out of reach of the sun, whose energy is running down, the worm survives, blind and damp, perfectly at home within its limited environment, surviving amidst more and more complex forms—and also surviving after them. Worms are the meek of the earth.[35]

Leslie Stephen picks up the anthropomorphism of Darwin's affectionate, even tender, regard for the worms he studied,[36] as does Punch in an 1882 cartoon of Darwin as preacher on the text

---

[33] See n. 26.

[34] Charles Darwin, The Formation of Vegetable Mould, Through the Action of Worms, with Observations on their Habits (London, 1881), 313.

[35] A correspondent points out that the association of earthworms with anthrax in the 1880s meant that this was the end of the worm's era of innocence, and was thus threnody unawares.

[36] Leslie Stephen, Swift, English Men of Letters Series (London, 1882), 200.

'Man is but a Worm' (Fig. 10.1). Stephen compares Swift's *Polite Conversation* and *Directions to Servants* with Darwin's essay. Swift's essays:

show how closely Swift's sarcastic attention was fixed through life upon the ways of his inferiors. They are a mass of materials for a natural history of social absurdities such as Mr. Darwin was in the habit of bestowing upon the manners and customs of worms. The difference is that Darwin had none but kindly feelings for worms, whereas Swift's inspection of social vermin is always edged with contempt.

Darwin respects worms whereas Swift does not respect people. Does Darwin's respect turn them into humble folk? Is it class-bound, moving the 'higher–lower' organization anthropomorphically to and fro, celebrating and binding labour?

Andrew Lang, in his essay 'Apollo and the Mouse', enquires why it is that Apollo, particularly in his threatening aspect, is associated with the worship of insignificant creatures. He opens by asking 'Why is Apollo, especially the Apollo of the Troad, he who showered the darts of pestilence among the Greeks, so constantly associated with a mouse?'[37] He quotes sceptically De Gubernatio's solar suggestion (Zool. Myth II. 68): 'The Pagan sungod crushes under his foot the Mouse of Night', and instead substitutes a historical explanation in which totemism is overlaid with Apollonian worship. Another possible mode of explanation is that the conjunction of lowest and highest may have the function of warding off threats to stability by a fictional alliance of most and least powerful—that, I suggest, may be a function of Darwin's worm.

In 1850, turning away from dragon or serpent, Landor had written an 'Ode to the Worm', which appeared in *The Leader* (4 May 1851, reprinted 1853 and 1876). It opens 'First-born of all creation! yet unsung', and hymns the enduringness of the worm. Landor's poem ends 'Last of creation I will call thee now.'[38] For the worm survives meteors, feeds on prince and vulture, and is so lowly that it is the last surviving thing. Darwin may have read Landor's poem: it is quite probable, though not essential to this argument. What is striking is that Darwin's

---

[37] Andrew Lang, *Custom and Myth* (London, 1885), 103–20.
[38] W. S. Landor, *Poetical Works*, ed. S. Wheeler (Oxford, 1937), iii. 184–5.

FIG. 10.1. 'Man is but a Worm', from *Punch's Almanack for 1882* (December, 1881).

dismay at the oncoming death of the world (and his awareness of his own oncoming death too, perhaps) led him back to the primordial creature he had studied at the beginning of his career, in his initiating discipline. He domesticates the worm and through the delicate and detailed attention he pays to all its proceedings he also celebrates it. It becomes the object of *attention* after long disregard: worms select and show purposive intelligence, he claims. They are capable of bringing about the sinking of great stones. They produce tower-like castings of rococo form. They dash into their burrows like rabbits: they select like men and vary their habits as if in acts of choice.

The aesthetic choosiness of worms, and their great consequence for earth, despite their limitations, allows Darwin to comfort his readers with an image of the resourcefulness and unchanging stamina of fundamental life-forms: 'It may be doubted whether there are many other animals which have played so important a part in the history of the world, as have these lowly organized creatures.' Turning away from 'higher complexity' and from the changing future, Darwin gives pleasure and solace together. 'All sentient beings are doomed to complete annihilation after such long-continued slow progress',[39] he wrote of the cooling sun. But the obscure worm allows him an image, at once matter-of-fact and newly dignified, for the unchanging Saturnian world hidden away from the controversies of physics, forming (though this, I am sure, not consciously) a counter to solar myth. The almost blind worm shrinks from the light of the sun. It pulls down Stonehenge piece by piece beneath the ground. It pursues its subterranean pathways, least Apollonian of creatures. Such a reading of Darwin's essay in no way affects its status as scientific observation. It allows us though, I hope, some speculative insight into the reasons for the work's immense and immediate popularity, and into the powers of myth within other forms of knowledge.

[39] Darwin, *Earthworm*, 312.

11

Helmholtz, Tyndall, Gerard Manley Hopkins: Leaps of the Prepared Imagination

For the phenomenal world . . . is the brink, limbus, lapping, run-and-mingle of two principles which meet in the scape of everything.   (Hopkins on Parmenides, 1868)[1]

Newton's passage from a falling apple to a falling moon was, at the outset, a leap of the prepared imagination.

(John Tyndall, 'On the Scientific Use of the Imagination', 1870)

Gerard Manley Hopkins was pre-eminently a religious writer, of that no doubt. The vicissitudes of his calling and his sufferings have preoccupied many who respond to his life-story. Between 1868, the year of his entry into the Jesuit novitiate at the age of 24, and 1876, the year of 'The Wreck of the Deutschland', he wrote no poetry. His major output dates from 1876 to 1889, when he died. His poetry expresses the energies of the material world funnelled and focused to break through to a world beyond, or a world within. During his lifetime his poems were known only to those who knew him. There were no reviews to fan or snuff that very fiery particle, his mind, few responses to the words alone without thought of the writer. When Robert Bridges first published *Poems of Gerard Manley Hopkins* in 1918 the modernist movement claimed him as a displaced contemporary stranded among the Victorians with whom he was assumed to have had little in common. Roman Catholic scholars

---

[1] *The Journal and Papers of Gerard Manley Hopkins*, ed. Humphry House, completed by Graham Storey (London, 1959), 130. Hereafter referred to as *Journals and Papers*.

and readers have built up a hermeneutic tradition of reading his work which emphasizes his debt to Duns Scotus and Ignatius Loyola. That debt is undeniable, but athwart their presence in Hopkins runs also an intellectual and emotional engagement with current ideas.

In this essay I concentrate on the force of scientific discovery and speculation within Hopkins's poetry, both in its sense and sound. Physics in particular was offering detailed new cosmologies. In the vast amount of attention that has been given to the impact of evolutionary theory on Victorian consciousness those other interpretative urgencies are in danger of being lost to sight. The present essay, necessarily limited in its examples, is part of a larger-scale study in progress concerned with the diverse imaginative meanings that wave-theory produced among scientists and non-scientists in the later nineteenth century. As an outcome of new work by major figures such as Helmholtz in Germany and Faraday, Thomson, and Clerk Maxwell in the British Isles, optics, acoustics, and (above all) the laws of thermodynamics were transforming Victorian perceptions.[2] The work of all these writers was rapidly presented and discussed in general journals by co-workers such as John Tyndall.

The invaluable and long-awaited complete edition of *The Poetical Works of Gerard Manley Hopkins*, with its greatly expanded references and commentaries by Norman H. MacKenzie, offers some exposition of ornithological, geological, and astronomical material.[3] Even here, however, physics gets short shrift. Helmholtz is mentioned only once (409) and then as the object of an attack by Edmund Gurney,[4] while Tyndall is referred

---

[2] Patricia M. Ball, *The Science of Aspects: The Changing Role of Fact in the work of Coleridge, Ruskin and Hopkins* (London, 1971) is disappointingly unspecific, seeing Hopkins as 'a sensitive observer' only (115) and setting up a contrast between 'imaginative logic' and 'a more strictly scientific process of thought' that she does not pursue (118–19).

[3] *The Poetical Works of Gerard Manley Hopkins*, ed. Norman H. Mackenzie (Oxford, 1990). All references to the poetry are to this edition, hereafter referred to as *Poetical Works 1990*. For the editor's general remarks on the scientific allusions, see Preface, pp. viii–ix. See also his 'Hopkins and Science', *Studies in the Literary Imagination* (special Hopkins issue), 21 (1988), 41–56.

[4] An essay by Hopkins's friend George Simcox entitled 'An Empirical Theory of Free Will' immediately precedes the Gurney essay on Helmholtz, *Mind*, 4 (1879), 469–81. Simcox illustrates the problem of free will by means of the example of averages and adjustments, a field familiar to Hopkins since his father, Manley Hopkins, was by profession an average-adjuster for shipping. Manley Hopkins

to only as author of the 1874 Belfast address, which MacKenzie says Hopkins found 'maddening' (373). (Hopkins wrote, with subtle difference, 'I thought it interesting and eloquent, though it made me "most mad".')[5]

What fresh experience did writers like Helmholtz and Tyndall open up and bring into question for Hopkins? How did his reading of *Nature* and other journals, such as *The Academy* and the *Nineteenth Century*, feed his mind and emotions? J. Hillis Miller suggested in *The Disappearance of God* that for Hopkins, 'The words of the poem incarnated the things they named, just as the words of the Mass shared in the transformation they evoked.'[6] Scientific materialism was not as much at odds with his thinking as might be anticipated. But working alongside, and athwart, that emphasis on the stabilized and material was a fascination with motion, flux, and the disorderly. How does Hopkins's appetite for discovery work with, and averse from, his respect for authority? The troubled urgency of sense-experience seeks an intelligible form in science, a sacralized in religion: the two patterns for the Victorians sometimes cohere, sometimes lurch apart.

The question of authority—civil, religious, scientific—might seem to be settled early for Hopkins. But even the double and conflicted action of words like 'buckle' (collapsing and containing) indicates how the irresolvable energies of counter-explanation continue to propel his poetry. For Hopkins faith dominated; but the urgency of his writing is coiled upon contesting forces. An early poem, written in 1864 in Wales, clenches long-standing philosophical questions (pursued by Locke and Berkeley) of empiricism, individualism, mentalism. It does so in the image of the rainbow: both prism and idea, each of the group seeing a separate bow:

> It was a hard thing to undo this knot.
> The rainbow shines, but only in the thought

published a classic manual on average-adjustment in 1857, wrote *A Manual of Marine Insurance* (1867) and *The Port of Refuge, or Advice and Instructions to the Master Mariner in Situations of Doubt, Difficulty, and Danger* (1873). It seems not to have been remarked that questions of chance, fatality, and providence surrounding shipwrecks (the *Deutschland*, the *Eurydice*) would therefore have had a particular (and conflicted) intensity of significance for Hopkins from childhood on.

[5] *Further Letters of Gerard Manley Hopkins*, 2nd edn., ed. Claude Colleer Abbott (London, 1956), 128. Hereafter referred to as *Letters*, III.

[6] J. Hillis Miller, *The Disappearance of God* (Cambridge, Mass., 1975), 3.

Of him that looks. Yet not in that alone,
For who makes rainbows by invention?
And many standing round a waterfall
See one bow each, yet not the same to all,
But each a hand's breadth further than the next.
The sun on falling waters writes the text
Which yet is in the eye or in the thought.
It was a hard thing to undo this knot.[7]

That knot of explanation and experience persistently tied itself anew throughout his strenuous poetry. Reading Hopkins's work in relation to the scientific writing of his time makes us aware of how much he was beset by entropy and azure, delighted by optics and acoustics, and roused to combat and to embrace caprice.

Hopkins, as I shall demonstrate, was increasingly fascinated by scientific issues, particularly those under discussion in the field of physics. In the 1880s he participated directly in discussion through his letters to *Nature* and his proposed, though never completed, works on the scientific basis of metre and music, on light and the ether. In late poems like 'Spelt from Sybil's Leaves' and 'That Nature is a Heraclitean Fire' the dissonances between scientific articulations of the universe, their compacting in human experience, and the demands of faith form 'the brink, limbus, lapping, run-and-mingle of two principles which meet in the scape of everything'.

The prevalence of Helmholtzian physiological optics and acoustics as a reference-point in English Victorian intellectual life has received singularly little attention from scholars or theorists.[8]

---

[7] *Poetical Works 1990*, 31.

[8] Helmholtz's work became much better known outside—and even within—scientific circles during the 1870s after the publication in English translation of his *Popular Lectures on Scientific Subjects* (first series), translated by E. Atkinson with an introduction by Professor Tyndall (London, 1873). Series 2 appeared in 1884. However, his key essay formulating the laws of thermodynamics 'Über die Erhaltung der Kraft' (Berlin, 1847) had been collected in English translation as long ago as 1853, in John Tyndall and William Francis, (eds.), *Scientific Memoirs Selected from the Transactions of Foreign Academies of Science and from Foreign Journals: Natural Philosophy* (London, 1853). Peter Dale, in *Towards a Scientific Culture* (Madison, 1990), argues for Helmholtz's influence on G. H. Lewes during the 1860s. Compare William Baker (ed.), *The George Eliot–George Henry Lewes Library: An Annotated Catalogue of their Books at Dr. Williams's Library, London* (New York, 1977), 91–2, for the list of the Helmholtz volumes they owned in German, and one

Even Tom Zaniello (whose valuable contextual study *Hopkins in the Age of Darwin* I read only after writing this essay) refers to Helmholtz slightly, and, in relation to Tyndall, as 'one of his colleagues, another outstanding experimenter in light and sound, H. L. F. von Helmholtz' who 'stated in *On the Sensations of Tone as a Physiological Basis for the Theory of Music* (English edition 1877) that "the phenomena of mixed colours present considerable analogy to those of compound musical tones".'[9] Although Helmholtz's fundamental masterpiece on acoustics *Die Lehre von den Tonempfindungen als physiologische Grundlage für die Theorie der Musik* was indeed translated into English first in the 1870s, his ideas had long been represented and popularized in the work, particularly, of John Tyndall. For example, his ground-breaking 1847 essay formulating the second law of thermodynamics, 'Über die Erhaltung der Kraft', was published in English in 1853, and Tyndall's *Sound*, first published in 1867 and going through numerous editions, opens with this tribute:

Four years ago a work was published by Professor Helmholtz, entitled 'Die Lehre von den Tonempfindungen', to the scientific portion of which I have given considerable attention. Copious references to it will be found in the following pages; but they fail to give an adequate idea of the thoroughness and excellence of the work. To those especially who wish to pursue the subject into its aesthetic developments, the Third Part of the Tonempfindungen cannot fail to be of the highest interest and use. (p. viii)[10]

in French. Helmholtz's great works on optics and acoustics first reached a wider English public through the medium of John Tyndall's expositions, *Sound* and *Light*. *Tonempfindungen* appeared in German (Braunschweig, 1863) and went through numerous editions. Alexander Ellis prepared an English translation, first in 1875, based on the third German edition of 1870 and a second edition based on the fourth German edition of 1877, which appeared in English in 1885: *On the Sensations of Tone as a Physiological Basis for the Theory of Music* (London, 1885). Ellis was both a mathematician and a philologist, a point of some consequence for my general argument.

  [9] Tom Zaniello, *Hopkins in the Age of Darwin* (Iowa City, 1988), 68–9. Another brief discussion of Helmholtz occurs, on pp. 45–6, in relation to vortex rings. Zaniello's study offers very little direct discussion or analysis of Hopkins's poetry.

  [10] John Tyndall, *Sound, A Course of Eight Lectures delivered at the Royal Institution of Great Britain* (London, 1867). Helmholtz in turn translated Tyndall's writing into German and paid liberal tribute to his work, particularly on light and on the processes of re-gelation. See e.g. his *Popular Lectures on Scientific Subjects*, first series (London, 1873), 138.

Even before Tyndall's exposition in *Sound* Max Müller had, in his *Lectures on the Science of Language*, offered an account in English of Helmholtz's acoustical work, published only a year after *Tonempfindungen*. Müller, already a fellow of All Souls at Oxford, was Sanskrit scholar, philologist, and the dominant interpreter of the history of language and the signification of myth during the 1860s and 1870s in England. In the *Science of Language* he discusses not only historical and metaphysical questions of language but the business, too, of physical voice production. As part of that discussion he considers that 'a most important discovery of Professor Helmholtz' is 'that we can now determine the exact configuration of many compound vibrations, and determine the presence and absence of the harmonics which, as we saw, caused the difference in the quality, or colour, or timbre of sound'.[11] This discussion of the 'colour, or timbre of sound' is a major preoccupation in *Nature* in the 1870s and of crucial importance to Hopkins, who wrote his poems for the voice:

> As tumbled over rim in roundy wells
> Stones ring; like each tucked string tells, each hung bell's
> Bow swung finds tongue to fling out broad its name . . . [12]

The 'thisness' or inscape, the identity, of things is a matter for Hopkins of the particular *sounds* they make quite as much as of the pictures they form. That is true, too, of his own verse.

By the end of the 1870s Helmholtz is, with Darwin, the recurrent point of reference for writers in *Nature* and *Mind*, where the weight of his presence is felt within very diverse arguments. In the fourth volume of *Mind* (1879), for example, almost all the essays allude to or discuss his work. William James in 'Are we Automata?' refers to 'Helmholtz's immortal work on

---

[11] F. Max Müller, *Lectures on the Science of Language delivered at the Royal Institution of Great Britain in February, March, April, and May, 1863* (London, 1864), 108. I am grateful to Dr Catherine Phillips for drawing my attention to this discussion. For discussion of Müller's mythography in relation to then current physics and evolutionary theory, see my 'The Death of the Sun: Victorian Solar Physics and Solar Myth', in *The Sun is God: Painting, Literature and Mythology in the Nineteenth Century*, ed. Barry Bullen (Oxford University Press, 1989), 159–80; repr. as Ch. 10, above.
[12] *Poetical Works 1990*, 141. See also p. 368, note on ll. 6–8, for comments on Müller's theory of root syllables and his analogy with the 'law . . . that everything which is struck . . . has its peculiar ring'.

Physiological Optics' (9); the next essay, by Hopkins's acquaintance Edmund Gurney, 'On Discord' concentrates on Grant
Allen's *Physiological Aesthetics* and 'Helmholtz's *Tonempfindungen*' (25); O. Plumacher, reviewing Sully, refers to Helmholtz
with others for his work on 'the relatively unconscious . . . the
consciousness of the different nervous centres within an organism' (75); while in 'Philosophy in the United States', immediately
following, G. Stanley Hall discusses Helmholtz's influence on the
philosopher C. S. Peirce (103).

Nor was it only in such relatively specialized journals that
Helmholtz's presence was felt. Tyndall's advocacy of Helmholtz's work in general journals meant that his influence was
more rapidly evident *outside* scientific circles than that of his
great contemporary James Clerk Maxwell. Whereas Tyndall's
personal relations with Maxwell were guarded, his admiration
for Helmholtz was unbounded. For example, already in 1866
Tyndall's essay 'On the Relations of Radiant Heat to Chemical
Constitution, Colour, and Texture', which draws extensively on
Helmholtz's work on the conservation of energy, took pride of
place in the fourth volume of *The Fortnightly Review*.[13] Billie
Inman, indeed, suggests that this essay had an impact on Pater's
writing, particularly 'Sebastian van Storck', 'Conclusion', and
'Winckelmann'. Pater was both Hopkins's tutor and his friend at
this period.[14]

John Tyndall was probably the most important single figure
among the scientific community for those concerned with the
relations between ordinary human perceptions and science. Thomas Henry Huxley had more combative presence, but whereas
Huxley concentrated on evolutionary and anthropological processes Tyndall was principally concerned with heat, light, sound,
ether, matter. Through his writing the cosmological was articulated near at hand, and through his demonstrations the invisible
and inaudible reaches of vibration that make up life were manifested, with the production of artificial blue skies and singing

[13] *Fortnightly Review*, 4 (15 Feb. 1866), 1-15. G. H. Lewes was editor of this
volume of the journal.

[14] Billie Inman, *Walter Pater's Reading: A Bibliography of his Library Borrowing
and Literary References 1853-1873* (New York, 1981), 104-5, 133-4. Hopkins
took a First in Greats in the spring of 1867. In July 1867 he writes: 'I have no plans
till sometime in August, when Pater is going to ask me down to Sidmouth' (*Letters*,
III, 16 n.). He saw a good deal of Pater again in Feb.-Oct. 1879.

rods. It is not altogether surprising that spiritualists, whom he detested, sought to claim Tyndall as a medium. For the physical sciences, he asserted, it is necessary not only empirically to demonstrate but also to find a way beyond experience: 'The Germans express the act of picturing by the word *vorstellen*, and the picture they call a *Vorstellung*. We have no word in English which comes nearer to our requirements than *Imagination*.'[15] So although he emphasizes always materialism he is able to give a transcendental edge to that ordinarily unmystical concept: despite denying vitalism—and indeed all religious authority—he contrived to keep some dark space for an ordering, though not a pre-emptive, Intelligence.

This ambiguous position was not enough to ward off charges of atheism but it softened his cultural role and made his voice audible in circles that might otherwise have shut their ears. The distinguished mathematician J. J. Sylvester spoke of him as one 'whom Science and Poetry woo with an equal spell, and whose ideas have a faculty for arranging themselves in forms of order and beauty as spontaneously and unfailingly as those crystalline solutions from which . . . he drew so vivid and instructive an illustration'.[16] Tyndall's imaginative eloquence and his power of seemly yet unexpected exposition gave him a major interpretative role in Victorian culture. He wrote in a style that gave pleasure to an extraordinary variety of readers and he published in a great array of journals, both technical and general.[17] Science, he held, 'not unfrequently derives motive power from an ultra-scientific source'.[18] He was both a highly respected and an innovative worker, constantly referred to in *Nature* during the 1870s particularly. His scientific education in Germany and his friendship with Helmholtz gave him, moreover, a much broader awareness of current possibilities in European science than a

---

[15] *The Academy: A Weekly Review of Literature, Science, and Art* (22 Aug. 1874), 211.

[16] J. J. Sylvester, *The Laws of Verse together with the Inaugural Presidential Address to the Mathematical and Physical Section of the British Association at Exeter* (London, 1870), 103.

[17] Generalist journals to which Tyndall contributed include: *The Westminster Review, The Academy, The Contemporary Review, Macmillan's Magazine, The Fortnightly Review, Fraser's Magazine, Longman's Magazine, The Nineteenth Century, New Review.*

[18] *The Academy* (22 Aug. 1874), 216.

cultural chauvinist like P. G. Tait, whose later book on *Light* so irritated Hopkins.[19]

The particular urgency for Hopkins of John Tyndall's writing, in the light of Helmholtz, on sound, colour, the conserving and dissipation of energy, has been effaced. That effacing has obscured sources of conflict within Victorian experience, which find a peculiarly intense form in Hopkins's poetry and in his journals. Tyndall was not only an exceptionally alluring and widely published writer on scientific questions, he was also well known as a materialist, as one who refused the idea of miracles, and one who was not afraid to accept the epithet 'atheist'.[20] The present essay therefore brings to the surface a network of allusion and controversy, shared with other Victorian intellectuals, that in Hopkins's work becomes vehemently condensed.

'He was intimately versed in the whole range of scientific expression, and showed a preference for such terms as were most recondite and but seldom used.' So wrote Father John MacLeod, a younger contemporary, in the internal journal of the Jesuits in 1906.[21] This strain in Hopkins was no mere quaint attachment to the out-of-the-way; it was rather an expression of his earnest familiarity with a field of experience more openly available to the Victorians than it is to us: the current work of scientists and the difficult, world-embracing meanings of their work. It is also a sign of his abiding fascination with the specificity of things, a specificity that is only at great cost brought into temper with authority.

[19] P. G. Tait, *Light* (Edinburgh, 1884). Hopkins disliked what he perceived as Tait's tone of condescension and—strikingly—his mentalism rather than materialism, his failure to apprehend the richness of the material world: 'they end in conceiving only of a world of formulas, with its being properly speaking in thought, towards which the outer world acts as a sort of feeder, supplying examples for literary purposes' (*Letters*, III, 139–40, 7 Aug. 1886). Tait was an important correspondent and friend for Clerk Maxwell, but Tyndall's obdurate enemy. Despite Hopkins's impatience with the book he might have found (and perhaps did) the discussion of different kinds of light valuable: 'Reflection from the surface of metals, and of very highly refractive substances such as diamond, generally gives at all incidences elliptically polarised light' (230).

[20] In response to a Catholic critic of his Belfast Address Tyndall wrote: 'I do not fear the charge of Atheism; nor should I even disavow it, in reference to any definition of the Supreme which he, or his order, would be likely to frame.' *Fragments of Science*, vol. II, 10th impression (London, 1889), 205.

[21] Fr. John MacLeod, 'The Diary of a Devoted Student of Nature', *Letters and Notices* (Apr. 1906), 390, collected in Gerald Roberts (ed.), *Gerard Manley Hopkins: The Critical Heritage*, (London, 1987), 64–5.

In Roman Catholic circles at the time new developments in scientific theory were by no means always seen as being in conflict with established doctrine. In the late 1870s *The Month*, the main organ of educated Catholic opinion, was sanguine about the possibility of reconciling evolutionism with the teachings of the Church. In a review essay on St George Mivart's *Lessons from Nature, as Manifested in Mind and Matter*, which refers back also to Mivart's earlier *Genesis of Species*, John Rickaby claims that Mivart 'had previously shown the complete harmony between the strictest orthodoxy and the theory of evolution'.[22] Hopkins himself had taken the same view of Mivart's work in a letter to his mother two years earlier in 1874: 'You should read St. George Mivart's *Genesis of Species*: he is an Evolutionist though he combats downright Darwinism and is very orthodox' (*Letters*, III, 128). Rickaby continues in *The Month*: 'It would be well too if Catholics would learn more accurately the real bearings of the relations between science and religion, and would never forget that it is impossible that dogma can conflict with physical science.'

This sanguine view is tempered in the next paragraph which looks back towards earlier conditions of Church authority: 'We are fortunate that in these troubled days of her journey through time, the Church has had no need to shield the faith of her children by laying restraint, as she has sometimes been obliged to do, on the free discussion of the discoveries of science.' Be that as it may, St George Mivart was eventually excommunicated as a result of articles he wrote from the mid-1880s on, repudiating ecclesiastical authority.

That sequence of events illustrates both the openness of Catholicism to the latest scientific discoveries and the dangerous borderland trodden by all those within the Church who were interested in scientific explanation. All was well so long as the discoveries could be appropriated to an earlier body of approved knowledge or shown to issue from the words of earlier teachers—as the article under discussion concludes: 'It has been shown that the possibility of this latest discovery of the gradual evolution of species was prepared for in the teaching of the most honoured among the great minds which in all ages have devoted

---

[22] *The Month and Catholic Review*, 8 (May–Aug. 1876), 107.

themselves to her service.' Indeed, in an article a few months later, 'St. Augustine and Scientific Unbelief', the writer invokes the difficulty of belief in recent physics as an analogy to difficulties of belief in transubstantiation. In each case it is necessary, he argues, to rely upon the authority of teachings that one cannot, unless especially trained and long practised, encompass. The writer invokes Helmholtzian theory:

What pupil would be allowed to interrupt the very first lectures of his professor of physics by such premature questions as these: If heat is a mode of motion, how do we cool hot tea by stirring it? If light is propagated by modulations, how do we actually see the rays in straight lines? If musical harmony depends upon a certain regularity, proportion, and interlacement of atmospheric waves, how is it that these conditions are not utterly destroyed by the ever-varied modifying obstacles encountered in different concert rooms, and by the ever-varied relative position of the several instruments?[23]

The difficult novelty of current physics—whose formulation here draws directly on Tyndall's writing in *Sound*—demonstrates that the universe is full of unexpected and hidden phenomena for which authoritative interpretation is required.

An often-repeated claim among Victorian scientists, on the other hand, was that science was the love of truth 'for its own sake'. For example, in *Nature*, 1 May 1884, adjacent to a long article on 'The Krakatoa Eruption' whose after-sunsets so fasci-

---

[23] *The Month* 9 (Sept.–Dec. 1876), 202–3. This discussion appears to draw directly on Tyndall's *Sound*, esp. at 282–3 where Tyndall discusses Helmholtz and uses the same example. The same writer, John Rickaby, whose brother Joseph had earlier written a critique of Tyndall's Belfast Address in *The Month*, gives a hostile account of Tyndall in his next essay 'The Reign of Mist', 281–96, but a much more appreciative account in the following volume, 10, (Jan.–Apr. 1877), in an essay on 'Evolution and Involution' (269–85). There he writes that the physicist has been able to reduce the 'primary phenomena' of 'material force' 'to undulations or modes of motion; and by discovering the principle of 'the conservation of energy'—the counterpart to the principle of the indestructibility of matter—he has come to see the close bond of union—that exists between the workings of the several forces of nature, and the constant transformations that take place between them, at least as regards their outward manifestations. The pure physicist, as such, goes no further than the external effects; according to Professor Tyndall 'the convertibility of natural forces consists solely in the transformations of dynamic into potential and of potential into dynamic energy. In no other sense has the convertibility of force, at present, any scientific meaning' (276). Zaniello, *Hopkins in the Age of Darwin*, has an informative discussion of the Rickaby brothers in his chapter on 'The Stonyhurst Philosophers'.

nated observers, including Hopkins, S. Newcomb distinguishes different attitudes to authority:

If called upon to define the scientific spirit, I should say that it was the love of truth for its own sake. This definition carries with it the idea of a love of exactitude—the more exact we are the nearer we are to the truth. It carries with it a certain independence of authority; because, although an adherence to authoritative propositions taught us by our ancestors, and which we regard as true, may, in a certain sense, be regarded as love of truth, yet it ought rather to be called a love of these propositions, irrespective of their truth. The lover of truth is ready to reject every previous opinion the moment he sees reason to doubt its exactness. (10)

The emphasis here on exact observation chimes in with Hopkins's work. Certainly, Hopkins was insistent that new circumstances heighten observation: in one of his contributions to *Nature* he points out that many attribute to the Krakatoa eruption effects already observable but not then paid much attention to: 'It is, however, right and important to distinguish phenomena really new from old ones first observed under new circumstances which make people unusually observant' (30 Oct. 1884, 636). Other of his contributions to *Nature* make essentially the same point: 'I may remark that things common at home have sometimes first been remarked abroad. The stars in snow were first observed in the polar regions; it was thought that they only arose there, but now everyone sees them with the naked eye on his coatsleeve' (*Nature* (16 Nov. 1882), 53). 'There seems to be no reason why the phenomenon should not be common, and perhaps if looked out for it would be found to be. But who looks east at sunset?'

You must first expect to find, or you must look from a point of view contrary to the ordinary, to make such discoveries, Hopkins indicates. New circumstances—the encounter with phenomena strained within the language and metrics of a poem, for example—can make things fresh. But though de-familiarization can make things *seem* new, Hopkins emphasizes that many of them were already there, all about us. The good sense of this argument also serves to keep most phenomena within the bounds of established knowledge. Newcomb's emphasis on the need to respond to new observations and discard old authorities tells against all that Hopkins had committed himself to.

The problem becomes clear in Hopkins's tart remarks on Tyndall's references to authoritative sources in the Belfast Address: 'I notice that he has no sense of the relative weights of authority: he quotes Draper, Whewell and other respectable writers for or against Aristotle, Bacon etc as if it were just the same thing and you were keeping at the same level—the Lord Chief Justice rules this way, his parlourmaid however says it should be the other, and so on.'[24]

Hopkins takes for granted that major writers of the past carry most weight and that there is a permanent class hierarchy in knowledge. Tyndall assumes that the more recent writers are more likely to be correct. This is not only a matter of Hopkins being authoritarian and Tyndall flexible—though it may be that too. It is, rather, a confrontation between two *forms* of authority, one of them the more familiar to us now. Hopkins assumes that truth has a stable, though hermeneutic, form, whereas Tyndall adopts a progressive heuristic. In this pattern science steadily accrues true knowledge and discards error: the most recent is taken to be the most correct.

Hopkins was both fascinated by and resistant to evolutionism wherever he found it. He calls it 'a philosophy of continuity or flux' and insists on the need to uncover stable mathematical principles that will sustain difference within these chromatic patterns. Indeed, Hopkins's formulation of such distinctions in acoustical terms in 1867 (before the start of *Nature* in 1869 when the discussion of such topics became widespread) suggests that he already knew something of the arguments in Helmholtz's *Tonempfindungen*, published in Germany four years earlier, most probably through Tyndall's *Sound* (1866), though also, less wide-rangingly, through Müller's work on the science of language.[25]

To the prevalent philosophy and science nature is a string all the differences in which are really chromatic but certain places in it have

---

[24] *Letters*, III, 128. Hopkins read Tyndall's essay in *The Academy* (19 Aug. 1874), 209–19. This journal devoted a quarter of its space to science, which 'includes Natural Philosophy, Theology, and the Science of Language'.

[25] For discussion of the relations between evolutionary and language theory in this period see my 'Darwin and the Growth of Language Theory' in John Christie and Sally Shuttleworth (eds.), *Nature Transfigured: Essays in Literature and Science* (Manchester, 1989), 152–70. repr. as Ch. 5 above.

become accidentally fixed and the series of fixed points becomes an arbitrary scale. The new Realism will maintain that in musical strings the roots of chords, to use technical wording, are mathematically fixed and give a standard by which to fix all the notes of the appropriate scale.[26]

Yet that insistence, that need for fixing, springs from Hopkins's fascination with changeful forms, dappled things: whatever is fickle, freckled. Within Hopkins's responsiveness intellectual fields, expressed as physical and linguistic desires, knot and waver. He is drawn to natural history by its prinked exactness of observation, to physics by its charged meteorological interpretations and its insistence on waves, vibrations, patterns, beyond the ordinary range of our senses: above all, perhaps, by its recognition that light, heat, and sound are all modes of motion. In the later poetry particularly that motion reveals itself threateningly as entropy, the rapid and increasing disorganization that makes less and less of energy available, squandering difference.

Down roughcast, down dazzling whitewash, wherever an elm arches,
Shivelights and shadowtackle in long lashes lace, lance, and pair.
Delightfully the bright wind boisterous ropes, wrestles, beats earth
    bare
Of yestertempest's creases; in pool and rutpeel parches
Squandering ooze to squeezed dough, crúst, dust; stánches, stárches
Squadroned masks and manmarks treadmire toil there
Fóotfretted in it. Million-fuelèd, nature's bonfire burns on.
But quench her bonniest, dearest to her, her clearest-selvèd spark
Mán, how fást his fíredint, his mark on mind, is gone!

In Hopkins's poetry all parts of speech incline to verbs. Not only does he form verbs such as 'swarthed', 'sheaved', but adjectives and nouns often take on simultaneously the functions of verbs and present participles so that everything is de-stabilized, rushing onwards or oscillating. Everything is charged with motion. To take a typical, and lesser-known, example (c.1878),

---

[26] 'The Probable Future of Metaphysics', *Journals and Papers*, 120. See e.g. the discussion, in Part 3, of *On the Sensations of Tone*, 2nd edn. (London, 1885), 369: 'Then, again, we have seen that the reason why a chord in music appears to be the chord of a determinate root, depends as before upon the analysis of a compound tone into its partial tones, that is, as before upon those elements of a sensation which cannot readily become subjects of conscious perception.'

where even the first word 'furl' is a record of process, feasibly either verb or noun as the eye alights upon it, and the line-ending poises 'down' momentarily as substantive, the soft covering of the leaf, before the enjambement loosens it as adverbial, downward motion:[27]

> The furl of fresh-leaved dogrose down
> His cheeks the forth-and-flaunting sun
> Had swarthed about with lion-brown
> Before the Spring was done.
>
> .   .   .
>
> Or like a juicy and jostling shock
> Of blue bells sheaved in May
> Or wind-long fleeces on the flock
> A day off shearing day.

The fascination with the manifest and with its hidden energy of form, the suggestion that light and pitch are related, that out of the white solar rays kingfishers catch fire and shining comes from shook foil, the discussion of the blue of the sky and its meaning (Mary's colour) are not Hopkins's alone. All these concerns are spread through the pages of *Nature* in the 1870s and 1880s, and are explored from the mid-century in the writing of people like Tyndall and greater theorists such as Faraday, Rayleigh, Clerk Maxwell, and Helmholtz. They vibrate in Hopkins's language and in his metrical experiments too. Those metrical experiments have been profusely studied; more remains to be thought through in relation to energy physics. From considerations of space, however, I have chosen to reserve that topic for a future essay.

Nor were the pages of *Nature* entirely devoid of poetry themselves. Hopkins's first letter to the journal (16 Nov. 1882, 53) was triggered by a discussion of 'rayons de crépuscule' in the previous issue, 9 November 1882 (30). Immediately adjacent in that issue is an article on James Clerk Maxwell's life and major scientific contribution which ends by quoting the opening of Maxwell's 'Paradoxical Ode to Hermann Stoffkraft'. Maxwell's sardonic survey of his contemporaries' (unsuccessful) attempts to dislodge the soul from matter and energy, though metrically more conservative, has a semantic vigour and precision not unlike Hopkins's own:

---

[27] *Poetical Works* 1990, 154.

My soul's an amphicheiral knot,
Upon a liquid vortex wrought
By Intellect, in the Unseen residing.
And thine doth like a convict sit,
With marlinspike untwisting it,
Only to find its knottiness abiding;
Since all the tools for its untying
In four-dimensioned space are lying,
Wherein thy fancy intersperses
Long avenues of universes,
While Klein and Clifford fill the void
With one finite, unbounded homaloid,
And think the Infinite is now at last destroyed.

The temper of *Nature* in its early days was open, various, conversational, enquiring, making room for interested amateurs and conducting controversies without great pulling of rank. *Nature*'s early ideals were set out in the first issue (4 Nov. 1869):

Men of science work not for themselves, or for their scientific fellows, but for mankind; and that only mischief can come of it if they whose business it is to ask Nature her secrets are hindered from telling the world all that they think they hear. It is impossible to separate science from other knowledge and from daily life: all new discoveries especially must have ties with every part of our nature. (13)

During the first volumes of *Nature* a spirited correspondence recurred concerning the correlations of music and colour, alongside meteorological observations, discussion of comets and sunspots, the flight of birds and 'wingmanship' (*Nature*, 1870, 431), the flowering of winter plants, lumeniferous ether, electrical shining. The laws of thermodynamics, in particular, set a puzzle that moved in contrary directions and engaged those outside the scientific community, suggesting at once an energetic rush towards inertia and a teased-out system of interpenetrating waves that produced systems of extraordinary complexity without losing the individual impulse. These, at least, were the terms in which writers like Tyndall made such knowledge available to their contemporaries, as I shall illustrate. So my argument here is not a matter of finding single sources, or of simply assigning priorities (though I do seek to establish the reading of particular and hitherto undiscussed works and their significance in Hopkins's creativity). As important is feeling the energy available to

Hopkins in the scientific, secular world around him, and in which he participated.

Hopkins's fascination with philology, and the importance of language history to his poetry, is well known. Scientists, like Maxwell and Clifford and Sylvester, were as much fascinated in this period with philology as were poets. The mathematician W. K. Clifford, following William Barnes, translated *Erkenntnistheorie* as 'Ken-lore'; J. J. Sylvester in his Presidential Address to the Mathematical and Physical Section of the British Association in 1869 argued that there is a close connection between mathematics and philology:

The relation between these two sciences is not perhaps so remote as may at first appear; and indeed it has often struck me that metamorphosis runs like a golden thread through the most diverse branches of modern intellectual culture, and forms a natural link of connection between subjects in their aims so remote as grammar, philology, ethnology, rational mythology, chemistry, botany, comparative anatomy, physiology, physics, algebra, versification, music, all of which under the modern point of view, may be regarded as having morphology for their common centre.[28]

Hopkins writes sympathetically of William Barnes's re-made Anglo-Saxon English in which 'degrees of comparison' become 'pitches of suchness'.[29] The quaint phrase, in which 'degrees of comparison' take on an acoustical intensity, has a particular aptness for my discussion. Hopkins's ear is tuned to 'sensations of tone' in his contemporaries' scientific work.

Hopkins several times alludes directly to Tyndall in his letters (whose name he spells Tyndal), and always with mixed responses. Tyndall generated in Hopkins an uneasy crossing of emotions—admiration of his eloquence, fellow feeling with a fine observer, enjoyment of his imaginative passion, dismay at his materialist system of explanation, and an unfettered enjoyment of Tyndall's power of imaging fresh knowledge.

Writing to his mother on 20 September 1874, Hopkins added a long postscript concerning John Tyndall's Belfast Address to

---

[28] *The Laws of Verse or Principles of Versification Exemplified in Metrical Translations: together with The Inaugural Presidential Address ... of the British Association* (London, 1870), 130.

[29] *The Letters of Gerard Manley Hopkins to Robert Bridges*, ed. Claude Colleer Abbott, rev. edn. (Oxford, 1955), 163. Hereafter *Letters*, I.

the British Association for the Advancement of Science. This Address roused widespread controversy because of Tyndall's insistence that materialism offered a sufficient creative explanation of the history of the universe and of mankind. Tyndall warned of the tendency of religion, both in the past and potentially, to 'exercise despotic sway over . . . intellect' (216). In the Address he outlined a history of the search for knowledge, seeing it as a primal impulse, a desire for causality. Within that history, religion had the role of adversary—first anthropomorphizing, and then inhibiting, the free exploration of observed phenomena. In particular, Tyndall dwells on the case of Giordano Bruno: 'Struck with the problem of the generation and maintenance of organisms, and duly pondering it, he came to the conclusion that Nature in her productions does not imitate the technic of man' (212).

This recognition of a disjunction between natural processes and human patterns of expectation and design Tyndall sees as one of the characterizing gains of science. Bruno was, Tyndall recounts, a martyr to these values. Originally a Dominican monk, he was accused of heresy, fell into the hands of the Inquisition, and was eventually burnt at the stake. It is not surprising that Hopkins found the piece disquieting, not to say infuriating.

It is Tyndall's willingness *not* to know that troubles Hopkins: 'It is not only that he looks back to an obscure origin, he looks forward with the same content to an obscure future—to be lost "in the infinite azure of the past" (fine phrase by the by).'[30] Yet Tyndall casts epistemophilia as profoundly natural and emphasizes its evolutionary capacity: 'An impulse inherent in primeval man turned his thoughts and questionings betimes towards the sources of natural phenomena. The same impulse, inherited and intensified, is the spur of scientific action today' (209).

Tyndall proves, nevertheless, to be unwilling quite to shed the passional life that finds expression equally in religion, in sexual love, in 'Awe, Reverence, Wonder'. 'You who have escaped from these religions into the high-and-dry light of the understanding may deride them' (216). But high-and-dry light is not Tyndall's

---

[30] *Letters*, III, 128.

medium; he prefers the liberal oscillation within sentences, the vigour of metaphor, and the ardent re-composition of ideas. To that degree his views temptingly ran alongside the religious, even while they repudiated religious authority. That makes it possible for Hopkins to sustain a fellow feeling with him which gives sustained access to a range of ideas apparently at odds with Hopkins's own profession: 'I fear he must be called an atheist, but he is not a shameless one: I wish he might come round' (*Letters*, III, 128) Moreover, for Hopkins, confident of the incarnation and to whom the mass was an act of transubstantiation, materialism was always less threatening than was mentalism. Materialism simply did not go far enough: it understood inscape but not instress.

Hopkins had already made Tyndall's acquaintance when they were both in the Alps in 1868, that intense summer of freedom before Hopkins began his novitiate in the September. The meeting occurred at the foot of the Matterhorn as Tyndall was about to set out for his third attempt on the mountain. Apart from any conversation they may have had, two circumstances made the meeting notable to Hopkins: first, Hopkins's companion fell ill and Tyndall 'very kindly saw E. B. and prescribed a treatment' (*Journals*, 182). The other happening was the mass held specially at two in the morning for the guides who would accompany Tyndall's ascent. Both men record this event: Hopkins in the journal, Tyndall in *Hours of Exercise in the Alps*, the book of travel and scientific meditation that he published in 1871 and which recorded his active years of scientific exploration among mountains. Hopkins remarks:

There was no church nearer than Valtournanches, but there was to be mass said in a little chapel for the guides going up with Tyndal at two in the morning and so I got up for this, my burnt face in a dreadful state and running. We went down with lanterns. It was an odd scene; two of the guides or porters served; the noise of a torrent outside accompanied the priests. Then to bed again. (182)

Tyndall records that after first refusing to climb on a Sunday his guide was persuaded by the suggestion of an early mass: 'On Saturday Maquignaz saw his confessor, and arranged with him to have a mass at 2 A.M. on Sunday; after which, unshaded by the sense of duties unperformed, he would commence the ascent.'[31] Tyndall is unlikely to have been at the service himself.

The strangeness of the scene lingered with Hopkins. The rest of the day was spent very differently by the two writers but they each observed the energies of the physical world, in patterning, flux, and decay. Hopkins walked down the valley:

We passed a gorge at the end of which it was curious to see a tree rubbing and ruffling with the water at the neck just above a fall. Then we saw a grotto, that is deep and partly covered chambers of rock through which the torrent river runs ... Further, across the valley a pretty village ... and above, a grove of ash or sycamore or both, sprayed all one way like water-weed beds in a running stream, very English-looking. Beyond again, in the midst of a slope of meadow slightly pulled like an unsteady and swelling surface of water, some ashes growing in a beautifully clustered 'bouquet'. (*Journal*, 182)

The hidden energies of the scene produce swerves and tensions, but all grouped as pattern, chance aiding art, as Hopkins remarks. The next day they walked through 'pleasant groves of Spanish chestnut full of great scattered rocks'.

Much higher up the face of the mountain Tyndall looked on the starting-place of those rocks and describes the cataract of boulders: 'Their discharge ... was incessant ... and by detaching a single boulder, we could let loose a cataract of them, which flew with wild rapidity and with a thunderous clatter down the mountain' (290). Tyndall continues brooding on the implications of the laws of thermodynamics:

As long as our planet yields less heat to space than she receives from the bodies of space, so long will the forms upon her surface undergo mutation, and as soon as equilibrium, in regard to heat, has been established we shall have, as Thomson has pointed out, not peace, but death. Life is the product and accompaniment of change, and the selfsame power that tears the flanks of the hills to pieces is the mainspring of the animal and vegetable worlds. Still, there is something chilling in the contemplation of the irresistible and remorseless character of those infinitesimal forces, whose integration through the ages pulls down even the Matterhorn. Hitherto the impression that it made was that of savage strength, but here we had inexorable decay. (291)

---

[31] John Tyndall, *Hours of Exercise in the Alps* (London, 1871), 276.

The 'inexorable decay' that Tyndall describes strains against the wind-tossed life of trees and their shadows: 'shivelights and shadowtackle', 'Million fueled, nature's bonfire burns on.'[32]

Perhaps Hopkins did later read Tyndall's published account of the day they had started together. (The imbalance in all these reading-relations is expressed in the fact that Tyndall could not have read Hopkins's journal or, more strikingly, his poetry.) Whether or not Hopkins read that particular passage he could not have failed to respond to the discussions and the dreads ('world's wildfire, leave but ash') released by the laws of thermodynamics: and did not, as one of his last and greatest poems, written in July 1888, 'That Nature is a Heraclitean Fire and of the Comfort of the Resurrection', makes clear.

The later part of Tyndall's Belfast Address as printed in *The Academy* in 1874 concentrates on the 'great generalisations' of the present: 'The theory of the origin of species is but one of them. Another, of still wider grasp and more radical significance, is the doctrine of the Conservation of Energy' (214). The passage quoted above from *Hours of Exercise* brings out the new terrors released by the second law of thermodynamics and widely discussed during the 1870s: particularly, that disorder tends to increase and that equilibration brings not equity or peace but death irrecuperable. Energy is transformed, dissipated, absolutely irretrievable: 'vastness blurs, and time beats level'. In the universe as described by entropy there can be no resurrection. That much is acknowledged in *The Unseen Universe* (1875) a work of scientific Christian apologetics by the physical mathematicians Stewart and Tait.

While it is very easy to change all of our mechanical or useful energy into heat, it is only possible to transform a portion of this heat-energy into work. After each change too the heat becomes more and more dissipated or degraded, that is, less and less available for any future transformation.

---

[32] James Leggio, 'The Science of a Sacrament', *The Hopkins Quarterly*, 4 (1977), 63, suggests that 'The transformation of bread and wine into body and blood provided a model for change that served as an alternative to the physicist's model of thermodynamic decline. In the transubstantiation there is a change from a lower to a higher state of charge instead of the reverse; therein lay the action of grace.' The analogy, though pleasing, does not seem to me to encompass the passionate apprehension of entropy in 'Spelt from Sybil's Leaves' and 'That Nature is a Heraclitean Fire'.

In other words, the tendency of heat is towards equalisation; heat is, par excellence, the communist of our universe, and it will undoubtedly bring the present system to an end. (126)

To right this political difficulty for the universe, they invoked an 'unseen universe' out of which our present one arose and whence all energy flowed and is returned for renewal: a dramatic invocation of the scientific imagination indeed. In the poetry that begins to flow again after 1876, and particularly in that of the 1880s, Hopkins eschews the pathway into the unseen. Instead, he more and more takes in the implications of thermodynamics. In 'That Nature is a Heraclitean Fire' he breaks out of the dilemma of the earth's self-consuming energy to the most concentrated fusion within the palpable and physical world, the enduring outcome of heat: the diamond. The poem ends:

This Jack, joke, poor potsherd, patch, matchwood,
                                                            immortal diamond,
          Is immortal diamond.[33]

The evanescent flare of readily consumed matchwood, the friability of the pot even when it has been through the kiln, are matched and surpassed by the condensation of the diamond, itself a form of coal, here become—through Christ—immortal in Nature's Heraclitean fire.

Between the time of the encounter between Tyndall and Hopkins and the publication of the Belfast Address Tyndall had published other highly controversial Addresses, particularly 'On the Scientific Use of the Imagination'—a piece first presented to the British Association in 1870 that he revised a number of times and that appears at intervals in different forms. The tenor of Tyndall's argument was that imagination is essential if the hidden physical properties of the universe are to be revealed. Only thus will new prospects of knowledge open: 'Newton's passage from a falling apple to a falling moon was, at the outset, a leap of the prepared imagination . . . In fact, without this power, our knowledge of nature would be a mere tabulation of coexistences and sequences. We should still believe in the succession of day and night, of summer and winter; but the soul of Force would be dislodged from our universe' (6).

[33] *Poetical Works 1990*, 198.

The binding energy of the imagination induces causal relations while the limits of imagination and language constrain representation: 'Strictly speaking, the spectrum embraces an infinity of colours, but the limits of language and of our powers of distinction cause it to be divided into seven segments: red, orange, yellow, green, blue, indigo, violet' (13). Tyndall's discussion, here and elsewhere, of the relations between thermodynamics, acoustics, and optics, his figuring of sound waves, air waves, the waves in ether and the sea, his emphasis on imagination and particular demonstration, on energy and flux, his emphasis on 'the emotion of the intellect' all would strike chords in Hopkins's consciousness: 'By myriad blows (to use a Lucretian phrase) the image and superscription of the external world are stamped as states of consciousness upon the organism.'[34]

A major topic in 'The Scientific Use of the Imagination' is again light, particularly the reason for the sky's azure colour. Tyndall argued that the sky is not air stained blue. This may seem obvious enough to us, but at the time it provoked considerable excitement and some adverse commentary. When George Eliot, in a metaphor in *Middlemarch*, referred to the relations between signs and interpretation as being like a sky 'coloured by a diffused thimbleful of matter', R. H. Hutton in 1871 demurred at the allusion to 'Professor Tyndal's speculations as to the cause of the blueness of the sky'.[35] Tyndall writes: 'Pure unsifted solar light is white' but 'turned into their equivalents of sensation, the different light-waves produce different colours' (13). 'The light of our firmament', Tyndall argues, 'is reflected light.'

The light of the firmament comes to us across the direction of the solar rays, and even against the direction of the solar rays . . . In accounting for the colour of the sky, the first question suggested by analogy would undoubtedly be, is not the air blue? But . . . How if the air be blue, can the light of sunrise and sunset, which travels through vast distances of air, be yellow, orange or even red? (15)

---

[34] *The Academy* (22 Aug. 1874), 215.

[35] *Spectator* (16 Dec. 1871), 1,528–9. The discussion began with Rudolf Clausius's argument in the late 1840s that the light of the sky is due to reflection from water bubbles. Tyndall, and subsequently Rayleigh, rejected this theory, demonstrating instead that sky blue is the result of scattering by particles of small dimensions as compared with the wavelength of light. I am grateful to Dr Peter Harman for discussion of this matter.

Tyndall's answer is that minute particles in the air reflect the ripples of ether-waves: 'Turned into their equivalents of sensation, the different light-waves produce different colours. Red, for example, is produced by the largest waves . . . blue, of the small waves'; 'an undue fraction of the smaller waves is scattered by the particles, and, as a consequence, in the scattered light, blue will be the predominant colour' ('Imagination', 13–14). White light, he argues, is directly transmitted light, azure is the result of reflected light. (One of his most popular demonstrations was to produce an artificial blue sky, a feat he performed, for example, in the Cambridge Senate House.)

In 'The Blessed Virgin compared to the Air we Breathe' Hopkins draws an extended metaphor from this discussion: 'look overhead how air is azured'. Mary is the medium. The sunbeams shine perfect through the blue, not stained by colour. Yet the solar rays are reflected so that colour is produced, a bath of air, that wards off the concentrated vehemence of the sun, of godhead.

> Yet such a sapphire-shot,
> Charged, steeped sky will not
> Stain light. Yea, mark you this:
> It does no prejudice.
> The glass-blue days are those
> When every colour glows,
> Each shape and shadow shows.
> Blue be it: this blue heaven
> The seven or seven times seven
> Hued sunbeam will transmit
> Perfect, not alter it.
> Or if there does some soft,
> On things aloof, aloft,
> Bloom breathe, that one breath more
> Earth is the fairer for.
> Whereas did air not make
> This bath of blue and slake
> His fire, the sun would shake,
> A blear and blinding ball
> With blackness bound, and all
> The thick stars round him roll
> Flashing like flecks of coal,
> Quartz-fret, or sparks of salt,
> In grimy vasty vault.

Mary (like the azure sky a protective veil to ward off from us the stark heat of the sun) both reflects and transmits. Such reflection produces colour, which makes possible the apprehension of what otherwise would be dark. 'The limits of language and of our powers of distinction', as Tyndall wrote, lead us to describe the spectrum in seven colours though it may be 'seven or seven times seven' or 'an infinity of colours'. The paradox of Mary is that she sustains the sunbeam 'perfect' (she carries the godhead of Christ without staining it), yet, as air in which earthly particles are suspended, she deflects the unbearable light of godhead.

During the 1880s, as Hopkins's interest in scientific matters intensified, his work on metre and music grew more systematic:

Coming to the point where I must go deep into scientific first principles I had a happy thought of putting my ideas for the purpose into the shape of a Paper to be read before a physical and mathematical science club which meets at the Royal Dublin Society once a month . . . Writing it has naturally cleared my mind and indeed opened out a sort of new world. I believe that I can now set metre and music both of them on a scientific footing which will be final like the law of gravitation.[36]

So he writes to Coventry Patmore, and finishes the letter with a postscript offering to send him the paper after it has been read and briskly upbraiding him for his attitude to science. Patmore in *Love and Poetry* had written loftily, 'The greatest and perhaps the only real use of natural science is to supply similes and parables for poets and theologians.' Hopkins rejoins 'The only use of natural science! It is a hard saying, who can hear it?'[37] Hopkins responded energetically both to precise observations and to the implications of physical and biological sciences, rather than dismantling them into decorative embellishments for poetry. Those other systems of understanding drive deep into his thought and form conflicts that propel his poetry.

[36] 'For the purpose of grounding the matter [his discussion of metre] thoroughly I am subjecting the terms of geometry, line, surface, solid and so on, many others to a searching examination', *Letters*, III, 379. This fascination with geometry in 1887 may in fact go some way to explain his scornful references a year later to George Minchin's *Uniplanar Kinematics of Solids and Fluids* (London, 1882). So may his being on holiday ('Besides we have no books except the farce of the fellow reading Minchin's *Kinematics* . . . this book I leave to him entirely, as you may suppose' *Letters*, I, 279). Perhaps, too, having just completed 'That Nature is a Heraclitean Fire' he felt he had grasped the principles of kinematics in another tongue!

[37] *Principles in Art* (London, 1913), 336, quoted *Letters*, III, 377 (20 Jan. 1887).

The sun on falling waters writes the text
Which yet is in the eye or in the thought.
It was a hard thing to undo this knot.

It is fitting, then, that the strongest evidence that Hopkins had read Helmholtz himself (rather than always Tyndall's, or Müller's rendering of his ideas) came through my pursuing an unconsidered aside in an 1882 letter to Bridges chiefly concerned with William Barnes. This, Hopkins's last reference to Tyndall, is to one of his invented compounds not chemical but linguistic.[38] Hopkins is discussing Barnes, the Dorset poet and philologist whose search for an English refreshed by dialect and loosed from abstraction fascinated him with a kind of pathos. Hopkins speaks scornfully of Tyndall's invention: 'The very worst compound ever I heard in English was Tyndal's word *clangtint* = *klangfarbe* in German = *timbre* in French for the quality of musical instruments' (*Letters*, 1, 166, 1 Dec. 1882). Hopkins is here alluding to Tyndall's translations of Helmholtz's terms in Tyndall's *Lectures on Sound* (2nd edn. (1869), 117). Tyndall's neologism had been commented on earlier by Max Müller and used by a number of later Victorian musicologists, but Hopkins's criticism, and its terms, are drawn straight from Alexander Ellis's translation of Helmholtz, *The Sensations of Tone* (24–5).

Ellis's work appeared first in 1877 and was extensively revised for a second edition in 1885 (see note 8 above). Ellis's own career shows how closely ideas concerning philology and mathematics ran. He was not only the translator of Helmholtz but an authority on language to whom Max Müller pays tribute, one of the founders of the Early English Text Society, the author of *Early English Pronunciation* and also of *Algebra Identified with Geometry*. Ellis, in an extremely long critique both of the philological and the scientific problems of Tyndall's neologism, discusses the three terms, *clangtint, klangfarbe*, and *timbre* side by side. The arguments he adduces are drawn from acoustics, philology, and the controversy concerning the relations between sound and

---

[38] Hopkins teases Bridges by inventing his own pseudo-scientific compounds to replace the word 'domeless' that he dislikes in Bridges's poem: 'No: better to say the kamp-tuliconless courts or Minton's-encaustic-tileless courts or vulcanised-india-rubberless courts . . . that Prometheus, who was at once a prophet and as a mechanic more than equal to Edison and the Jablochkoff candle and the Moc-main Patent Lever Truss with self-adjusting duplex gear and attachments . . .' (p. 167).

colour. He quotes, censoriously, Tyndall's discussion of Thomas Young (1773–1829) who developed the analogies between primary colours and simple tones and quotes Young's suggestion that 'this quality of sound is sometimes called its register, colour, or timbre'.[39] Ellis brushes aside the sustained controversies concerning the relations between the colour spectrum and the musical scale and their suggested 'tonal' analogies as 'a passing metaphorical expression'.

Hopkins, it would seem then, was almost certainly reading directly in Helmholtz's own work when he was himself considering the scientific basis of metre, sound, and music in the mid-1880s. By then, as Ellis's footnotes show, Helmholtz had also been caught into a number of thriving controversies of great urgency in England at the time, controversies that expanded from philology to nationhood, acoustics to the ordering of the universe: as do the concerns of Hopkins's poems. The fascination with the relations between sound and sight, and between the sound and colour of words, that we find throughout Hopkins's career, was not an idiosyncratic concern. It was in the mainstream of scientific debate at the time.[40] So, of course, was the

[39] The note occupies more than a page of small print. The general tenor is indicated by the following passage: 'Prof. Helmholtz uses the word *Klang* for a *musical tone*, which generally, but not always, means a *compound tone*. Prof. Tyndall . . . therefore proposes to use the English word *clang* in the same sense. But *clang* has already a meaning in English, thus defined by Webster: "a sharp shrill sound, made by striking together metallic substances, or sonorous bodies, as the *clang* of arms of any like sound, as the *clang* of trumpets." This word implies a degree of harshness in the sound, or more harshness than *clink*. Interpreted scientifically, then, *clang*, according to this definition, is either *noise* or one of those *musical tones with inharmonic upper partials*, which will be subsequently explained. It is therefore totally unadapted to represent a *musical tone* in general, for which the simple word *tone* seems eminently suited, being of course originally the tone produced by a *stretched* string . . . Of course, if *clang* could not be used, Prof. Tyndall's suggestion to translate Prof. Helmholtz's *Klangfarbe* by *clangtint* fell to the ground . . . Prof. Tyndall quotes Dr. Young to the effect that "this quality of sound is sometimes called its register, colour, or timbre." . . . Timbre . . . is a foreign word, often odiously mispronounced, and not worth preserving. *Colour* I have never met with as applied to music, except at most as a passing metaphorical expression.' Ellis, *On the Sensations of Tone*, 24.

[40] Clerk Maxwell's presentation of the fundamental basis of colour theory, 'On the Theory of Compound Colours', *Philosophical Transactions* (1860), is often cited in scientific journals of the time alongside Helmholtz. Attempts were frequently made to link the development of colour-sense to evolutionary processes. See e.g. Grant Allen, *The Colour-Sense: Its Origin and Development, An Essay in Comparative Psychology* (London, 1879).

emphasis on energy in its varying forms, as heat, light, sound—to which Hopkins triumphantly added, metre.

> thrush
> Through the echoing timber does so rinse and wring
> The ear, it strikes like lightnings to hear him sing;
> The glassy peartree leaves and blooms, they brush
> The descending blue; that blue is all in a rush
> With richness; the racing lambs too have fair their fling.[41]

Music and light for Hopkins give relief from bared opposition in which 'thoughts against thoughts in groans grind'.[42] They chime out inherent order without the striving after ethical choices:

> For good grows wild and wide,
> Has shades, is nowhere none;
> But right must seek a side
> And choose for chieftain one.
>
> Therefore this masterhood,
> This piece of perfect song,
> This fault-not-found-with good
> Is neither right nor wrong,
>
> No more than red and blue,
> No more than Re and Mi,
> Or sweet the golden glue
> That's built for by the bee.

Those carefree verses come from an untitled poem written after 1876, called by Bridges 'On a Piece of Music'. But the poem is unfinished and was set out in the manuscript in what Gardiner calls a 'dubious two-column arrangement'.[43] That arrangement

---

[41] *Poetical Works 1990*, 142.

[42] The possible analogies between colour and music were a continuing preoccupation of correspondents in *Nature*. Among the authorities cited and the contributors, professional and amateur, to the debate in the first volume, for example, were Herschel, Brewster, Grove, Helmholtz, Sedley Taylor, J. J. Murphy, Deas, C. J. Monro, Clerk Maxwell. The most frequent reference points are the current work of Clerk Maxwell and Helmholtz (neither of whom contributed directly and therefore do not appear in the index to the volume). The significance of this wide range of names for a study of reception and dissemination is that no pointers were offered to the non-scientific reader as to the comparative standing of the participants within the scientific community.

[43] *The Poems of Gerard Manley Hopkins*, ed. W. H. Gardner and N. H. MacKenzie, 4th edn. (Oxford, 1970), 313. *Poetical Works 1990* rearranges the verses: 159–60.

has been juggled into different orders by editors of differing religious views and moralized to insist that 'the "right" is the higher perfection'. The two-column manuscript form of the poem springs free, momentarily, of that dilemma.

The poem alludes to primary forms of difference: between red and blue ('Turned into their equivalents of sensation, the different light waves produce different colours. Red, for example is produced by the largest waves . . . blue, of the smaller waves', wrote Tyndall in 'The Scientific Use of the Imagination').[44] The 'absolutely pure fundamental colours' are, Helmholtz writes, most nearly approached in 'scarlet-red, yellow-green, and blue-violet'. He goes on to compare the spectrum with 'the ultimate simple elements of the sensations of tone, simple tones themselves' that are rarely heard alone.[45]

Hopkins's musical example of perfect difference is from abutting intervals in the sol-fa system 'Re and Mi'. As Ellis observes in a long note to Helmholtz's chapter on 'Just Intonation in Signing': 'The twenty years which have elapsed since Prof. Helmholtz's first acquaintance with the Tonic Sol-fa movement have made a struggling system, slowly elaborated by a Congregationalist minister in connection with his ministry, into a great national system of teaching singing.' It 'had the cordial approval of Prof. Helmholtz'.[46]

The last example of goodness without the strain of right and wrong takes up the instance of the honeycomb. Tyndall in the Belfast Address writes at length on Darwin's example of the hexagonal cell as non-teleological perfection achieved within the natural order, not by 'the "technic" of a man-like Artificer' but by means of the gradual processes of natural selection.[47] The example teased Hopkins and he returned to it in letters to Bridges in 1888. In the poem he eludes the controversies surrounding instinct and natural selection. He celebrates honey itself, the absolute 'golden glue' so perfectly stored.

The purity and directness of these verses need not be lost within the range of references I am drawing into the light. Quite

---

[44] In John Tyndall, *Essays on the Use and Limit of the Imagination in Science* (London, 1870), 23, 24.
[45] Ellis, *On the Sensations of Tone*, 64–5.
[46] Ibid. 423–6.
[47] *The Academy* (22 Aug. 1874), 214.

the contrary: Hopkins concentrated and absorbed such discussion. From it he drew both simple tones and resonance. Sometimes the world of perception studied by the scientists of the time seemed to offer repose from the struggle of endless ethical choices: a world that *is*, rather than a world of right and wrong. Sometimes, though, such studies provoked anxiety, threatening the collapse of more than individual creativity.

Hopkins in the 1880s is involved in an ever-widening search for an expression that can keep control and encompass the unravelling of the world in his own life, in the universe. All Hopkins's letters to *Nature* concern sunset, the oncoming of dark, the surge and foundering of colour:

I have witnessed, though slightly, the phenomenon of a blue setting. The sunset was bright this evening, the sun of a ruddy gold, which colour it kept till nothing was left of it but a star-like spot; then this spot turned, for the twinkling of an eye, a leaden or watery blue, and vanished.[48]

SPELT FROM SIBYL'S LEAVES

Earnest, earthless, equal, attuneable, vaulty, voluminous, . . .
    stupendous
Evening strains to be tíme's vást, womb-of-all, home-of-all,
    hearse-of-all night.
Her fond yellow hornlight wound to the west, her wild hollow
    hoarlight hung to the height
Waste; her earliest stars, earlstars, stárs principal, overbend us,
Fíre-féaturing héaven. For éarth her béing has unbóund; her dápple
    is at énd, as-
Tray or aswarm, all throughther, in throngs; self ín self stéepèd and
    páshed—qúite
Disremembering, dísmémbering áll now. Heart, you round me right
With: Óur évening is óver us; óur night whélms, whélms, ánd will
    énd us.
Only the beakleaved boughs dragonish damask the tool-smooth
    bleak light; black,
Ever so black on it. Óur tale, O óur oracle! Lét life, wáned, ah lét
    life wínd

---

[48] *Nature* (30 Oct. 1884), 633.

Off hér once skéined stained véined varíety upon, áll on twó spools;
  párt, pen, páck
Now her áll in twó flocks, twó folds—bláck, white; ríght, wrong;
  réckon but, réck but, mínd
But thése two; wáre of a world where bút these twó tell, éach off
  the other, of a ráck
Where, selfwrung, selfstrung, sheathe- and shelterless, thóughts
  agaínst thoughts ín groans grínd.[49]

Evening strains towards night. In the language of night's oncoming, words like 'equal' and 'waste' brood on the dissipation and final equilibration of energy which brings death. Earth 'her being has unbound'. The oncoming of night, the loss of variety, her dapple at an end 'our night whelms, whelms, and will end us'. The entropic movement is towards the degradation and loss of differentiating energy.[50] Fire both is, and consumes, energy. Only the principles of opposition sustain the tension of life—and they, unmitigated by 'skeined stained veined variety', grapple and grind upon each other without outcome or ending.

  'Truth is often of a dual character, taking the form of a magnet with two poles', wrote Tyndall in the Belfast Address. What to Tyndall is a liberating oscillation, to Hopkins can become a life-destroying clench. Hopkins needs the veined, dappled, varying phenomena of the world; he lives through their realization in language, through the extensions and turns of sprung rhythm. Condensing and prolonging are both ways of evading those bared opposites in which two explanations intolerably grind against each other, more like joints or passions than arguments.

[49] 'Spelt from Sybil's Leaves' was completed in Nov. 1886 (*Letters*, I, 245–6).
[50] J. Leggio, 'The Science of a Sacrament' (n. 32 above), also reads this poem as playing between Lucretian and entropic concepts.

12

The Reader's Wager: Lots, Sorts, and Futures

Reading Peter Carey's novel, *Oscar and Lucinda* (1988), provoked me to think about the fascination with gambling in the late nineteenth century, both in society and fiction. It made me also pursue the question of the reader's wager. What do we stand to gain or lose in entering and playing out a fiction? The reader's task (and joy) is not only participation but prediction, the weighing of multiple futures, and the knowledge that we never can foresee enough. No sentence, even, can be confidently foretold though we master all the skills of predication.

What particular beliefs and anxieties were at stake for later nineteenth-century readers and writers that were figured in the frequent scenes of gambling in Victorian fiction? Let me move back to that question through Carey's novel. Carey takes as hero and heroine two committed gamblers. The starting-point from which the writing later swerves is Edmund Gosse's *Father and Son: A Study of Temperaments*, first published in 1907 but describing a childhood of the 1850s and early 1860s. The 8-year-old boy, having questioned his father on idolatry, performs a variant on Pascal's wager, one of the two founding documents of probability theory. Pascal in the mid-seventeenth century expressed the problem of belief in the form of a wager; he argued that no matter how small the odds of God's existence we must make the effort of belief since the outcome is infinite: bliss against damnation.[1]

---

[1] See Ian Hacking, *The Emergence of Probability: A Philosophical Study of Early Ideas about Probability, Introduction and Statistical Inference* (Cambridge, 1975); Gerd Gigerenzer, *et al.*, *The Empire of Chance: How Probability Changed Science and Everyday Life* (Cambridge, 1989).

The young Edmund decides to test belief under experimental conditions:

One morning, when both my parents were safely out of the house, I prepared for the great act of heresy. I was in the morning-room on the ground-floor, where with much labour, I hoisted a small chair on to the table close to the window. My heart was now beating as if it would leap out of my side, but I pursued my experiment. I knelt down on the carpet in front of the table and looking up I said my daily prayer in a loud voice, only substituting the address 'O chair!' for the habitual one.

Having carried this act of idolatry safely through, I waited to see what would happen. It was a fine day, and I gazed up at the slip of white sky above the houses opposite, and expected something to appear in it. God would certainly exhibit his anger in some terrible form . . . I breathed the high, sharp air of defiance. But nothing happened; there was not a cloud in the sky, not an unusual sound in the street. Presently I was quite sure that nothing would happen. I had committed idolatry, flagrantly and deliberately, and God did not care. (1913 edn., 46–7)

His act does not at that time so much unsteady the child's belief in God as his 'confidence in my Father's knowledge of the divine mind'.

The child and the father in Gosse's autobiography typify a particularly Victorian dilemma: the father is Philip Gosse, the respected mid-nineteenth-century zoologist, who brought down ridicule on his head by countering Darwin with his own theory that God had implanted the fossils already formed in the rocks at the instant of creation, so providing earth with a false history, demanding belief against the odds, and enforcing Pascal's wager from the other side.

The child's mother, who died early, believed (Gosse tells us in an episode not referred to by Carey) 'that to "tell a story", that is, to compose a fictitious narrative of any kind, was a sin'. As a child she had a passionate skill in such story-telling and it remained a violent longing in her. Her secret diary records: 'Even now [at the age of 29] tho' watched, prayed and striven against, this is still the sin that most easily besets me' (20–21).

Carey uses these elements—fiction-making, gambling, the risks of faith, and the questions of genetic descent—to spring the traps he lays for the reader in the work. The novel is full of allusions to the historical world of Victorian England, including such

phenomena as the Crystal Palace and George Eliot. Lucinda buys
a glassworks with her inheritance, and the paradoxical fragility
and strength of glass is cross-set with questions of chance and
endurance in the book. (Indeed, the glass-rolling equipment
comes from a firm nonchalantly named Chance Brothers.) Pascal's wager is an intermittent, sometimes oblique, point of reference: when Oscar makes his first bet he thinks 'Perhaps he could
open an account at Blackwell's. He would like to purchase his
own copy of Mr. Paley's *Evidence*' (118). When Lucinda asks
him, a clergyman, to absolve her of the sin of gambling he
demands 'Where is the sin?' . . .

'Our whole life is a wager, Miss Leplastrier. We bet—it is all in Pascal
. . . We bet that there is a God. We bet our life on it. We calculate the
odds, the return, that we shall sit with the saints in paradise. Our
anxiety about our bet will wake us before dawn in a cold sweat. We are
out of bed and on our knees, even in the midst of winter. And God sees
us, and sees us suffer. And how can this God, a God who sees us at
prayer beside our bed . . .' His hands were quite jerky in their movements. (261)

The reader is invited to enter a tumultuous, and old-fashioned,
intimacy with the two principal characters. Oscar's goodness is
affirmed and Lucinda's lovingness, against the odds. Their love
energizes the work. The bet between them is a form of marriage
vow. The outcome seems certain: they are the narrative pair and,
by inference, the genetic pair in this tale told by Oscar's great-
grandson. Both must have survived for the narrator to exist. By
a trick of plot, managed with malign dexterousness, Oscar is
brought to death and yet manages to be the great-grandfather of
the narrator. Not by Lucinda. Lucinda loses Oscar, the wager,
her inheritance. She becomes, we are told, a heroine of the
Australian labour movement.

   This fiction uses ingenious and specious forms to lay claim to
truth. Like Oscar, like the wasps caught inside glass, the reader
also has—in both senses—'the wrong intelligence'. The wasps
'bashed against "nothing" as if they were created only to demonstrate to Oscar Hopkins the limitations of his own understanding, his ignorance of God, and that the walls of hell might
be made of something like this, unimaginable, contradictory,
impossible' (494). Oscar Hopkins's name itself imagines an

almost impossible—but suddenly revealing—condensation of Oscar Wilde and Gerard Manley Hopkins.

The reader of this novel is placed in a primary narrative dilemma, strapped across two systems, the teleological and the stochastic (a matter of numerical frequency rather than law). Parenting, authoring, and godhead are entangled in particular ways in the later nineteenth century, a period when evolutionary theory was making classification itself a narrative of change rather than an enduring system of types but when patterns of genetic inheritance had not yet been established. For the Victorians the new ideas abroad in evolutionary theory and in thermodynamics intensified the difficult relations between design and causation, futurity and chance.[2]

Both evolutionary and thermodynamic theory dramatize the oncoming future and yet make it hard to imagine it. According to the second law of thermodynamics, entropy (disorganization) tends to a maximum; according to evolutionary theory, variation is the medium of radical change. Future patterns therefore become difficult to descry. The new theories unsettled knowledge of the past and prediction of the future. Instead of constant rediscovery of stable norms the future became irregular, chancy, peopled by speculative types whose relation to the present might repeat and extend the scandal of our relation to other earlier species.

In such an erratic situation games of chance and novels may both figure and circumscribe the dilemma of interpreting the future. Marilyn Strathern in *The Gender of the Gift* (Berkeley, 1989) points out how endemic to modern Western cultures is the idea of incompleteness, and thus of futurity. The world is not finished and replenishing, nor in sustained equilibrium. Rather, it is unravelling or diversifying. Both patterns, in different ways, challenge design. As a character puts it in Tom Stoppard's play *Hapgood* (1988):

Quantum mechanics made everything finally go random, things can go this way or that way, the mathematics deny certainty, they reveal only

---

[2] Helmholtz's first paper on the conservation of energy appeared in 1847 and was being discussed in generalist journals by the late 1850s; *The Origin of Species* (1859) generated immediate controversy. For discussion of the connections between physics and mythography in the period see my 'The Death of the Sun', in Barry Bullen (ed.), *The Sun is God* (Oxford, 1989); repr. as Ch. 10, above.

probability and chance, and Einstein couldn't believe in a God who threw dice. He should have come to me, I would have told him. 'Listen, Albert, He threw you—look around, he never stops.' (49)

Many recent writers of fiction pinpoint this problem of what we may call narrative genetics, in which the unlikely outcome is no less determined than the likely and the writer cannot shake off the authorial talent for fixing: so, Julian Barnes in *A History of the World in Ten and a Half Chapters* (1989) writes:

As in most of the Old Testament, there's a crippling lack of free will around—or even the illusion of free will. God holds all the cards and wins all the tricks. The only uncertainty is how the Lord is going to play it this time: start with the two of trumps and lead up to the ace, start with the ace and run down to the two, or mix them around. And since you never can tell with paranoid schizophrenics, this element does give the narrative some drive. (176–7)

Reader and gamester ignore that parsimony, persistently inventing possibilities and alternatives as they play, conjuring an experience of freedom before the game concludes. Ian Stewart asserts in *Does God Play Dice? The Mathematics of Chaos* (Oxford, 1989) that 'We are beginning to discover that systems obeying immutable and precise laws do not always act in predictable and regular ways. Simple laws may not produce simple behaviour. Deterministic laws can produce behaviour that seems random. Order can produce its own kind of chaos' (2). Like much new knowledge, this has been long known. But it takes new intensity and new terms from fresh technology. Carey gambles with the Victorian novel, playing Einstein, pinpointing anxieties, rifling rules. The unforeseeable (and yet predicted) conclusion reveals to the reader the risks we take in fulfilling the fictions of belief, of law, of chaos. His brilliant and painful book raises questions and constrains response. But other questions remain to be asked about the meaning of gambling in Victorian fiction—questions that will include the self-aware interpretative acts of nineteenth-century readers and writers themselves.

From time to time, when there is a crash on the stock-market or a storm blows off our roof we become aware of those under-pinning forms of gambling, aggressive and defensive, common in bourgeois life: shareholding and insurance. To nineteenth-century people gambling could bring dereliction more immediately.

The Victorians were very well aware that the stock-market is a form of gambling—as the fate of Mr Merdle and the unknown others affected by his bankruptcy grimly shows in *Little Dorrit* (1858). Stockpiling goods is a dangerous game, as the mayor of Casterbridge discovers when the bumper harvest brings down the price of grain.

Gambling puts goods in jeopardy in hope of gain. That's a succinct, though insufficient, definition of the practice. Risk and hope are essential to its power in human experience. So is fascination with the future: prediction; chance or design, chance *as* design, a causal or stochastic universe. Speculation includes the ideas of hypothesizing, surveying, watching, risking goods against future events. These are the urgencies ritualized in games of chance and in the act of betting or wagering.

Underpinning them is play, both the rule-bound observances that come close to religious ritual and the eroticism that seeks to discover more and more spontaneous possibilities within a narrowly determined field. Repetition, rule, and the unforeseen are, at this other level of explanation, essential to the meaning of games of chance. In my argument here I concentrate on the *scene* of gambling in fiction: that scene concerns the spectator as often as the player. It frequently makes manifest the hidden activities of the reader reading: it encodes as event the reader's inner speculative theatre.

To take one further recent example to clarify this point before I turn to nineteenth-century examples: a powerful condensation of gambling, eroticism, and what I am calling the reader's wager is to be found in the scene of strip-poker near the beginning of Thomas Pynchon's *The Crying of Lot 49*. Oedipa Maas wagers against her companion her skill in predicting the plot of the old film they are watching on television. Oedipa loses her clothes item by item as she fails to guess or half-guesses the twists and turns of the plot. She is confident, though, that she can predict the final outcome and so save her underwear. She knows that in such a story and such a genre, the heroes (one of them a boy-child) *must* be rescued from the drowned submarine. They are not. She is naked. The reader begins to experience, from that point on, triumph and paranoia at once, taking both parts in this unsound wager where the rules display the fictiveness of rule.

The *addictiveness* of reading comes from this presaging endeavour. Why do we read on? Why do we turn the next page? Why are we not satisfied with the munificence of the page spread under our eye? Some writers do offer a textual abundance that toys with satiety; we may then indeed grow languorous, hardly able to stir the next sheet. Most fiction, though, generates its promise by giving to the reader the power moment by moment to amplify the text with multiple alternative outcomes, to weigh chances, to foresee and determine, to experience loss and gain, to *hope*, particularly against the odds. To take a very basic and extreme story, one told (and suspended) as an example in John Venn's influential book on probability theory, *The Logic of Chance* (1866):

A man finds himself on the sands of the Wash or Morecambe Bay in a dense mist, when the spring-tide is coming in; and knows therefore that to be once caught by the tide would be fatal. He hears a church-bell at a distance, but has no means of knowing whether by following its sound he will be led out into the mid-stream and be lost, or led back to dry land and safety. Here there can be no repetition of the event, and the cases are indistinguishably alike, to him . . . is not then his prospect of death, it will be said, necessarily equal to one half? (118)

Venn leaves the tale half-told. It has served his purpose, which is to produce a limiting case to demonstrate that 'we always entertain a certain degree of belief on every question that can be stated'.

The urgency of the situation brings that point home, Venn claims. But for the reader the half-toldness of the tale is perturbing: not to know the outcome forces us into baffling calculation without closure. The iterative present tense of its telling both distances it, as a signalled example, and brings it close, as a circumstantial event. The mist is the condition of the story: both climatic and symptomatic it is at once the main reason for the man's predicament and a representation of his decision-making dilemma. As Venn says, 'To stand still and wait for better information is certain death'; but that, formally, is the position that the reader of the tale is left in. What assurance or what irony is in the sound of that *church* bell, its sound perhaps brought closer by water or safely 'at a distance' across land? Strain as we may at these redundant clues we do not know what the man decides, nor what comes of it.

The frustration experienced is out of scale with the function of the example in the argument and tells us something about the habit of reading and the limits of the reader's hypothesizing powers. Here is the simplest of futures: only two. And only one possibility of further sequence: death or life. Yet with all our skills as readers we are unable to settle the outcome.

A short, end-stopped answer to the first question I posed earlier (why is gambling so frequent a topic in late-nineteenth-century fiction) might be that Victorian people gambled a good deal, at all levels of society. Betting on the horses, or on prize-fights, was a form of gambling across a wide social range. Gaming rooms had been made illegal in 1845, but they persisted behind the façades of private houses. Card-games such as whist rose in popularity in the later nineteenth century.

There are many moralistic Victorian novels about the dangers of gambling—and of that gambling on a larger scale, financial speculation. They range from J. H. Parker's *Speculation: A Tale* (reviewed in 1851 as showing 'the dire consequences of a reckless lust of gain') to the dust-heaps of Dickens's *Our Mutual Friend* (1865). George Moore's *Esther Waters* (1894) concerns a young girl of strict religious upbringing who enters service in the house of a great stable-owner. Gambling in this novel is shown to bring pleasure, hope, and gaiety to the poor, as well as disaster. George Meredith opens his last novel, *The Amazing Marriage* (1894), with a grotesque expressionist description of a gambling salon, while Trollope managed to combine various strains together in the ingenious plot of his late *Mr. Scarborough's Family* (1883)—which is preoccupied with a father's attempts to evade the laws of primogeniture and to lay bets both ways on the future behaviour of his sons. One of those sons is himself a gambler:

During the last fortnight or more Captain Scarborough's name had been subjected to many remarks and to much disgrace. But this non-payment of the money lost at whist was considered to be the turning-point. A man might be declared illegitimate, and might in consequence of that or any other circumstance defraud all his creditors. A man might conspire with his father with the object of doing this fraudulently . . . All this he might do and not become so degraded but that his friends would talk to him and play cards with him. But to have sat down to a whist-table and not to be able to pay the stakes was held to be so foul a disgrace than men did not wonder that he should have disappeared. (ch. 4)

It is precisely the triviality of the occasion that invests it with so much ritual meaning. Those meanings draw on family relations, on hermetic social groups and their bonds, on class distinctions, on eroticism, and on the fear of losing control. (It was probably not idleness that made card-games and gambling so prominent among the pleasures of those sent out to manage the Empire.)

Gambling was on the increase in that period. Certainly that was what James Greenwood claimed in *The Seven Curses of London* (1869): 'There can be no doubt that the vice of gambling is on the increase amongst the English working-classes' (241). As soon as we begin to look at his description of that phenomenon other questions break through. The suggestion of a rite pervades his purportedly disinterested account.

After the Epsom races 'the Fleet-street crowd begins to gather':

Butcher-lads from the neighbouring great meat market, come bare-headed and perspiring down Ludgate-hill, and at a pace that tells how exclusively their eager minds are set on racing: all in blue working-smocks, and with the grease and blood of their trade adhering to their naked arms, and to their hob-nailed boots, and to their hair. Hot and palpitating they reach the obelisk in the middle of the road, and there they take their stand, with their eyes steadfastly fixed on that at present blank and innocent window that shall presently tell them of their fate. (257)

The crossing of bounds between pure and impure, hidden and open, steadfast and violent, is enacted in the butcher boys' Gadarene rush. The hidden blood of Smithfield is seen on the public streets. Guilt and innocence ceremonially mingle. The suggestion of a rite is reinforced in the gathering at the obelisk, and the 'blank and innocent' window becomes the oracle of fate. A curious connection surfaces between gambling, appetite, and supplication: the future is devoured as it becomes present infor-mation. What seems at first to be straightforward description implies continuities with a remote past of religious experience, a René Girard-like emphasis on occluded violence. That same condensation of sang-froid and violence, private and public, is in the grain of Edith Wharton's *The House of Mirth* (1905), where

the highly polished surface of Lily Barth's milieu is crazed with
dirt, figured in the scenes of near rape, desperate gambling, and,
finally, botched sleep or suicide. All are offered at the altar of a
respectability that exists as ritual only.

George Eliot will have none of this occulting of gambling, at
least in her letters: 'Gambling being a vice I have no mind to, it
stirs my disgust even more than my pity . . . Burglary is heroic
compared with it' (*Selections from George Eliot's Letters*, ed.
G. Haight (1985), 406). So she writes from Bad Homburg in
1872 where she has watched Geraldine Leighton, among others,
gambling at the casino. But when she turns to write the opening
of *Daniel Deronda* (1876) the vexing questions raised cannot so
easily be brushed aside. Instead that opening scene at the casino
transcribes issues of causal sequence, of knowing, of your future
as an emerging past controlled and set in motion elsewhere, of
voyeurism. The power and gender relations between the watcher
of play and the watched player will occupy the 700-odd pages of
the book. Deronda crosses the zone between watcher and player
when he *redeems* Gwendolen's necklace, acting providence.
Watching and playing, without being able to redeem, describes
the reader's predicaments in that particular novel.

The involvement of women with gambling, whether as watchers or participants, intensifies the anxiety generated by the
theme. Gwendolen Harleth in *Daniel Deronda*, Lily Barth in
Edith Wharton's *The House of Mirth*, Polina in Dostoevsky's
The Gambler, Esther Waters in George Moore's novel of that
name, all focus the social disapproval that centred on the idea of
a woman taking chances, risking all, asserting the identity of
eroticism and money, flouting the slow pace of that other self-
defensive form of gambling: insurance—which in the marriage
market must mean for women the preservation of reputation and
the search for a secure husband. An undertow of sado-masochist
negotiation is given its social form in the gambling scenes in these
novels. A violation of prescribed gender roles is acted out. In
Vanity Fair, earlier, Becky Sharp plays all these different markets
simultaneously, the intervening narrator provoking the reader's
elation and chagrin at her behaviour. In *Oscar and Lucinda*,
Peter Carey teases out the degree to which the horror at a
woman's gambling is horror at a woman out of society's control,
concentrated in her own desires and miseries, recklessly sorting

the chances—and, worst, perhaps winning. Fascination with laws of inheritance underpins the plot of very many nineteenth-century novels, and is part of their enquiry into kinship, women's rights, hegemony—and the body.

Another reason for the horror generated by the sight of women gambling seems to be the helpless self-display of obsession. At the gambling table the body is both possessed and self-revelatory, as Charles Cotton observed long before in *The Compleat Gamester* in 1674. The book opens thus, seeming in some measure to anticipate Freud's diagnosis of gambling as a substitute for masturbation:

Gaming is an enchanting *witchery*, gotten between *Idleness* and *Avarice*: An itching Disease, that makes some scratch the head, whilst others, as if they were bitten by a Tarantula, are laughing themselves to death: Or lastly, it is a paralytical distemper, which seizing the arm the man cannot chuse but shake his elbow . . . it renders a man incapable of prosecuting any serious action, and makes him always unsatisfied with his own condition; he is either lifted up to the top of mad joy with success, or plung'd to the bottom of despair by misfortune, always in extremes, always in a storm.

It is that extremity that the gambler, male or female, seeks. As Dostoevsky, himself for a time an addicted gambler, observes, orgiastic failure is sought as passionately as winning. Moreover, gambling generates a refined discourse of its own: in 'The Character of a Gamester' Cotton comments that 'He speaks the language of the Game he plays at, better than the language of his Country; and can less indure a solecism in that than this' (21).

Games of chance and gambling concern more fundamental gains and losses than money, even. Commodity fetishism finds its similar in gambling—but gambling accommodates also the shadow of fetishism, the longing to destroy the fetish: the desire to spend, to be expended, to lose everything.[3] Reification makes it easier to destroy, as well as to worship: you can see what has to go. The familiar condensation of economic and erotic meaning in the word *spend* is, in the history of gambling, not particularly concealed.

[3] See Andrew Feenberg, 'Fetishism and Form: Erotic and Economic Disorder in Literature', in Paul Dumouchel (ed.), *Violence and Truth: On the Work of René Girard* (1987), 134–51. See also André Orlean, 'Money and Mimetic Speculation', 101–12.

Games of chance may restore to the adult the child's passion for play itself, which in Winnicott's terms must be established before identity can stabilize or any interpretation usefully take place. The sickness of the game that has not been played out in infancy reaches its most wretched form in Victorian fiction in Nell's grandfather in *The Old Curiosity Shop* (1841), who is reduced to cringing infantilism by his passion for gambling, 'anxious . . . eager . . . ravenous'. 'Le jeu pour le jeu' is the tag of the obsessional gambler as much as of the infant.

Such games have, moreover, similarities with the game of the infant that Freud observed: the 'fort–da' game. The child throws an object out of the cot, beyond its own reach; the adult retrieves it and gives it back—and so on, again and again. Not only is the loved object repeatedly restored, but insecurity is allayed and autonomy and power both are gained. But what if there is no adult?—no mother, no father, no god? Or an adult with better things to do? That is the dilemma that much fiction of the last fifty years has concerned itself with, Beckett's supremely, in whose fiction repetitive games function to keep objects safely within the cot.

There were other reasons, then, besides the divide between poverty and affluence why games of chance, and gambling in its many forms, became part of the ague of Victorian fiction—and of the reading habits it has bequeathed to us. Gambling and reading are both acts of desire whose longing is to possess and settle the future, but whose pleasure is in active uncertainty. Yet, of course, reading fiction also offers reassuring constrained choices. The number of variables presented is far fewer than in the world outside fiction. Similarly, gambling is rule-bound, preoccupied with niceties of parlance and with systems, though these may be ineffective against loss.

The reader of the novel is invested with foreknowledge by means of plot conventions already established and by the sometimes dispersed, but in Victorian fiction often knowingly present, figure of a narrator. Moreover the future of the reader within the book is the past of the writing. But the reader can always be worsted. We sustain our skills of moment-by-moment speculation; we multiply futures, select and delay. These reading-acts can be brushed aside by a turn of the page when the writer chooses to break the sequence of our expectations. Still, there are rules to this game, as Michel Serres points out in relation to Zola's Rougon-Macquart series, and writers of fiction tend to become habituated to them as much as do their readers.[4] The energy of fiction, though, comes from there being a number of different sets of rules which may all be in play at once.

In the period that particularly concerns me here scientists moved beyond Laplace's certainty that with the evidence current-ly available he could predict all future movements of the planets. They came as far as to Clerk Maxwell's emphasis on anti-determinism: Maxwell expressed the hope that 'the intelligent public' would be weaned from determinism by being 'led in pursuit of the arcana of science to the study of the singularities and instabilities, rather than the continuities and stabilities of things' (444). William James in his lecture 'The Dilemma of Determinism' (delivered 1884) mocks the magical terror deter-minists feel in the face of probability theory:

This notion of alternative possibility, they say, this admission that any one of several things may come to pass, is, after all, only a roundabout name for chance [and chance is] barefaced crazy unreason, the negation of intelligibility and law? And, if the slightest particle of it exist any-where, what is to prevent the whole fabric from falling together, the stars from going out, and chaos from recommencing her topsy-turvy reign. (21)

Many people, he remarks, 'talk as if the minutest dose of discon-nectedness . . . the faintest tremor of ambiguity about the future . . . would turn this godly universe into a sort of insane sand-heap or nulliverse'.[5]

The topic of prediction preoccupied scientists and nonscientists alike in the last part of the nineteenth century. Calendar apoca-lypse (in Kermode's phrase) may have had something to do with that. But more immediately the preoccupation had to do with the conflicts between ideas of strict causal sequence and the

    [4] Michel Serres, *Hermes: Literature, Science, Philosophy* (Baltimore and London, 1982), 40. Hermes, whom Serres brilliantly discusses as messenger and information theorist, was also the god of gambling and astronomy.
    [5] Lewis Campbell and William Garnett, *The Life of James Clerk Maxwell with a Selection from His Correspondence and Occasional Writings and a Sketch of His Contributions to Science* (1882); William James, 'The Dilemma of Determinism', in C. W. Allen (ed.), *The William James Reader* (Boston, 1971).

preoccupation with hazard, or chance, in a number of different fields: in evolutionary theory, astronomy, physics, and sociology.

Among middle-class intellectuals, readers of the generalist journals like the *Nineteenth Century* or the *Cornhill* or the *Fortnightly Review*, such philosophical matters were freely and knowledgeably discussed, as in the well-known meeting between Leslie Stephen and Hardy when they spoke of vortex rings, theologies decayed and defunct, the origins of matter, and so on. Richard Proctor, in particular, is a mediating figure here. He wrote extensively on whist and mathematics, chance and the transits of Venus, astronomy and social order. His controversy with Forbes as to whether the stars in the galaxies were scattered or sorted is cited in Venn's book on probability theory and provides material for Hardy's imagination in *Two on a Tower*. His professional interest in astronomy and his fascination with the theory and practice of games of chance did not seem to him—nor it seems, his readers—to be disparate. His collections of essays, *Transits of Venus* (1874), *Chance and Luck* (1887), and *The Universe of Suns* (1884), overlap in argument and material. The laws of luck and the movements of planets were part of the same set of concerns—though Proctor drew the line at what he called 'Dream-Space', attacking Cayley's non-Euclidean mathematics. Most of Proctor's articles were first published in generalist journals with a large distribution. George Eliot took notes from his essay on gambling superstitions as well as his astronomical writing.

The developing field of statistics offered new methods for assessing the present and for predicting the future, methods that sorted ill with the ideal of individualism. Playing between these two (statistics and individualism) was the figure of the gambler. The gambler refuses what Locke called 'the twilight of probability', staking all on an outcome.

The question of religious belief permeated all these concerns. During the later Victorian period uneasiness about older metaphors for causality combined with a fascination with prediction. John Venn in *The Logic of Chance* pointed out that we might do better to substitute 'for the familiar "chain of causation", such an expression as a "rope of causation" ' (228). A chain suggests sequence, a single event that can be broken off, or apart, but the rope represents the multiple simultaneous strands of thought and occurrence that, twisted together, tighten into bonds. W. K. Clifford questioned the view that Nature is reasonable, 'inasmuch as every effect has a cause'. 'What', he asks 'do we mean by this?' (170) 'The word represented by "Cause" has sixty-four meanings in Plato and forty-eight in Aristotle.' Clifford suggested that induction is often simply simile-making and that prediction is an unsound gridding of past patterns of event upon the future. He offers an account of habits of mind that take for granted laws 'so familiar that you seem to see how the beginning must have been followed by the end' (as did Oedipa Maas). That pattern of expectation and confirmation, he argues, is then applied across the board: when events and sequences will not conform to the simile the majesty of mystery is invoked (172)[6]

Inheritance and prediction, induction and similes, are all recognized as unstable. But what continues to be insisted on in late-nineteenth-century fiction is the need to compress the kinship network and to control the inheritance of property. To do that, the slow gambling of family was required: with entails, and inheritances, with nephews and natural sons, with capital, and the profitable marrying of daughters. As Venn points out, the terms of insurance and of gambling are identical. Genetic laws were as yet unknown.

The fore-doom of Balzac's *La Comédie humaine* broods over later nineteenth-century fiction. This great series shares with Zola's Rougon-Macquart novels a preoccupation with inheritance, in all its senses, economic, genetic, and national. The strange story of *La Peau de chagrin* takes its propulsive force from its first scene of gambling. Technically, gambling is a powerful mechanism for setting a plot in motion, with its isolation of factors, its evocation of a variety of futures. It can also function as a pithy satire on the lumbering fortunes of human life elsewhere so tardily played out. Only in fiction could the heavy hand of determinism be so openly exposed and satirized. For that, the speeding up of several generations is necessary. The family proves to be a form of extended gambling: gambling, one might say, as vegetable empire.

In Dostoevsky's *The Gambler* (first translated into English and published by the radical Vizetelly and Co. in 1887) that is how

[6] 'On the Aims and Instruments of Scientific Thought' (1872), W. K. Clifford, *Lectures and Essays*, 2 vols. (1901), Vol. 1.

the family is described. The hero vituperatively denounces the system of family servitude from generation to generation in the service of wealth-gathering and sees it all as sacrifice to the god 'Vater': the instructive books read within the family and the book of family descent are one and the same. Both are tales of ruined happiness in the service of vicious 'honesty': marriage delayed in the service of capital, younger sons enslaved, the same story endlessly repeated: 'The eldest son now becomes himself a virtuous *Vater*, and the same story starts all over again'. 'Well, sir, that's what it amounts to: I'd much rather indulge in debauchery, Russian style, or make my fortune at roulette' (36).[7] Notice that he assumes that he will make his fortune.

Let me turn now to demonstrate from the writing of Freud and of Hardy some of the analogies between the gambling scene and the reader's practice that I have been indicating. That practice includes interpretation, hypothesizing, and prediction. It includes also intense hope, desire, and anxiety.

Freud's essay on 'Dostoevsky and Parricide' (1928) seems to be about to conclude with an analysis of Dostoevsky's novella *The Gambler* when, instead, he embarks on an account of Stefan Zweig's short story 'Twenty Four Hours in the Life of a Woman'. A young widow, with sons newly grown, lonely and aimless, visits, Freud writes, 'the Rooms at Monte Carlo. There, among all the remarkable impressions which the place produces, she is soon fascinated by the sight of a pair of hands which seem to betray all the feelings of the unlucky gambler with terrifying sincerity and intensity.' Realizing that he has lost all and plans suicide she approaches him when he leaves the rooms. He takes her for a prostitute. In her effort to persuade him to give up gambling she returns to his hotel with him. They spend the night together.

After this improvised night of love, she exacts a most solemn vow from the young man . . . that he will never play again, provides him with money for his journey home and promises to meet him at the station before the departure of his train . . . Various mischances delay her, so that she misses the train. In her longing for the lost one she returns once more to the Rooms and there, to her horror, sees once more the hands

7 Fyodor Dostoevsky, *The Gambler, with Polina Suslova's Diary* (Chicago, 1972).

which had first excited her sympathy: the faithless youth had gone back to his play.[8]

Freud's analysis of this gripping tale elides the difference between author and subject: in the unconscious the writer *is* the young man, changing mother to prostitute in order to render her accessible, breaking through the Oedipal taboo in a night of love, after which nothing is changed. The woman gives herself twice over, as money and as person. But these gifts also seek to generate control. She longs to save the young man from his gambling habit. She is the worsted gambler. The narrative return to the gambling table makes of this story 'a serpent with its tail in its mouth'—the ancient figure for eroticism and also Coleridge's specification of the ideal form that narrative should take.

The woman's account, predominant in the first-person form of the Zweig story, is in Freud set to one side. 'It is true', he remarks concessively, 'that Zweig's story is told by the mother, not the son.' But he immediately interprets this as the unconscious self-flattery of the writer who identifies with the son. Freud continues: 'it is extremely questionable whether the erotic life of women is dominated by sudden and mysterious impulses' (193). Freud, therefore, produces a clinching motivation for her behaviour: she has unconsciously substituted the young man for her own son. She plays the part of Jocasta to Zweig's Oedipus.

However, the reader of Freud may note that the analyst's own professional predicament is closer to that of the woman than the young man. The therapeutic urge of the analyst, the perils of uncontrolled counter-transference, and the obstinate triumph of the recidivist patient who loves obsession more than cure, all express the ailments to which the analytic condition is subject. The tale tells the story of a failure to heal, in which the woman, like the analyst, is jilted. The young man, like the young woman Dora, cannot be prevented from walking out, unsaved and self-determining. Control is lost.

Strikingly, this essay is Freud's only discussion of gambling, apart from two letters of the 1890s where he simply mentions it in a list of substitutes for masturbation. Through literary analysis—as with the Schreber case also—Freud reaches a more

---

[8] James Strachey, (ed.), *The Standard Edition of The Complete Psychological Works of Sigmund Freud*, vol. 21. (1961), 192.

chequered and subtle understanding, tinctured with his own anxieties. Will the past of the patient yield to treatment—to a new beginning? Analysis cannot predict securely the length of those seemingly interminable, iterative stories on which it thrives. The future haunts the analytical scene, less demonstratively than the past, but generating its own anxieties.

So much for Freud's reading of the tale. But the story also presents a number of characteristic features that may take us further into understanding what gambling can signify in fiction—and may take us back into the particular period of writing on which much of my argument has concentrated. The tale is called 'Twenty Four Hours in a Woman's Life': that intense condensation of experience within a narrow timespan parallels the experience of game-playing, and of reading a compelling fiction.

This night was so crowded with struggle and conversation, with passion and anger and hatred, with imploring and frenzied tears, that it seemed to me to last a thousand years, and I fancied that we—one of whom had entered the abyss animated by a mad craving for death; the other all unsuspecting—emerged from the death-struggle utterly transformed, with different senses and different feelings. (38)[9]

As perhaps the reader may for a time feel after reading Dostoevsky. The reader's expectation of being transformed will equally prove unfounded. This is to remain a hidden adventure whose consequences are hard to track in the woman's future. The young man's fate remains unchanged by the episode. An obdurate sense of the importance, and the impotence, of the reader's experience is figured in this tale of gambling, of twenty-four hours packed with experience, and then of an untransformed afterlife.

This is the spectator's story. Watching the play (in all senses) is the reader's initial position in a novel—a position dramatized in the opening of *Daniel Deronda* where Deronda, existing so far only as a question (existing that is in the same grammar as the reader at the start of the text) muses in the casino: 'Was she beautiful or not beautiful?' The woman in Zweig's story intervened, disastrously, as it proved, for her own happiness. The

---

[9] Stefan Zweig, *Stories and Legends* (1955). First published in Great Britain in 1927.

reader is threatened and incapacitated at once by her experience. The analyst here parallels the reader, enacting passivity, unable, apparently, to intervene though he or she may inwardly undergo. The reader is the silenced partner in the text, silently performing it. The multiple futures potentiated by the work engage our ingenuity and anxiety at once, here only to return to their starting point.

What do we risk, then, as readers? The field of play is contracted. We can evade the immediate consequences of the narrative, as in dream. A gap remains between emotion and outcome. We do not stand to lose everything. We are not at the gambling table, though gripped by some of the same anxieties in the face of a future condensed within a little span. Reading fiction, though, puts hope at risk and courts defeat.

In the *Return of the Native* Hardy grippingly combines and satirizes many of the extended hopes that people reading invest in fiction. Fiction seems to offer a teleological future, in which hidden plans will declare themselves and all that is jostled and awry will prove to have been held within the cognizance of the great (or even the lesser) author. But what if the plan is itself jostled and awry? What if the voyeur of the scene is unconcerned and curious, a wild pony fascinated by light without signification? Should the reader emulate the heath-cropper?

The double gambling scenes in that novel uncover the hidden hopes of order, of magical righteousness, that fiction harbours. The episode takes place half-way through the work, occupying the last two chapters of the book called 'The Fascination'. That fascination is erotic, but in these chapters the game accelerates the reader's own involvement in that experience. The innocent and timorous 'maphrotight' Christian Cantle is carrying two bags of fifty guineas, Mrs Yeobright's life-savings, fifty for Thomasin, married to the faithless Wildeve, fifty for her son, Clym, just marrying Eustacia against Mrs Yeobright's wishes. For safe keeping Christian distributes them in his boots. Christian is the man no woman will wed. He is haplessly outside the round of courtship and desire. In the scenes that ensue Christian is first persuaded to take part in a 'raffle' at the inn, at which he wins 'the gown-piece' but has no one to give it to. The vocabulary of the game is full of sly parallels to amorous affairs: it is played with three dice and the winning throw is 'a pair-royal'—three of a kind. Christian, newly persuaded of his luck, gives up the only power he has: the secret of the money he carries. Through this quirky relationship between secrecy and gambling, the uttering of the chances, Hardy embroils the reader in the power-play of reading his fiction.

Can people be predicted? The distaste that many Victorians felt for statistics was for the suggestion that it is possible, given large enough numbers, to predict the life-moves of individuals. The human capacity for keeping secrets disturbs that control. The uttering of a secret is the hedonistic moment of power; its aftermath is most often powerlessness. The lust to *tell* is the expense of spirit in a waste of shame. (In the Zweig/Freud story the whole is generated by an elderly woman's confessional impulse. She tells the secret tale of her experience twenty years before to the narrator, the talking cure rendered harmless by the long gap of time between secret and utterance.) Christian *tells* because he feels buoyed up with his gambling success. Wildeve then tells him persuasively formulaic stories that bring to light the fantasies of desire fuelled by gambling. Fortune reverses at the last moment before disaster and the debtor wins back his money on the way to sell all his stock. The poor man crossing class-bounds gains wealth and love conjoined, respectability, the transformation of the powerless watcher (the waiter at the gentlemen's gaming house) into the central figure:

Then there was a man of London, who was only a waiter at White's club-house. He begin to play first half-crown stakes, and then higher and higher, till he became very rich, got an appointment in India, and rose to be Governor of Madras. His daughter married a member of parliament, and the Bishop of Carlisle stood godfather to one of his children. (238)[10]

As he plays for 'higher and higher' stakes his social position—by the magic of narrative—effortlessly rises 'higher and higher' too. The excluded spectator enters the game and wins. Last is the story of the man who lost all his money, staked his watch and chain, his umbrella

'his hat; lost again: staked his coat and stood in his shirt-sleeves; lost again. Began taking off his breeches, and then a looker-on gave him a

---

[10] Thomas Hardy, *The Return of the Native* (New Wessex Edition, 1974).

trifle for his pluck. With this he won. Won back his coat, won back his hat, won back his umbrella, his watch, his money, and went out of the door a rich man. (238–9)

Risking all, reaching the nadir, courting humiliation and exposure, retrieving the self intact and enhanced; the strange erotics of gambling are here succinctly set out. Wildeve and Christian dice, out on the heath by lantern-light with the coins hot from Christian's boots, in moist mild air, brushed by ferns and moths. The writing marks the contrasts between the softly conjoined bodily world of the heath, and the sharp, discrete set of objects that pattern the play.

Wildeve wins, first all Christian's money and then Mrs Yeobright's entire store. The chapter ends with Christian's despair; then just as Wildeve is shutting the lantern, 'a figure rose from behind a neighbouring bush and came forward into the lantern light. It was the reddleman approaching' (241). And so the tale begins its fore-ordained recuperation. Now the reddleman will play Wildeve. This chapter is entitled 'A New Force Disturbs the Current'. This time the play is recounted in detail and the reddleman (who has been the hidden watcher and listener for the first exchange) taunts Wildeve with the story he has recounted, 'won back his coat'; a magic repetition is acted out. Each time it seems that the game is concluded, they play on at Wildeve's urging.

Gradually the night-world closes in on them. The gazing reader and the gazing ponies are quaintly likened. A death's-head moth douses the candle. Wildeve collects glow-worms and places them like watchers round the stone. The ponies return 'and were looking on with erect heads just as before, their timid eyes fixed on the scene' (246). Nature begins a satire, so that the last phases of the gaming are comic and desperate at once. The prolonged description raises the excitement and the uneasiness for the reader. Repeatedly the conclusion seems reached, with the reddleman triumphant, yet they play on. This iterative endlessness of gambling and of description is presumably what Freud characterizes as its masturbatory function. But many other things besides are going on here: the organization of the narrative makes it impossible for the reader to escape, though quailing under its urgent repetition. Hardy prevents us simply skimming the surface of the text, hastening on to ease our anxiety, by emphasizing changes of light and texture: 'Amid the soft juicy vegetation of the hollow in which they sat, the motionless and the uninhabited solitude, intruded the chink of guineas, the rattle of dice, the exclamations of the reckless players.'

They change the game and play for lowest, letting God 'mix it around' in Julian Barnes's terms. Throughout this scene a half-assurance has been proferred to the reader that Venn must win. The story patterns of Wildeve's tales promise that fulfilment. That's how such stories end. The whole is determined. The reddleman does win. He does so by virtue of his virtue: the cards connive, under the ordering hand of the writer. The reddleman is impassive, Wildeve agitated; these moral attitudes appear to control success and failure. Christian loses because he is weak and Wildeve because he is unstable. A moral drama is enacted, a popular story. Gambling is under the sway of some larger law that orders the chances.

But the chapter and the book 'The Fascination' ends with a vertiginous loosing of hazard again. Venn meets in the darkness first Clym and Eustacia, and then Thomasin. To Thomasin he gives all the money he has won, not aware that half of it was meant for Clym: now the narrative becomes predictive: 'it was an error which afterwards helped to cause more misfortune than treble the loss in money value could have done'. Venn's intercession, or meddling, is 'a new force' that 'disturbs the current', not channels it for good. The next book is ominously entitled 'The Closed Door'.

The reader is balked of control, forced to survey the reassuring expectations with which we habitually people the future. The re-telling of fictions seems to assure their truth—or at least their efficacy. Hardy displays the absurdity of that belief, while his own novel sardonically performs another narrative prediction: bad luck is good for story. 'So the subject recurred: if he (Clym) were making a fortune and a name, so much the better for him; if he were making a tragical figure in the world, so much the better for a narrative' (186).

Hardy here leagues his narrative to the new forces that disturb the current of the 1870s, those of uncertainty and entropy, the cosmic lottery. But he pins it also into that other antique yearning gratified by play: the longing for disaster, the full but fictive experience of obliteration. That desire is contained and gratified, for the moment, by gaming, or the bounds of a book.

13

Wave Theory and the Rise of Literary Modernism

When I first imagined this essay I set it in the late 1920s and 1930s, the period when the elegant expositions of Eddington and Jeans, and the fame of Einstein, were communicating to non-scientists how modern physics crazed categories and dislimned boundaries. As Eddington wrote: 'In the scientific world the conception of substance is wholly lacking . . . For this reason the scientific world often shakes us by its appearance of unreality. It offers nothing to satisfy our demand for the concrete. How should it, when we cannot formulate that demand?' (274)

By the late 1920s waves in motion are all the universe consists in—and they are probably fictitious, 'ondes fictives', as de Broglie called them, or as Jeans suggests in *The Mysterious Universe*: 'the ethers and their undulations, the waves which form in the universe, are in all probability fictitious . . . they exist in our minds' (79). He is thus led, long before Baudrillard, to equalize representations and enactments: 'The motion of electrons and atoms does not resemble those of the parts of a locomotive so much as those of the dancers in a cotillion. And if the "true essence of substances" is for ever unknowable, it does not matter whether the cotillion is danced at a ball in real life, or on a cinematograph screen, or in a story of Boccaccio' (136). 'The universe', he asserts, 'is best pictured . . . as consisting of pure thought.'

How does literary realism engage with a scientific system that denies substance, dissolves difference, and in the early 1930s insists that the universe is best understood as mind? The problem is that in such a formation all realism's work has, paradoxically, been done for it: the difficult forging of likeness between symbol and substance is prematurely accomplished; indeed, there is an 'always already' complete fusion between represented and representable. The loss of the contradictions at the heart of the realist enterprise saps its energy even while it ensures its continuance.

Wave theory seems to make a single process a sufficient explanation of all phenomena. This universalizing impulse is counterset in later nineteenth-century scientific writing by an insistence on relativizing, the relativizing both of our knowledge and of possible descriptions. The relativizing of description is crucial both for advances in quantum mechanics and in modernism. Wave–particle duality and complementarity and *The Waste Land* alike draw on this resource.

Realism in writing is founded on paradox. The term 'real*ism*' declares itself as approximation, or servitor: an attempt to mimic an 'other' which it must also match. The twin goals of realism are cohering and observing, at once. The 'other' that realism serves is assumed as prior, already *there:* out there, in there. If necessary, to be made there.

Sometimes the impossible nature of that 'other' is manifest. Such is the case with 'psychological realism', which is predicated on the fiction that we can enter another person's consciousness. Sometimes, as in social realism, the project is predicated on a contradiction: on the reader's supposed ignorance of low-life or of technical vocabularies, which that reader is yet then also to recognize so as to vouch for the authenticity of the text.

Realism is stretched further when its topic is the unseen, the unheard, the unregistered: that which lies beyond the reach of our unaided senses. It is also then released from some of the constraints of mimesis. Many nineteenth-century scientists hypothetically filled the zones of space with a transmissive medium, lumeniferous ether, using an old term, aether, in a new guise. Wave theory, acoustics, radiation, all seemed to indicate that our senses are contracted and that we are battered by continuous events beyond their registration: sound waves, air waves, the irreversible transformations of thermodynamic energy. Such theories produced also a space for the idea of the unconscious.

As I approached the topic of realism and representation, therefore, it seemed to me that it might be more productive to focus on a period when realism is usually described as being in the ascendant and to illustrate through a single example, that of the great physicist James Clerk Maxwell, the restiveness about representation in the later nineteenth century—a restiveness shared, and crossing to and fro, between physicists, philosophers, and poets. Maxwell is most often held up as an example of the modes of thought and the attitudes to physical models before quantum mechanics (see Harman). As I shall demonstrate, he was acutely aware of problems of representation and was averse to materialism. Clerk Maxwell is, moreover, a particularly apt choice for those of us living in the postmodern era in which he has become more broadly famous through the trope of Maxwell's Demon, and its figuring in Pynchon's *The Crying of Lot 49*. Like many others of my literary generation I first heard of him and his work through that book—and, at the time, was not sure whether he was a figment of Pynchon's imagination.

My remarks here, therefore, are primarily concerned with the conditions for modernism rather than with samples of literary works. Among Victorian scientists we uncover anxieties about the relativity of knowledge, about determinism, about imaging a stochastic universe instead of a teleological one, about manifestation, symbol, and discourse (see Ch. 12, above). These anxieties refined (and shared) the conditions necessary to the rise of modernism and of quantum mechanics alike. They were argued at large in the major generalist journals of the time, such as the *Academy*, the *Westminster Review*, the *Nineteenth Century*, and the *Cornhill Magazine*.

Key terms, I would suggest, are often formulated at the moment that their explanatory power begins to wane. 'Realism' and 'determinism' would be strong nineteenth-century examples. The *OED*'s first example for 'determinism' is 1846, and for 'realism' it is the late 1830s in philosophy, the late 1850s in art and literature. Multiple, non-dualistic forms of representation were proving to be necessary to the advance of the physical sciences. Probability and statistics were the means of stabilizing laws from the random behaviour of molecules. C. S. Peirce, arguing for a 'universe of chance' in 'The Doctrine of Necessity Examined' (1892), was, as Ian Hacking points out, impressed by the statistical mechanics of Maxwell.

Maxwell derived the classical deterministic laws of gases from the postulation of purely random behaviour of molecules. Peirce conjectured that something similar would prove to be the case with all the most firm deterministic laws of physics. Hacking goes on to observe the interplay between sociology and physics in this invocation of statistical explanation: 'Maxwell had been led to his model and his analysis after reading an account of Quetelet's research into social phenomena. In a sense he modelled his random distribution of molecular motion on social interactions. Maxwell himself may have held, at least for a time, that his models were more than models' (Olby: 70).

In the period that concerns me in this essay the margins between models, thought experiments, social occurrences, and mechanical events were a central topic for dispute. How to represent the relations between the all-inclusive laws of thermodynamics and their incommensurate, diverse, and evanescent manifestations? 'She arrived in tears and a sedan chair'—the rhetorical figure of zeugma is, I think, useful here. The acceptance of multiple, incommensurable outcomes driven by a single verb opened the way alike to modernist literature and thought and to wave–particle theory.

Nineteenth-century scientists from Helmholtz to Thomson, Clausius to Clerk Maxwell, were pursuing a single explanation of cosmic processes that would include light, heat, and sound and that would construe them all as motion, passing irreversibly beyond the reach of the senses and dissipating irregularly through the ether (that crucial explanatory substance that ebbed quietly out of the universe early in the twentieth century, going the way of eighteenth-century *phlogiston*, the material principle of combustibility) (Cantor and Hodge passim, esp. 309–40).

Ideas of flux were of course in no way new: all things fleet away; we never step into the same river twice; *alles geht vorbei*. Such Heraclitean tropes were familiar, and were themselves resources, and assurances, for working scientists of the time. What was unfamiliar was the universalizing of wave theory (as thermodynamics continued to be called) to account for all phenomena. Unfamiliar, too, were the twin emphases in the laws of thermodynamics on the constancy of energy within a system and the tendency to increasing disorganization (entropy always tends to increase to a maximum).

There is no need for agreement between legendary and scientific accounts for the release of new imaginative energies. It helps, though, if the phenomena under description are already familiar both in canonical literature and in daily life. This is the case both in thermodynamics and in chaos theory, where observed but hitherto excluded phenomena move into the centre of meaning. Even phenomena like the sun and the waves and tides are, after all, inflected differently at different times in the same place.

Educated people in Victorian Britain read Heraclitus, Lucretius, and Ovid in their youth, and often continued to read them in adulthood. All these writers emphasized the wavelike flow of energies. Moreover, people in nineteenth-century Britain were far more conscious of the manifest waves of the sea than we are. They experienced their action. They, or their kin and acquaintance, were obliged to take sea voyages, often long ones. Emigration, imperialism, and trade depended on protracted sea journeys. Even crossing the Channel to Europe in unstabilized boats gave—and can still give—an unforgettable physical experience of wave activity. Fishing was a major industry with a high death-toll, the matter of Victorian ballads such as Kingsley's 'Men must work and women must weep'. The fashion for sea bathing was, in the mid-nineteenth century, still sufficiently new to add a *frisson* to being buffeted on chill British shores. (Lying on the beach was *not* then an acceptable alternative.) So there was a manifest social complex of referents which could overlap, incompletely but persuasively, with fresh scientific theory. Waves were not only the visible waves of the sea, now, but any kind of periodic disturbance in a medium or in space. The physicist John Tyndall, travelling to the Alps, describes in a continuous implied argument seasickness, heat as a mode of motion, the intellect as a function of temperature, a thunderstorm, the sound of agitated water, the 'sonorous vibrations' of air bubbles, reflected light, and human sleepers in a carriage 'each burning the slow fire which we call life' (*Hours of Exercise*: 59–65).

In 1858 Herbert Spencer, the economist and philosopher, wrote to Tyndall, shaken by Tyndall's exposition to him of the second law of thermodynamics: 'That which was new to me in your position . . . was that equilibration was death. Regarding, as I have done, equilibration as the ultimate and *highest* state of society, I had assumed it to be not only the ultimate but also the highest state of the universe. And your assertion that when equilibrium was reached life must cease, staggered me' (Duncan: 104). The assumption that a congruity must exist between ideal representations of society and the universe is not peculiar to the Victorians. Such congruity is sought persistently, even at high cost, as now chaos theory has been eagerly seized upon by non-scientists as reinvesting the erratic with meaning and thus surcharging social description with significance—a significance that need no longer depend upon equilibration.

When familiar ideas and phenomena become the focus of scientific theory and research they acquire, for the moment, a new dignity. Half understood and rapidly received, they move across into other fields of enquiry, and they cluster, unstably transformed, amidst the needs and anxieties of a community. I have argued elsewhere that that process informed the new significations of solar physics in Victorian society: the coming death of the sun was no longer a matter of legendary history only, though those precedent legends (Balder dead, the fall of the Incas, Max Müller's solar interpretations of Aryan myth) inform the scientific enquiry, and its reception. Helmholtz, Thomson, Clerk Maxwell made that heat death of the universe seem imminent not by moving it forward temporally, but by changing the level of assent demanded. No longer an as-if story, nor a foundational one, the new physics counted up the number of years likely to intervene before the death of the sun. Their sums varied (anything from 25 to 20 million years) but their totals did not: the earth will become too cold for life.

Stephen Brush, in his invaluable two-volume study *The Kind of Motion We Call Heat: A History of the Kinetic Theory of Gases in the Nineteenth Century*, observes the inductive problem of thermodynamics: 'It is difficult to conceive of a time when people did not know that heat flows from hot bodies to cold bodies. Our problem is to understand how this apparently trivial example of irreversibility was translated into an illustration of a general law of nature, the Principle of Dissipation of Energy, and as such was seen to be in conflict with Newtonian mechanics.' (551). One might turn that argument around and say that for most people, once observed, it was not easy to know where the application of the principle stopped. It could be made into a description of mind; it could become grounds for spiritualism; it could provide a vocabulary for degenerationism; it could dislimn all boundaries and disturb all organizations. Happily, it began to play all these parts in early modernism. As Pater puts it in *Plato and Platonism*:

These opinions too, coming and going, these conjectures as to what under-lay the sensible world, were themselves but fluid elements on the changing surface of existence.

Surface we say; but was there really anything beneath it . . . Was not the very essence of thought itself also such perpetual motion? . . . The principle of disintegration [is] inherent in the primary elements alike of matter and of the soul . . . the principle of lapse, of waste, was, in fact, in one self. (14–15)

Such lapsing could also produce resistance, a flow to be staunched, as T. E. Hulme later attempted to do.

At the end of his essay on Helmholtz, Clerk Maxwell invites the reader to join him in observing Helmholtz observing the waves of the sea.

Now that we are no longer under the sway of that irresistible power which has been bearing us along through the depths of mathematics, anatomy, and music, we may venture to observe from a safe distance the whole figure of the intellectual giant as he sits on some lofty cliff watching the waves, great and small, as each pursues its independent course on the surface of the sea below. (*Scientific Papers*: ii. 598)

The scene is heroic and dizzying: Helmholtz is a 'giant', Maxwell and the reader are at 'a safe distance', released momentarily from 'that irresistible power which has been bearing us along' in an imaginative likeness to the action of thermodynamics; the waves are each 'independent.'

Maxwell continues by quoting Helmholtz, taking us into the pleasures and difficulties of vision, in the double sense peculiarly apt for Helmholtz, who for so long worked on optics, on acoustics, on energy:

'I must own,' he [Helmholtz] says, 'that whenever I attentively observe this spectacle, it awakens in me a peculiar kind of intellectual pleasure, because here is laid open before the bodily eye what, in the case of the waves of the invisible atmospheric ocean, can be rendered intelligible only to the eye of the understanding, and by the help of a long series of complicated propositions.' (Ibid. 598)

Instead of series and complexity, Helmholtz here delights in instantaneity. The visible waves *vouch for* as well as represent the 'invisible atmospheric ocean'. They give it the effortless 'reality' of the manifest. The intensity of the scene is imbued also with Maxwell's own scientific nostalgia, for manifestation, for models, for sufficient equivalence, for an escape from the impasse of theories which mean that 'we are once more on a pathless sea, starless, windless and poleless' (letter to Tait, 11 Nov. 1874, Add 7655/Ib/72).

Many later-nineteenth-century scientists, and in particular Maxwell, were scrupulously aware of the problems of representation, problems not only intrinsic to language but specific to the theoretical work in which they were engaged. In *The Meaning of Truth* (1904) William James argued that 'up to about 1850 almost everyone believed that sciences expressed truths that were exact copies of a definite code of non-human realities'.

But the enormously rapid multiplication of theories in these latter days has well-nigh upset the notion of any one of them being a more literally objective kind of thing than another. There are so many geometries, so many logics, so many physical and chemical hypotheses, so many classifications, each one of them good for so much yet not good for everything, that the notion that even the truest formula may be a human device not a literal transcript has dawned upon us. We hear scientific laws now treated as so much 'conceptual shorthand,' true so far as they are useful but no farther. Our mind has become tolerant of symbol instead of reproduction, of approximation instead of exactness, of plasticity instead of rigor. 'Energetics,' measuring the bare face of sensible phenomena so as to describe in a single formula all their changes of 'level,' is the last word of this scientific humanism. (40–1)

We do not need entirely to agree with James's view of science before 1850 to find some reinforcement of what he is arguing in the work of late-nineteenth-century scientists, especially those concerned with 'energetics'. Not only in the social theorizing-out from evolutionary ideas, but in the fields of physics and mathematics, we find a heightened awareness of the instability of language, certainly, and also—more strikingly—of the insufficiency of symbol and of algebra.

In the number of the *Westminster Review* in which Walter Pater's important early essay 'Coleridge's Writings' was first published (NS 29, Jan. 1866) George Grote reviewed John Stuart Mill on *The Philosophy of William Hamilton*. This is *not* the same William Hamilton whose initiating work on quaternion vectors Maxwell was studying at that same time (a useful reminder of the principle that things do not fit neatly but remain recalcitrant). But all these writers, philosophers, and mathematicians alike, are concerned with the issue of the relativity of knowledge. Pater in his essay argues that 'modern thought is distinguished from ancient by its cultivation of the "relative" spirit in place of the "absolute".' Hamilton, says Grote, advances the doctrine of the Relativity of Knowledge and yet elsewhere (in his dissertation on Reid) argues 'that our knowledge is only partly, not wholly, relative; that the secondary qualities of matter, indeed, are known to us only relatively, but that the primary qualities are known to us as they are in themselves, or as they exist objectively, and that they may be even evolved by demonstration *a priori*' (12).

The argument concerning the relativity of knowledge is absolutely necessary to the emergence of modernism. And it is particularly in the cognate confusion between method and findings that connections between late-nineteenth-century physics and mathematics and proto-modernist texts can, I believe, be uncovered.

Take, for example, Cayley's mathematics. These caused extreme distress to more conservatively minded astronomers, such as the highly effective scientific writer Richard Proctor. In particular, Proctor attacked Cayley's 'Address at the opening of the 1883 meeting of the British Association' (*Universe of Suns*: 303). In his essay 'Dream Space' Proctor challenged what he saw as the *unreal* nature of the non-Euclidean geometry that Cayley pursued, in which Cayley considered four-dimensional space, worlds in which two and two make three, and inhabitants of 'a perfectly smooth sphere' who would with 'a more extended experience and more accurate measurements' be taught 'that any two lines, if produced far enough each way, would meet in two points; they would in fact arrive at a spherical geometry, accurately representing the properties of the space in which they lived' (308).

Proctor is appalled by these alternative worlds and by Cayley's disturbance (by his interposing of the word *seems*) of axioms such as that odd and even numbers succeed each other alternately *ad infinitum*. Cayley pointed out that 'because a proposition is observed to hold good for a long series of generations, 1,000 numbers, 2,000 numbers, as the case may be, this is not only no proof, it is absolutely no evidence, that the proposition is a true proposition holding good for all numbers whatever; there are in the Theory of Numbers very remarkable instances of propositions observed to hold good for very long series of numbers which are nevertheless untrue' (quoted in Proctor: 306).

The mathematician W. K. Clifford similarly argued in his essay 'Aims of Scientific Thought' (1872) that the apparently stable generalizing process of scientific induction is often only simile-making, and that prediction is an unsound gridding of past events upon the future. He questioned the view that Nature is reasonable, 'inasmuch as every effect has a cause' (i. 170). 'What,' he asks, 'do we mean by this?' 'The word represented by "Cause" has sixty-four meanings in Plato and forty-eight in Aristotle' (i. 170–1). We develop habits of mind that take for granted laws 'so familiar that you seem to see how the beginning must have followed from the end'. When sequences of outcome will not conform to the established simile, the majesty of mystery is invoked: 'The cause of that event is a mystery which must remain for ever unknown to me.' With some asperity he observes, 'On equally just grounds the nervous system of my umbrella is a mystery which must for ever remain unknown to me. My umbrella has no nervous system' (172).

This emphasis among mathematicians on conditionality and relativity is a far cry from the position of a contemporary such as T. H. Huxley, who claims 'that there is not a curve of the waves, not a note in the howling chorus, not a rainbow glint on a bubble which is other than a necessary consequence of the ascertained laws of nature; and that with sufficient knowledge of the conditions competent physico-mathematical skill could account for, and indeed, predict, every one of these "chance" events' (Darwin: 553–5). Realism was put in question in this debate since it depends not only upon representations of interlocked events laterally, but upon the reader's acquiescence in the logic of sequence.

What most disquieted Proctor intellectually (and what most materially makes for my argument that scientific questioning and proto-modernism are closely interconnected) is that, as Proctor observes, Cayley's paper was enthusiastically taken up by *The Times*, the *Globe*, and the *Spectator*. The generalist journals and the newspapers made new ideas rapidly available to people throughout the country. Demonstrations by travelling lecturers such as Proctor and Tyndall, with experiments set up on stage, made a dramatic impact on their audiences. Such lectures were arresting entertainment, expanding the scope of the senses and putting credence to the test. Yet such demonstrations also asserted the real presence of unforeseen phenomena 'out there': singing flames, invisible rays made visible, artificial blue skies. Materialism became a form of magic spectacle, and the spectacle implied both the relativity of knowledge and the actuality of phenomena beyond the customary reach of our unaided senses.

In the Conclusion to *The Renaissance* Pater presents physical life as perpetual motion, perpetually unobserved: 'the passage of the blood, the waste and repairing of the lenses of the eye, the modification of the tissues of the brain under every ray of light and sound—processes which science reduces to simpler and more elementary forces' (233). At the same time, Helmholtzian optics newly established the eye as an uncertain arbiter, an imperfect organ. Helmholtz, indeed, argued that 'the impressions of sense are the mere *signs* of external things' (quoted in Tyndall, *Fragments of Science*: i. 193).

Rosalind Krauss has recently emphasized in *The Originality of the Avant-Garde and Other Modernist Myths* that painters from the 1870s and Impressionism 'had to confront a particular fact: the physiological screen through which light passes to the human brain is not transparent, like a window pane; it is like a filter, involved in a set of specific distortions' (15). In the last edition of *The Origin* Darwin pinpoints Helmholtz's emphasis on the imperfection of the eye as according with the processes of natural selection which do not guarantee absolute perfection. The contradictions between these various recognitions were themselves startling representations of the relativity of knowledge.

Human beings are adept at living in multiple and conflicted epistemologies, or we could not survive. In postmodernism we have even attempted to domesticate that awareness of conflicted multiplicity, as Don DeLillo demonstrates in his novel *White Noise*. In the late nineteenth century, play, vertigo, and denial were all provoked in readers by the disequilibrium and illimitability that the new physics was attempting to grip in symbols.

Clerk Maxwell indeed hoped that 'the intelligent public' would be weaned from determinism by being 'led in pursuit of the arcana of science to the study of the singularities and instabilities, rather than the continuities and stabilities of things' (Campbell and Garnett: 444).

Among scientific workers themselves the referentiality of language became a dilemma to be argued through. Nor was mathematics naïvely seen as an escape from the problems of language. The correspondence between Faraday and others concerning the term 'force' makes that clear.

'Relativism' of representation need not at all, of course, infringe upon a belief in the actuality of phenomena under description. Indeed, an awareness of slippages within representation—the scrupling at terms and disavowal of any exact reference—may be a form of hyper-realism: an assertion that there is an 'out there' so powerfully *sui generis* that it cannot be captured by already existing terms. The race in science between neologism and agreed nomenclature shows that tendency in action.

In the late 1850s Tyndall thanks Maxwell for offprints in dynamics, the perception of colours, and for his monograph 'The Lines of Force.' His tone seems a trifle tart: 'I never doubted the possibility of giving Faraday's notions a mathematical form, and you would probably be one of the last to deny the possibility of a totally different imagery by which the phenomena might be represented' (7 Nov. 1857, Add 7655/II/13).

Clerk Maxwell's correspondence with Tait in particular (now in the Cambridge University Library, to whom I am grateful for permission to quote the material in this essay) is a fruitful source of these debates concerning representation and phenomena. Maxwell's struggle to establish exact terms is undertaken with a serious merriment that is alert to the multivocality of language and tries to yoke that to his purposes. He is both lighthearted and exacting in his attempts to control what he calls 'plurality'. In the following passage he seeks the apt and stringent word. He toys with sexual reference and escapes it. He controls the *pace* implied by the chosen term.

The discussion is about the vocabulary of vector quantities. (Vector quantities are measures of motion in which both magnitude and direction must be stated: displacement and velocity are examples of vector quantities.)

the vector part I would call the twist of the vector function (Here the word twist has nothing to do with a screw or helix.) If the words *turn* or *version* would do they would do better than twist for twist suggests a screw. Twirl is free from the screw notion and is sufficiently racy. Perhaps it is too dynamical for pure mathematicians so for Cayley's sake I might say curl (after the fashion of Scroll). (7 Nov. 1870, Add 7655/Ib/16; Beer, Introduction)

Maxwell is chary of the over-abundance of connotation and recognizes the difficulty of honing any word to one limited notion, particularly when a field is new. How to say little enough is the problem. But he is also well aware that mathematical symbols are no simple alternative to the communicative problems of language. Language, after all, is composed of grammar and syntax quite as fundamentally as of semantics, and Maxwell felt the lack of a secure grammar in the current mathematical field of quaternions derived from W. R. Hamilton's work. He complained of the want of a 'Grammar of Quaternions' and 'the proper position of . . . Contents, Notation, Syntax, Prosody, Nablady' (4 and 9 Oct. 1872, Ib/49, 50).

By the end of that sentence he has moved across the spectrum into his own punning habit of mind, between music and geometry. Tait, in Maxwell's repertory, is the 'Chief Musician upon Nabla' because 'Nabla was the name of an Assyrian harp of the shape ▼.▼ is a quaternion operator . . . invented by Sir W. R. Hamilton, whose use and properties were first fully discussed by Professor Tait' (Campbell and Garnett: 634, n. 1).

Maxwell was an extraordinarily skilful parodic poet. In his poem addressed 'To the Chief Musician Upon Nabla: A Tyndallic Ode', he uses quaternion rhymes in a performance, half celebration, half mockery, of John Tyndall's scientific demonstrations. The opening stanzas of this long ode run:

> I come from fields of fractured ice,
>   Whose wounds are cured by squeezing,
> Melting they cool, but in a trice,
>   Get warm again by freezing.
> Here, in the frosty air, the sprays
>   With fern-like hoar-frost bristle,
> There, liquid stars their watery rays
>   Shoot through the solid crystal.

I come from empyrean fires—
From microscopic spaces,
Where molecules with fierce desires,
Shiver in hot embraces.
The atoms clash, the spectra flash,
Projected on the screen,
The double D, magnesian b,
And Thallium's living green.

Precisely equivalent passages to the scenes described in these and the ensuing stanzas of this poem can be found in Tyndall's 1865 Rede Lecture on radiation (*Fragments of Science*: i. 28–73), in his *Heat as a Mode of Motion*, and in his paper 'On the Blue Colour of the Sky, and the Polarisation of Skylight' (*Fragments*: i. 109–30).

A week later, in his correspondence with Tait, Maxwell returns to the problem of representational orders: 'the interaction of many is necessary for the full development of a new notation . . . Algebra is very far from O.K. after now some centuries . . . We put down everything, payments, debts, receipts, cash, credit, in a row or column and trust to good sense in totting up' (9 Oct. 1872, Add 7655/Ib/50). In 1873 he proposed a spoof question for the Cambridge Natural Sciences Tripos: 'General Exercise: Interpret every 4ion [i.e., Quaternion] expression in literary geometrical terms.'

Maxwell is careful to preserve a distinction between our knowledge of the world and the possible nature of the world, as did Schrödinger and Einstein later. Thus, in his *Britannica* article 'Diffusion', Maxwell argues that the idea of entropy depends on our knowledge of the system and is not itself an observable property of the system: 'Now, confusion, like the correlative term order, is not a property of material things in themselves, but only in relation to the mind which perceives them' (quoted in Brush: 592–3).

Maxwell repeatedly uses the tardy and distanced form of denomination that Helmholtz also recommended to the scientist: 'the motion *called* heat.' This power of distancing himself from terms allows a limber play of attention across even those concepts most necessary to his projects. He jokes about the ether, which yet (as his contemporary R. T. Glazebrook wrote concerning Maxwell) seemed to be for scientists at the time the remaining secret to be unlocked: 'In light waves periodic changes in the ether are taking place . . . The laws of these vibrations, when they are completely known, will give us the secret of the ether' (*DNB*: xv. 120).

Maxwell combines the extreme of scepticism with the extreme of faith, remaining always devout while teasing out the obduracies of the invisible material world. Indeed, for his theological comfort he needs that distinction between what he calls in another letter 'the ignorance and finitude of human science' and the enduring energies and dissipations of the universe. In the space between them his God can remain stable, even while Maxwell himself experiences through his study of Clausius, as he remarks wryly, 'that state of disgregation in which one becomes conscious of the increase of the general sum of Entropy' (12 Feb. 1872, Ib/43).

Maxwell struggles, with great self-discipline and scepticism, against a temptation in epistemology, where, for example, evolutionism employs the branching model to represent the procedures by which theory is formed as well as the theory that is formed, thus confirming its own theorization. This tendency, I have already suggested, proved fruitful in modernist writing where it could be reconceived as imitative form. Maxwell avoided merging his mode of explanation with the topic studied, but he was highly conscious of the changing functions of metaphor as they extend across scientific fields, shifting from technical description toward generalization that allows productive switching to take place between two fields.

By means of the finitude of mathematical symbols and theorems Maxwell sought to wrest his own representation away from any likeness to the entropic processes he described. But he was also acute about the instability even of mathematical symbols. To Tait he wrote that he 'should make a supplementary book on Quaternions explaining the true principles of dots and brackets and defining the limits of the sway of symbols' (14 June 1871, Ib/30).

He concludes this postcard by writing out a 'Sylvestrian sonnet', 'Tasso to Eleonora', without remark. The poem is thereby made to bear upon the theoretical problems they are surveying in their study of thermodynamics. The octave runs:

> Calm, pure, and mirroring the blue above
> To whom comminglingly my life's streams flow,
> Making that one which many seemed but now,

Thou art the sum and ocean of my love.
What though my soul rebellious pulses prove:
These are the gusts that o'er the surface play,
The fleeting colours painted on the spray;
They cannot in its depths the oceans move.

The writing-out of the poem in the context of this correspond-ence produces an implicit analysis that he need not spell out. Here, current topics in science are serenely re-imagined in the traditional tropes of love sonnets: the blue of the sky (which Tyndall had recently shown to be the result of the polarization of sunlight by particles in the upper atmosphere), the expanding of a single explanatory system to encompass light, heat, sound; the conserving of energy through the whole system; the fleeting colours of the spectrum in the turning wave; and the recognition that the particles of water do not move forward but simply up and down, the disturbances being at right angles to the direction of propagation. All these subjects are to be found in the work of Helmholtz and Maxwell, and are set forth with ravishing clarity in Tyndall's essays gathered in *Fragments of Science*. The tropes of Renaissance poetry are the current topics of science, Maxwell indicates. Recontextualizing the sonnet draws attention to the complexities of limiting 'the sway of symbols'. Language is fertile with fresh reference.

Maxwell has an unusual spatial capacity in his thought that allows him to hold geometry, poetry, logic, statistics, and joke alongside each other without seeking resolution or hierarchy among them, in a manner that actualizes Bakhtin's idea of the polyphonic. This ranging is achieved without muddle. Even his puns are models of precision.

Maxwell warns against popular expository rhetorics, which he calls 'the sensationalist' and 'the hierophantic':

The sensationalist says 'I am now going to grapple with the Forces of the Universe and if I succeed in this extremely delicate experiment you will see for yourselves exactly how the world is kept going.' The Hierophant says 'I do not expect to make you or the like of you understand a word of what I say, but you may see for yourselves in what a mass of absurdity the subject is involved.' (23 Dec. 1867)

Up to now in this argument I have concentrated on the writings of Clerk Maxwell, partly because he is so clear and adept a thinker about communicative questions and also because his work has continued to be of profound importance in the development of physical theory. But Clerk Maxwell's influence took time to be felt and acknowledged in cultural circles beyond science.

John Tyndall, in the physical sciences, was the writer who most spoke to his contemporaries, conveying to a general readership information about current scientific work and illuminating its penumbra of meaning. His effect can still be felt in the writing of Virginia Woolf, particularly *The Waves*, as I have argued elsewhere ('Victorians in Virginia Woolf'). He wrote in a style at once easy and incandescent. He was the person whom Pater read, Hopkins read, and in her youth Woolf read—indeed, he was the one writer you could scarcely have avoided scanning on scientific subjects if you read the generalist journals of the later nineteenth century.

Tyndall provoked controversy by his atheism, materialism, and insistence upon the imagination: itself an intriguing mix of preoccupations. He was from Ireland, not part of the social establishment, making his way from the ordnance survey of Ireland to the Preston Mechanics' Institute and thence as a mature student to Marburg University in Germany where he studied chemistry and mathematics. He was an atheist but 'redeemable', Hopkins hoped, and a materialist of a lofty, even transcendent, cast of mind (see Ch. 11 above). Much of the power in his writing came from his making visible to the imagination forces beyond the reach of sense. These paradoxical qualities meant that his work posed questions about cosmic order and extent. His work on radiation emphasized 'the incessant dissolution of limits' (*Fragments*: i. 2). His picturing of the outmost reaches of space was figured as sensation: 'It is the transported shiver of bodies countless millions of miles distant, which translates itself in human consciousness into the splendour of the firmament at night' (i. 4). Heat and light are both modes of motion and

in the spaces of the universe both classes of undulations incessantly commingle. Here the waves issuing from uncounted centres cross, coincide, oppose, and pass through each other, without confusion or ultimate extinction. Every star is seen across the entanglement of wave-motions produced by all other stars. It is the ceaseless thrill caused by those distant orbs collectively in the ether, that constitutes what we call the 'temperature of space.' (i. 34)

Tyndall prefers words that are at once precise, sensational, and evaluative: here, 'thrill' technically signifies penetration and oscillation, and also communicates excitement. This talent for rousing sensation in the reader meant that, despite his specifying precise meanings for terms such as force, radiation, absorption, his work offered mental images that could be symbolically reapplied, even though his own position was firmly grounded in materialism. He sets as epigraph to his most famous essay, 'The Scientific Use of the Imagination' (1870), a passage from Emerson whose last four lines run:

> The rushing metamorphosis
> Dissolving all that fixture is,
> Melts things that be to things that seem,
> And solid nature to a dream.

The tendency of Tyndall's own rhetoric was not dissolution but making visible. His particular major contribution to research was on the 'obscure rays' of the sun and their powers, as well as on ice crystallization, and on the blue of the sky.

Tyndall's making visible, in his theoretical and experimental demonstrations, of the 'dark rays' of the sun was—for some beholders—not unlike the appearance of the aura in spiritualism. Azure and wave motion, the stirring topics of then current scientific enquiry, enter early modernism alongside spiritual emanations. If ether, why not aura? If dark rays, why not invisible presences? And if a 'medium' of transmission (the ether) is required for energy, why not for voices from beyond? Spiritualist seances and scientific demonstrations did not seem very different in their effects. Signs; science; seances: how were they to be distinguished? Photography, with its apparent authenticity of real presences, could be used to confirm spiritualism. The Victorian camera takes snapshots of emanations, by an optical and chemical process that seemed to parallel spiritualism's insistence on 'manifestation'.

The 'dark rays' of Tyndall's own experimental work manifested otherwise invisible presences and claimed for them a more than symbolic form. In an essay, 'Science and the Spirits' (*Fragments*: 444–52), Tyndall sets himself in competition with the medium at a seance. Both claim to bring hidden 'real' phenomena within the scope of the senses. In this unremarked essay

Tyndall gives a vivid account of a tussle between himself and the medium for control of interpretation. He and she are, equally, storytellers. Whose narratives more satisfyingly expound wave processes? Whose please the listeners more? Whose describe a 'real' world?

Our host here deprecated discussion, as it 'exhausted the medium.' The wonderful narratives were resumed; but I had narratives of my own quite as wonderful. These spirits, indeed, seemed clumsy creations, compared with those with which my own work had made me familiar. I therefore began to match the wonders related to me by other wonders. A lady present discoursed on spiritual atmospheres, which she could see as beautiful colours when she closed her eyes. I professed myself able to see similar colours, and, more than that, to be able to see the interior of my own eyes. The medium affirmed that she could see actual waves of light coming from the sun. I retorted that men of science could tell the exact number of waves emitted in a second, and also their exact length. The medium spoke of the performances of the spirits on musical instruments. I said that such a performance was gross, in comparison with a kind of music which had been discovered some time previously by a scientific man. Standing at a distance of twenty feet from a jet of gas, he could command the flame to emit a melodious note; it would obey and continue its song for hours . . . These were acknowledged to be as great marvels as any of those of spiritdom. The spirits were then consulted, and I was pronounced to be a first-class medium. (i. 447)

(This 'siren song' is alluded to in the Maxwell poem I quoted earlier.) Tyndall triumphs, or believes himself so to do, but the exchange also takes us back to his early letter to Maxwell, arguing for variety of representations. Tyndall's materialism makes room for variety of interpretation and representation, but within the pale of scientific debate. Single truth and hyper-realism prevail. That scene of debate between scientist and medium, both conjurors of demonstrations, both claiming a higher validity for their performance, suggests also a context (which I shall not here develop further) for Yeats's early poetry.

The idea of the universe as waves, of the parallels between light, heat, and sound, and the single process expressed through them, enters late-nineteenth-century writing with a fresh urgency. Flux, the vortex, the ocean, the aura, the 'sea of forces flowing and rushing together', as Nietzsche called it, so important in modernism, are all elements of a repertoire shifting across fields.

In this I have concentrated on issues of representation among British scientific writers of the later nineteenth century concerned with wave theory, rather than on the famous philosophical examples of Nietzsche and of Bergson in the formation of early modernism. One of the oddities of modernist chronology is the frequency of time-warps, delays of reception which have sustained the insistence on novelty so important to modernist ideology. Let me conclude by glancing at this oddity since it has its bearing on questions of representation and realism. In French writing of the later nineteenth century science and symbolism are not at odds: witness Mallarmé's 'L'azur', and the great and hideous invocation of the ocean in Lautréamont's *Maldoror*. Lautréamont idealizes mathematical signs in his sado-masochistic ecstasies which, in a series of cantos, flow associatively through reformations and deformations of the human body and psyche: 'Ainsi, les êtres humains, ces vagues vivantes, meurent l'un après l'autre, d'une manière monotone; mais sans laisser de bruit écumeux (1.9) . . . "Les bras nageant aveuglement dans les eaux ironiques de l'éther" ' (2.5). Lautréamont, like Gerard Hopkins (and, so far as non-scientific circles go, like Clerk Maxwell too), is a curious example of the time-crumpling nature of modernist reception. (When Woolf came to write *The Waves* she was responding both to Einstein and to Tyndall simultaneously.) Lautréamont died in the 1870s yet his heyday was in the period of Surrealism in the 1920s. Similarly Hopkins appears as the first poet in the *Faber Book of Modern Verse*, reft away from the period in which he himself lived among the surrounding languages of poets like Swinburne, writers like Maxwell and Tyndall.

The force of scientific ideas in literary works is to provoke resistance as often as it is to persuade acquiescence or extension. In his essay 'Bergson's Theory of Art' in *Speculations*, T. E. Hulme describes the activity of the mind through a forced extension of the waves metaphor:

It is as if the surface of our mind was a sea in a continual state of motion, that there were so many waves on it, their existence was so transient, and they interfered so much with each other, that one was unable to perceive them. The artist by making a fixed model of one of these transient waves enables you to isolate it out and to perceive it in yourself. (150-1)

The important modernist principle here is that of *falsification*: to model or to fix a wave is to interfere fundamentally with its representation. The violent seizure of the provoked image is one important strain in modernism: as in the vortex, the interpenetrating cones. Hulme sees science, and indeed all thought, as the art of reduction in the service of power: 'to reduce the complex and inevitably disconnected world of grit and cinders to a few ideal counters, which we can move about and so form an ungritlike picture of reality—one flattering to our sense of power over the world . . . In the end this is true too of mathematics' ('Cinders', *Speculations*: 224). That emphasis on arrest and power is one important element in modernism. It is set in energetic opposition to entropy and to the evanishing of substance. Yet the metaphor of cinders also recalls the degradation of energy through the entropic process and calls on that as the 'real' against the stylization of art. A different expression of modernist creativity, which does draw on wave theory without quarrel, is that of oceanic communality. It is voiced alike by Woolf in *The Waves* and by Schrödinger. Schrödinger, like Woolf, like Jung indeed, wrote of 'conscious awareness as something emerging in individuals like tips of waves from a deep and common ocean' (quoted in MacKinnon: 221).

The questioning of substance in twentieth-century physics, and the formulation of wave–particle theory, gave realism a new lease of life (if in a manner somewhat analogous to the move in theology from literalism to the hermeneutics of myth). It is harder to deny an 'out there' that is undifferentiated, or irresolute, or composed of 'ondes fictives' than it is to challenge substantive phenomena. Realism spurns paradox: it seeks referential (and reverential) equivalence, the one-to-one locking of word and thing. But it has come to depend on paradox and on the logic of zeugma.

REFERENCES

Beer, Gillian, 'The Death of the Sun: Victorian Solar Physics and Solar Myth', in B. Bullen (ed.), *The Sun Is God: Painting, Literature, and Mythology in the Nineteenth Century* (Oxford 1989). (Repr. as Ch. 10, above.)

Beer, Gillian, 'Helmholtz, Tyndall, Gerard Manley Hopkins: Leaps of the Prepared Imagination', *Comparative Criticism*, 13 (1991). Repr. as Ch. 11, above.

—— Introduction, to Rhetoric and Science special number, edited with Herminio Martins, *History of the Human Sciences* (May 1990).

—— 'The Reader's Wager: Lots, Sorts, and Futures', *Essays in Criticism*, 40:2 (Apr. 1990). Repr. as Ch. 12, above.

—— 'The Victorians in Virginia Woolf', *Arguing with the Past* (London, 1989).

Benson, Donald R., ' "Catching Light": Physics and Art in Walter Pater's Cultural Context', in George Levine (ed.), *One Culture* (Madison, 1989), 143–63.

Brush, Stephen G., *The Kind of Motion We Call Heat: A History of the Kinetic Theory of Gases in the Nineteenth Century*, 2 vols. (Amsterdam, 1976).

Campbell, Lewis, and Garnett, William, *The Life of James Clerk Maxwell with a Selection from His Correspondence and Occasional Writings and a Sketch of His Contributions to Science* (London, 1882).

Cantor, G. N., and Hodge, M. J. S., *Conceptions of Ether: Studies in the History of Ether Theories, 1740–1900* (Cambridge, 1981).

Churchland, Paul, *Scientific Realism and the Plasticity of Mind* (Cambridge, 1979).

Clifford, W. K., *Lectures and Essays*. 2 vols. (1879; repr. London, 1901).

Darwin, Charles, *Life and Letters of Charles Darwin*, ed. F. Darwin, 2 vols. (New York, 1959).

DeLillo, Don., *White Noise* (Harmondsworth, 1988).

Dictionary of National Biography, ed. L. Stephen, vol. 15 (London, 1888).

Duncan, David, *The Life and Letters of Herbert Spencer* (London, 1908).

Eddington, Arthur, *The Nature of the Physical World* (Cambridge, 1928).

Girard, René, *'To double business bound': Essays on Literature, Mimesis, and Anthropology* (Baltimore and London, 1978).

Goethe's Theory of Colours, trans. Charles Lock Eastlake (London, 1840; reissued Cass, 1967).

Harman, P. M., *Energy, Force, and Matter: The Conceptual Development of Nineteenth-Century Physics* (Cambridge, 1982).

Helmholtz, H. von., *Epistemological Writings*, the Paul Hertz/Moritz Schlick Centenary Edition of 1921 with notes and commentary by the editors Robert S. Cohen and Yehuda Elkana (Dordrecht, 1977).

—— 'On the Conservation of Force; a Physical Memoir' (1847), in *Scientific Memoirs Selected from the Transactions of Foreign Academies of Science: Natural Philosophy*, ed. John Tyndall and William Francis (London: 1853).

—— *Popular Lectures on Scientific Subjects*, series 1 and 2 (London, 1870, 1881).

Holton, Gerald, *The Thematic Origins of Scientific Thought: Kepler to Einstein* (Cambridge, Mass., 1973).

Hopkins, Gerard M., *The Journals and Papers of Gerard Manley Hopkins*, ed. Humphry House and Graham Storey (Oxford, 1958).

Hulme, T. E., *Speculations: Essays on Humanism and the Philosophy of Art*, ed. Herbert Read with a foreword by Jacob Epstein (London, 1924).

Inman, Billie A., *Walter Pater's Reading: A Bibliography of His Library Borrowing and Literary References, 1853–1873* (New York, 1981).

James, William, *Pragmatism* and *The Meaning of Truth*, Introduction by A. J. Ayer (Cambridge, Mass., 1978).

Jeans, James, *The Mysterious Universe* (Cambridge, 1930).

Karl, Frederick R., *Modern and Modernism: The Sovereignty of the Artist, 1885–1925* (New York, 1985).

Krauss, Rosalind E., *The Originality of the Avant-Garde and Other Modernist Myths* (Cambridge, Mass., 1985).

Lautréamont [Isidore Ducasse], *Maldoror*, trans. A. Lykiard (London, 1970).

Levenson, Michael H., *A Genealogy of Modernism: A Study of English Literary Doctrine, 1908–1922* (Cambridge, 1984).

Lyotard, J.-F., *The Post-Modern Condition: A Report on Knowledge* (Manchester, 1984).

McGrath, F. C., *The Sensible Spirit: Walter Pater and the Modernist Paradigm*. (Tampa, Fla., 1986).

MacKinnon, Edward M., *Scientific Explanation and Atomic Physics* (Chicago and London, 1982).

Maxwell, James Clerk, Holograph Correspondence, Cambridge University Library.

—— *The Scientific Papers of James Clerk Maxwell*, ed. W. D. Niven, 2 vols. (Cambridge, 1890).

—— *The Scientific Letters and Papers of James Clerk Maxwell*, ed. P. M. Harman, vol. I, 1846–1862 (Cambridge, 1990).

Nietzsche, Friedrich, *The Will to Power* trans., Walter Kaufmann and R. J. Hollingdale, ed. Walter Kaufmann (New York, 1968).

Olby, Robert, *et al.* (eds.), *Companion to the History of Modern Science* (London, 1989).

Pater, Walter, *Plato and Platonism: A Series of Lectures* (1893; repr. London, 1967).
—— *The Renaissance* (London, 1910).
Popper, Karl R., *Quantum Theory and the Schism in Physics* (London, 1982).
Proctor, Richard, *The Universe of Suns and Other Science Gleanings* (London, 1884).
Pynchon, Thomas, *The Crying of Lot 49* (Harmondsworth, 1967).
Schrödinger, Erwin, *Science and the Human Temperament* (London, 1935).
Schwartz, Sanford, *The Matrix of Modernism: Pound, Eliot, and Early Twentieth-Century Thought* (Princeton, NJ, 1985).
Simons, Herbert W. (ed.), *Rhetoric in the Human Sciences* (London, 1988).
Tyndall, John, *Fragments of Science: A Series of Detached Essays, Addresses, and Reviews.* 2 vols. (10th impression, London, 1899).
—— *Hours of Exercise in the Alps* (London, 1871).
Wheaton, Bruce R., *The Tiger and the Shark: Empirical Roots of Wave–Particle Dualism* (Cambridge, 1983).
Zaniello, Tom, *Hopkins in the Age of Darwin* (Iowa City, 1988).

IV

Coda

Square Rounds *and Other Awkward Fits: Chemistry as Theatre*

From this day natural philosophy, and particularly chemistry, in the most comprehensive sense of the term, became nearly my sole occupation. I read with ardour those works, so full of genius and discrimination, which modern enquirers have written on these subjects.[1]

So writes Victor Frankenstein of his studies, studies that eventually led to the production of a monster. His description communicates enthusiasm, intelligence, obsession. He is both neophyte and initiate, looking back from a burdened knowledge to the outset of his studies. The language also exempts his creator, or producer, Mary Shelley, from needing to describe his studies in detail. 'In the most comprehensive sense of the term' gives leeway to the unknown—and while it suggests inclusiveness and knowledge (comprehension) it also veils the activities described, extending them beyond the gaze of the non-scientist. The incommensurate terms 'genius' and 'discrimination' have the effect of pairing transcendence and reason. The sealed laboratory lies at the centre of social fantasy. What goes on there? Do we wish to know? Are we responsible for it? Or is the knowledge generated there the responsibility—and the property—of those who produce it?

Such questions have dogged our culture and writing over the past 200 years, presenting themselves often in a positive form for the Victorians, more often as dread in this century. Partly this has to do with the mathematicization of scientific knowledge. This has speeded up communication between

---

[1] Mary Shelley, *Frankenstein: or the Modern Prometheus* (Oxford, 1980), 50. First published 1818.

scientists to a startling degree, as if the Tower of Babel had been built in a day once the workers found a common discourse. The admonitory force of the story of Babel has swung, for many, to suggest that perhaps after all the barriers of language were heuristically benign, slowing the pace at which knowledge can be acquired so as to give time for sensibility to catch up. The language of formulae and theorems seals knowledge in secret codes to which the uninitiated are debarred access. So the laboratory is figured as fortress, or even as Bluebeard's castle—places of unaccountable power. Thus, paradoxically, metrication seems to exceed counting; it mystifies (and is mystified); it is exempted from accountability. Yet its consequences count.

Such images are one side of the imagining of science: occult, sequestered, yet invasive, changing the world before that change can be measured or controlled. Many works of fiction thrive on those communal fears. Nevertheless, science—and particularly perhaps chemistry—is understood not only as *unheimlich*, uncanny, but as *heimelig*, humdrum and homely, caught into the ordinary processes of living: cooking and consuming, excreting and fertilizing. It can become a figure also for living itself, the body a cauldron of chemical activity. Indeed, in a book like Michael Maier's alchemical treatise *Atalanta Fugiens*, published in the 1620s, the alchemist is urged to note the procedures of housewives, their methods of going about domestic tasks, as a model for his own work. The woodcuts in this volume show a woman at work cooking over a kitchen fire, and boiling laundry in a great cauldron. The scientist here is urged to acquire techniques from the household skills by which he is surrounded. The Paracelsian emphasis on the human figure as a homology with the universe continues to leave its mark. The metaphor of alchemy survives as commentary on the processes of transformation within the human cycle.

That association between the human body and chemical process intensifies the appeal of chemistry even while it tends to relate it in its starkest form to people's childhoods, as in a poem by the poet Leonard Nathan called 'Alchemy' which remembers the world of 'stinks', of fantasies that threaten adulthood. Chemistry in ordinary recollection often figures as an interest outgrown, associated with a time before puberty—a time of sexual latency and apparent irresponsibility.

The materials and the outcomes of science are the stuff of literature, more often than are the procedures of scientific activity. The longing for transmutation persists. Chemistry can provide compelling metaphors for transformation. Less genially it can be made to yield metaphors and examples of another kind of transformation: the vacillations between good and evil outcomes in the world from apparently neutral experiment in the laboratory. Transformation is the most familiar and fascinating life-experience that we all share. It is the allure of transformation, in magic performance, that gave Tony Harrison the way in to his extraordinary theatre-piece (he does not call it a play) *Square Rounds*, produced for the National Theatre.[2] The piece appeals to the pantomime-child in the adult. It is a display of wonderful stage-effects (scarves changing colour, endless ribbons that spew over the stage, spirit instruments, a Chinese festival in which the magician's clothes pass through all the colours of the rainbow as we watch—though always with a sinister insistence on yellow, nitrous oxide). The piece is often very funny. It catches the pleasures of being amazed, the hopefulness for miracles that persists past childhood in even sober adults. It theatricalizes the way science looks like magic—and, sometimes, magic like science. It is also a pedagogic history of fertilizer from Liebig to Haber, taking in the new and wasteful British imperial habit of flushing away excrement while ignoring taboos about the use of human bones in making fertilizer phosphates. One of Harrison's many targets is the imperial habit of mind, whether in Britain, Germany, or China, and its effects within the science of the country.

But above all—or rather within all, since everything is instinct with this story—the piece is about the power of scientific discovery for good and ill at once. Harrison homes in on the life-story of Fritz Haber to provide his example of this oscillation and, by doing so, he is able to take in much of the most terrible European history of this century, partly by allusion, partly by representation. We see the First World War and the gassing of the troops; we do not see the Second World War and the gas chambers. But they are there, in a single poignant and chilling couplet as Haber's wife Clara fades from sight, singing:

[2] Tony Harrison, *Square Rounds* (London, 1992).

He'll never live to see his fellow Germans use
his form of killing on his fellow Jews.[3]

The doubled 'fellow' in that couplet condenses a question that
the play persistently sets before us, implicit already in its title
Square Rounds with its allusion to the puckle gun, invented
by Mr James Puckle (1667?–1724) in 1718, which used round
bullets for Christians and square bullets (more painful) for
Moslems.[4]

What is fellowship? And following from that first question,
then: Who belongs to whom? What kind of unit is a nation?
What is a marriage? Is science autonomous? What loyalty does
evidence demand? Are there elective affinities in life also? Are
women averse to war? Can consequences ever be quite unforeseen? And what of the communality of bones in fertilizer? These
questions dance before our eyes as we watch, rather than being
debated in set form. They are themselves constantly put under
stress, shape-shifted, made part of magic play.

Though many readers may be familiar with the life of Fritz
Haber, it may be worth reminding you of some of the salient
incidents if you have not seen the play. Harrison is selective, of
course, in what he uses: this is not biography; rather, it is a kind
of bared myth. Oddly, there is one feature of Haber's life that he
does not allude to (which, following the form of magic tricks and
scientific papers, I will reveal later on). What Harrison does
show us is Haber, who by fixing nitrogen will:

> ... harness its newly freed fantastic power
> to make infertile fields and wastelands flower.[5]

This is the Haber who was in 1919 awarded the 1918 Nobel
Prize for his contribution to the solution of world hunger problems by the development of the synthesis of ammonia.[6] But the

---

[3] Ibid. 52.
[4] A diagram of the gun is reproduced on the title-page of the programme for the
National Theatre production. This programme extends the material of Harrison's
piece in a number of revealing ways through quotations from the eighteenth century
to the present and through photographs. On Puckle, see *DNB*.
[5] *Square Rounds*, 6.
[6] Information about Fritz Haber's life and work is excellently summarized in U.
Emrich and R. Gerwin (eds.), *Fritz-Haber-Institute of the Max-Planck-Society Berlin*
(Munich: Max-Planck-Gesellschaft, English trans. 1989). I have drawn on this
booklet and on the experience of a brief visit to the institute in preparing this essay.
See also Henry Harris, 'Fritz Haber', *German History*, 10 (1992), 24–38.

same Fritz Haber was at the end of the war labelled as a 'war criminal' by the Allies. He it was who made possible the use of chlorine gas as a weapon in the First World War. Haber believed that gas would quickly end the war. His wife, the chemist Clara Immerwahr (whose surname with extraordinary aptness means 'ever true'), resisted his plans.[7] When he persisted, she killed herself. All this is presented with kaleidoscopic immediacy and tact. Harrison does not pursue the later ironies of Haber's life: that when the Nazis came to power he was in 1933 ordered (himself a Jew) to 'dismiss all racially undesirable staff members'.[8] Rather than do so, he resigned his post and sought exile in England. Within a few months he was dead, on his way to visit the recently founded Daniel Sieff Research Institute in Palestine, later to become the Weizmann Institute. All the terrible poignancy of that later life is condensed in the couplet I have quoted, which comes as the culmination of Clara's persistent awareness that as Jews they are simply of use to the Kaiser, to be jettisoned at will. Harrison alludes also (though not by name) to the reluctance of the German staff officers to use the services of Haber's friend and fellow-Jew Richard Willstätter who developed the respiratory filter for the gas mask.[9]

The story of Haber's double contribution—to replenishment and to destruction—is supported and paralleled by the more comically rendered figures of the Hiram brothers, makers of both the maximite gun for TNT and of the anti-asthma glass pipe. And the marriage of Clara and Fritz is set alongside that of the late-nineteenth-century chemist and physicist Sir William Crookes and his wife Nellie. Crookes announces:

> At the Great Exhibition William Perkin the inventor
> showed crude coal tar makes marvellous magenta.
> Both Lady Crookes and I were so impressed
> by the Perkin process that Lady Crookes is dressed
> in a mauve derived by it from disgusting tar
> to remind us how redeemable even foul things are.

---

[7] There is a recent biography: G. v. Leitner, *Der Fall Clara Immerwahr. Leben für eine humane Wissenschaft* (Munich, 1993). See the review by Jeffrey Johnson in *Ambix*, 41 (1994), 57–8.

[8] Emrich and Gerwin, 18–19.

[9] L. F. Haber, *The Poisonous Cloud: Chemical Warfare in the First World War* (Oxford, 1986).

. . .

And from these radiant colours by extension
how Science redeems the world with its invention
Poisons that made the clouds above us blacker
and coated the flowing brook with stinking lacquer
that poisoned fish in tranquil stream and pond
converted by the chemist's magic wand.[10]

Crookes's buoyant address concerning the redemptive wonders
of chemistry, figured in Harrison's play by wonderful magenta
dyes, singing voices, material transformations, is then set in
doubt by the death of his wife. Can scientific knowledge hold its
significance in the face of personal death? Crookes, the distinguished physical and empirical scientist (OM, FRS, D.Sc., LLD,
as the stage directions inform us) converts to spiritualism in his
anguished search for his lost wife. Scientific evidence will not
suffice his need. Is he a traitor to science?—and is Haber one?

Thematic survey, uncovering parallels (such as I have just
offered), still cannot quite do justice to the freedom of the play's
arrangement, the speed with which the audience is drawn into a
world where transformation is always possible for good or ill,
functioning equally as the basis of scientific experiment, of
magic, of sewage plant, or in quite other guises. And this is where
two of Harrison's most particular theatrical and literary
strategies become crucial. These two strategies are (1) the use of
women to play almost all the parts, and (2) the use of rhymed
quatrains and rhymed couplets, often loaded with further internal rhymes, for almost all the speech.

To consider first the deployment of women: all the characters
are played by women, except the prose-speaking lavatory attend-
ant and the shell-shocked man (who doubles late in the play as
the Chinese conjuror). The transvestism allies the play to music-
hall, with principal boy Haber, and true woman heroine Clara,
the chorus of munitionettes (women who were drafted into
munitions factories in the First World War), and the comic turn
of the fat and thin Maxim brothers. The music-hall transvestisms
in some ways ease the grip of history, but the cross-gender
theatrical role-playing also raises questions about social roles.
What are the responsibilities of women as well as of men? Do

[10] *Square Rounds*, 19.

women figure in the scientific process as part of the construction of knowledge? and of responsibility? or are they simply subsequent—driven to sacrifice or salvation by its effects? No clear single answers are given: nor can they be. Clara Haber is the lodestar of the play, but a woman plays Fritz Haber—not to feminize him but to raise the issue of all that is usually absent, as Evelyn Fox Keller has shown, in the epistemological habits of scientists.[11] Moreover, members of the munitionettes also play Sir William Crookes, Hiram Maxim, Hudson Maxim, Fritz Haber, Justus von Liebig as well as Clara Haber and Lady Nellie Crookes. Women (Harrison suggests) are the general term out of which emerge particular instances, both male and female. Moreover, women were not absent from the production of the First World War, as the programme makes doubly clear when it lists some of the military inventions patented by women in the Great War: 'automatic pistol, bomb-launching apparatus, cane-gun, cartridge tube filter, flashlight attachment for firearms, front sight for firearms, incendiary ball, loading device, ordnance, percussion and ignition fuse, primer, railway torpedo, rear sight for guns, resilient missile, single trigger mechanism, submarine mine, top for powder cans, torpedo guard, woven carriage carrier.'[12]

Harrison's point is less to accuse women of complicity than to challenge the kind of essentialism that emphasizes women's passivity. The omnipresence of women in the play's acting shifts the way things were and are. Another meaning of his title 'square rounds' is the way stereotypes constrict actuality, until actuality is so powerfully transformed as to break open stereotype: that transformation may be the outcome of communal catastrophe quite as often as of reasoned progress. In the First World War a million women took the places of men in the factories; after the First World War women got the vote and things never were quite the same again:

All the discoveries the scientists thought they had made about her, all the reports the sociologists solemnly filed over her, and all the jokes the punsters wrote about her—everything has gone to the scrap-heap as

[11] Evelyn Fox Keller, *Reflections on Gender and Science* (New Haven, Conn., 1985), *passim*.
[12] Quoted in the theatre programme from Fred Amram 'The Innovative Women', *New Scientist*, 102 (24 May 1984), 10–12.

repudiated as the one-time theory that the earth was SQUARE instead of ROUND. Everything they said she wasn't and she couldn't and she didn't, she now is and she can and she does.[13]

This quotation raises issues of how social narratives are transformed. How do things hang together? Are there secure and identifiable causal sequences, at least in science if not in history?—or is that expectation of severe causal explanation part of science's myth of itself? In this theatre-piece Harrison uses rhyme that plays on the rim of doggerel and often is unabashed (though technically brilliant) doggerel. So he brings forward questions about chance and likeness, about the way activities, things—and words too—may be set in apposition and so may transform each other without any of the expected reasoned links.

The play opens with the flushing of a water closet and in prose. Much comedy is derived at the start from the wastefulness of this early British invention. As Liebig later remarks:

> Your nation, Britain, has left the world less green
> by making universal the use of the latrine.

When Haber enters, hey presto, like a magician he exacts rhyme from all he meets. Harrison here uses the fact that the historical Fritz Haber used to enjoy talking in rhyme, would keep it up for several hours, and challenged his juniors to meet his skill. Harrison's use of rhyme is itself a brilliant metaphor for the slippery world of transformations. Rhyme rescues fleeting concords from unlike terms. It suggests kinship where none has before seemed to exist. It flouts hierarchy, matching words from very diverse linguistic registers. It marries low and high, familiar and arcane. In Harrison's skilled hands it sounds casual, pantomimic, refusing to fix or dignify for ever, yet impressing on the ear unforgettable concurrences that we might otherwise resist.

> The war I detest in which all the best
> and bravest of men meet their fate
> I do what I can not for Deutschland, but MAN
> and save him before it's too late.
>
> Something that shocks, unorthodox
> a weapon not thought of before

[13] Quoted in this form in the theatre programme from Mabel Potter Daggett, *Women Wanted* (1918).

a sudden surprise out of the skies
to bring a quick end to this war.[14]

The knocked-together internal rhymes (detest/best; can/MAN; shocks/unorthodox; surprise/skies) grip the couplets together more tightly and more covertly than end-rhyme alone can ever achieve. Here the end-scheme seems quite loose and permissive (abcb) but hidden connections occupy the run of the lines. Or take Clara's sinuously long-lined couplets:

> The shades you adore to see us women wear
> are converted into cankers that corrupt the living air,
> the green of undergarments, the green of a chemise
> born as deadly poison on the April breeze.
> Into the top hat vats the coloured silks went in
> and out came something most unfeminine.[15]

Alliteration, (those cs and gs), assonance, and end-rhymes in the first four lines draw together and transform words in ways that imitate the process described. The awkward stumble of close internal rhyme (hat, vats) and of iteration (Into, in) and of incommensurate rhyme (in/unfeminine) disturbs the macabre lulling of the reader. It wakes us momentarily out of the sound-induced inevitability of accepting beauty and corruption without being able to keep them apart. The incantatory is here not only persuasive but performative: it makes us enact as well as listen. In the theatre we have no time, certainly, to analyse the auditory affect produced by rhyme, but that makes it more, not less, powerful in its persuasions. It acts out transformation in our ear, just as the conjuring tricks do for our eyes. It may remind us again of the alchemist Michael Maier who wanted his text sung polyphonically for the full meaning to emerge.

And what was the episode in Haber's life that Harrison makes nothing of? Perhaps the project seemed to him too far out into the world of magic itself. As a non-scientist Harrison may have been chary of seeming to impute alchemy to chemistry. For in 1920 Haber had 'the idea of electrochemically extracting the gold supposedly present in solution in sea-water in relatively high concentrations' in order to pay off the German reparation debts. He formed a secret team and developed new methods of extraction and new techniques for analysis. Only after several

---

[14] *Square Rounds*, 39.   [15] Ibid. 47.

years of effort did it turn out 'that the older and at first apparently very promising values (it was estimated that 8 thousand million tons of gold were dissolved in the sea) were too high by a factor of 1,000'.[16] The alchemical remains within and still resists the chemist's hopes.

Harrison's theatre-piece is both challenging and uneasy. Cutting across generic bounds, it is poised between farce, tragedy, Peking opera, and music-hall, reminding us that the link between magic and chemistry cannot readily be broken in the public mind. Nor indeed can it securely be broken even for scientists themselves. It reminds us, too, that the human body is implicated in chemical processes: on the stage the body is presented as masquerade, as magician and as magic material, but also as human person. Harrison does not allow his audience to ignore the appalling actualities of mustard-gas or gas chamber; instead he insinuates them on stage as a kind of malign magic. There are risks here: of sentimentality, of aestheticism, of a stage-crafted alienation that produces pedagogic whimsy rather than intensity. But I think he just avoids this and makes the audience flinch at the possibility of trivialization rather than wallow in it.

In the National Theatre production a healing transformation was introduced at the play's ending that shifted its meaning toward hope—an illicit hope, perhaps, and not there in the stage directions. The last scene combines ancient China and 1992. In the preceding chorus the audience is reminded that science does not belong only to the West, and neither does destruction:

(The CHINESE MAGICIAN walks down with the black top hat. Some poppy petals fall from it on to the white stage).
CHINAMAN 1 TO 21
(Singing)

> To you it appears that all pioneers
> of science were men who wore these
> but all that you've seen, munition, machine,
> had all been first made by Chinese.
> The first rocket occurred when we took a bird
> and harnessed fire to its claws.
> These expendable doves set fire to foes' roofs

---

[16] Emrich and Gerwin, 16. On this issue see also, Roy M. MacLeod, 'Gold from the Sea: Archibald Liversidge, F.R.S. and the Chemical Prospectors', *Ambix*, 35 (1988), 53–64.

and helped us to win many wars.[17]

CHINESE MAGICIAN

> Now by slow stages through ages and ages
> the rockets fly faster and higher
> the problem is now to find a way how
> to free the first dove from the fire.

There is an explosion and we are back with the sweeper and the toilet cabin. Then the stage-directions read:

The SHELL-SHOCKED MAN comes out of the Toilet Cabin with a dead bird in his hand. He walks up the centre gangway of the theatre and exits.

But in the theatre, in the performance, as the shell-shocked man gently holds it, the dead pigeon flutters, is released, and flies freely—actual and alive, a dove. The dead do not come back to life. Chemistry tells us that, and experience. But in theatre everything becomes possible. Did Harrison agree to the change? His many-faced text holds contradictory possibilities: perhaps he felt relief at this final theatrical, natural, riddle.

The piece is surrounded by riddles as well as working with them. Perhaps the answer to one of them, and to the move towards hope, is contained in the work's dedication: 'For my son Max.' The play is a gift and a warning at once. Max, like many others world-wide, grows up in the consequences of both of Haber's major achievements: fertilizer and genocidal weapon (fertilizer also now as weapon). And, like many of his generation, Max may well have been taking the National Curriculum science programme. One of the booklets produced for that curriculum concentrates on the figure of Fritz Haber.[18] Was that the starting-point for father and son? If so Harrison's theatre-piece is an extraordinary transformation of homework: but that's a major part of what he is saying. There is no secure divide between the domestic world and the laboratory. Both look like private spaces; both produce and are involved in communal consequences, world-wide transformations.

---

[17] *Square Rounds*, 60.
[18] See e.g. A. S. Travis, 'The High Pressure Chemists', *Wembley: Brent Schools and Industry Project* (1984).

Index